Jack Burd's

Civil War Source Book

1999-2000

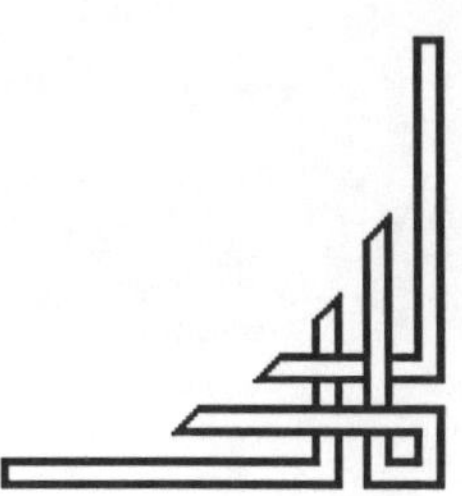

Rockbridge Publishing
Charlottesville, Virginia

Published by
Rockbridge Publishing
an imprint of
Howell Press, Inc.
1713-2D Allied Lane
Charlottesville, VA 22903

(804) 977-4006
http://www.howellpress.com

The cavalry engages in a saber fight in the opening
action of the 135th anniversary program
of the battle of Gettysburg.

ISBN 1-57427-087-7
ISSN 1091-1618

CONTENTS

Dear Readers,

Just when we thought we had a pretty good listing of people, places, and things related to the war between the states, our intrepid researchers and net warriors went back to work, gleaning more listings and updating those already included. The result is the book you have in your hand—**MORE THAN THREE THOUSAND ENTRIES** and twenty-six more pages than the 1998 edition!

We appreciate our readers who took the time to let us know about incomplete or outdated information due to the many new area codes and the proliferation of e-mail and internet addresses. We tried to catch as many as we could and apologize for the few we may have missed.

The Civil War Source Book is the most complete guide to people, places, events, and products of the war that you'll find anywhere, but it's only as current as the day we go to press. We suggest you use this book as a starting point in your search. If you don't see exactly what you're looking for, call one of the businesses that specializes in a related subject area and ask if they can point you in the right direction. Take a little time to look over the table of contents, then skim through the book itself and see how it is organized. As you become familiar with the contents you'll soon know where to look to satisfy your needs for all things Civil War.

Many of the listings throughout the book have been updated to include e-mail addresses and/or internet web site URL addresses. And while a fair number of internet sites in the last directory have gone *poof*, the remaining sites and some strong new ones in the **Internet Addresses** section have been around long enough to establish themselves as reliable sources of information and excellent places to begin searching for more information.

Now that the telephone companies seem to have called a moratorium on new area codes and the flurry of new web sites seems to have steadied, the information in these pages should remain up-to-date for a while. For that reason we expect this directory to have a shelf-life of more than a year. We'll be gathering information for the next edition in 2001, and we're hoping our readers will let us know about new companies and organizations that should be included.

We're revising constantly as we look toward the next edition. Let us know what you'd like to see here. We'll make every effort to make it so!

Sincerely,

Jack

Jack Burd

20TH MAINE, INC.
207-865-4340
207-865-9575 Fax
Patricia Hodgdon
49 West St • Freeport ME 04032-1127
Specialized bookstore devoted to Civil War with new & old books, art, music, videos, antiques & much more.

ALPHAEUS H. ALBERT
PO Box 5266
Clinton NJ 08809-0266

ALTUS INTERNATIONAL, LTD.
612-922-6948
5609 Interlachen Cir
Edina MN 55436-1331
Civil War chess set - wooden, hand-carved, painted, lacquered. Historically accurate. Board is plate glass, beveled edges. Players stands 6-1/2" tall.

AMERICA'S COVERED BRIDGES
PO Box 516 • Lightfoot VA 23090-0516
22-piece collection of replicas, incl. "Old Humpback Bridge," a covered bridge saved from destruction by a negotiated agreement between Union & Confederate forces. $45 ea. Write for complete list.

THE AMERICAN HISTORICAL FOUNDATION
800-368-8080 • 804-353-1812
804-359-4895 Fax
http://www.ahfrichmond.com
1142 W Grace St
Richmond VA 23220-3613
Firing reproductions of Lee's 1851 Navy Revolver (Ltd). Colt's 34d Model Dragoon Revolvers, Jackson LeMat, JEB Stuart Le Mat, Lee/Grant Henry Rifles, etc.

AMERICAN MILITARY ANTIQUES
410-465-6827
Courtney B. Wilson & Assoc.
8398 Court Ave
Ellicott City MD 21043-4514
Appraisers & dealers in fine 19th-century military Americana. Civil War memorabilia, books, photos, swords, forearms, relics. Buys/sells.

AMERICANA SOUVENIRS & GIFTS
http://www.americanagifts.com
302 York St • Gettysburg PA 17325-1930
Most complete line of Civil War souvenirs & memorabilia for both USA & CSA. Cannons, bullets, patches, toys, books, flags, videos, documents, insignias, & much more.

AMES INSTRUMENT COMPANY
PO Box 651
Ames NY 13317-0651
Signalman's compass - 2" solid brass with level & "slit and window" sights in lined walnut box.

DALE C. ANDERSON CO.
4 W Confederate Ave
Gettysburg PA 17325
Firearms, edged weapons, uniforms, accoutrements, & 1000s of other objects touching all periods & significant events, 1776-1945. Emphasis on Civil War era. Our 37th year. Photo-illus. militaria catalog issued bi-monthly - $12/yr.

ANDERSONVILLE ANTIQUES
912-924-2558
912-924-1044
Peggy & Fred Sheppard
PO Box 26
Andersonville GA 31711-0026
Authentic Civil War guns, swords, buttons, documents; books on the Civil War.

ANTIQUE AMERICANA
PO Box 389
Whitman MA 02382-0389
Civil War documents, books, autographs, maps.

THE ANTIQUE CENTER OF GETTYSBURG
717-337-3669
7 Lincoln Sq
Gettysburg PA 17325-2205
100 showcases of quality antiques & collectibles, including large selection of Civil War memorabilia, artifacts, weapons & medical supplies. In historic Wills House on the square in Gettysburg.

ARROWHEAD FORGE
605-938-4814
RR 1 Box 25 • Wilmot SD 57279-9718
Tools, fire irons, candle holders, grills, eating utensils, tomahawks, & much more.

ARSENAL ARTIFACTS, INC.
800-483-1861
486 W Main St • Sylva NC 28779-5545
Limited edition prints by Bob Graham, John Warr, Mort Kunstler, John Paul Strain & others. Large selection of dug artifacts. Specialize in artillery.

ARTCAST
770-270-9659
PO Box 28561 • Atlanta GA 30358-0561
1861 reproduction West Point class ring. Original reproductions of the May & June class. (Only year with 2 graduations.) Sterling - $59.95; gold - $169.95.

ATLANTA ARSENAL
6005 State Bridge Rd Apt 1434
Duluth GA 30097-6463
Reproduction Confederate painted canvas accoutrements, copy from originals, incl. cartridge boxes, cap boxes, bayonet scabbards, slings, belts. Free price list.

THE BAG MAN
615-859-9658
Patrick Strickland
588 Dividing Ridge Rd
Goodlettsville TN 37072
Best possible reproductions. Knapsacks - $50 & up; S&K copper or tin canteens - $39 & $55.

BALLANTYNES OF WALKERBURN (USA), INC.
888-269-8720 • 910-323-4872
910-323-0214 Fax
bowusa@aol.com
Tracey Lindsay • PO Box 35001
Fayetteville NC 28303-0001
Fine quality, 8" hand-painted porcelain resin statues. Ask about our collectors club. Free catalog.

BARRY'D TREASURE
502-448-8772
http://www.iglou.com/btreasure
PO Box 16569
Louisville KY 40256-0569
Civil War accoutrements, books, bullets, cartridges, dug items, other relics & artifacts. Extensive, illustrated catalog.

BARTLETT'S COLLECTIBLES
PO Box 545
Mechanicsburg PA 17055-0545
Civil War trading cards; superb photography, educational, collectible. Sample card & catalog - free.

BELL CONSULTING, INC.
352-753-0219
Ted & Pat Bell
PO Box 579 • Lady Lake FL 32158-0579
Antique handguns, Bowie knives, cartridge belts & holsters, rifles, deringers, swords. Buy/sell/trade. Cat. - #10 SASE.

BELLINGER'S MILITARY ANTIQUES
770-992-5574
Bill Bellinger
PO Box 76371-SB • Atlanta GA 30358FULL-TIME DEALER of antique firearms, edged weapons, belt plates, leather goods, books & miscellaneous from the 17th-19th C. Civil War a specialty. Catalog - $3; 4 issues/$10 (overseas - $20).

BENCKENDORF PIPES
515-255-0838
PO Box 30062
Des Moines IA 50310-9402
Finest reproduction & collectible pipes & smoking accoutrements. Free catalog.

D. BIGDA ANTIQUES
803-722-0248
http://bmark.com/bigda.antiques
dbigda@awod.com
178 King St
Charleston SC 29401-2212
Specializing in matching period & modern sterling silverware. Many patterns in stock. Tea sets, perfume bottles, etc.

BLACKSWORD ARMOURY, INC.
352-495-9967
102 Depot Rd
Hawthorne FL 32640-5613
Replicas of historical weapons & armor from ancient to Civil War. Catalog - $3.

BLUE/GREY MILITARIA
860-749-3407
PO Box 296 • Somers CT 06071-0296
GAR, Regimental & Veteran Association reunion ribbons & badges. Collections & single items bought. Catalog/list - $1.

BORDER STATES LEATHERWORKS
501-361-2642 • 501-361-2851 Fax
1158 Apple Blossom Ln
Springdale AR 72762-9762
Civil War collectibles, original weapons & equipment. Reproduction cavalry saddles & equipment. Custom hand-forged bits.

MIKE BRACKIN
203-647-8620
PO Box 23
Manchester CT 06045-0023
Large assortment of Civil War & Indian War autographs, accoutrements, memorabilia, insignia, medals, buttons, GAR, documents, photos & books. Catalog - $6/yr for 5 issues.

THE BRADFORD EXCHANGE
9345 N Milwaukee Ave
Niles IL 60714-1393
The Heart of Plate Collecting. Limited edition collector's plates featuring historic events.

BRITISH COLLECTIBLES LTD.
1727 Wilshire Blvd
Santa Monica CA 90403-5509
Authentic collectibles for serious collectors, 1800s-WWII. Catalog - $15.

KEN BROWN
614-498-8379
17261 Sligo Rd • Kimbolton OH 43749Quality, handmade, reproduction cavalry tack, equipment & accoutrements. Free brochure.

WALTER BUDD
3109 Eubanks Rd
Durham NC 27707-3622
Finest selection of US military antiques, firearms, swords, uniforms, head gear, cavalry equipment, McClellan saddles, mess gear, horse-drawn army wagons & rolling stock, etc. Subscription rate - $5 for 8 issues.

BUFFALO ROBE TRADING POST
520-457-2322
George Henry
9 N 5th St • PO Box 741
Tombstone AZ 85638-0741
Civil War, local history, American Indian, western lawmen & outlaws. Gift shop, artifacts, video & audio tapes. Historian in attendance.

THE BUGLE CALL
630-350-1116
630-350-1606 Fax
http://www.infinitiv.com/BugleCall
Robert C. Trownsell
1241 N Ellis St
Bensenville IL 60106-1118
Fine military antiques. Shoulder straps a specialty.

RICH BURNHAM
310-832-3252
PO Box 4056
Torrance CA 90510-4056
Union & Confederate dug & non-dug buttons. Many rare. Large list - $2.

STANLEY BUTCHER
4 Washington Ave
Andover MA 01810-1724
Buys Confederate generals' autographs, letters, & other Civil War documents.

CALDWELL & CO. COLLECTIBLES
765-482-6280
civilwr@in-motion.net
816 Pleasant St
Lebanon IN 46052-2853
Edged weapons, firearms, Civil War items & general antiques. Buy/sell. Free catalog.

KEITH CANGELOSI
4201 Frenchman St
New Orleans LA 70122-3839
CW military antiques. Longarms, carbines, handguns, edged weapons. List $2.

CARDS WITH MY PARDS (TM)
877-443-1863 (toll free)
cardswithmypards@yahoo.com
Tony & Pat Fantilli
PO Box 6186 • Clearwater FL 33758 Buys & sells CW playing card decks; repro CW card decks. Historically accurate, colorful & informative "CW Playing Cards" newsletter. (See ad page 263)

CAROLINA COLLECTORS CIVIL WAR RELICS
http://www.collectorsnet.com/ccrelics/index.htm
Rick Burton or Warren Vestal
PO Box 1177
Kernersville NC 27285-1177
Dug & non-dug relics from battlefields & camp sites. Photo-illus. catalog.

THE CARRIAGE HOUSE
918-367-6425
PO Box 8
Slick OK 74071-0008
Wooden wheels for cannon, old auto, carriage & decor.

CAT'S MEOW VILLAGE
717-359-8608
717-359-7411
1295 Frederick Pike
Littlestown PA 17340-9380
Historic Gettysburg series, collectable painted wooden buildings include Jenny Wade House, Lee's HQ, Meade's HQ, Pa. Monument, Lutheran Seminary Chapel, several others.

THE CAVALRY SHOP
804-266-0898
T.E. Johnson, Jr.
9700 Royerton Dr
Richmond VA 23228-1218
Civil War leather goods, buckles; horsegear. Catalog - $2. (See ad page 259)

CEDAR CREEK RELIC SHOP
540-869-5207
Rex & Mary Bailey
PO Box 232 • Middletown VA 22645 Largest selection of authentic Civil War relics in the Shenandoah Valley. Next to battlefield. Catalog - $6 for 4 issues/yr.

CIVIL WAR "THINGS 'N FRAMES"
615-952-3672
http://www.i285.com/civil/index.html
sonny_c@bellsouth.net
Sonny Collins
PO Box 422
Kingston Springs TN 37082-0422
Forrest, Davis, Mosby & Stuart prints & notecards from orig. museum pieces painted from life. Also, antique medical equipment & Civil War artifacts.

CIVIL WAR ANTIQUES
419-878-8355
419-882-5547
David W. Taylor
PO Box 87 • Sylvania OH 43560-0087
Pedigreed Civil War antiques, guns, swords, uniforms, buckles, flags, drums, letters, diaries, etc. Bought/sold. Catalog - $10.

CIVIL WAR ANTIQUITIES
614-363-1862
http://www.civilwarantiquities.com
Todd Rittenhouse, Prop.
PO Box 1411
Delaware OH 43015-1411
Quality CW items. Guns, swords, letters, currency, books, prints. Buy/sell/trade. Full service custom framing & matting; specializing in conservation framing. Shop located at 13-1/2 N Sandusky St., Delaware, Ohio. Free catalog.

CIVIL WAR BULLET COLLECTOR NEWSLETTER
oma00077@mail.wvnet.edu
Chuck Haislip
66 W Main St Apt 3
White Sulphur Springs WV 24986-2437
Newsletter with classified section distributed by Civil War Bullet Collector Association. $10/yr. for 6 issues.

CIVIL WAR CATALOG
Bob & Pat Bartosz
PO Box 226
Wenonah NJ 08090-0226
Attention Civil War Collectors - $3 for next 3 issues. Letters, documents, slave papers, hires, etc. Historical documents, ephemera.

CIVIL WAR EMPORIUM, INC.
408 Mill St
Occoquan VA 22125
From harmonicas to working cannons. Working repros. Decorator models. Consignments welcome. Buy/sell.

CIVIL WAR TABLE
716-632-4603
Michael Valentic
52 Mill St
Williamsville NY
Buy/sell. Free appraisal.

STAN CLARK MILITARY BOOKS
717-337-1728
717-337-0581 Fax
915 Fairview Ave
Gettysburg PA 17325-2906
Buys/sells Civil War books, ltd. edition prints, autographs, letters, documents, postcards, soldiers' items; special interest in U.S. Marine Corps items.

CLARK'S GUN SHOP, INC.
540-439-8988
10016 James Madison Hwy
Warrenton VA 20186-7820
Retailer of books, Civil War relics, kepis, flags, buttons, Confed. souvenirs, original Confed. money & state notes, CW prints.

CLASS COLLECTIBLES
2005 Route 35 N Ste 124
Oakhurst NJ 07755
Repros of death certificates.

COLLECTING THE CIVIL WAR
800-440-8478
PO Box 18844
Denver CO 80218-0844
2 videotapes - "Collecting the Union Soldier" vol. 1, & "... Confederate Soldier" vol. 2. Expert descriptions, close-up color photography. 100s of items. $19.95 ea.; set $29.95. Add $4 S&H.

COLLECTOR'S ARMOURY
800-544-3456 x515
703-684-6111
703-683-5486 Fax
James W. Hernly
PO Box 59, Dept CWB
Alexandria VA 22313-0059
Full line of "non-firing" reproduction pistols, rifles, cannons, Civil War swords, knives, bayonets, canteens, cap boxes, bugles & flags. Free catalog.

COLLECTORS HERITAGE, INC.
PO Box 355
Bernardsville NJ 07924-0355
Reproduction museum-quality military swords, knives, & bayonets. Catalog - $5 (ref.).

COLLECTORS' ANTIQUITIES, INC.
60 Manor Rd Ste 2000
Staten Island NY 10310-2626
American military antiques & memorabilia. Catalog - $12 for 3 issues. $15 overseas.

COLUMBUS ARMORY
706-327-1424 Ph & Fax
David S. Brady
1104 Broadway
Columbus GA 31901-2429
Complete Civil War store featuring books, relics, art, muskets & supplies. Buy/sell/trade. Free price list.

DAVID CONDON, INC.
540-687-5642
800-364-8416 Orders only
540-687-5649 Fax
PO Box 7
Middleburg VA 20118-0007
Dealing in fine antique firearms since 1957. Store located at 109 E Washington St (Route 50), Middleburg, Va.

CONFEDERATE ARTS
8301 Alvord St Dept. C
Mc Lean VA 22102-1736
Great Seal of the Confederacy minted in exact detail in solid bronze. Limited ed. - $69.95.

THE CONFEDERATE MBR NEWSLETTER
770-270-0542
Peter Bertram, Editor
PO Box 451421
Atlanta GA 31145-9421
6-pg illustrated newsletter cataloging UCV, SCV Reunion Medals, badges & ribbons. $12/yr. ($17 outside USA), 4 issues. Free sample copy - large SASE.

CONFEDERATE STATES MILITARY ANTIQUES
888-724-0512
http://www.collectorsnet.com/confedstates • jjackson@collectorsnet.com
2905 Government St
Baton Rouge LA 70806-5502
Civil War relics & memorabilia; metal detector sales.

CRANE MERCANTILE & MFG. CO.
314-231-4163
1212 Allen Ave • Saint Louis MO 63104-3914
Purveyor of finest cavalry saddle hardware. Iron frame coat strap buckles. McClellan saddle kit, tree & all hardware. Brochure - $2.

CSA
PO Box 570060
Whitestone NY 11357-0060
Confederate passports. Accurate, historical, might-have-beens. $4.

RON DACUS
800-868-0339
719 Turkey Trl • Fortson GA 31808-7227
"General Order #9: Lee's Farewell to the Confederacy" displayed in 18"x22" solid wood, gold-trimmed frame. $99.95 + $10 S&H.

DALESAND
PO Box 513 • Norge VA 23127-0513
Civil War bullets excavated from battlefield areas. 2 for $9. (1 Union & 1 Confederate).

DEAD HORSE FORGE
1220 Price Station Rd
Church Hill MD 21623-1315
All types of knives, Hawks & other ironware, powder horns & gourd canteens. Brochure - send SASE.

DER DIENST
PO Box 221
Lowell MI 49331-0221
Confederate officer's hat insignia, exact full-size repros - $21.50. Over 400 authentic metal & badge replicas. Cat. $5 (free w/ order).

DR. K. DIETRICH
PO Box 994
Stockbridge MA 01262-0994
Buy/sell Civil War memorabilia, soldiers' letters, weapons & accoutrements, images. Listing - 2 stamps.

DIXIE DEPOT
706-265-7533 • 706-265-3952 Fax
http://www.ilinks.net/~dixiegeneral
Dixie_Depot@stc.net
John Black
PO Box 1448 • 72 Keith Evans Rd
Dawsonville GA 30534-0027
Pro-Southern educational products: video/audio tapes, new/old books, bumper stickers, flags, wearables, lapel pins, exclusive Great Seal items. More than 600 items! Catalog. (See ad page 260)

DIXIE LEATHER WORKS
502-442-1058 • 800-888-5183 Orders only
502-448-1049 Fax
PO Box 8221
Paducah KY 42002-8221
Military & civilian museum-quality repros. 60+ hard-to-find leather items. Documents, maps, printed labels & stationery. Swords, firearms, & hats. Handmade chairs, desks; leather medical cases & bottle roll-up kits. Photo- illus. catalog - $6.

THE DIXIE SUTLER
PO Box 5162 • Mobile AL 36605
Specializing in CW-period supplies & collectibles for the reenactor or collector.

DOBI PUBLISHING
716-372-8687
1662 Haskell Pkwy
Olean NY 14760-9510
New edition of *Directory of Buyers* - lists 1000s of collectors & dealers who are anxious to buy. $14.95 + $3 S&H.

R. STEPHEN DORSEY ANTIQUE MILITARIA
541-937-3348 • PO Box 263
Eugene OR 97440-0263
Largest western dealer in pre- & post-Civil War, Civil War, & post-1900 U.S. militaria. Guns, accoutrements, edged weapons, etc. Catalog - $8 for 4 issues.

DRUM & MUSKET
906-842-3549
RR 1 Box 95A • Republic MI 49879-9758
Buys/sells/trades Civil War memorabilia by appointment, or send for free catalog.

DRUMMER BOY AMERICAN MILITARIA
717-296-7611
Christian Hill Rd • RR 4 Box 7198
Milford PA 18337-9713
CW repros: uniforms, buttons, leather goods, insignia, firearms, tinware, canteens, flags, books, sabers, etc. Cat. $1.

EARLY AMERICAN HISTORY AUCTIONS, INC.
619-459-4159 • 800-473-5686
619-459-4373 Fax
http://www.cts.com/browse/ean
PO Box 3341 • La Jolla CA 92038-3341
Mail bid auctions every two months; approx. 1,000 lots in each. Historic Americana & Civil War-related material. Always buying collections & accepting important consignments. Catalog - $36/yr. for 6 issues. Free on Internet.

THE EARLY AMERICAN HISTORY SHOPPE
603-772-7973
225 Water St • Exeter NH 03833-2417
Books (antiquarian & in-print), ephemera, prints, antique memorabilia & collectibles, T-shirts, CD-Rom, flags, games, tapes, maps, mugs, miniatures, genealogies & more. Specialize in the Civil War. Free catalogs.

AN EARLY ELEGANCE
717-338-9311
61 Steinwehr Ave • Gettysburg PA
17325American-made items & authentic reproductions. CW-era writing box, fabrics. Gifts at reasonable prices. Product guide - business-size SASE. Fabric swatch book - $2.50.

GEORGE ESKER
PO Box 100 • La Place LA 70069-0100
Civil War memorabilia (especially Confederate), currency, images, relics, bullets, buttons, projectiles, documents. Catalog - $9 for 3 issues.

PETER EVANS PIPES
305-361-5589
285 W Mashta Dr • Dept F
Key Biscayne FL 33149-2419
Custom-made period pipes, reproductions, clays, quality pipe accessories. For smokers, reenactors, collectors, historians. Free brochure.

EXCELSIOR PRESS
516-475-7069 • 516-874-2489 Fax
Don Roberts
PO Box 926 • Bellport NY 11713-0926
Civil War Cabinet Cards. Color art prints of 24 famous regiments include period battle maps & regimental histories. Boxed set - $23.95 + $3.50 S&H (30-day money-back guarantee). Catalog/brochure - $1 (ref. w/ purchase).

FEDERAL HILL ANTIQUITIES
410-584-8185 / 8329
14 Glen Lyon Ct • Phoenix MD 21131-1212
Purveyors of fine autographs & collectibles. Letters & documents, photos, relics & artifacts, ephemera. Buy/sell/trade.

FIELDS OF GLORY
800-517-3382 Orders
717-337-2837 • 717-337-9315 Fax
http://www.collectorsnet.com/fog/index.htm • foglory@cvn.net
55 York St • Gettysburg PA 17325-2302
Best in Civil War memorabilia. Visit our store. Catalog - $10 for 12 issues.

N. FLAYDERMAN & CO., INC.
305-761-8855
PO Box 2446
Fort Lauderdale FL 33303-2446
Antique guns, swords, & knives. Nautical, western & military collectibles from Revolutionary through Spanish-American wars. Catalog - $15.

THE FLINTLOCK ROOM
201-543-1861
201-543-1865 Fax
http://www.flintlockroom.com
6 Hilltop Rd
Mendham NJ 07945-1238
Collectibles for Connoisseurs - classic firearms, fine cigars, military figurines, prints & militaria, Victorian miniatures.

TIM FORTIER
15 Ramblewood Dr
Newbury NH 03255-6109
Confederate passports. Lifelike document allows safe passage. Customs information, Southern institutions, photo page, entries/departures, etc. $4.

FOUR WINDS TRADING COMPANY
1010 California Dr
Columbia SC 29205-4219
Buys/sells War Between the States art & memorabilia. Open & ltd. ed. prints. Catalog - $4.

FRENCH'S STORE & TRADING CO.
717-530-5037
PO Box 454
Shippensburg PA 17257-0454
Authentic Civil War reproductions of trade goods, 17th-19th century. Specializing in cavalry & leather goods & saddles. Catalog - $1.

FRONTIER SADDLE
941-322-2560
Gabriel Libraty
5530 Juel Gill Rd
Myakka City FL 34251-9234
Replica saddles of the Old West & military; from mountain man to Civil War to classic Western saddles. Free catalog.

GALVANIZED YANKEE
540-373-1886
10611 Heather Greens Cir
Spotsylvania VA 22553-1717
Military collectibles from the Civil War. Catalog - $10 domestic/$20 overseas.

GETTYSBURG CIVIL WAR & ANTIQUE CENTER
717-337-1085
705 Old Harrisburg Rd
N Gettysburg Plaza
Gettysburg PA 17325-3401
Multi-dealer complex in heart of antique country. Civil War memorabilia, military art, antiques & fine collectibles. Open 7 days/wk. Free parking.

JOHN S. GIMESH, MD
910-484-2212
PO Box 53788
Fayetteville NC 28305-3788
Authentic Civil War-era medical, surgical, dental & apothecary items; Civil War-era medical texts. Buy/sell.

CARL GIORDANO, TINSMITH
330-336-7270
tinsnip@newreach.net
PO Box 74 • Wadsworth OH 44282-0074
18th- & 19th-century reproductions. Hand-wrought, custom work. Brochure - send SASE.

WILL GORGES CIVIL WAR MILITARIA
919-636-3039 • 919-637-1862 Fax
http://www.collectorsnet.com/gorges/index.htm
rebel!@abaco.coastalnet.com
2100 Trent Blvd
New Bern NC 28560-5326
Largest active inventory of authentic items in the Southeast. Fine quality uniforms & weapons our specialty. Buy/sell/appraise/broker. Catalog - $10.

GREAT CIRCLE FORGE
PO Box 9040
Lexington OH 44904-9040
Hand-forged ironwork: tent stakes, tripods, potted plant stands, coat racks, decorative hooks, trammel hooks, & more. Cat. $1.50.

GREAT WAR OF THE CONFEDERACY
704-739-5862 • 704-739-1809 Fax
243 Oak Grove Rd
Kings Mountain NC 28086-7720
Civil War memorabilia & collectibles, including historic Confederate art.

GREEN RIVER TRADING CORP.
502-531-3115 Ph & Fax
ekelle@scrtc.net
PO Box 2 • Bonnieville KY 42713-0002
Original & repro Civil War relics, clothing, weapons.

W.D. GRISSOM, SR.
medals@cei.net
PO Box 59
Cabot AR 72023-0059
Medals, documents, related items. Regimental research, reasonable price. Specialist for US & foreign military medals. Catalog - $1 (ref.).

GWYN'S COLLECTIBLES & BOOKS
717-957-4141
717-957-9208 Fax
Gwyn L. Irwin
211 Front St • Marysville PA 17053-1413
Civil War books. Roster of soldiers in the "War of the Rebellion" from Monroe County, New York. 26 pp., 3 columns - $12 ppd.

THE HAMILTON COLLECTION
4810 Executive Park Ct
PO Box 44051 • Jacksonville FL 32231
Collectible plates, featuring CW Gens.

THE HAVERSACK DEPOT
210-620-5192
1236 River Acres Dr
New Braunfels TX 78130-3529
Museum-quality products at reasonable prices, incl. US haversack, CS cartridge box sling & CS leather belt with Ga. frame brass buckle. Satisfaction guaranteed.

HEART OF HISTORY & VARIABLE HEART
540-234-9031 (mall)
John & Miriam Heatwole, Dick Swanson
Simonetti's Antique Center
Rt 11 (at exit 235 on I-81)
Weyers Cave VA 24486
One of the best Civil War shops in the Shenandoah Valley - museum-quality photos & artifacts, wrought iron, pharmaceutical relics, buttons, books, documents, & much more.

DENNIS HEATH
919-569-8781
RR 1 Box 55A
Deep Run NC 28525
Civil War weapons, relics, accoutrements. Catalog - $7/yr.

HERITAGE CLASSICS
800-357-8548
718-218-8587
543 Bedford Ave # 163
Brooklyn NY 11211-8511
Wood Collector's plate, laser-cut inlay of Lincoln & others - $34.95 ea. + $4.95/order S&H.

HERITAGE DRUM CO.
256-533-5498
http://fly.hiwaay.net/~tpalmer
/heritage2.htm • ropedrum@juno.com
Terry Cornett
4021 Apollo Dr SW
Huntsville AL 35805-5601
Custom order, period repro snare & bass drums. Hand-crafted.

HERITAGE STUDIO
540-659-1070 • 540-374-1872
606 Caroline St
Fredericksburg VA 22401-5902
Donna J. Neary's *Even to Hell Itself* - $130. *A Terrible Gale* - $150. *Till Death Do Us Part* - $125. *Do Your Duty, Boys* - $175. *Edge of the Storm* - $150.

THE HISTORIAN'S GALLERY
770-522-8383 • 770-522-8388 Fax
history@atl.mindspring.com
3232 Cobb Pkwy Ste 207
Atlanta GA 30339-3896
Brokers & dealers in maps, autographs, selected relics.

HISTORIC FRAMING & COLLECTIBLES
410-465-0549
Joe Parr
8344 Main St • Ellicott City MD 21043Civil War weaponry & assorted items. Military art by all major artists, including aviation & WWII. True conservation-quality framing.

HISTORIC MIDWAY MUSEUM STORE
606-846-4214
PO Box 4592 • 124 E Railroad St
Midway KY 40347-4592
Civil War newspapers, books on Kentucky. Scale model cannons.

HISTORICAL AMERICANA
718-409-6407
Peter Hlinka
PO Box 310 • New York NY 10028-0017
Military & civilian decorations, medals, award certificates, insignia items, books, & other Americana collectibles. Free catalog.

HISTORICAL COLLECTIBLE AUCTIONS
336-570-2803 • 336-570-2748 Fax
PO Box 975
Burlington NC 27215
Quarterly auctions of Civil War collectibles including photography, manuscripts, autographs, weapons, etc. Consignments encouraged. Catalog - $20/issue; next 3 for $45.

HISTORICAL DOCUMENTS INTL., INC.
603-472-7040
603-472-8773 Fax
PO Box 10488
Bedford NH 03110-0488
Museum quality historical documents originally signed by many of the most famous individuals in history: Washington, Lee, Lincoln, Edison, Twain, Churchill, etc.

HISTORICAL MILITARY ART & COLLECTIBLES
PO Box 1806
Lafayette CA 94549-8006
Collector books, limited edition military art, & military & political collectibles, including medals, flags, badges, pins, & patches. Free catalog.

THE HISTORICAL SHOP
504-467-2532
504-464-7552 Fax
Yvonne & Cary Delery
PO Box 73244 • Metairie LA 70033-3244
Photos, documents, autographs, CSA currency, letters, slavery ads & items, relics, framed displays & other collectibles. Buys/sells. Illus. catalogs - $8/yr.

THE HISTORY WORKS
800-717-7359
vjackson@select.net
2788 Loker Ave W
Carlsbad CA 92008-6612
Reproductions of Muster Roll forms, stationery, art, & Regimental Action Reviews. Call/write for complete details. Free catalog.

HISTORY-MAKERS
4040 E 82nd St Dept 44
Indianapolis IN 46250-4209
Historic letters & documents signed by the greatest history makers who ever lived. Free report.

THE HORSE SOLDIER
717-334-0347
717-334-5016 Fax
http://www.bmark.com
/horsesoldier.antiques
hsoldier@mail.wideopen.net
PO Box 184 • Cashtown PA 17310-0184
Buying, selling & appraising Civil War military antiques: firearms, edged weapons, photographs, documents, battlefield relics & more! All items unconditionally guaranteed. Soldier research service available. Semi-annual catalog - $10/yr.

HUGHES
717-326-1045
717-326-7606 Fax
tim@rarenewspapers.com
PO Box 3636
Williamsport PA 17701-8636
Newspapers; rare, historic - 1600s-1985. Extensive catalog of genuine issues - $2.

THE INDIAN SHOP
606-441-0773
Von Hilliard
PO Box 246
Independence KY 41051-0246
Authentic Civil War newspapers - $10 ea. Indian relics. Catalog - $5 (ref.).

J & B, INC.
910-674-2999
520 Hwy 62 E
Pleasant Garden NC 27313
Fine quality, hand-painted resin Civil War figurines. List - $1 (ref.).

J. J. B. LTD.
PO Box 507
Shamokin PA 17872-0507
Civil War print/calendar of the year 1861. Day-to-day events. 20"x17-1/2" - $29.95.

JACQUES NOEL JACOBSEN, JR.
718-981-0973
60 Manor Rd
Staten Island NY 10310-2626
Antiques & military collectibles, insignia, weapons, medals, uniforms, Kepis, relics, photos, paintings, & band instruments. Catalog - $12 for 3 issues. $15 overseas.

JEBCO CLOCKS
800-635-3226
301 Industry Dr
Carlisle OH 45005-6309
Leading manufacturer of collectibles. Artwork by Kunstler & Gnatek now available on plaques or limited ed. clocks. Clocks - 11"x23", $69.95 ppd. Plaques - 11"x14", $44.95 ppd.

THE JEWELER'S DAUGHTER
301-733-3200
301-733-5076 Fax
24 W Washington St
Hagerstown MD 21740-4804
1860 VMI (Virginia Military Institute) class ring. Repro from original museum piece. 10K gold, wax seal style, "Let Virginia Choose" - $259.95.

JOHN'S RELICS
843-549-7751
cwrelics@lowcountry.com
John Steele
227 Robertson Blvd
Walterboro SC 29488-2752
Civil War & colonial relics, arms accoutrements, veteran memorabilia, newspapers, books, CW tokens, photography, buttons & related memorabilia. Catalog - $1 (ref. w/ purchase).

JPL ANTIQUES
914-896-6006
211 Main St
Fishkill NY 12524-2209
CSA currency, bonds, documents, letters, CDVs, newspapers, accoutrements, CSA/Union imprints. Price list - $1.

K & P VALLEY COLLECTIBLES
540-635-8564
499 Osprey Ln
Front Royal VA 22630-8336
Original, Civil War excavated relics & artifacts, incl. weapons & newspapers. Specialize in original Harper's Weekly issues. List available.

KAWARTHA MARKETING COMPANY
705-639-2572
705-639-1809 Fax
RR 1 Station W
Norwood Ontario, KOL 2VO Canada
Firearms, cannons, knives, helmets, bayonets, daggers, swords, surplus, uniforms, etc. Including originals that have seen battle. Catalog - $4 (ref. w/ order).

J. E. KELLY & CO.
9 Langdon St
Montpelier VT 05602-2903
Recruiting posters of famous Civil War regiments reproduced from rare, mint-condition originals, 18"x 24" - $12.95 ea. 1st U.S. Sharpshooters, 1st Penn. Cavalry, 5th N.Y., Lincoln's Assassin Wanted poster.

KENNESAW MOUNTAIN MILITARY ANTIQUES
770-424-5225
770-424-0434 Fax
CANNONBALL@aol.com.
3017 Butler Creek Rd NW
Kennesaw GA 30152-3327
Civil War relics & complete list of books available. New, reprints, & reference books. Catalog subscription - $10.

KEYA GALLERY
212-366-9742 • Orders 800-906-KEYA
http://www.KeyaGallery.com
Key15@aol.com
110 W 25th St Gallery 304A
New York NY 10001-7401
Excavated relics - bullets, tokens, buckles, buttons, insignia, & more. Catalog.

KINGSTON MILITARY ANTIQUES
770-336-9354
Jerelhook@aol.com
Jere Hook
PO Box 217 0149 • Kingston GA 30145
Buy/sell/trade pre-1898 militaria, mostly CW. By appt. only. Catalog - 32¢.

L & G EARLY ARMS
2049 Clermont Laurel Rd
New Richmond OH 45157-9557
Authentic Civil War guns. Free list w/ business-size SASE.

PHILLIP B. LAMB, LTD.
504-899-4710 • 800-391-0115 Orders
504-891-6826 Fax
http://www.LambRarities.com
lambcsa@aol.com
PO Box 15850
2727 Prytania St
New Orleans LA 70175-5850
Buy/sell Confed. memorabilia; CDVs, currency, documents, photos, art, bonds, slave items, swords, buttons, bullets, autographs, & more.

DEBORAH LAMBERT
1945 Lorraine Ave
Mc Lean VA 22101-5331
Slavery documents, Civil War newspapers, prints, letters, autographs, battle maps. List - $1.

LAWRENCE OF DALTON
706-226-8894
4773 Tammy Dr NE
Dalton GA 30721-6936
Civil War bullets, projectiles, buttons, buckles, plates, bayonets, bottles, hat pins, dug relics. Growing into one of South's largest mail order dealers. Buy/sell. 4 mail order lists - $4.

LEE-GRANT, INC.
804-352-5234
Harry A. Lillie
RR 4 Box 102 • Appomattox VA 24522-8916
Limited ed. prints. Dug & undug artifacts from in & around Appomattox, Va. Flags of all sorts.

LEGENDARY ARMS, INC.
800-528-2767
908-788-7330
908-788-8522 Fax
PO Box 479
Three Bridges NJ 08887-0479
Museum-quality, authentic duplication. Finest repros: swords, knives, battle axe, & bugle, uniforms of the Civil War.

LEXINGTON HISTORICAL SHOP
540-463-2615
Bob Lurate
PO Box 1428 • Lexington VA 24450Civil War memorabilia. Buy/sell books, relics, flags, currency, ephemera. Appraisals. Visit shop Mon-Sat 10-6, College Square Shopping Center, Route 11N, Lexington, Va.

LOGAN CREEK DESIGNS
800-944-5684 • 540-944-5555
540-944-3504 Fax
10347 Lindell Rd
Abingdon VA 24210-8985
Stonewall Jackson's field desk, handmade. Licensed through VMI Museum. Solid cherry, limited ed. Cherry table - perfect complement to desk. Desk - $1,863; table - $350 + S&H. Color brochure.

LOOK BACK IN TIME
803-986-9097
803-986-9297 Fax
PO Box 572
Port Royal SC 29935-0572
Civil War newspapers, engravings, books, relics, & much more. Want lists welcome. Free catalog.

LOST MOUNTAIN RELICS
800 Wyntuck Dr NW
Kennesaw GA 30152-4057
Battlefield bullet set - 3 dropped minies in display case, $12 ppd. Illus. relic list - 3 stamps.

M.J.M. COLLECTIBLES
879 W Park Ave # 244
Ocean NJ 07712-7205
Reproduced copy of Lee's death certificate, suitable for framing. $10.

ROBERT J. MADISON
PO Box 582
Claymont DE 19703-0582
Civil War collectors' watches in color. Gold-plated case, black leather band, quartz movement. Select Grant, Lee or Jackson. $40 ea. + $5 S&H.

MAGIC TOWN
800-878-4276
49 Steinwehr Ave
Gettysburg PA 17325-2811
Bradford Exchange plates - Battles ... & Gallant Men of the Civil War. Michael Garman sculptures at great prices!

JOSEPH L. MARTIN
1125 Kennesaw Springs Ct
Kennesaw GA 30144
Buying, selling, trading fine Civil War swords, guns, uniforms, flags, etc. Over 35 yrs of experience in dealing military items. Competent appraisals available.

MATUSZEK'S
847-253-4685
Frank Matuszek • 126 E Wing St # 210
Arlington Heights IL 60004-6064
Civil War & Indian War firearms, swords, uniforms & other collectibles. Sample catalog - $2. Mention the CW Source Book!

MC GOWAN BOOK CO.
919-968-1121 • 800-449-8406
919-968-1644 Fax
http://www.mcgowanbooks.com
mcgowanbooks@mindspring.com
R. Douglas Sanders
PO Box 4226 • 106 S Christopher Rd
Chapel Hill NC 27515
Always buying. Highest prices paid for fine & rare CW books, autographs, documents, photographs, etc. Cat. subs. - $3.

MEEHAN MILITARY POSTERS
212-634-5683
PO Box 477 • New York NY 10028-0018
Genuine war posters. Catalog - $10 (ref.)

ROD MENCH STUDIOS, LLC
719-380-1126
800-987-1126
719-380-8815 Fax
5967 Omaha Blvd
Colorado Springs CO 80915
Ltd. ed. CW sculpture. Highly detailed, historically accurate, unsurpassed in quality. Pewter sabers, carbines & hardwood base with black brass plate. Cat. $2.

MILES OF HISTORY
423-337-2540
http://www.collectorsnet.com/miles
huskey@usit.net
Miles Huskey • PO Box 599
Sweetwater TN 37874-0599 (cont'd next pg.)

Buy/sell/trade Civil War items. Images, buttons, weapons, documents, personal items, & authentic period jewelry available through internet auction on website.

MILITARY BOOK CATALOG
PO Box 4470 • Cave Creek AZ 85327 Military history, medals, uniforms, weapons, collectibles. More than 1,000 titles. Catalog - $2. Medals catalog - $1.

THE MILITARY COLLECTION
PO Box 830970M
Miami FL 33283-0970
Helmets, uniforms, field gear, awards, medals, flags, weapons, swords, photos, etc. Cat. $8.

JERRY MOSES
3601 Vanderwood Dr
Memphis TN 38128-3417
Shiloh bullets. Authentic Civil War bullets excavated in the vicinity of Shiloh Battlefield. 3 for $10.

MTM RELICS
32 Edgehill Rd • Birmingham AL 35209
Fine Civil War relics, reasonably priced. Catalogs - $6/yr.

MULLINS ANTIQUES
320 Davis Ave • Elkins WV 26241-3894
Reproduction CW state medals - $20 ea.

MUSEUM OF AMERICAN CAVALRY
540-740-3959
Peter & Jane Comtois
298 Old Cross Rd • New Market VA 22844
History of the Horse Soldier from colonial through Vietnam & modern times. Gift shop with books, flags, weapons, relics, other items. Formerly Indian Hollow Antiques.

MUSEUM REPLICAS LIMITED
800-883-8838 • 770-388-0246 Fax
PO Box 840
2143 Gees Mill Rd
Conyers GA 30012-0840
Reproductions of authentic museum quality, historically accurate replicas of weapons & period battle wear. Cat. $3.

SUSAN A. NASH
304-876-3772
PO Box 1011 • Shepherdstown WV 25443
Paper conservation. Specialist in historic documents, photographs, prints, drawings, maps, letters, broadsides. Cleaning, mending, deacidification, museum matting. By appt.

NESHANIC DEPOT
610-847-5627
610-847-8618 Fax
283 Durham Rd
PO Box 367
Ottsville PA 18942-0367
Historic artifacts, muzzleloading guns & supplies, originals, reproductions, & historic flags.

NEW MARKET BATTLEFIELD MILITARY MUSEUM
540-740-8065 • 540-740-3663 Fax
John Bracken
9500 Collins Dr • PO Box 1131
New Market VA 22844-1131
Comprehensive museum shop featuring CW relics, flags, uniforms, bullets, buttons, swords, muskets, currency, memorabilia, etc. More than 1200 book titles. Open Mar. 15-Dec. 1.

NMC ENTERPRISES
800-591-2999 (24 hrs.)
913 18th St Apt 2
Santa Monica CA 90403-3251
Civil War blackpowder accessories; fine, handcrafted leather. Holsters, belts, pouches, bags, buckles. Free catalog.

THE NOBEL COLLECTION
800-806-6253
PO Box 3444 • Merrifield VA 22116-3444
Historic reproductions & collectible swords. From King Arthur to Samurai. Free catalog.

NORTH & SOUTH RECREATIONS
603-629-7192
122 Laura Ln
Hampstead NH 03841-2331
Civil War-era antique reproductions including uniform corps badges & lapel pins, ladies' scroll brooch & pennant corps badge, pipes, etc. Catalog - $1.

NORTH SOUTH TRADERS CIVIL WAR
540-67-CIVIL • 540-672-7283 Fax
nstcw@msn.com
PO Box 631 • Orange VA 22960-0370
Illustrated, bi-annual *Civil War Collectors' Price Guide* - $25 + $3 S&H. Bi-monthly magazine, heavily illustrated - $25/yr.

OHIO SILVER
301-834-5389
PO Box 124
Brunswick MD 21716-0124
Silver bullet key chains & necklaces. Minie bullet replicas (.575 cal.) on key ring or sterling silver chain.

THE OLD PAPERPHILES
401-624-9420
401-624-4204 Fax
PO Box 135
Tiverton RI 02878-0135
Offering 100s of accurately described paper collectibles. Great variety, wide price range. Autographs, documents, books. Catalog - $8 for next 10.

OLD SOUTH MILITARY ANTIQUES
919-523-7181
Dennis Heath
403A E New Bern Rd
Kinston NC 28504-6737
Full line of Civil War muskets, swords, accoutrements & artifacts at reasonable prices. Shop open Mon-Sat. Catalog - $7/yr.

OLDE AMERICAN COLLECTIBLES, INC.
13 Nathalie Ct
Peekskill NY 10566-6240
Semi-annual auctions, mail/telephone. Collections purchased outright or accepted on consignment. Fully illus. catalog - $20 for 2-issue subscription.

ORIGINAL FRAMEWORKS
800-654-1861
540-953-1655
http://ptiweb.com/civilwar
civilwar@nrv.net
Jay Rainey
Gables Shopping Center
1300 S Main St
Blacksburg VA 24060-5526
All Civil War artists at discount; signatures, documents, 19th-century steel engravings, relics. Will find any artwork. Always looking to purchase. Also at 4 E Washington St, Lexington, Va. (See ad page 259)

PALMETTO HISTORICAL WORKS
803-699-6746
Tim Bradshaw
120 Branch Hill Dr
Elgin SC 29045-9383
Civil War researcher. Union & Confederate letters, 6th East Tenn VI muster roll, tintypes.

PALMETTO PRESENCE
803-641-2382
http://www.21mall.com/ppresence.htm
jarnett@seescape.net
Jim Arnett
PO Box 527
Montmorenci SC 29839-0527
Confederate relics, ephemera. Online catalog.

PECARD ANTIQUE LEATHER CARE
541-937-3348
R.S. Dorsey
PO Box 263
Eugene OR 97440-0263
Finest antique leather care. Moisturizes, softens, preserves - absolutely safely. Colorless, odorless, long-lasting. 6 oz. tub - $9.50 ppd. 16 oz. tub - $17 ppd. 32 oz. tub - $28 ppd.

ALEX PECK
217-348-1009
PO Box 710
Charleston IL 61920-0710
Medical antiques. Surgery, military, other fields. Buy/sell. Send SASE for info.

PEMBROKE INK
PO Box 445
Chesterfield VA 23832-0445
For the discriminating collector. Dealer of documents & rare books. Extensive list.

PERRYVILLE CW RELICS & MUSEUM
Ken Hamilton & Dr. Craig Knox
302 S Buell St
Perryville KY 40468-1026
Authentic Civil War artifacts & collectibles, 1861-1865. Guns, swords, photographs, belt buckles, buttons, dug relics, etc.

THE PICKET POST
540-371-7703
Tim Garrett & Bill Henderson
602 Caroline St
Fredericksburg VA 22401-5902
Civil War military antiques: canteens, buttons, swords, guns, images, buckles, uniforms. Buys/sells. Photo-illus. catalog - $10 for 3 issues.

PICTURE THAT ANTIQUES & COLLECTIBLES
414-361-0255 • 414-361-2992 Fax
107 W Huron St
Berlin WI 54923-1516
Large selection of tintypes, CDVs, ambrotypes & cabinet cards of Civil War soldiers & civilians. Books.

THE POWDER HORN GUN SHOP, INC.
540-687-6628 • 540-687-6431 Fax
Robert M. Daly, Pres.
200 W Washington St
PO Box 1001 • Middleburg VA 20118-1001
Buy/sell. Dealers in antique firearms & militaria, Revolutionary War-WWII. Civil War a specialty. Catalog - $20 for 6 issues.

PRESERVATION PRODUCTS
608-839-4038
preservprod@yahoo.com
Jeffery C. Remy
3813 Bass Ln • Cottage Grove WI 53527
Wooden ammunition boxes, shipping containers, traveling chests, officers' & regimental desks, & more. Historically accurate reproductions of Civil War & Indian War. Photo-illus. catalog - $2 (ref.).

THE PROFESSIONAL TREASURE HUNTERS HISTORICAL SOCIETY
603-357-0607 • 800-447-6014 (New England)
603-352-1147 Fax
George Streeter
14 Vernon St
Keene NH 03431-3440
Info. about treasure hunting in US. Metal detecting info. Treasure club activities in US. Newsletter - *Treasure Hunter's Gazette*.

R & L PUBLISHING
28 Vesey St Ste 2116C
New York NY 10007-2906
Bottles of Old New York and *New York City's Buried Past* dealing with Civil War & Rev. War bottles. $22.95 & $27.95 ppd.

STEVEN S. RAAB AUTOGRAPHS
800-977-8333 • 610-446-4514 Fax
http://www.raabautographs.com
raab@netaxs,com
PO Box 471
Ardmore PA 19003-0471
Serious collectors, respected dealers. Top dollars paid for collection & quality individual autographs, documents, manuscripts, signed photos, & interesting letters. Catalog sample - $5; $15/yr.

RAPINE BULLET MANUFACTURING CO.
215-679-5413
9503 Landis Ln
East Greenville PA 18041-2541
Civil War bullet molds. Catalog - $2.

M.S. RAU ANTIQUES
800-544-9440
504-523-5660
504-566-0057 Fax
http://www.bmark.com/rau.antiques
sjtl@aol.com
630 Royal St
New Orleans LA 70130-2116
Authentic Civil War Surgery Kits incl. amputation kit, post-mortem kit, & neurosurgeon's kit - the real things! Catalog - $5.

THE RAVEN'S DEN
860-623-9470
Chet Mulka
PO Box 178 • East Windsor CT 06088-0178
Repro Civil War box plates & medals. Buy/sell Civil War relics. Catalog - $2 (ref.).

REB ACRES
540-377-2057
rebacres@cfw.com
57 Steeles Fort Rd
Raphine VA 24472-2503
Specializing in Civil War artifacts. Priced right for beginning collectors. Comprehensive, 32-pg catalog - send 3 first-class stamps.

J. REB'S CIVIL WAR RELIC GALLERY
706-377-2057
513 Battlefield Pkwy
Fort Oglethorpe GA 30742-3848
Located near Chickamauga Battlefield. Fine quality Civil War artifacts. Excavated & non-exc. Art gallery houses one of finest CW collections. Authorized metal detector dealer. Buy/sell. Catalog - $10/yr.

REBEL STAND
PO Box 4972 • Falls Church VA 22044-0972
Hand-lettered reproduction of authentic Confederate Officer's Commission/Appointment - $25 ea. Include name, officer rank, & CS unit desired on your frameable document with order.

RED BULL ANTIQUES
304-535-2259
staneagl@intrepid.net
Stan Hadden
PO Box 131 • Harpers Ferry WV 25425-0131
Civil War bullets, swords, muskets, pistols, buttons, belt buckles, etc. Original Schneider & Glassick Revolver.

RED CLAY RELICS
770-445-8631
Ray McMahan
PO Box 420
Dallas GA 30132-0420
Buckles, buttons, bullets, shells. Buy/sell/trade. Inventory list - send SASE.

RICHIE'S ARTIFACTS OF THE WEST
719-783-9028 Ph & Fax
PO Box 627
Westcliffe CO 81252-0627
Replicas of old carbon knives. 31 models. Perfect for reenactors. Reasonably priced - $6.95 & up.

RICHMOND ARSENAL
804-272-4570 Ph & Fax
7605 Midlothian Tpke
Richmond VA 23235-5223
100% authentic Civil War antiques, from common bullets & buttons to museum quality weapons, accoutrements, uniforms, drums & flags. Photo-illus. catalog - $10 for 3 issues.

RICHMONVILLE TINWARE
800-501-1675 • 541-678-1675
PO Box 407
21328 Highway 99E
Aurora OR 97002-0407
Highest quality, historically correct tinware obtainable. Custom orders welcome. Catalog - $3.

ROCHESTER CHESS CENTER
800-ON-CHESS
Civil War chess sets. Grant & Lee 5" tall! Choose from various styles.

MIKE RUSSELL
401 Virginia Ave
Herndon VA 20170-5437
Quarterly catalog of Victorian artifacts & relics, emphasis on obsolete currency, bottles & pipes - $2. *The Collector's Guide to Clay Tobacco Pipes, Vol. I* - $20.45 ppd.

S & S FIREARMS
718-497-1100 • 718-497-1105 Fax
7411 Myrtle Ave
Glendale NY 11385-7433
Military Americana. Antique gun parts, carbines, Enfield, buttons, insignia, books, equipment, appendages, headdress, etc. Reenactor supplies. Original & reproduction. Photo-illus. catalog - $3.

SCENIC EFFECTS, INC.
510-235-1955
510-235-9901 Fax
Wendy Schuldt
PO Box 70332
Port Richmond CA 94807-0332
Ltd. ed. of historically accurate buildings, ea. handmade. Some include figures & are hand-painted; unpainted available. Catalog/listing - send SASE.

SCHOOLHOUSE ANTIQUES
717-334-4564
Gettysburg PA 17325
Antique guns, relics, swords, uniforms, souvenirs. Close to battlefield - 5 mi. on Business Rt. 15 South.

CARL SCIORTINO MILITARIA
PO Box 29809
Richmond VA 23242-0809
700-item catalog of Civil War militaria - $2 (ref.). Military books - 600 titles. Catalog - $2 (ref.).

SCOTT'S ANTIQUES & CIVIL WAR RELICS
717-624-2088
121 Lincoln Way E
New Oxford PA 17350-1210
Buy/sell Civil War antiques & relics. Come in & see the shop.

SCS PUBLICATIONS
PO Box 3832
Fairfax VA 22038-3832
Civil War Artifacts: A Guide for the Historian. More than 1700 items pictured, common to very rare. Data includes history, issuance, etc. 240 pp. $39.95.

EDWARD SEMMELROTH
517-278-2214
415 Fleming Rd
Tekonsha MI 49092-9660
Antique iron sales, restoration & reproductions, incl. 1820s-1870s style kitchen cookstove. Custom casting & restoration in any medal; no job too big or small.

SHARPSBURG ARSENAL
301-432-7700 • 301-432-7440 Fax
101 W Main St
PO Box 568
Sharpsburg MD 21782-0568
Purveyors of fine Civil War militaria; firearms, edged weapons, buttons, bullets, leather accoutrements, battlefield relics, books, flags, personal & camp items, paper, letters, framed prints. Buy/sell. (See ad page 264)

SHILOH'S CIVIL WAR RELICS
901-689-4114 • 901-926-3637 Fax
http://www.shilohrelics.com
relics@shilohrelics.com
4730 Highway 22 N
Shiloh TN 38376-4310
Authentic Civil War artifacts. Something for every level of collecting. Catalog - $5 for 4 issues.

SHIPS & SOLDIERS
603-742-1886
PO Box 912
Dover NH 03820-0912
Antique-toy-style toy soldiers, boats, etc. Brochure - $2.

R.J. SIMARD
PO Box 514
Bristol RI 02809-0514
Custom-made ornamental 6" Civil War dolls made to your specifications. $10 ea. (send detailed description or snapshot). Civil War drum pins, enameled red, white & blue - $10 ea. Catalog - $2 (deductible).

SOUTHERN ENCAMPMENTS
504-751-0757
tcld04@premier.net
Tim Rochester
16380 S Fulwar Skipwith Rd
Baton Rouge LA 70810-5743
Civil War antiques; autographs, buttons, documents, period glass, insignia, letters, projectiles, books & more. Photo-illus. catalog - $2.50.

SOUTHERN GUN WORKS
757-934-1423
757-925-1177 Fax
109 Cherry St
Suffolk VA 23434-5306
Civil War prints, autographed military books, memorabilia. Art by Troiani, Spaulding, Kunstler, Gallon, others.

SOUTHERN YANKEE VETERANS MEMORABILIA
409-264-1865 Dan Reed
409-852-2822 Mike Carter
Buy/sell/trade GAR & UCV relics, postcards, Civil War books. Catalogs - $10 (3 issues/yr.).

SPITZ MOUNTAIN ENTERPRISES
Steven Spitz
3013 S Washington St
Naperville IL 60540
Great generals & legendary heroes. Wooden military collectibles. Hand-carved & crafted. Authentically detailed. Grant, Lee, Jackson, Custer, Stuart, many more. $49.95 ea. Color brochure. Catalog - $2.50 (ref.).

DEAN SPROWL
210-816-2590
Boerne TX
Civil War Collector specializing in Civil War images, dug relics & forts of Texas artifacts.

STARS & BARS MILITARY ANTIQUES
540-972-1863
9832 Plank Rd • Spotsylvania VA 22553-4243
Civil War militaria: edged weapons, uniforms, accoutrements, medals, weaponry, prints, etc. On Chancellorsville battlefield, est. 1976.

STONEMAN TREASURERS
PO Box 15309
Philadelphia PA 19111-0309
Musket & trapdoor Springfield parts. Affordable historical collectibles, incl. bayonets, swords, tools, relics, etc. 6-pg. list - $1 + stamp.

STONEWALL ENTERPRISES
800-856-6071
706-321-0020 Fax
Kim Hightower
205 Hickory Chase
Carrollton GA 30117-3522
Ltd. ed., museum-quality bronze sculptures representing the battles of the Civil War by world-renowned sculptor, Eric H. Baret, MD. Call for free brochure.

SUMTER MILITARY ANTIQUES & MUSEUM
803-577-7766
803-856-4629 Fax
http://www.collectorsnet.com/sumter/index.html
585 Chimney Bluff Dr
Mout Pleasant SC 29464-8167
Authentic artifacts from the Civil War. List - $10/yr.

SUTLERS WAGON
Stamatelos Bros, Prop.
PO Box 390005
Cambridge MA 02139-0001
Fine quality American military items, 1775-1900. Civil War uniforms, headgear, accoutrements, buckles, tack, photos, swords, documents. Buy/sell.

SWORD & SABER
717-334-0205
2159 Baltimore Pike
Gettysburg PA 17325-7015
Specializing in original Confederate & Union documents, framed items, relics, weapons & swords. 5 illus. catalogs - $10.

T5 ENTERPRISES
208-788-3348
Larry & Wende Thornton
4 Freedom Loop
Bellevue ID 83313-5012
Buy/sell/trade U.S. cavalry & horse-related equipment (1833-1943).

TEXANA RELICS
PO Box 717
Boerne TX 78006-0717
Trans-Mississippi Civil War relics & images. Photo-illus. catalog - three 32¢ stamps.

THOROUGHBRED FIGURES
3833 Buckhorn Pl
Virginia Beach VA 23456-4927
Ship models (1/600 scale) - antiques, assembled on walnut base. Send SASE for more info.

TIME TRAVELERS ANTIQUES
717-337-0011
http://www.tias.com/stores/gettysburg
gettysburg@mail.wideopen.net
312 Baltimore St
Gettysburg PA 17325-2601
Fine general line of quality Americana, collectibles & decorative arts in ca.1901 Victorian house. Costumed Civil War walking tours of Old Baltimore Street sites.

TL SPECIALTIES
RR 4 Box 336B
Wynantskill NY 12198
Civil War clocks & plaques. Reproduced prints from *Leslies* and *Harpers* magazines of 1860s. Walnut/burnt wood stain. Free brochure - SASE.

TRADEMARK MILITARIA
2800 NW 10th St
Oklahoma City OK 73107-5314
Dealers of historical military artifacts & memorabilia. Trade/sell/appraise. Catalog - $5 for 3.

TRANS-MISSISSIPPI MILITARIA
972-517-8111 Ph & Fax
http://www.collectorsnet.com/transmiss/index.html
charlucv@flash.net
Charles Brecheisen
1004 Simon Dr
Plano TX 75025-2501
UCV, GAR, Civil War & Indian War period relics, books & diaries, papers, letters, covers & records, medical instruments. Always buying. Catalogs - $10 (min. 3 large lists).

TWIN OAKS SADDLERY
407-790-2461
11580 46th Pl N
Royal Palm Beach FL 33411-9141
American-made Civil War goods/reproductions. Cartridge box plates, carbine box, cap box, sword belts, sashes, holsters, saddlebags, saddles & parts, belts & buckles, tinware. Catalog - $2.

U.S. GAMES SYSTEMS, INC.
203-353-8400
203-353-8431 Fax
USGames@aol.com
Lee Stockwell
179 Ludlow St
Stamford CT 06902-6900
Heavily illustrated, informative & entertaining CW playing cards & card games. Facsimile decks of cards originally published in the 1860s. Award-winning Civil War series. Catalog - $2. (See ad page 264)

UNCLE DAVEY'S AMERICANA
904-730-8932 Ph & Fax
http://www.collectorsnet.com/uncledv/index.htm
uncledv@southeast.net
6140 Saint Augustine Rd
Jacksonville FL 32217-2511
Original Civil War collectibles - full range of items for collector & historian. Catalog.

THE UNION DRUMMER BOY
610-825-6280
717-334-2350
http://www.uniondb.com
civilwar@uniondb.com
Bill & Brendan Synnamon, Prop.
420 Flourtown Rd
Lafayette Hill PA 19444-1002
Specializing in authentic Civil War artifacts. Shop located at 34 York St., Gettysburg, PA 17325. Catalog - $6 for 3 issues.

VALHALLA ANTIQUES & COLLECTIBLES
9792 Edmonds Way Ste 255
Edmonds WA 98020-5940
Visit the 508 Main St, Edmonds, Washington, location for the largest & best Civil War selection in the Northwest.

VILLAGE TINSMITHING WORKS
336-468-1190 • 330-468-1191 Fax
Bill & Judy Hoover
PO Box 539
Hamptonville NC 27020-0539
Quality reproduction & period items. Lead-free solder on potable items. More than 80 items. Custom orders. Catalog - free w/ long SASE.

VIRGINIA STEREOSCOPIC EMPORIUM, INC.
PO Box 1718
Stafford VA 22555-1718
Civil War Stereoscopic cards. Beautiful 3D image when viewed through stereo viewer. Set of 6 cards - $19.95 + S&H. Catalog - $2.

THE VOLUNTEERS
207-384-1911
19 York Woods Rd
South Berwick ME 03908
Civil War militaria & antiques. Good selection, many items. Also a shop at RR1 Box 3428, Sanbornville, NH 03872 - Tel. 603-473-8345. Free lists.

WAR BETWEEN THE STATES MEMORABILIA
717-337-2853
Len Rosa
PO Box 3965
Gettysburg PA 17325-0965
Buy/sell soldiers' letters, envelopes, documents, CDVs, photos, autographs, newspapers, badges, ribbons, relics, framed display items, currency, & more. Estab. 1978. Illus. catalogs - $10/yr for 5 issues. Active buyers receive future subscriptions free.

WARPATH MILITARY COLLECTIBLES
910-425-7000
Ed Hicks
3805 Cumberland Rd
Fayetteville NC 28306-2439
United Confederate Veterans Southern Cross of Honor. WWI, WWII crosses of military service. Sell/trade.

WATSON ENTERPRISES
PO Box 392
North Pembroke MA 02358-0392
Letter from Sullivan Ballou to wife Sarah, 1861, as heard on Civil War series on TV. Reproduced on yellow, blue, or gray parchment. $12.95.

WILDMAN'S CIVIL WAR SURPLUS
770-422-1785
2879 S Main St
Kennesaw GA 30144-5624
Rare & antique guns, books, & other Civil War collectibles. Price list - $2. (See ad page 258)

WISCONSIN VETERANS MUSEUM & STORE
608-264-6086
608-266-1680
http://badger.state.wi.us/agencies/dva/museum/wvmmain.html
30 W Mifflin St
Madison WI 53703-2558
Authentic reproduction tinware from originals in our collection. Coffeepot, tin cups, canteens, etc. Blankets. Museum - 2 main galleries & various displays.

CRAIG WOFFORD ANTIQUES
2101 Harrison Ave
Orlando FL 32804-5467
Civil War memorabilia bought/sold, appraisals; specializing in autographs, letters, documents, diaries, photographs. Identifies items, soldiers groupings. Est. 1975.

WORLD EXONUMIA
815-226-0771 • 815-397-7662 Fax
http://www.exonumia.com
Rich Hartzog
PO Box 4143BWX
Rockford IL 61110-0643
Civil War & sutler tokens, medals, slave tags, Civil War dog tags, corps badges, sutler paper, GAR reunion badges, etc. Buy/sell; mail bid sales. Publisher of *Sutler Paper Money*.

YANK & REB TRADER
740-345-4092
PO Box 4704
Newark OH 43058-4704
Civil War artifacts. Buy/sell. Large inventory of reference books not available in bookstores. Catalog - $5 for 6 issues (ref. w/ purchase).

YANKEE FORAGER
517-263-3925
137 Park St
Adrian MI 49221-2528
Civil War specialty books, documents, photos, relics, & more. Catalog - $2.

YE OLDE POST OFFICE
334-928-0108
17070 Scenic Hwy 98
PO Box 9 • Point Clear AL 36564-0009
Dealer in antique & military collectibles, guns, swords, uniforms, books, etc.

YESTERDAY'S NEWS, USA
612-721-5526
5344 34th Ave S
Minneapolis MN 55417-2167
Civil War autographs, books, documents, images, militaria, & identified items. 19th & 20th-cent. newspapers & magazines. Catalogs.

YESTERYEAR
615-893-3470
Larry W. Hicklen
3511 Old Nashville Hwy
Murfreesboro TN 37129-3094
Quality dug & non-dug Civil War artifacts of all types. Buckles, buttons, swords, guns, paper, leather, etc. Mail order subscription - $5/yr.

ALABAMA STATE ARCHIVES & HISTORY DEPT.
334-242-4363 • 334-242-4435
334-240-3433 Fax
http://www.asc.edu/archives/agis.html
Reference Room
624 Washington Ave • PO Box 300100
Montgomery AL 36130-0100

ALASKA DEPT. OF EDUCATION
907-465-2275 • 907-465-2270
907-465-2465 Fax
Archives Division • 141 Willoughby Ave
Juneau AK 99801-1720

ARIZONA LIBRARY, ARCHIVES & PUBLIC RECORDS DEPT.
602-542-4159
602-542-4972 Fax
http://www.lib.az.us/archives/archdiv.html
1700 W Washington St Rm 442
Phoenix AZ 85007

ARKANSAS HISTORY COMMISSION
501-682-6900
http://www.state.ar.us/ahc/ahc.html
State Archives
1 Capitol Mall
Little Rock AR 72201-1049

CALIFORNIA STATE ARCHIVES
916-653-7715
1020 O St
Sacramento CA 95814-5704

COLORADO ADMINISTRATIVE DEPT.
303-866-2055
303-866-2257 Fax
Archives & Public Records Div.
1313 Sherman St Rm 1B20
Denver CO 80203-2236

CONNECTICUT STATE LIBRARY
860-566-3690 • 860-566-5650
860-566-2133 Fax
http://www.cslnet.ctstateu.edu/handg.htm
Archives / History & Genealogy Unit
231 Capitol Ave
Hartford CT 06106-1548

DELAWARE DEPT. OF STATE
302-739-5318 • 302-739-5314
302-739-6711 Fax
http://del-aware.lib.de.us/archives
archives@state.de.us
Historical & Cultural Affairs
Hall of Records, Public Archives
Dover DE 19903

SECRETARY OF THE DISTRICT OF COLUMBIA OFFICE
202-727-2052
202-727-6076 Fax
Office of Archives / Public Records
1300 Naylor Ct NW
Washington DC 20001-4225

FLORIDA STATE ARCHIVES
904-487-2073
904-488-4894 Fax
R.A. Gray Bldg
500 S Bronough St
Tallahassee FL 32399

GEORGIA DEPT. OF ARCHIVES & HISTORY
404-656-2393 • 404-651-9270 Fax
http://www.state.ga.us/SOS/Archives
330 Capitol Ave SE
Atlanta GA 30334-9002

HAWAII STATE ARCHIVES
808-586-0329
808-586-0330 Fax
Iolani Palace Grounds
Honolulu HI 96813

IDAHO HISTORICAL LIBRARY & ARCHIVES
208-334-2120
208-334-4059 Fax
450 E 4th St
Boise ID 83702-6027

ILLINOIS OFFICE OF THE SECRETARY OF STATE
217-782-3556 • 217-782-4682
217-524-3930 Fax
Illinois State Archives
Norton Bldg
Springfield IL 62756-0001

INDIANA STATE ARCHIVES
317-232-3660 • 317-232-3373
317-232-3154 Fax
http://www.ai.org/acin/icpr/index.html
Commission on Public Records
140 N Senate Ave Rm 117
Indianapolis IN 46204-2207

STATE HISTORICAL SOCIETY OF IOWA
515-281-3007 • 515-281-5111
515-242-6498 Fax
http://www.uiowa.edu/~shsi/library/library.htm
State Archives
600 E Locust, Capitol Complex
Des Moines IA 50319-0001

KANSAS STATE HISTORICAL SOCIETY
785-272-8681 x117
http://history.cc.ukans.edu/heritage/kshs/kshs1.html
Library & Archives Division
6425 SW 6th Ave
Topeka KS 66615-1099

KENTUCKY LIBRARY & ARCHIVES DIV.
502-875-7000 • 502-564-8300
502-564-5773 Fax
PO Box 537 • 300 Coffee Tree Rd
Frankfort KY 40602-0537

LIBRARY OF CONGRESS
202-707-9779
http://www.loc.gov
101 Independence Ave SE
Washington DC 20540-0002
Collection of Civil War-related photos, documents, manuscripts, books, more.

LOUISIANA STATE ARCHIVES
504-922-1206
504-922-1209 Research Library
504-342-5577 Fax
3851 Essen Ln • Baton Rouge LA 70809

MAINE STATE ARCHIVES
207-287-5795 • 207-287-5790
207-287-5624 Fax
http://www.state.me.us/sos/arc/general/admin/mawww001.htm
84 State House Sta
Augusta ME 04333-0084

MARYLAND STATE ARCHIVES
410-974-3914 • 410-974-3867
410-974-3895 Fax
http://www.mdarchives.state.md.us
Hall of Records Bldg • 350 Rowe Blvd
Annapolis MD 21401-1686

MASSACHUSETTS STATE ARCHIVES
617-727-2816 • 617-727-8730 Fax
http://www.magnet.state.ma.us/sec/arc
220 Morrissey Blvd
Boston MA 02125-3384

MICHIGAN DEPT. OF STATE
517-373-1408
517-373-0851 Fax
http://www.sos.state.mi.us/history/archive/archive.html
Michigan Historical Center
State Archives Unit
717 W Allegan St
Lansing MI 48915-1730

MINNESOTA HISTORICAL SOCIETY
612-296-6980 • 612-296-6126
612-297-7436 Fax
Libraries & Archives • 345 Kellogg Blvd W
Saint Paul MN 55102-1906

MISSISSIPPI ARCHIVES & HISTORY DEPT.
601-359-6876 • 601-359-6850
601-359-6964 Fax
PO Box 571 • 100 S State St
Jackson MS 39205-0571

MISSOURI STATE ARCHIVES
573-751-3280 • 573-526-7333 Fax
http://mosl.sos.state.mo.us/gov-ser/arch.html
PO Box 778 • 600 W Main St
Jefferson City MO 65102-0778

MONTANA HISTORICAL SOCIETY
406-444-4774 • 406-444-2694
406-444-2696 Fax
Division of Archives & Manuscripts
225 N Roberts St • Helena MT 59601-4514
Photographs, library, genealogy resources.

NATIONAL ARCHIVES & RECORDS ADMINISTRATION
202-501-5400 • 202-501-5410
http://www.nara.gov
inquire@arch2.nara.gov
7th St & Pennsylvania Ave
Washington DC 20408-0001

NEBRASKA STATE HISTORICAL SOCIETY
402-471-4751
http://www.nebraskahistory.org
Library/Archives Division
PO Box 82554 • 1500 R St
Lincoln NE 68501-2554
Checks GAR memberships & burials, rosters of Neb. soldiers, & 1890 Census of veterans & widows. Research fee.

NEVADA STATE LIBRARY & ARCHIVES
702-687-5160 • 702-687-8311 Fax
http://www.clan.lib.nv.us/docs/nsla.htm
100 Stewart St, Capitol Complex
Carson City NV 89710

NEW HAMPSHIRE DEPT. OF STATE
603-271-2236
603-271-2272 Fax
http://www.state.nh.us/state/archives.htm
Division of Records Mgmt. & Archives
71 S Fruit St • Concord NH 03301-2410

NEW JERSEY STATE ARCHIVES
609-633-8334 • 609-530-3200
609-396-2454 Fax
http://www.state.nj.us/state/darm/darmidx.html
185 W State St Ste Cn307
Trenton NJ 08625

NEW MEXICO STATE RECORDS CENTER & ARCHIVES
505-827-7332 • 505-841-4399
505-827-7331 Fax
404 Montezuma Ave
Santa Fe NM 87502

NEW YORK STATE ARCHIVES
518-474-8955 • 518-473-9985 Fax
http://www.sara.nysed.gov
11D40 Cultural Ctr
Albany NY 12230-0001

NORTH CAROLINA STATE ARCHIVES
919-733-3952 • 919-733-1354 Fax
http://www.ah.dcr.state.nc.us
109 E Jones St
Raleigh NC 27601-2806

NORTH DAKOTA STATE ARCHIVES & HISTORICAL RESEARCH LIBRARY
701-224-2668 • 701-328-2666
701-328-3710 Fax
http://www.state.nd.us/hist
North Dakota Heritage Ctr
612 E Boulevard Ave
Bismarck ND 58505-0830

THE OHIO HISTORICAL SOCIETY
614-297-2510
http://www.ohiohistory.org
Gary J. Arnold, Chief Bibliographer & Ref. Specialist • Archives-Library Division
1982 Velma Ave
Columbus OH 43211-2497

OKLAHOMA DEPT. OF LIBRARIES
405-521-2502 • 405-522-5209
405-525-7804 Fax
Archives & Records Office
200 NE 18th St
Oklahoma City OK 73105-3298

OREGON SECT. OF STATE
503-373-0701 x1
503-373-0953 Fax
http://arcweb.sos.state.or.us
reference.archives@state.or.us
Archives Division
800 Summer St NE
Salem OR 97310-1347

PENNSYLVANIA STATE ARCHIVES
717-783-3281 • 717-787-3362
717-787-4822 Fax
http://www.state.pa.us/PA_Exec/Historical_Museum/DARMS/overview.htm
PO Box 1026 • 3rd & Forster Sts
Harrisburg PA 17108-1026

RHODE ISLAND STATE ARCHIVES DIVISION
401-277-2353
401-277-3199 Fax
gopher://archives.state.ri.us
337 Westminster St
Providence RI 02903

SOUTH CAROLINA ARCHIVES & HISTORY DEPARTMENT
803-734-8596 • 803-734-7918
803-734-8820 Fax
http://www.scdah.sc.edu/homepage.htm
PO Box 11669
Columbia SC 29211-1669

SOUTH DAKOTA STATE HISTORICAL SOCIETY
605-773-3804
605-773-6041 Fax
http://www.state.sd.us/state/executive/deca/cultural/archives.htm
State Archives • 900 Governors Dr
Pierre SD 57501-2200

TENNESSEE STATE LIBRARY & ARCHIVES
615-741-7996 • 615-741-6471 Fax
http://www.state.tn.us/sos/statelib/tslahome.htm
referenc@mail.state.tn.us
403 7th Ave N • Nashville TN 37219-1409

TEXAS STATE LIBRARY & ARCHIVES COMMISSION
512-463-5463 • 512-463-5455
512-463-5436 Fax
http://www.tsl.state.tx.us
PO Box 12927
1201 Brazos St / Capitol Station
Austin TX 78711-2927

U.S. ARMY MILITARY HISTORY INSTITUTE
http://carlisle-www.army.mil/usamhi
Carlisle Barracks
22 Ashburn Dr
Carlisle PA 17013-5008
Civil War books, photos, manuscripts, etc., in the army's central historical repository.

ARCHIVES

UTAH STATE ADMINISTRATIVE SERVICES DEPARTMENT
801-538-3012
801-538-3354 Fax
http://www.state.ut.us/html/Records_&_Archives.htm
Archives Division • State Archives Bldg
Salt Lake City UT 84114

VERMONT SECRETARY OF STATE
802-828-2369
802-828-2496 Fax
http://www.sec.state.vt.us/archives/archives.htm
State Papers Archives Div.
109 State St
Montpelier VT 05609-1103

VIRGINIA STATE ARCHIVES
804-692-3500
http://leo.vsla.edu
Library of Virginia
800 E Broad St • Richmond VA 23219

WASHINGTON SECRETARY OF STATE
360-753-5485 • 360-664-8814 Fax
State Archives
1120 Washington St SE
Olympia WA 98504-0238

WEST VIRGINIA DEPT. OF CULTURE & HISTORY
304-558-0230 • 304-558-0220
304-558-2779 Fax
http://www.wvlc.wvnet.edu/history/historyw.html
Archives & History Section
The Cultural Ctr, State Capitol Complex
1900 Kanawha Blvd E
Charleston WV 25305-0009

WISCONSIN HISTORICAL SOCIETY
608-264-6460 • 608-264-6400
608-264-6577 Fax
http://www.wisc.edu/shs-archives
Archives Division
816 State St
Madison WI 53706-1482

WYOMING DEPARTMENT OF COMMERCE
307-777-7826
307-777-7044 Fax
http://commerce.state.wy.us/cr/archives/
Archives Division
6101 Yellowstone Rd
Cheyenne WY 82002

20TH MAINE, INC.
207-865-4340 • 207-865-9575 Fax
Patricia Hodgdon
49 West St
Freeport ME 04032-1127
Specialized bookstore devoted to Civil War with new & old books, art, music, videos, antiques & much more.

A & K HISTORICAL ART
800-286-3084
AandKart@aol.com
12 Kilburn Ave
Huntington Station NY 11746-1508
Large inventory of Civil War art - Troiani, Kunstler, Strain, many more. New & secondary market.

ACCENTS & PRINTS
231 Winslow St
Fayetteville NC 28301-5515

ALLEN'S CREATIONS, INC.
800-669-2731 • 864-654-3594
864-653-4568 Fax
http://www.allenscreations.com
aci@innova.net
R. Trent Allen
PO Box 452 • Clemson SC 29633-0452
Frame & art gallery. One of the nation's largest Civil War print collections with more than 500 prints in stock.

ALLEN'S FRAMEWORKS & GALLERY
919-438-3799
RR 8 Box 386
Henderson NC 27536-9808

AMERICAN ANTIQUES & ARCHITECTURALS
Sue Phillips
3863 Old Shell Rd
Mobile AL 36608-1345
Civil War reproduction prints.

AMERICAN ART & ANTIQUES, INC.
800-242-1994
PO Box 1994 • Staunton VA 24402-1994
Limited ed. prints by Rick Reeves & other artists; sculptures, memorabilia. Visit our gallery, 5312 R.E. Lee Highway, in heart of the Shenandoah Valley, Civil War country.

AMERICAN EPIC STUDIO
717-337-1814 • ka-epic@cvn.net
PO Box 3994
241 N Stratton St
Gettysburg PA 17325-0994

AMERICAN FRAME SHOPPE
717-334-2924
717-334-5549 Fax
39 Queen St
PO Box 3821
Gettysburg PA 17325-0821
Military, contemporary, & wildlife. Stivers, Gnatek, Troiani, Harvey, Kunstler, Phillips, Kidd, Reeves, Landry, Doolittle, Hirato, Lamb, Wilson, Strain, etc.

AMERICAN MASTERS GALLERY
800-547-9232
5222 Rolling Rd
Burke VA 22015-1654
Civil War prints - buy/sell/trade.

AMERICAN PUBLISHING GROUP & PRINT GALLERY
800-448-1863
PO Box 4477
Gettysburg PA 17325-4477
Publishers of Mort Kunstler's fine art prints, America's most collected historical artist.

AMERICANA GALLERY
800-892-6119
541-895-2678
541-895-3679 Fax
83647 N Pacific Hwy
Creswell OR 97426-9712

AMERICAST
800-360-5772
http://www.AmericastUSA.com
AmcastUSA@aol.com
121 24th Ave NW
Norman OK 73069-6320
Limited edition hand-painted figurines (5,000) of great military leaders. $195.

AMIRIAN'S FINE ART & FRAMING
919-735-9128
118 E Walnut St
Goldsboro NC 27530-3649

THE ANCIENT PAGE
290 Macon Ave
Asheville NC 28804-3711

ANTIETAM GALLERY
301-432-5868
17320 Shepherdstown Pike
Sharpsburg MD 21781-1626
Distinctively framed & displayed prints by Kunstler, Strain, Troiani & others. Battlefield gift items.

ARCHIVE ARTS
760-723-2119 Ph & Fax
http://www.archivearts.com
George@primemail.com
PO Box 2455
Fallbrook CA 92088-2455
Clip art, 62 editions for Mac & PC; 8 Civil War editions. More than 450 CW images - $25/edition or CD with 3600 images - $99. Free catalog.

ARMISTEAD CIVIL WAR COLLECTIONS LTD.
310-280-3507
310-472-6081 Fax
8306 Wilshire Blvd Ste 684
Beverly Hills CA 90211-2382
Authentic 19th-century CW map engravings - extremely rare. Civil War-related art.

ARSENAL ARTIFACTS, INC.
800-483-1861
486 W Main St
Sylva NC 28779-5545
Limited edition prints by Bob Graham, John Warr, Mort Kunstler, John Paul Strain & others. Large selection of dug artifacts. Specialize in artillery.

ARSENAL GALLERY
1716 Owen Dr
Fayetteville NC 28304
Gallery featuring the artwork of Dale Gallon.

ART & FRAME CLASSICS
404-270-0542
Northlake Square
4135 Lavista Rd Ste 220
Tucker GA 30084-5325
Specializing in Civil War, military art prints. Over 45 artists in stock, bronzes, Russ Norgan artillery pieces, etc. Free listing - SASE.

ART RECOLLECTIONS
800-278-7746
703-525-2805 Fax
109 N Fairfax St
Alexandria VA 22314-3223
Prints by Paul McGehee. Color catalog - $5 (free w/ purchase).

ART TO GO
888-ART-TO-GO
Ltd. ed. prints at wholesale prices, incl. *Hope of the Confederacy* by G. Harvey.

BACK IN TIME PORTRAIT & FINE ART STUDIO
800-484-1163 x2119
770-631-6533
P. Hardin
PO Box 181
Tyrone GA 30290-0181
"Go Back in Time." Your photo converted into a B/W or full color portrait as CW soldier, mountain man, etc. Any era. Oil, pencil, acrylic. Start at $75.

BALLANTYNES OF WALKERBURN (USA), INC.
888-269-8720
910-323-4872
910-323-0214 Fax
bowusa@aol.com
Tracey Lindsay
PO Box 35001
Fayetteville NC 28303-0001
Fine quality, 8" hand-painted porcelain resin statues. Ask about our collectors club. Free catalog.

BARWICK PUBLISHING
423-984-3581
PO Box 5355
Maryville TN 37802-5355
Black & white charcoal, full-figure ltd. ed. portraits of Jackson, Lee, Stuart, Grant, Sherman & Custer by the late George I. Parrish, Jr. $35/$50 A/P.

BATTLEFLAGS OF THE CONFEDERACY
800-639-2957
Steve Bishop
Franklin TN 37068
Print designed to honor all those who fought for Dixie & banners they followed. 10 flags featured.

BLUE MOON IMAGES
18 Washington St Ste 210
Canton MA 02021-4004
Set of 8 Civil War watercolor notecards - 4 scenes. $8.95 ea. set + $2.50 S&H.

BOHEMIAN BRIGADE BOOKSHOP
423-694-8227
423-531-1846 Fax
Ed Archer
7347 Middlebrook Pike
Knoxville TN 37909-3108
Specializing in 1st edition & out-of-print Civil War books, hard-to-find CW titles & popular reprints. Also, CW prints. Collection assistance. Catalog - $3.

BONNIE'S GIFT WORLD OF PRODUCTS
800-650-5350 • 619-789-6485
619-789-1551 Fax
Bgwhp@aol.com
Keith Bonney
117 Los Banditos Dr
PO Box 1978
Ramona CA 92065-1978
Complete line of 54mm soldiers & sets as well as sculptures, casting molds, kits, corgi vehicles, ships, prints, etc. Catalog - $3.

BOOKMARK
414-646-4499 • 414-646-4427 Fax
PO Box 335
Delafield WI 53018-0335
Mort Kuntsler's Civil War & *Legends in Gray* calendars & notecards. Catalog - $2.

BOXER GALLERY & FRAME CO.
330-494-2348 Ph & Fax
PO Box 2362
North Canton OH 44720-0362
Prints by Troiani, Kunstler, Strain. Mounted officers (15"H) & other Gettysburg figures (9"H) in full color. Free list of swords, bayonets, belts, buckles, insignia.

BROUTHERS & KEEFE "CHAMPION" HOUSE
315 E 86th St
New York NY 10028-4714
Ltd. ed. framed reprints of the original 1890 H. Ellis & Co.'s *Recruit.* Cigarette-Pack-Cards highlighting Lee, Grant, Sheridan, etc. $31.23 ppd. ea.

BUCKLEY MARTIN GALLERY
4617 Montrose Blvd
Houston TX 77006-6101
Limited edition prints by P. Buckley Moss. Subjects include children of the Civil War.

BUDGET FRAMER
888-343-7263
Larry Skaff - Photographry
940 North Ave
Grand Junction CO 81501
Civil War living history fine art prints & photography. Catalog - $1 (ref. w/ order).

BUTTERFIELD & BUTTERFIELD
213-850-7500 x286 • 800-223-2854 x525
Greg Shaw
7601 W Sunset Blvd
Los Angeles CA 90046-2753
Fine art auctioneers & appraisers since 1865. Call for more info. or to order catalog.

DOUG BYRUM/CUSTOM ART
614-459-2622
Creative Illustration & Graphic Design
5413 Bennington Woods Ct
Columbus OH 43220-2221
Historical & reenactor portraits, battle scenes, home-front life. CW photos rendered as custom color art, contemporary art. Commissions accepted, fees based on B&W/color, size, media/subject matter. Prints available.

C & C MILITARY FINE ART
703-904-9320 • 703-904-9718 Fax
PO Box 3514
Reston VA 20195-1514
Original oil paintings by Mark Churms, oil & pencil sketches. More than 750 military fine art prints by Cranston Fine Arts available. 5 vol. color catalog - $65.

CALDWELL STUDIOS
618-747-2655
RR 2 Box 160
Tamms IL 62988-9605
Professional reproductions of regimental flags constructed & hand-painted. Reasonable prices. Reenactment tested. Call Zac for free information.

CANON PRINTS
800-303-6086 • 412-746-1573
James Sulkowski
PO Box 45 • Canonsburg PA 15317-0045
Limited edition prints.

CARDINAL PRINTS
414-784-8348 • 414-7884-7994 Fax
Best prices on Gallon, Harvey, Kunstler, Rocco, & Troiani prints. Free list.

CHICKAMAUGA BRONZE & MARBLE, INC.
PO Box 595
Chickamauga GA 30707-0595
Legends of History Series sculptures. Confederate generals Jackson, Forrest, Stuart & Lee. 16½", cold-cast bronze, patina finish. Ltd. ed. $600 ea.

CIVIL WAR "THINGS 'N FRAMES"
615-952-3672
http://www.i285.com/civil/index.html
sonny_c@bellsouth.net • Sonny Collins
PO Box 422
Kingston Springs TN 37082-0422
Forrest, Davis, Mosby & Stuart prints & notecards from original museum pieces which were painted from life. Also, antique medical equipment & Civil War artifacts.

CIVIL WAR ANTIQUITIES
614-363-1862
http://www.civilwarantiquities.com
Todd Rittenhouse, Prop.
PO Box 1411
Delaware OH 43015-1411
Quality CW items. Guns, swords, letters, currency, books, prints. Buy/sell/trade. Full service custom framing & matting; specializing in conservation framing. Shop located at 13-1/2 N Sandusky St., Delaware, Ohio. Free catalog.

CIVIL WAR ART CENTER
912-929-3018
Warner Robins GA

CLARK ART
919-756-3937
646 E Arlington Blvd
Greenville NC 27858-5837
Framed & unframed prints.

CLASSIC AVIATION ART
770-419-2678 • 770-419-3882 Fax
http://www.warart.com
444 Manget St SE Ste 800
Marietta GA 30060-2759
Recognized leader in aviation & Civil War art. New & secondary market Kunstler, Stivers & Strain prints. Buy/sell/trade. Sign website guestbook for weekly updates. Extensive list - free.

CLASSIC PORTRAITS MILITARY FINE ARTS
800-677-3257 Orders only & Fax
410-747-8780
Michael H. Sullivan
4 Marshs Victory Ct
Baltimore MD 21228-2425
Museum-quality oil paintings & prints of Civil War figures. Custom painted portraits by leading artists from photos. Oils from $225. Prints from $30. Free catalog.

CLUB'S COLLECTIBLES
10029 243rd Pl SW
Edmonds WA 98020-5751
Museum-quality framed prints, produced from archive negatives, & authentic Confederate currency mounted & framed. Many generals.

COLLECTOR HISTORICAL PRINTS, INC.
813-877-9334
PO Box 18661
Tampa FL 33679-8661
Limited edition prints by Reeves & others. Free catalog.

THE COLLECTOR'S ART GALLERY
919-977-0883 • 919-443-4737
1200 S Browntown Rd
Rocky Mount NC 27804-9213
Huge selection of Kunstler, Prechtel, Troiani, Cole, Gallon, Strain, DeMott, Stivers, Rocco, Griffing.

COLUMBUS ARMORY
706-327-1424 Ph & Fax
David S. Brady
1104 Broadway • Columbus GA 31901-2429
Complete Civil War store featuring books, relics, art, muskets & supplies. Buy/sell/trade. Free price list.

CONFEDERATE LEGENDS
703-616-5759
PO Box 2565
Leesburg VA 20177-7764
All the Confederate legends in one magnificent portrait: Davis, Lee, A.P. Hill, Hood, Johnston, Jackson, Stuart, Longstreet, etc.

JAMES H. COOKE & SON, INC.
201-327-1482
PO Box 403
Allendale NJ 07401-0403
Civil War prints, new & secondary market. Price list.

COTTON & CO.
800-994-5366
4 Penny Ct • Hendersonville NC 28739-6871
Tapestries picturing Lee, with Lt. Col. Marshal, leaving McLean House at Appomattox CH. Choose wall hanging ($39.95) or afghan throw ($45). Machine washable 100% cotton.

COUNTRYSIDE PRINTS, INC.
35 W Prospect Ave
Washington PA 15301-6346
Ltd. ed. Civil War art.

COVERED BRIDGE GALLERY
68 S Washington St
Waynesburg PA 15370-2036
Offering America's high-quality collectible artists such as Rick Reeves.

CREATIVE FRAMING
814-266-3477
http://www.citipage.com/minimall/creativeframing
106 College Park Plz
Johnstown PA 15904-2831
Art prints of U.S. history. Kunstler, Stivers, Troiani, Griffing & Buxton. 24-hr. gallery.

CSA GALLERIES, INC.
800-256-1861 • 803-744-1003
http://www.csagalleries.com
2401 Mall Dr Unit A4
North Charleston SC 29406-6597
Confederate prints by Kunstler, Troiani, Strain, Gallon, Stivers, Reeves, Gnatek, Rocco, Nance, etc.

CYPRESS SHADOWS
1060 E County Line Rd Ste 9
Ridgeland MS 39157-1937
Featuring the works of John P. Strain. Write or call for complete listing of all works/artists available.

D & B STUDIO
PO Box 18959
Memphis TN 38181-0959
Civil War art at affordable prices. Price list $1.

DECK THE WALLS
2000 Riverchase Galleria Ste 180
Birmingham AL 35244-2319
Rick Reeves, limited edition historical prints.

DECOYS & WILDLIFE
47 Ridge Rd
Frenchtown NJ 08825-4100
Specializing in Civil War arts & prints. Featuring artists such as Rick Reeves. Call for other listings.

DESIGN TOSCANO
800-525-1733 xA711
17 E Campbell St
Arlington Heights IL 60005-1472
The Lincoln Life Mask, Hands & Draped Bust by Leonard Wells Volk. Replicas of the original works in iron, [illegible]ze green, & bronze. Free catalog.

DOMINICK'S ART WORLD
610-759-9121
224 Nazareth Pike • Trolley Station Mall
Bethlehem PA 18020-9080
Gallery featuring prints by Jeremy Scott.

DON'T KNOW MUCH ABOUT HISTORY
800-531-9173
http://members.aol.com/p20IL/index.html
P20IL@aol.com • Phil Lauricella, President
316 Franklin St
Geneva IL 60134-2639
More than 200 prints by well-known artists such as Kunstler, Rocco, Troiani & Stivers. Carry 300+ CW titles; will research out-of-print or rare items. Free catalog.

EAGLES NEST/ITP
PO Box 6087
Frazier Park CA 93222-6087
Grant & Lee bust sculptures on alabaster. 3-7/16"x6"x1-1/4". Hand-painted with brief biography. $25 ea. ppd.

ECLIPSE
PO Box 773
Cleburne TX 76033-0773
Civil War Series starting with Lincoln & McClellan, cold cast in bronze - 13" tall, ltd. ed. priced from $295.

ELEGANZA, LTD
206-283-0609
Magnolia Village • 3217 W Smith # 573
Seattle WA 98199
Busts of famous people. Lincoln bronze patinated bonded stone, 12-3/4" on alabaster base - $181 ppd. Washington, Jefferson, Franklin, Plato, etc. 128-pg color catalog of museum repros - $6.

EXCELSIOR PRESS
516-475-7069 • 516-874-2489 Fax
Don Roberts
PO Box 926
Bellport NY 11713-0926
Civil War Cabinet Cards. Color art prints of 24 famous regiments include period battle maps & regimental histories. Boxed set - $23.95 + $3.50 S&H (30-day money-back guarantee). Catalog/brochure - $1 (ref. w/ purchase).

FARNSWORTH HOUSE MILITARY GALLERY
717-334-8838 • 717-334-5862 Fax
farnhaus@mail.cvn.net
Loring H. Shultz
401 Baltimore St
Gettysburg PA 17325-2623
Large selection of Don Troiani art - Gettysburg's exclusive dealer for over 10 yrs. New, used & rare books on Civil & Indian wars. Buy/sell/trade. Catalog - $2. (See ad page 272)

FOUR WINDS STUDIO
366 Summit Ave
Ligonier PA 15658-1427
Classic art of the Civil War.

FOUR WINDS TRADING COMPANY
1010 California Dr
Columbia SC 29205-4219
Buys/sells War Between the States art & memorabilia. Open & ltd. ed. prints. Cat. - $4.

FOX INTERNATIONAL, INC.
800-767-8851
PO Box 80037 • Portland OR 97280-1037
Limited ed. bronze casting of Lincoln, by Nano Lopez, 19.5"x12"x8" - $1,950. Also available in bonded marble - $695.

FRAME GALLERY OF STATESVILLE
704-873-6097 Ph & Fax
Carol Chappell
110 W Broad St • Statesville NC 28677-5256
Framed & unframed prints. Offering Mort Kuntsler & Troiani prints, Civil War accessories, encapsulation services utilizing current archival technology. Books.

FRAME MAKER
15 Wade Hampton Blvd
Greenville SC 29609-5656
John Paul Strain's works are featured.

FRAMED EXPRESSIONS
1618 Lincoln Way
Mc Keesport PA 15131-1714
Offering America's high-quality collectible artists such as Rick Reeves.

FRAMING FOX ART GALLERY
800-237-6077
148 Main St • PO Box 679
Lebanon NJ 08833-0679
Troiani, Kunstler, Strain, Gallon, Reeves, Rocco & all others. Inventory of more than 1,000 prints. One of America's largest Civil War art galleries. Custom picture framing.

FREDERICKSBURG HISTORICAL PRINTS
540-373-1861 • 888-FHP-9499 Orders only
540-371-9197 Fax
829 Caroline St
Fredericksburg VA 22401-5805
All major Civil War artists. Oils, prints, sculptures, engravings, montages, memory boxes, books, custom framing. Layaway plans.

FRUDAKIS STUDIO
215-884-9433
2355 Mount Carmel Ave
Glenside PA 19038-4103
Life-size Abraham Lincoln half-round bust suitable for hanging on wall. Call for details.

GALLERY SOUTH
864-461-9038
13 Crestmore Dr • Greenville SC 29611-4519
Prints by Robert W. Wilson S/N - $125. Artist's proofs - $175 for *The Final Farewell*, R.E. Lee at Stonewall Jackson's Gravesite.

DALE GALLON HISTORICAL ART
717-334-0430
9 Steinwehr Ave
Gettysburg PA 17325-2811
More than 75 limited edition prints of Civil War scenes.

GETTYSBURG CIVIL WAR & ANTIQUE CENTER
717-337-1085
705 Old Harrisburg Rd
N Gettysburg Plaza
Gettysburg PA 17325-3401
Multi-dealer complex in heart of antique country. Civil War memorabilia, military art, antiques & fine collectibles. Open 7 days/wk. Free parking.

GETTYSBURG FRAME SHOP & GALLERY
717-337-2796
717-337-2481 Fax
Paul Selmer
25 Chambersburg St
Gettysburg PA 17325-1102
Limited prints by most noted Civil War artists. Originials by Rocco, Reeves, Gnatek, Bender, Umble, Wikoff, Prechtel, Forquer. Civil War books. Catalog - $1.

THE GETTYSBURG GIFT CENTER
800-887-7775
717-334-6245
297 Steinwehr Ave
Gettysburg PA 17325-2815
In the lobby of the National Civil War Wax Museum. Pewter sculptures of the Civil War by Barnum. For a complete listing and more info., write, call, or stop in.

GETTYSBURG HISTORICAL PRINTS
717-334-3800
888-GHP-2515 Orders only
717-334-7562 Fax
ghprints@erols.com
219 Steinwehr Ave
Gettysburg PA 17325-2801
America's oldest military art gallery. Civil War art of most popularly collected historic artists; prints & originals. Montages, memory boxes, sculptures. Custom framing; layaway plans.

GETTYSBURG MILITARY PUBLISHING
800-900-1862
1 White Oak Trl
Gettysburg PA 17325-8039
Limited edition fine art prints by John Paul Strain.

GNATEK STUDIOS
202-363-6803
6642 Barnaby St NW
Washington DC 20015-2357
Michael Gnatek's latest offerings.

CRAIGIE GORDON STUDIO
717-657-8628
717-657-5073 Fax
279 Linglestown Rd
Harrisburg PA 17110
Your Civil War art alternative. Representing Don Troiani & Dale Gallon. Call for listings of many other prints.

GRAY STONE PRESS
615-327-9497
800-251-2664
615-320-1389 Fax
205 Louise Ave
Nashville TN 37203-1896
Limited ed. collector art prints by David Wright & various other artists. Large variety of artwork available. Free catalog.

GREAT WAR OF THE CONFEDERACY
704-739-5862 • 704-739-1809 Fax
243 Oak Grove Rd
Kings Mountain NC 28086-7720
Civil War memorabilia & collectibles, including historic Confederate art.

GREEN FLAG PRODUCTIONS
800-739-6464
PO Box 7757
Greenwich CT 06836-7757
Art series celebrating the Irish Brigade, by Bradley Schmehl.

GREENPOINT GALLERY
704-844-8026
http://www.greenpointart.com
Rob Miller
908 W John St • Matthews NC 28105-1324
Charlotte's largest selection of Civil War & aviation art. New issue & secondary market prints. Custom framing.

GREYSTONE'S HISTORY EMPORIUM & GALLERY
717-338-0631 • 717-338-0851 Fax
http://www.GreystoneOnline.com
461 Baltimore St
Gettysburg PA 17325-2623
Producers of *CW Journal* have created a store, gallery & museum. Military miniatures, books, videos, collectibles, art, exhibits, story theatre. Unique merchandise.

HALLOWED GROUND PRINTS
800-576-7409
919-872-7111
http://www.jps.com/hgp
PO Box 61322
Raleigh NC 27661-1322
Limited edition prints by Jeremy L. Scott.

NESTA HARPER
PO Box 12
Rapidan VA 22733-0012
19th-century engravings of Civil War leaders & battle scenes. Hand-tinted & signed by artist. 9x12 - $11.95 ea. + $3.60 S&H. Price list - send SASE.

HEDGEROW GALLERY
800-433-4376
Civil War prints - Kuntsler, Strain, Summers, Casteel & others.

HENDRICKSEN STUDIO
800-313-7701
Unit 4B The Shipyard
8 Western Ave Ste 18
Kennebunk ME 04043-2878

HERITAGE EMBROIDERY
402-488-7913
402-488-8167 Fax
http://WWW.CivilWarMall.com/Image.htm
Heritage@navix.net
Tom & Dorothy Rivett
PO Box 22424
Lincoln NE 68542-2424
Exclusive Mort Kunstler art images embroidered on quality American-made garments. Personalization available for reenactors, round tables, museums & galleries. Visit our online catalog.

HERITAGE STUDIO
540-659-1070
540-374-1872
606 Caroline St
Fredericksburg VA 22401-5902
Donna J. Neary's *Even to Hell Itself* - $130. *A Terrible Gale* - $150. *Till Death Do Us Part* - $125. *Do Your Duty, Boys* - $175. *Edge of the Storm* - $150.

HERITAGE WEST PUBLISHING
800-303-6629
2501 S Mason Rd
Katy TX 77450-5936

HISTORIC FRAMING & COLLECTIBLES
410-465-0549
Joe Parr
8344 Main St • Ellicott City MD 21043-4653
Civil War weaponry & assorted items. Military art by all major artists, including aviation & WWII. True conservation-quality framing.

HISTORIC PRINT & MAP CO.
888-824-5777
http://www.civilwarprints.com
85 Riberia St • Saint Augustine FL 32084
Famous historic lithographs; repros.

HISTORICAL ART PRINTS
203-262-6680 • HAPRINTS@aol.com
PO Box 660
Southbury CT 06488-0660
Limited edition Civil War & military art prints by one of America's most respected military artists, Don Troiani. Contact for more info.

HISTORICAL HOUSE PRESS
615-297-4357
2805 Westmoreland Dr
Nashville TN 37212-4714

HISTORICAL IMPRESSIONS
888-603-0100 • 970-256-0157 Fax
lskaf@iti2.net
PO Box 60323
Grand Junction CO 81506-8758
PC & Mac standard & multimedia Civil War screensavers for Union, South or mixed versions. Limited ed. art, posters, bookmarks, magnets, postcards. Dealer inquiries welcome. Catalog. (See ad page 264)

HISTORICAL MILITARY ART & COLLECTIBLES
PO Box 1806 • Lafayette CA 94549-8006
Collector books, limited edition military art, & military & political collectibles, including medals, flags, badges, pins, & patches. Free catalog.

HISTORICAL MILITARY GALLERIES
219-534-4858
Civil War art prints by Troiani, Gallon, etc.

HISTORICAL PAINTINGS & SCULPTURE
817-478-3926 Ph & Fax
105420.2351@compuserve.com
Ron Moore
326 Spring Branch Ln
Kennedale TX 76060-5212
Carefully researched & visually compelling fine art. Strong narrative style.

HISTORICAL PRINTS, INC.
800-882-8864
PO Box 18661
Tampa FL 33679-8661
Limited edition art.

HISTORICAL SCULPTURES
518-622-3508
PO Box 141
Cairo NY 12413-0141
Ron Tunison sculptures in cold cast and hot bronzes. Free brochure.

HISTORY IN PRINT
800-816-3571
219-465-5778 Fax
PO Box 1295
Valparaiso IN 46384-1295
World's largest seller of Civil War books, videos, audio tapes, maps & fine art prints. Delivered to your door - select from 100s of titles! Free catalog.

HISTORY UNLIMITED
540-459-3921
1374 Jadwyn Rd
Maurertown VA 22644-2404
Trilogy to honor Chamberlain by Gary Casteel. Cold-cast, hot-cast, or cold-cast hand-painted bronzes. $975 to $3,500 each. Exquisite detail.

THE HOLLOW LOG
800-927-0718
4 Clarksville Hwy
Cornelia GA 30531
Prints by John P. Strain. Call or write for listing of all art available.

HOSPITAL HILL HISTORICAL
800-335-8571
145 Presidents Ln
Quincy MA 02169-1917
Distributors of *Timeless Spirit*, sepia portrait of Lee after the war. 11"x17" - $75.

HRM & COMPANY, INC.
800-511-3864
http://www.apex-ephemera.com
hrmco@praxis.net
PO Box 775
Silver Springs FL 34489-0775
Civil War engravings - more than 1,000 original hand-colored newspaper engravings - $55 & up.

MURRAY HUDSON - ANTIQUARIAN BOOKS & MAPS
800-748-9946 • 901-836-9057
901-836-9017 Fax
mapman@usit.net
109 S Church St
PO Box 163
Halls TN 38040-0163
Large selection of Civil War authentic maps & prints. 1300+ items (priced $25-$7,500). Rare Forrest bust; large Lee print. Catalog - $10 (ref.).

ISI PRINTS
2821 Minot Ln
Waukesha WI 53188-4525
Limited ed. prints of Civil War battle flags, by J.B. Collins.

J R FRAMING
703-878-1036
4390 Kevin Walker Dr
Dumfries VA 22026-1635
Gallery featuring the work of Dale Gallon. Also at 6050 Gorgas Rd, Fort Belvoir, Va.

J.J.B. LTD.
PO Box 507
Shamokin PA 17872-0507
Civil War print/calendar of the year 1861. Day-to-day events. 20"x17-1/2" - $29.95.

J'S GALLERY & FRAME SHOPPE
800-448-1861
515-448-4012
http://www.netins.net/showcase/art
406 E Broadway St
Eagle Grove IA 50533-1817
Civil War prints by Strain & others. Gallery located at 109 S Commercial, Eagle Grove, Iowa.

JEBCO CLOCKS
800-635-3226
301 Industry Dr
Carlisle OH 45005-6309
Leading manufacturer of collectibles. Artwork by Kunstler & Gnatek now available on plaques or limited ed. clocks. Clocks - 11"x23", $69.95 ppd. Plaques - 11"x14", $44.95 ppd.

TERRY JONES
610-353-2210
234 Hickory Ln
Newtown Square PA 19073-3326
Solid cold-cast bronze and hot bronze sculptures available. Works include Stonewall Jackson, Chamberlain, Gen. John Gibbon, etc.

JUNCTION SOFTWARE
970-256-0194
751 Horizon Ct Ste 244
Grand Junction CO 81506-8718
ArtCollector for Windows. Track your art collection, invoices, inventory, for-sale lists & much more. Living history Civil War screensavers by Historical Impressions.

K & E OUTLET
900 Conference Dr
Goodlettsville TN 37072-1923
Prints by John Paul Strain.

ERIC KAPOSTA STUDIO
800-247-3550
6109 W 34th St
Houston TX 77092-6407
Gen. R.E. Lee, 13" tall bust in cast stone with terra-cotta finish - $175. Call for details.

KATE GALLERY
652 Great Plain Ave
Needham MA 02192-3305
18th-20th century architecture, furniture & decorative art prints. Framed & unframed. Fine notecards. Illus. catalog - $2.

J. E. KELLY & CO.
9 Langdon St
Montpelier VT 05602-2903
Recruiting posters of famous Civil War regiments reproduced from rare, mint-condition originals, 18"x24" - $12.95 ea. 1st U.S. Sharpshooters, 1st Penn. Cavalry, 5th N.Y., Lincoln's Assassin Wanted poster.

KIDD HISTORIC GALLERY
100 Waterfront Dr
Colonial Heights VA 23834-2180
Henry Kidd's moving & romantic set of prints. Color brochure - free.

JANE KUNSTLER
516-624-2830
PO Box 311
Oyster Bay NY 11771-0311
Kunstler Civil War artist's proofs - most prints available. Western, Native American, & other subjects.

LANG GRAPHICS
414-646-2211
PO Box 99
Delafield WI 53018-0099
Mort Kunstler's new Civil War calendar & notecards. Beautifully done, fully illustrated. $12.95 + $5 S&H. Catalog - $2.

THE LAST SQUARE
800-750-4401
http://www.lastsquare.com
questions@lastsquare.com
5944 Odana Rd
Madison WI 53719-1214
Dedicated to military history. Gaming supplies, miniatures, books, fine prints. Call for info.

MICHAEL L. LEE
1981 Stonewood Dr
Cithia Springs GA 30057-2776
General R.E. Lee, by artist Michael L. Lee. Limited edition. 11"x14" B/W print - $35. Framed - $99.95.

LEE-GRANT, INC.
804-352-5234
Harry A. Lillie
RR 4 Box 102 • Appomattox VA 24522-8916
Limited ed. prints. Dug & undug artifacts from in & around Appomattox, Va. Flags of all sorts.

LIMITED EDITION ART
800-468-0153 Ph & Fax
1066 Lizabeth Cir
Newark OH 43056-1626
Art prints by Gallon, Duillo, Gnatek, Kidd, McGrath, Rocco, Umble, Vann.

LONE WARRIOR
800-767-3498
Olathe KS
T.M.L. Peterson, *Soldier in the Rain*, 24"x30" S/N $150; A/P $175.

MAGIC TOWN
800-878-4276
49 Steinwehr Ave
Gettysburg PA 17325-2811
Bradford Exchange plates - Battles ... & Gallant Men of the Civil War. Michael Garman sculptures at great prices!

MAGNUM CREATION
310-659-3077
835 S Wooster St Apt 315
Los Angeles CA 90035-1758
Original sculptured soldiers, 6"-12" tall, Civil War & WWI. Certificate with ea. $39.95.

THE MARKS COLLECTION
800-849-3125
http://www.markscollection.com
8601 Dunwoody Pl Ste 510
Atlanta GA 30350-2551
Resurrection Morn - ltd. ed. 1250 - $95. *Honor in Darkest Hour* - ltd. ed. 2000 - $95.

RON MARLETT
904-269-1940
Bob Marlett
PO Box 40192
Jacksonville FL 32203-0192
Limited ed. prints.

MAYO RIVER ART & FRAME
910-427-5735
206 S Lonesome Rd
Madison NC 27025-1842
18"x24" framed, ltd. ed. print of *Lee's Flag* by Tom Butler. Includes original Civil War commemorative 1st day-issue stamped envelope. S/N - $150 ppd.

MAZE CREEK STUDIO
800-432-1581
1495 E 13th St
Carthage MO 64836-9317
Trans-Mississippi print series - $50 ea. Pea Ridge, Westport, Wilson's Creek, etc.

JANET MC GRATH STUDIO
800-346-9398
904-697-3543
PO Box 731
Lanark Village FL 32323-0731
Lee and His Valiant Men - Longstreet, Forrest, Stuart, Jackson. Ltd. ed. S/N - $95; Artist proof - $150. $10 flat S&H.

MEADOWBROOK PUBLISHING
717-263-3282
43 S Main St
Chambersburg PA 17201-2237

MEEHAN MILITARY POSTERS
212-634-5683
PO Box 477
New York NY 10028-0018
Genuine war posters. Catalog - $10 (ref.).

MELROSE TRADING
912-742-0620
912-741-3864 Fax
PO Box 6292
Macon GA 31208-6292
Robert E. Lee bronze sculpture with walnut frame, ltd. ed. Library of Congress 1937 copyright. $1995 ea.

MEMORIAL GRAPHICS
4461 W Flamingo Rd # 180
Las Vegas NV 89103-3703
Silk screened prints reproduced from the original headstone rubbings of Civil War greats - Lee, Stuart, Davis, etc. Free brochure.

ROD MENCH STUDIOS, LLC
719-380-1126
800-987-1126
719-380-8815 Fax
5967 Omaha Blvd
Colorado Springs CO 80915
Ltd. ed. Civil War sculpture. Highly detailed, historically accurate, unsurpassed in quality. Featuring pewter sabers, carbines & hardwood base with black brass plate. Catalog - $2.

DON MEREDITH'S CIVIL WAR ART
813-962-1225
PO Box 370020
Tampa FL 33697-0020
Ordinary photos turn into extraordinary CW-era portraits, with strict attention to detail. Prices vary from $75. Discounts for photos showing proper uniform, gear, pose, etc. Color brochure - free.

MERENS (USA) LTD.
800-793-9365
12 Twin Lakes Dr Ste 1200
Bedford NY 10506-1609
Civil War cartoon art from original comic book panels. Each limited edition of 750 cels. - $64.90 per cel.

MILITARY ART CLASSICS
256-435-6499 Ph & Fax
Steve McCracken
PO Box 423
Jacksonville AL 36265-0423
Limited edition military prints, new & secondary market. Civil War specialist. All popular artists. Competitive prices; layaway. Free price list.

THE MILITARY ART GALLERY
800-362-8567
57 Macomb Pl
Mount Clemens MI 48043-5624
Dealer of Cranston Fine Arts limited edition prints.

MILITARY ART SHOP
706 Edwards Dr
Harker Heights TX 76548-1340
Gallery featuring the art of Dale Gallon.

MIKE MINER'S GALLERY II
1235 Park Rd
Sevierville TN 37862-2805
Professional gallery representing most national & regional artists. One of largest selections of Civil War art in the nation.

MOMENTS IN HISTORY
800-328-5865
5483 Beaujolaise Ln
Fort Myers FL 33919-2703
Authentic woodcut prints of Civil War scenes as witnessed & created by the nation's finest artists of the period. Complete, illus. catalog.

MONUMENTS OF AMERICA
321 Baltimore St
Gettysburg PA 17325-2602
Work of sculptor Gary Casteel in "Commanders of the Shenandoah Valley" series.

C. W. MORGAN CO.
757-631-5393
3419 Virginia Beach Blvd Ste B14
Virginia Beach VA 23452-4419
Series of Civil War generals & naval commanders in 19th-century-style art.

DAN NANCE PRINTS
704-543-1115
http://www.civil-war.net/nance.html
10433 Kilmory Ter
Charlotte NC 28210-8349
The Bloody Lane (Sharpsburg, MD) by Dan Nance - $173 (artist's proofs).

NATIONAL GLASS & MIRROR CO.
540-647-3806
205 Virginia Ave
Collinsville VA 24078-2268
Framed & unframed prints.

NATURE'S IMAGE
800-333-0395
95 8th Ave SW
Forest Lake MN 55025-1877
Civil War arts & prints. Featuring artists such as Rick Reeves & others.

NEWFIELD PUBLICATIONS
PO Box 16613
Columbus OH 43272-0001
Set of Civil War cards. Many scenes, incl. *Battle of Gettysburg: Pickett's Charge*, by Mort Kunstler.

NEWMARK PUBLISHING, USA
800-866-5566
502-266-6752
11700 Commonwealth Dr Ste 900
Louisville KY 40299-6363
Featuring Robert Summer, Gary Lynn Roberts, & Wayne Justus. Catalog - $3.50.

DAVID I. NORWOOD, ARTIST
504-344-7249
2247 Oleander St
Baton Rouge LA 70806-5326
Poster-size aerial view depicting siege of Port Hudson in great detail. B&W - $10.

OLD GLORY GALLERIES
706-556-0677
174 N Louisville St
PO Box 1327
Harlem GA 30814-1327
Specializing in the Civil War. Kunstler, Stivers, Strain, Gallon & others. Cat./price list - free.

OLD GLORY GALLERY & FRAME SHOPPE, INC.
800-731-0060 • 817-923-5576
http://www.oldgloryprints.com
Robert Rubel
2966 Park Hill Dr • Fort Worth TX 76109-1143
Civil War prints. Troiani, Kunstler, Strain, Gallon, Stivers, Reeves, Heron, Gnatek, Freeman, Kidd, Wright, & others. Chilmark Civil War sculptures. Send for list.

THE OLD GUARD MILITARY ART
519-432-8410
136 Emery St, W. London
Ontario CANADA N6J 1S1
Dealer of Cranston Fine Arts limited edition prints.

OLD SOUTH ART & FRAME
770-471-3621
2695 Emerald Dr
Jonesboro GA 30256-5231
Fine art prints by Reeves, Gallon, Gnatek, Troiani, Kunstler, Neery, Rocco, Umble, McGrath, Strain. Sculptures by Tunison, Casteel, Krebs, etc.

ORANGE HISTORICAL ARTWORKS
PO Box 828 • Pine Bush NY 12566-0828
Series of watercolor prints by Civil War artist/reenactor Dianne Drewes.

ORIGINAL FRAMEWORKS
800-654-1861 • 540-953-1655
http://ptiweb.com/civilwar
civilwar@nrv.net • Jay Rainey
Gables Shopping Center • 1300 S Main St
Blacksburg VA 24060-5526
All CW artists at discount; signatures, documents, 19th-century steel engravings, relics. Will find any artwork. Always looking to purchase. Also at 4 E Washington St, Lexington, Va. (See ad page 259)

OSAGE PRESS
815-398-0602
PO Box 5082
Rockford IL 61125-0082
Repro of 1860 Spencer Repeating Rifle Patent Drawings - start at $13.95. Free catalog.

P & L ENTERPRISE
301-449-5730
PO Box 518
Temple Hills MD 20757-0518
Buffalo Soldiers - ltd. ed. prints, statues, books. Color brochure - $2.

PANIOLO ART LTD.
7325 Henderson Ct SE
Tumwater WA 98501-6832

PARAMOUNT PRESS, INC.
716-789-3001
PO Box 226
Stow NY 14785-0226
Featuring Rick Reeves prints, proofs, & originals.

PARKER'S PICTURE FRAMING
800-648-2701
111 Erie St
Edinboro PA 16412-2208
Civil War arts & prints; featuring Rick Reeves. Call for other listings.

PHALANX STUDIO
608-437-6739
http://www.amtma.com/phalanxweb/phalanx.html
MThor1864@aol.com
414 Oak St
Mount Horeb WI 53572-1744
Ltd. ed. Civil War art by Mike Thorson.

PIECES OF HISTORY
602-488-1377
800-488-1316 Fax
PO Box 4470
Cave Creek AZ 85327-4470
Civil War historical art with CW medal. Gen. Custer or Citizen Corp of Wisconsin at South Mountain, MD. $89.95 ea. + $5 S&H. Military book or video catalog - $1 ea.

JOHN I. PISARCIK
1500 Annette Ave
Library PA 15129-9735
Reenactors - will draw your portrait from photo in "Battlefield Style." Special attention paid to details of uniforms, clothing & equipment.

DON PITCHER
75 Washington Ave Unit 7-204
Hamden CT 06518-6403
Offering original wood engravings as removed from Civil War-period newspapers. Locations, battles, leaders, maps, etc. Free catalog/list. (See ad page 260)

PIXELCHROME PROFESSIONAL
4304 Standridge Dr
The Colony TX 75056-4033
Gettysburg commemorative posters - 11"x17" - full color. Art prints of the Penn. & Va. monuments. Both posters - $15 + $3.95 S&H.

PORTRAIT SCULPTURE
217-422-6335
4 Ridge Ct • Decatur IL 62522-2539
Lincoln Sculptures by John McClarey. "Unfinished Work" - ltd. ed., 24"H bonded-bronze - $700. Individually crafted.

THE POTOMAC GALLERY
800-882-1861 • 703-771-8085
703-771-8161 Fax
17 S King St
Leesburg VA 20175-2903
Hand-painted pewter Civil War chess set. Limited editions by Stivers, Kunstler, Gallon, Strain, Troiani & more. Custom framing done on site. (See ad page 258)

PRECIOUS MEMORIES
919-639-2501
123 S Broad St • Angier NC 27501

THE PRESTON BROOKS SOCIETY
800-820-1860
PO Box 13012
James Island SC 29422-3012
Largest & best 100% Confederate Clip Art, Vol. 1. PC & MAC versions - more than 125 images on 5 disks, incl. flags, battles, soldiers, ships, weapons, stamps, forts, & much more!

THE PRINT PLACE
615-486-2929
1354 Gravel Hill Rd
Columbia TN 38401-1371
Civil War prints. Kunstler, Troiani, Strain, and others.

RAINBOW CARD CO.
800-473-5213 • 516-367-6790
516-367-3063 Fax
717 E Jericho Tpke Ste 315
Huntington Station NY 11746-7502
Official Currier & Ives "Civil War" card set. Limited edition (5,000 sets), individually serial numbered, 16 full-color cards - $14.95/set. Catalog - $1.

RAMCO FRAMING
7705C Saint Andrews Rd
Irmo SC 29063-2835
Framed & unframed prints.

J. REB'S CIVIL WAR RELIC GALLERY
706-377-2057
513 Battlefield Pkwy
Fort Oglethorpe GA 30742-3848
Located near Chickamauga Battlefield. Fine quality Civil War artifacts. Excavated & non-exc. Art gallery houses one of finest CW collections. Authorized metal detector dealer. Buy/sell. Catalog - $10/yr.

RED LANCER
PO Box 8056
Mesa AZ 85214-8056
Original 19th-century military art, rare books, Victorian-era campaign medals & helmets, toy soldiers. Catalog - $12 for 3-4 issues/yr.

RED'S MILITARY PRINTS
800-711-7337
PO Box 1071
Ringgold GA 30736-1071
Rare, historic full-color art prints - 8 Civil War, 24 Amer. Revolution. Illus. brochure - $1.

REMEMBRANCE ART
Ray Helmicki
1481 N Creek Rd
Lake View NY 14085-9516
Art gallery-quality Civil War shadow boxes in solid oak. Ltd. ed. of *Country Divided*, 30"x16" - $375. For more info, send SASE. Dealer inquiries welcome. Catalog - $3 (ref.).

RIVERDALE DECORATIVE PRODUCTS
PO Box 4959
1920 S Court St
Montgomery AL 36103-4959
Civil War battle scene pillows by Mort Kunstler. From $15.

ROUND TOP MINIATURES
301-330-3552
7766 Epsilon Dr
Rockville MD 20855-2555
Painted miniatures 15mm-120mm. Custom, shadow box & museum dioramas - realistic & historically accurate; ea. is unique with custom-designed figures. Catalog - $2 (ref.).

SANDLIN & ASSOCIATES
913-432-1705 • 913-432-5997 Fax
6405 Metcalf Ave Ste 420
Overland Park KS 66202-3929
Limited edition Civil War prints, more than 75 different types. Also available as etchings. Complete, illus. catalog - $3.50.

SCOTTISH IMAGES
800-700-0334 Orders • 916-362-3474 Ph/Fax
PO Box 160133
Sacramento CA 95816-0133
Dealer for Cranston Fine Arts limited edition prints.

SCULPTURES IN CLAY
8324 Mary Ave NW • Seattle WA 98117-4240
Limited edition ceramic sculptures by Richard Bowman.

SENECA RIDGE GALLERY
412-828-0240
426 Allegheny River Blvd
Oakmont PA 15139-1725
Civil War & 18th-century art, books, videos, games, music, more!

SENECA VALLEY FINE ART GALLERIES
301-898-5786
11639 Coppermine Rd
Union Bridge MD 21791-8437
All major artists represented. Civil War prints featuring Gallon, Troiani, Strain, Stivers, Reeves, etc.

SHARPSBURG ARSENAL
301-432-7700 • 301-432-7440 Fax
101 W Main St • PO Box 568
Sharpsburg MD 21782-0568
Purveyors of fine Civil War militaria; firearms, edged weapons, buttons, bullets, leather accoutrements, battlefield relics, books, flags, personal & camp items, paper, letters, framed prints. Buy/sell. (See ad page 264)

SHENANDOAH FRAMING, INC.
800-368-2171
215 Greenhouse Rd
Lexington VA 24450-3717
Framed & unframed prints. Prints by Tom Gallo, Michael Gnatek.

SILENT SENTINEL STUDIO
914-245-8903
Paul R. Martin III & Joanne F. Martin
PO Box 551
Yorktown Heights NY 10598-0551
Publishes ltd. ed. fine art prints by Paul R. Martin III. Color pencil drawings are contemplative images featuring battlefield monuments & landscapes. Commissions & dealer inquiries welcome. Credit cards accepted. Free catalog. (See ad page 259)

SIMMONS TPC
7011A Manchester Blvd Ste 165
Alexandria VA 22310-3202
Generals Grant & Lee in alabastrite sculptures. 6"x3-7/16"x1-1/4". Hand-painted (blue or gray). $25 ea. ppd.

SLAVIN'S GALLERY
800-448-9517 • 910-346-4105
http://slavin.onslowonline.net
201 Country Club Rd
Jacksonville NC 28546-6400
Finest illustrated Civil War history available. Fine art prints; original & ltd. eds. Sculptures; 1/8 & 1/4 scale model CS Artillery.

SM & S NAVAL PRINTS
410-893-8184 • 410-788-0660 Fax
PO Box 41 • Forest Hill MD 21050-0041
Lithographs. Call or write for complete listing.

SOMEWHERE IN TIME STUDIO
215-536-0143
PO Box 7 • Zionhill PA 18981-0007
Civil War sketches by artist Deborah George.

SOUTHERN/AMERICAN HERITAGE
PO Box 1894
Lancaster SC 29721-1894
Affordable portraits/prints. Beautiful, classic, professionally matted & framed. Lee, Jackson, Grant, Lincoln, Stuart, Forrest, etc. Gettysburg Address, Lee and Jackson's last meeting. Catalog - $4.

SOUTHERN GUN WORKS
757-934-1423 • 757-925-1177 Fax
109 Cherry St
Suffolk VA 23434-5306
Civil War prints, autographed military books, memorabilia. Art by Troiani, Spaulding, Kunstler, Gallon, others.

SOUTHERN HERITAGE PRINTS
256-539-3358
George Mahoney, Jr.
PO Box 503 • Huntsville AL 35804-0503
Civil War flags, memo pads, envelopes, bookmarks, paperweights, chronology chart/map, prints. *Last Charge at Brandy Station*, ltd. ed. print by C.E. Monroe, Jr. - $135 inc. S&H. Portion of proceeds goes to APCWS.

SOUTHERN HISTORICAL SHOWCASE
800-854-7832 • 615-321-0639
http://www.southernhistorical.com
southernhistorical@nashville.com
1907 Division St
Nashville TN 37203-2705
Southern military art & books, prints, original documents & autographs, photos, engravings. Artists: Prechtel, Reeves, Kunstler, Kidd, Gallon, Summers, Heron, Garner, Rocco. Catalog - $5.

SOUTHLAND HISTORICAL ART PRINTS
770-917-0177
4375 Willis St • Acworth GA 30101-5468
Art prints by Mark Lemn.

SOUTHPORT GALLERY
800-641-4901
PO Box 111405 • Stamford CT 06911-1405
George Pickett, Pride of the Confederacy, by Dale Gallon. 21"x28", $199 + $5 S&H. Complete with genuine Confederate bank note.

SOUTHWEST PASSAGE
603-895-3425
8 Bow St • Portsmouth NH 03801-3802
Offering prints by Mort Kunstler.

STIVERS PUBLISHING
540-882-3855
PO Box 25 • Waterford VA 20197-0025
Paintings by Don Stivers.

STONE SOUP GALLERY & SOLDIERS HAUNT INN
540-722-3976 • HAUNTINN@aol.com
107 N Loudoun St
Winchester VA 22601-4717
Original etchings, antique (1800s) furniture & quilts, antique reproductions. Bed & breakfast in building built in 1760. Showcase of regional talents.

STONES RIVER PRESS, INC.
800-207-8327
316 W Lytle St Ste 106
Murfreesboro TN 37130-3641

STONEWALL ENTERPRISES
800-856-6071 • 706-321-0020 Fax
Kim Hightower
205 Hickory Chase • Carrollton GA 30117
Ltd. ed., museum-quality bronze sculptures representing the battles of the Civil War by world-renowned sculptor, Eric H. Baret, MD. Call for free brochure.

STORY SLOANE'S GALLERY
713-782-5011
713-782-5048 Fax
2616 Fondren Rd
Houston TX 77063-2310
Generals of the Confederacy sculpture series by Edward L. Hankey. Hand-painted, crafted in fine porcelain.

STRICTLY SOUTHERN
912-454-1860
912-453-8483 Fax
http://www.accucomm.net/~theSouth
Ken Simpson
PO Box 1945
Milledgeville GA 31061
Confederate shop featuring books, T-shirts, souvenirs, Kunstler prints, jewelry. Mail orders available.

STUDIO OF SUNFLOWER LANDING
901-755-2391
800-423-0463
http://www.civilwarart.com
stratton@civilwarart.com
Harold Stratton
162 Leif Cv
Cordova TN 38018-7327
Civil War prints of Nathan Bedford Forrest, Robert E. Lee, & Stonewall Jackson. Total of 14 prints. Brochure.

SUNSHINE STUDIO
800-628-8004
2169 N Sunshine Rd
Fayetteville AR 72704-6342
Sculptor John Doty's limited editions in cold-cast bronze & hand-painted.

TAYLOR DESIGN, INC.
800-371-9452
304-876-1666 Fax
taylor@intrepid.net
PO Box 956
Harpers Ferry WV 25425-0956
Tom Taylor's mixed media technique combines intricate details with creative symbolism. *A Journey Through the Civil War*, open ed. print series, $17 ea. + S&H. Free brochure.

MARION SUE THOMPSON
501-972-0133
4300 Brenda St
Jonesboro AR 72401-8422
Sultana Disaster. Limited edition prints by Marion Sue Thompson, artist. Call for more info.

TIARA GIFTS
800-457-9911
1675 Rockville Pike
Rockville MD 20852-1619
Chilmark "sold out" & nearly "sold out" sculptures. Free catalog.

TRADITION STUDIOS
540-459-5469
540-459-5951
Keith Rocco
PO Box 779
Woodstock VA 22664-0779
Limited ed. prints by one of the finest historical artists working today, Keith Rocco. Free color catalog.

TREASURES
800-354-6393
PO Box 126
Kiawah Island SC 29455-0126
Chilmark sculptures. Visa, MC, American Express, & checks. Call/write for complete listing.

VALLEY FRAMING STUDIO & GALLERY
800-821-7529
540-943-7529
http://www.pointsouth.com/valframe.htm
valframe@cfw.com
328 W Main St
Waynesboro VA 22980-4509
Most comprehensive art gallery carrying largest inventory of art & artists in Shenandoah Valley. Civil War art, ltd. ed. prints. Free info.

VALOR ART & FRAME LTD.
540-372-3376
CWFugi@aol.com
Joe Fulginiti
718 Caroline St
Fredericksburg VA 22401-5904
Civil War artwork, artifacts & books. Featuring artwork of Don Troiani. Carry all major Civil War artists. Custom museum mount framing. 15 years of service. Free catalog.

VILLAGE GALLERY & FRAME SHOPPE
800-410-3608
Main Street
PO Box 608
Pleasant Valley NY 12569-0608
Military art & sculpture. Art broker. Ltd. ed. prints. Troiani, Kunstler, Neary, Kodera, Phillips, Tunison, Taylor, Gnatek, Strain, Stivers, etc.

DAVE WAGNER
619-789-5179
2027 S 10th Ave • Yuma AZ 85364-8355
A Raider's Return by new artist Dave Wagner. 1st of 4 limited edition prints - $35. Proofs - $45.

WALK ON THE WILD SIDE
1245 S Cleveland-Mass. Rd
Copley OH 44321
Offering America's high-quality collectible artists such as Rick Reeves.

WARNER LIMITED
800-371-9373
19 Seekonk Rd
Great Barrington MA 01230-1562
"Genovese: Civil War Gun series" prints. All prints shipped flat.

WARR ART GALLERY
http://www.websun.com/warr/
Confederate-themed prints for viewing & purchase.

WATSON ENTERPRISES
PO Box 392
North Pembroke MA 02358-0392
Letter from Sullivan Ballou to wife Sarah, 1861, as heard on Civil War series on TV. Reproduced on yellow, blue, or gray parchment. $12.95.

ANDREW WEISSMAN
325 Alexis Ct • Glenview IL 60025-4711
Oil paintings by commission, replicas. Color info. - $6.

WELL-TRAVELED IMAGES
414-896-0555
http://www.globaldialog.com/~eicher/index.htm
eicher@globaldialog.com
Lynda Eicher
S60 W24160 Red Wing Dr
Waukesha WI 53186-9508
Color photos of CW battlefields, sites. Books. Matted color prints of 10,000+ CW-related images, also available for publication. Call or email for catalog. See internet home page for samples & info. on books.

WELLINGTON MILITARY ART
800-889-4978
9508 Sappington Rd
Saint Louis MO 63126-3047
More than 1200 military prints available, Roman through Desert Storm. Free color flyers upon request. Catalog - $15.

C. PHILLIP WIKOFF REPRODUCTIONS
302-239-1457
302-239-5543 Fax
PO Box 132
Rockland DE 19732-0132
Impressions of the Civil War series. *Be Strong of Heart*, 19-1/4"x16", $85.

WRITINGS ON THE WALL
7950 Route 30
Irwin PA 15642-2725
Civil War arts & prints. Featuring artists such as Rick Reeves.

WRM GRAPHICS
216-491-9314
http://www.wrmgraphics.com
prints@wrmgraphics.com
3667 Traver Rd
Cleveland OH 44122-5165
Finest in limited edition Civil War naval prints by William R. McGrath. Color brochures.

YANKEE CAMP STUDIO
412-238-2776
404 E Main St
Ligonier PA 15658-1420
Ltd. ed. Civil War art prints & photos.

REX YOUNGER ENTERPRISES
910-984-2680
800-528-2117
3648 Clingman Rd
Ronda NC 28670-9174
The Last Stand - the State Capitol at Columbia, SC, by Ron Cockerham. 21"x28", S/N $150; A/P $200.

ABRAHAM LINCOLN BOOK SHOP
312-944-3085 • 312-944-5549 Fax
357 W Chicago Ave
Chicago IL 60610-3052
U.S. Military History, French & Indian War, Revolution, 1812, Mexican, Civil War, Indian Wars. Books, prints, autographs. Buy/sell. Catalog - $5.

ANTEBELLUM COVERS
301-869-2623 Ph & Fax
888-ANTEBEL (268-3235)
http://www.antebellumcovers.com
antebell@antebellumcovers.com
PO Box 3494
Gaithersburg MD 20885-3494
Civil War & 19th-century U.S. paper collectibles incl. soldiers' letters, images, general orders, patriotic envelopes, autographs, slavery documents & advertising paper; CD-ROMs of Civil War & historical titles. Free catalog. Internet customers can be notified by email each time auction is posted.

ANTIQUE AMERICANA
PO Box 389
Whitman MA 02382-0389
Civil War documents, books, autographs, maps.

AUTOGRAPH TIMES
1125 W Baseline Rd # 2-153
Mesa AZ 85210-9501
The only monthly newspaper for autograph collectors. Sample copy - $2 S&H.

BLACKJACK TRADING COMPANY
Chuck Hanselmann
PO Box 707
Blythewood SC 29016-0707
Buyer of family Confederate paper, stamps, letters, autographs, currency, slave documents, slave tags, & estates.

MIKE BRACKIN
203-647-8620
PO Box 23
Manchester CT 06045-0023
Large assortment of Civil War & Indian War autographs, accoutrements, memorabilia, insignia, medals, buttons, GAR, documents, photos & books. Catalog - $6/yr for 5 issues.

STANLEY BUTCHER
4 Washington Ave
Andover MA 01810-1724
Buys Confederate generals' autographs, letters, & other Civil War documents.

CIVIL WAR STORE
504-522-3328
212 Chartres St
New Orleans LA 70130-2215
Mail order catalog - weapons, currency, bonds, stamps, letters, diaries, CDVs, prints, slave broadsides & bills of sale, autographs, photos. Catalog - $4.

STAN CLARK MILITARY BOOKS
717-337-1728
717-337-0581 Fax
915 Fairview Ave
Gettysburg PA 17325-2906
Buys/sells Civil War books, ltd. edition prints, autographs, letters, documents, postcards, soldiers' items; special interest in U.S. Marine Corps items.

COHASCO, INC.
914-476-8500
914-476-8573 Fax
E. Snyder
Postal 821
Yonkers NY 10702
Semi-annual mail/phone auction catalogs containing varied CW memorabilia: generals, maps, letters, photos, ephemera, etc. Our 50th year in business. Catalog - $5.

COL. GROVER CRISWELL
352-685-2287
352-685-1014 Fax
PO Box 6000
Salt Springs FL 32134-6000
Buys/sells currency, stocks, bonds, money, slavery items, autographs. 51st year of business. *Comprehensive Catalog of Confederate Paper Money*, hardcover, 350 pp. - $35 (ppd.). 432-pp. price list of collectibles - $8 (ref.). Free book list.

FEDERAL HILL ANTIQUITIES
410-584-8185 / 8329
14 Glen Lyon Ct
Phoenix MD 21131-1212
Purveyors of fine autographs & collectibles. Letters & documents, photos, relics & artifacts, ephemera. Buy/sell/trade.

JAMES FUNKHOUSER
pres.connect@juno.com
1423 Macedonia Church Rd
Stephens City VA 22655-3710
Presidential autographs for sale. Listing - $1.

GIBSON'S CIVIL WAR COLLECTIBLES
423-323-2427
423-323-8123 Fax
Paul, Linda & Bryan Gibson
PO Box 948 • Bristol TN 37621-0948
Autographs, CSA bonds & currency, diaries, flags, letter groups, newspapers, photos, slave items, uniforms, any other paper items.

BRIAN & MARIA GREEN, INC.
336-993-5100 • 336-993-1801 Fax
http://www.collectorsnet.com/bmg/index.shtml
bmgcivilwar@webtv.net
PO Box 1816J
Kernersville NC 27285-1816
Civil War autographs, letters, documents, diaries, CSA stamps, covers, currency, etc. Catalog - $5/yr for 4 issues.

JIM HAYES
843-795-0732
PO Box 12560
Charleston SC 29422-2560
Civil War autographs. Bi-monthly list - $10/yr.
(See ad page 267)

GARY HENDERSHOTT
501-224-7555
PO Box 22520
Little Rock AR 72221-2520
Autographs, photographs, imprints, flags & memorabilia of the Civil War era. Catalog - $3.

THE HISTORIAN'S GALLERY
770-522-8383
770-522-8388 Fax
history@atl.mindspring.com
3232 Cobb Pkwy Ste 207
Atlanta GA 30339-3896
Brokers & dealers in maps, autographs, selected relics.

HISTORICAL COLLECTIBLE AUCTIONS
336-570-2803
336-570-2748 Fax
PO Box 975
Burlington NC 27215
Quarterly auctions of Civil War collectibles including photography, manuscripts, autographs, weapons, etc. Consignments encouraged. Catalog - $20/issue; next 3 for $45.

HISTORY-MAKERS
4040 E 82nd St Dept 44
Indianapolis IN 46250-4209
Historic letters & documents signed by the greatest history makers who ever lived. Free report.

HUGHES BOOKS
504-948-2427
PO Box 840237
New Orleans LA 70184-0237
Buy/sell rare books, documents, & autographs. Civil War, the South, Louisiana, New Orleans. 3 catalogs - $3.

INKWELL AUTOGRAPH GALLERY
717-337-2220
717-337-2221 Fax
imninkwell@aol.com
777 Baltimore St
Old Gettysburg Village
Gettysburg PA 17325-2600
Autographs bought/sold - entertainment, historical & sports. Autographs of the famous at surprisingly affordable prices. Open year-round; closed Wednesdays.

KEYA GALLERY
212-366-9742
800-906-KEYA Orders only
http://www.KeyaGallery.com
Key15@aol.com
110 W 25th St Gallery 304A
New York NY 10001-7401
Excavated relics - bullets, tokens, buckles, buttons, insignia, & more. Catalog.

KINGSTON MILITARY ANTIQUES
770-336-9354
Jerelhook@aol.com
Jere Hook
PO Box 217
Kingston GA 30145-0217
Buy/sell/trade pre-1898 militaria, mostly Civil War. By appt. only. Catalog - 32¢.

KUBIK FINE BOOKS
937-294-0253
3474 Clar Von Dr • Dayton OH 45430-1708
Buy/sell rare & out-of-print books on British, French, European, & U.S. military history. Autographs & historical fiction. 1st editions of 19th-century Civil War books. Catalog - $3.

PHILLIP B. LAMB, LTD.
504-899-4710 • 800-391-0115 Orders
504-891-6826 Fax
http://www.LambRarities.com
lambcsa@aol.com
PO Box 15850 • 2727 Prytania St
New Orleans LA 70175-5850
Buy/sell Confederate memorabilia; CDVs, currency, documents, photos, art, bonds, slave items, swords, buttons, bullets, autographs, & much more.

DEBORAH LAMBERT
1945 Lorraine Ave
Mc Lean VA 22101-5331
Slavery documents, CW newspapers, prints, letters, autographs, battle maps. List - $1.

HARDIE MALONEY
504-522-3328
212 Chartres St • New Orleans LA 70130
Civil War store. Confederate currency, bonds, stamps, covers, CDV.s, letters, diaries, documents, autographs, pistols & swords.

MC GOWAN BOOK CO.
919-968-1121 • 800-449-8406
919-968-1644 Fax
http://www.mcgowanbooks.com
mcgowanbooks@mindspring.com
R. Douglas Sanders
PO Box 4226 • 106 S Christopher Rd
Chapel Hill NC 27515
Always buying. Highest prices paid for fine & rare Civil War books, autographs, documents, photographs, etc. Catalog subs. - $3.

MENIG'S MEMORABILIA
708-258-9487
517 S Manor Dr
Peotone IL 60468-9129
Authentic Civil War autographs, newspapers, and documents. Free catalog.

THE MT. STERLING REBEL
606-498-5821
Terry Murphy
PO Box 481
Mount Sterling KY 40353-0481
Buy/sell since 1979 rare, out-of-print, & previously owned Civil War books. Limited inventory of Civil War paper items, ephemera, autographs & images. Catalog upon request.

NORTHERN CO. ARCHIVES/ACQUISITIONS
800-432-8777
18640 Mack Ave • PO Box 36793
Grosse Pointe Woods MI 48236-0793
Buyers of autographs, documents, photo collections, stock certificates, letters, contracts, etc. Lifetime member MS&D Society. Top $ paid.

HOWARD L. NORTON
PO Box 22821
Little Rock AR 72221-2821
Buy/sell/appraise. Autographs, Civil War items, Americana, historical documents, photographs, coins, currency, stamps, postal history. All transactions confidential. Catalog.

THE OLD PAPERPHILES
401-624-9420
401-624-4204 Fax
PO Box 135
Tiverton RI 02878-0135
Offering 100s of accurately described paper collectibles. Great variety, wide price range. Autographs, documents, books. Catalog - $8 for next 10.

OLDE SOLDIER BOOKS, INC.
301-963-2929
301-963-9556 Fax
Warbooks@erols.com
Dave Zullo
18779 N Frederick Ave Ste B
Gaithersburg MD 20879-3158
Largest selection of rare & hard-to-find books. Documents, letters, photographs, autographs, manuscripts. Buy/sell. Free catalog.

ORIGINAL FRAMEWORKS
800-654-1861
540-953-1655
http://ptiweb.com/civilwar
civilwar@nrv.net
Jay Rainey
Gables Shopping Center
1300 S Main St
Blacksburg VA 24060-5526
All Civil War artists at discount; signatures, documents, 19th-century steel engravings, relics. Will find any artwork. Always looking to purchase. Also at 4 E Washington St, Lexington, Va. (See ad page 259)

PROFILES IN HISTORY
800-942-8856
310-859-7701
310-859-3842 Fax
345 N Maple Dr Ste 202
Beverly Hills CA 90210-3859
Autographs wanted. Also buying original letters, documents, vintage photos, manuscripts, & rare books (signed). Illus. catalog - $45/yr. Sample - $10.

STEVEN S. RAAB AUTOGRAPHS
800-977-8333 • 610-446-4514 Fax
http://www.raabautographs.com
raab@netaxs,com
PO Box 471
Ardmore PA 19003-0471
Serious collectors, respected dealers. Top dollars paid for collection & quality individual autographs, documents, manuscripts, signed photos, & interesting letters. Catalog sample - $5; $15/yr.

JOSEPH RUBINFINE
561-659-7077
505 S Flagler Dr Ste 1301
West Palm Beach FL 33401-5951
American historical autographs. Catalog - $5 (ref.).

SOUTHERN ENCAMPMENTS
504-751-0757
tcld04@premier.net
Tim Rochester
16380 S Fulwar Skipwith Rd
Baton Rouge LA 70810-5743
Civil War antiques; autographs, buttons, documents, period glass, insignia, letters, projectiles, books & more. Photo-illus. catalog - $2.50.

SOUTHERN HISTORICAL SHOWCASE
800-854-7832
615-321-0639
http://www.southernhistorical.com
southernhistorical@nashville.com
1907 Division St
Nashville TN 37203-2705
Southern military art & books, prints, original documents & autographs, photos, engravings. Artists: Prechtel, Reeves, Kunstler, Kidd, Gallon, Summers, Heron, Garner, Rocco. Catalog - $5.

STAMPEDE INVESTMENTS
608-254-7751
1533 River Rd
Wisconsin Dells WI 53965-9002
Large inventory of original letters & documents from the most important people in U.S. History to fit every budget. Free catalog.

THEME PRINTS, LTD.
800-CIVL WAR
718-225-4067
PO Box 610123
Bayside NY 11361-0123
Books, antique arms, historic documents, photographs, letters & autographs from Revolutionary era to early Hollywood. Includes Civil War memorabilia. Fully illus. catalog - $5, or $12/yr. (5 issues).

UNIVERSITY ARCHIVES
Matthew McGarry, Dir. of Advertising
1406 Overlook Dr
Mount Dora FL 32757-3769
Buy/sell. Letters, documents, clipped signatures, 1400-present. Annual subscription of $29.95 yields at least 4 of the best catalogs in the industry.

WAR BETWEEN THE STATES MEMORABILIA
717-337-2853
Len Rosa
PO Box 3965
Gettysburg PA 17325-0965
Buy/sell soldiers' letters, envelopes, documents, CDVs, photos, autographs, newspapers, badges, ribbons, relics, framed display items, currency, & more. Estab. 1978. Illus. catalogs - $10/yr for 5 issues. Active buyers receive future subscriptions free.

CRAIG WOFFORD ANTIQUES
2101 Harrison Ave
Orlando FL 32804-5467
Civil War memorabilia bought/sold, appraisals; specializing in autographs, letters, documents, diaries, photographs. Identifies items, soldiers groupings. Est. 1975.

YESTERDAY'S NEWS, USA
612-721-5526
5344 34th Ave S
Minneapolis MN 55417-2167
Civil War autographs, books, documents, images, militaria, & identified items. 19th & 20th-cent. newspapers & magazines. Catalogs.

BOB ZABAWA
201-444-9653
201-444-8221 Fax
652 Ackerman Ave
Glen Rock NJ 07452-2422
Will buy or trade for Civil War autographs of famous & lesser known generals and naval officers.

ALABAMA BUREAU OF TOURISM & TRAVEL
800-ALABAMA
334-242-4554 Fax
http://www.touralabama.org
info@touralabama.org
Russell A. Nolen
401 Adams Ave
PO Box 4927
Montgomery AL 36103-4927
Birthplace of the most dramatic chapter in American history. Site of historic battles, parks, politics, & much more. Free travel guide.

AMERICA'S NATL PARK MUSEUM STORE
215-597-2569
316 Chestnut St
Philadelphia PA 19106-2708

ANDERSONVILLE NATL HISTORIC SITE
912-924-0343
RR 49 Box 196
Andersonville GA 31711

ANTIETAM BATTLEFIELD & BOOKSTORE
301-432-4329
Parks & History Association
PO Box 692
Highway 65 N
Sharpsburg MD 21782-0692

APPOMATTOX COURT HOUSE NHP
804-352-8987
PO Box 218
Appomattox VA 24522-0218
Includes visitor center, McLean House & Clover Hill Tavern. Admission fee.

ARKANSAS POST NATL MONUMENT
501-548-2207
1749 Old Post Rd
Gillett AR 72055-9733

ASSOCIATION FOR THE PRESERVATION OF CIVIL WAR SITES
888-606-1400
http://www.apcws.com
11 Public Sq Ste 200
Hagerstown MD 21740-5510
Not-for-profit membership organization that preserves Civil War sites for educational & recreational uses. Website: organizational news & membership info.

ATLANTA CYCLORAMA
404-658-7625
800C Cherokee Ave SE
Atlanta GA 30315-1440

BATTLE OF LEXINGTON STATE HISTORIC SITE
660-259-4654
PO Box 6
Lexington MO 64067-0006
Union earthworks & entrenchments, visitor center; restored Anderson House.

BE BOOKS
3712 Walnut Ave Ste 8135
Altoona PA 16601-1342
National Park handbooks: Gettysburg, Antietam, Fort Sumter, Vicksburg, etc. *Artillery Through the Ages*, *Fort Pulaski*, etc. Free catalog.

BEAUVOIR
601-388-9074
800-570-3818
http://www.beauvoir.org
2244 Beach Blvd
Biloxi MS 39531-5023
Last home of CSA president Jefferson Davis. Open daily 9AM-5PM (CST); closed for Thanksgiving & Christmas.

BELLE BOYD COTTAGE
540-636-1446
Warren Co. Heritage Society
101 Chester St • Front Royal VA 22630-3322
Lodging for Confederate spy Boyd on her visits to the area.

BELLE BOYD HOUSE
304-267-4713
Berkeley Co. Historical Society
126 E Race St • Martinsburg WV 25401-4310
Hosts the Boyd Mason Civil War Museum.

BENTONVILLE BATTLEGROUND STATE HISTORIC SITE
910-594-0789
5466 Harper House Rd
Four Oaks NC 27524-9125
Confederate cemetery, Union trenches, visitor center. Harper House.

BERKELEY COUNTY HISTORICAL SOCIETY
304-267-4713
Don C. Wood, Pres.
126 E Race St • Martinsburg WV 25401
Childhood home of Belle Boyd, famous Confederate spy. Civil War & military history museum; archives & genealogy section. Headquarters of historical society & landmarks commission. Free admission. Mon.-Sat., 10-4 PM.

BLANDFORD CHURCH
804-733-2396
111 Rochelle Ln
Petersburg VA 23803
18th-cent. parish church, memorial to Southern soldiers who died during Civil War. Displays 15 stained glass windows, 1 from ea. Confederate state, designed by L.C. Tiffany. Museums.

BRAEHEAD B&B
540-899-3648
123 Lee Dr • Fredericksburg VA 22401
1859 house within Fredericksburg Battlefield Park. Gen. Lee breakfasted here before the battle. 3 guest rooms; continental breakfast.

BRITTON LANE BATTLEFIELD
901-784-4227
199 Carriage House Dr
Jackson TN 38305-3952
Civil War-era cabin, Confederate mass grave, site where 213 Union prisoners captured.

CAMP NELSON
PO Box 1170 • Nicholasville KY 40340-1170
Site of Union supply depot & 3rd largest recruiting center for African-American troops.

CARNTON PLANTATION
615-794-0903
1345 Carnton Ln
Franklin TN 37064
Mansion housed more than 6,000 Confederate wounded after the battle of Franklin. Largest private Confederate cemetery located nearby. Gift shop. Admission charge.

THE CARTER HOUSE
615-791-1861 • 615-794-1327 Fax
julep19@mail.idt.net
Thomas Cartwright, Dir.
1140 Columbia Ave.
Franklin TN 37065
Restored museum house; new museum, gift shop complex. House was Union headquarters & in center of fighting during Battle of Franklin, Nov. 1864. Youth programs, living history, tours, etc.

CEDAR CREEK BATTLEFIELD FOUNDATION, INC.
540-869-2064
540-869-1438 Fax
http://www.winchesterva.com/cedarcreek
Suzanne Lewis
PO Box 229
Middletown VA 22645-0229
Visitors Center & bookshop overlooking battlefield. October reenactment. Reference library, large CW book selection, flags, prints, maps & square foot certificates. All proceeds go to preservation of battlefield.

CENTER STATE 29
800-732-5821
"Virginia's Civil War Connection." Follow Highway 29 to sample sites rich in Civil War heritage & history. Call for free brochure.

CHANCELLORSVILLE NATL HISTORIC SITE
RR 1 Box 125P
Route 3 W
Fredericksburg VA 22407-9751

CHATHAM MANOR NATL. PARK
540-373-4461
540-371-0802
120 Chatham Ln
Falmouth VA 22405
Served as Union HQs during Battle of Fredericksburg. Admission fee. Open 9 AM-5 PM.

CHICKAMAUGA / CHATTANOOGA NATL MILITARY PARK
615-821-7786
PO Box 2387
US Highway 27
Fort Oglethorpe GA 30742-2387

CHRISTMAS AT THE FORT
334-861-6992
Fort Gaines Historic Site
PO Box 97
Dauphin Island AL 36528-0097
Annual living history weekend; 1998 dates - December 5-6. Experience 1861 Christmas at the fort with Confederate soldiers -- authenticity stressed. Candlelight tour, feast, dance, drills, camp life, etc.

COLUMBUS-BELMONT STATE PARK
502-677-2327 • 502-677-4013 Fax
Bill Stevens, Park Mgr.
PO Box 8
Columbus KY 42032-0008
Civil War museum, activities, special events.

CONFEDERATE MEMORIAL HALL
423-522-2371
3148 Kingston Pike
Knoxville TN 37919-4627
Site of Longstreet's headquarters in 1862, now a Confederate museum & memorial.

CONFEDERATE MEMORIAL PARK
205-755-1990
437 County Road 63
Marbury AL 36051-3338
Cemetery w/ more than 300 Confederate soldiers & their widows. Civil War museum.

CONFEDERATE MEMORIAL SHS
660-584-2853
MO State Routes 20 & 13
Higginsville MO 64037
Memorial park area of Old Confederate Soldier's Home; honors 40,000 Missourians who fought for the Confederacy.

CONSTITUTION SQUARE HISTORIC SITE
606-239-7089
Becky Schnitzler
134 S 2nd St
Danville KY 40422-1802

CSS NEUSE STATE HISTORIC SITE
919-522-2091
PO Box 3043
2612 W Vernon Ave
Kinston NC 28502-3043
Remains of Confederate ironclad, artifacts. Guided tours of the gunboat.

CUMBERLAND GAP NATL HISTORIC PARK
606-248-7606
PO Box 156
Middlesboro KY 40965-0156

SAM DAVIS HOME
888-750-9524
1399 Sam Davis Rd
Smyrna TN 37167-2744
Antebellum home of the Boy Hero of the Confederacy, who was hanged as a spy in 1863 at the age of 21.

DICKSON-WILLIAMS MANSION
423-638-8144
114 W Church St
Greeneville TN 37745-3804
Gen. John Hunt Morgan spent his last night in this house, called "Showplace of East Tennessee."

FARLEY PLACE B&B
502-442-2488
166 Farley Pl
Paducah KY 42001-1442
Home of Aunt Em Jarrett, who saved local Confederate flag from destruction by Union gunboats. Single & double occupancy rooms; full or continental breakfast. Period antiques.

FIRST WHITE HOUSE OF THE CONFEDERACY
334-242-1861
644 Washington St
Montgomery AL 36104-4347
Home of President & Mrs. Davis, Feb.-April 1861. Period furnishings. Free.

FORD'S THEATRE NHS
202-426-6924
511 10th St NW
Washington DC 20004-1499
Photos, art & other memorabilia relating to Pres. Abraham Lincoln, housed in museum in theater's basement.

FORT CLINCH STATE PARK
904-277-7274
904-277-7225 Fax
2601 Atlantic Ave
Fernandina Beach FL 32034-2299
Living history demonstrations, tours of fort which fell into Union hands in 1862.

FORT DAVIDSON SHS
573-546-3454
MO State Route 21
Pilot Knob MO 63663
Site of 1864 Battle of Pilot Knob, between generals Ewing & Price. Visitor center.

FORT DONELSON NATL BATTLEFIELD
931-232-5706
PO Box 434
Dover TN 37058-0434
Free parking & admission.

FORT FISHER STATE HISTORIC SITE
910-458-5538
910-458-0477 Fax
PO Box 169 • 1610 Fort Fisher Blvd S
Kure Beach NC 28449-0169
Guided tours of fort's remains; visitor center.

FORT GAINES HISTORIC SITE
334-861-6992
PO Box 97 • Bienville Blvd
Dauphin Island AL 36528-0097
Visit fort's battlements, living quarters, bastions & tunnels. Admission.

FORT MC ALLISTER STATE HISTORIC PARK
912-727-2339
3894 Fort McAllister Rd
Richmond Hill GA 31324-4862
Civil War museum; best preserved Confederate earthworks.

FORT MIFFLIN ON THE DELAWARE
215-492-3395
Fort Mifflin Rd
Philadelphia PA 19153
Revolutionary fort which served as prison during the Civil War; reenactments held. Museum.

FORT PULASKI NATL MONUMENT
912-786-5787
PO Box 30757
Highway 80E
Savannah GA 31410-0757

FORT SUMTER NATL MONUMENT
803-883-9783
1214 Middle St
Sullivans Island SC 29482-9748

FORT WARD MUSEUM & HISTORIC SITE
703-838-4848
4301 W Braddock Rd
Alexandria VA 22304-1008
Museum in pattern of Union headquarters building, w/ various exhibits; tours. Research library available. Free admission. Closed Mon.

FORT WOOL
800-800-2202
757-727-1102
Hampton Visitor Center
710 Settlers Landing Rd
Hampton VA 23669
Civil War island fort, open Apr.-Oct. to pleasure boaters.

FREDERICKSBURG & SPOTSYLVANIA NMP
703-373-6122
http://www.nps.gov/frsp/frspweb.htm
1011 Lafayette Blvd
Fredericksburg VA 22401-5501
Visit the largest military park in the world without leaving home.

GETTYSBURG NATL MILITARY PARK
95 Taneytown Rd Electric Map
Gettysburg PA 17325-2804

GORDON-LEE MANSION
706-375-4728
800-487-4728
217 Cove Rd
Chickamauga GA 30707-1408
Rosecrans' headquarters & Civil War hospital now offers 6 rooms w/ private baths; full breakfast. Artifacts museum. Within minutes of Chickamauga battlefield & other Civil War-related sites.

ULYSSES S. GRANT NATL. HISTORIC SITE
314-842-3298
7400 Grant Rd
Saint Louis MO 63123
Open 9 AM-5 PM. Free admission.

GULF ISLANDS NATL SEASHORE
904-934-8742
1400 Fort Pickens Rd Bldg 5
Pensacola Beach FL 32561-5116

HARPER'S FERRY NHP
304-535-6298
PO Box 65
Route 340
Harpers Ferry WV 25425-0065
Museums, information center, hiking trails. Living history presentations & special events, 19th-cent. historic exhibits. Admission.

HISTORIC FORK INN
804-265-8591
Darrell Olgers
19621 Namozine Rd
Sutherland VA 23885
Site of Civil War hospital. Several rooms restored, with 19th-cent. furnishings. Main exhibit room houses unique Civil War relics.

HISTORIC JONESBOROUGH VISITORS CENTER
423-753-1012
117 Boone St
Jonesborough TN 37659-1345
Guided tours to Civil War sites. Maps available.

HISTORIC RICHMOND FOUNDATION TOURS
804-780-0107
804-788-4244 Fax
707 E Franklin St
Richmond VA 23219-2313
Civil War guided riding tour (includes battlefields). Reservations required. Open April-Oct. Call for prices.

HOLLYWOOD CEMETERY
804-648-8501
412 S Cherry St
Richmond VA 23220-6214
Richmond area's oldest active cemetery. Confederate Monument; more than 17,000 soldiers, as well as other famous Americans, buried here.

JEFFERSON DAVIS STATE HISTORIC SITE
912-831-2335 • 912-831-2060 Fax
338 Jeff Davis Park Rd
Fitzgerald GA 31750-6343
Confederate memorial & museum, containing relics from a Ga. battle flag to rare uniforms. Davis family's capture at this site on May 10, 1865, marked official end of the Confederacy.

KENNESAW MOUNTAIN NATL BATTLE-FIELD PARK
770-422-3696
900 Kennesaw Mountain Dr
Kennesaw GA 30152-4854

SIDNEY LANIER COTTAGE
912-743-3851
Middle Georgia Historical Society
PO Box 13358
935 High St • Macon GA 31208-3358
Birthplace of beloved Southern poet who served in the CSA & was imprisoned at Fort Lookout. Museum & gift shop.

LAUREL HILL CEMETERY
215-228-8200
Friends of the Laurel Hill Cemetery
3822 Ridge Ave
Philadelphia PA 19132-1881
Resting place of George Meade & John C. Pemberton. Public & private tours available.

THE ROBERT E. LEE MEMORIAL
703-557-0613
George Washington Memorial Pkwy
Turkey Run Park
McLean VA 22101
Incl. Arlington House, the Lees' home from 1831-1861.

LEE'S GETTYSBURG HEADQUARTERS
401 Buford Ave
US 30 W
Gettysburg PA 17325-1140
Civil War displays; period furnishings, original kitchen.

LEE-FENDALL HOUSE MUSEUM
703-548-1789
614 Oronoco St
Alexandria VA 22314
18th-century Lee home, used as Civil War hospital. Admission fee. Closed Mon.

LINCOLN HOME NATL HISTORIC SITE
217-523-3421
426 S 7th St
Springfield IL 62701

THE LINCOLN ROOM MUSEUM
717-334-8188
12 Lincoln Sq
Gettysburg PA 17325-2205
Historic Will House hosts room where Lincoln completed his Gettysburg Address. Museum contains collection of Lincoln & Gettysburg related artifacts.

LONE JACK CIVIL WAR MUSEUM
816-566-2272
Lone Jack MO 64070
Site of 1862 Battle of Lone Jack. Open daily, Apr.-Sept.; weekends, Oct.-Mar.

LOTZ HOUSE WAR BETWEEN THE STATES MUSEUM
615-791-6533
http://www.phoenix.w1.com/lotz
Lotzrebel@aol.com
Ronny Mangrum, Dir.
1111 Columbia Ave
Franklin TN 37064-3616
Area's most comprehensive Civil War collection. Tours of Lotz House, which was used as hospital after Battle of Franklin; genealogy services.

MACLAY HOME
660-433-2101
Highway B
Tipton MO 65081
1858 ladies' seminary; served as Union camp headquarters during Civil War. Open May-Oct. Small admission fee.

MANASSAS NATL BATTLEFIELD
703-754-7107
6511 Sudley Rd
Manassas VA 20109-2358

MEMORIAL TO VETERANS OF ALL WARS
Brookside Park, off Highway 61 N
Jackson MO 63755
Open chapel, block-granite wall honoring veterans of all American wars, including Civil War. Open year-round. Free admission.

MISSOURI DIVISION OF TOURISM
800-777-0068
Convention & Visitors Bureau
Cape Girardeau MO 63701
"Hearts of Blue & Grey" Civil War sites - Fort D, Union Monument & fountain, Confederate War memorial, CW hospital.

MONOCACY BATTLEFIELD & BOOKSTORE
301-662-3515
Parks & History Association
4801 Urbana Pike # B
Frederick MD 21704-7307

NATCHEZ NATL HISTORIC PARK
601-446-5790
1 Melrose Montebello Pkwy
Natchez MS 39120-4715

NEW MANCHESTER MANUFACTURING CO.
770-732-5871
Sweetwater Creek State Conservation Park
PO Box 816
Mount Vernon Rd
Lithia Springs GA 30122-0816
Ruins of Civil War-era textile mill. Walking trails & educational programs available.

NEW MARKET BATTLEFIELD HISTORICAL PARK
540-464-7323
PO Box 1864
8895 Collins Dr
New Market VA 22844-1864

NEWPORT NEWS, VA
888-493-7386
Battlefield tours, historic houses, harbor tours, museum exhibits & living history events. Free visitor guide & Civil War tour brochure.

OATLANDS PLANTATION & GIFT SHOP
703-777-3174
20850 Oatlands Plantation Ln
Leesburg VA 20175-6572

OLD CAHAWBA ARCHAEOLOGICAL PARK
334-872-8058
http://www.olcg.com/selma/cahawbah.html
9518 Cahawba Rd
Orrville AL 36767
Site of Civil War boom town & Castle Morgan prison. Nature trail & brochure.

OLD PHELPS COUNTY JAIL
573-364-5977
573-341-4874
3rd & Park Streets
Rolla MO 65401
1860 2-story jail that housed Civil War prisoners. Open May-Sept. Free admission.

PAMPLIN PARK: NATL. MUSEUM OF THE CIVIL WAR SOLDIER
804-861-2408 • 804-861-2820 Fax
http://www.pamplinpark.org
pamplinpark@mindspring.com
6523 Duncan Rd • Petersburg VA 23803Site of 1865 battle - preserved fortifications, walking trails, guided tours, living history, gift shop, restaurant. New high-tech museum (May 1999) focuses on common soldier. Website features museum gift shop.

PEA RIDGE NATL MILITARY PARK
501-451-8122
Highway 62E • Pea Ridge AR 72751

PETERSBURG NATL BATTLEFIELD PARK
804-732-3531
1539 Hickory Hill Rd • Petersburg VA 23803

THE PETERSON HOUSE
202-426-6924
516 10th St NW
Washington DC 20004-1401
House where Pres. Lincoln died, Apr. 15, 1865.

PICKETT'S MILL STATE HISTORIC SITE
770-443-7850
2640 Mount Tabor Rd • Dallas GA 30132
One of most well-preserved Civil War battlefields. Union & Confederate roads & earthworks; living history demonstrations, tours.

PORT HUDSON STATE COMMEMORATIVE AREA
504-654-3775
756 W Plains Port Hudson Rd
Zachary LA 70791-8701
View Civil War displays, original breastworks. Living history & weapons demonstrations.

PRAIRIE GROVE BATTLEFIELD STATE PARK
501-846-2990
PO Box 306 • Prairie Grove AR 72753-0306
Battlefield museum, historic houses. Self-guided tours. Bi-annual December reenactment. Located on U.S. Route 62. Various fees.

RHODES HALL
404-881-9980
Georgia Trust for Historic Preservation
1516 Peachtree St NW • Atlanta GA 30309
"The Rise & Fall of the Confederacy" - nine-paneled stained glass display depicting major scenes, famous persons & seals from the Confederacy.

RICHMOND NATL BATTLEFIELD PARK
804-226-1981
3215 E Broad St
Richmond VA 23223-7517

ROSEHILL CEMETERY
312-561-5940
5800 N Ravenswood Ave
Chicago IL 60660-3195
Self-paced & guided Civil War walking tours, visiting graves of 500 Union soldiers & sailors, incl. 14 generals.

SAILOR'S CREEK BATTLEFIELD HISTORICAL STATE PARK
804-392-3435
RR 2 Box 70
Green Bay VA 23942-9544
Site of Virginia's last major Civil War battle. Tours of the Hillsman House.

SHILOH NATIONAL MILITARY PARK
901-689-5696
shil_interpretation@nps.gov
RR 1 Box 9
US Highway 22
Shiloh TN 38376-9704
Self-guided tours of famous battlefield; museum & bookstore. Cemetery nearby. Open daily 8 AM-5 PM; closed Christmas Day. Admission - $2/person; $4/family.

STAUNTON RIVER BATTLEFIELD STATE PARK
804-454-4312
http://www.halifax.com/county/staunt1.htmp
RR 1 Box 183
Randolph VA 23962-9602
Earthworks, railroad bridge, artillery emplacement. Walking trail & visitor center.

A.H. STEPHENS STATE HISTORIC PARK
706-456-2602
PO Box 283
Crawfordsville GA 30631-0283
Site of Liberty Hall, home to Vice-President of the Confederacy Stephens; Confederate Museum.

STONES RIVER NATL BATTLEFIELD
615-893-9501
3501 Old Nashville Hwy
Murfreesboro TN 37129-8621
Self-guided tour; summer ranger programs. Open daily 8 AM-5 PM; closed Christmas. Free admission & parking.

STONEWALL JACKSON HEADQUARTERS MUSEUM
540-667-3242 • WFCH@shentel.com
Todd Kern
415 N Braddock St
Winchester VA 22601-3921
Gen. Jackson used this home during the winter of 1861-62.

STONEWALL JACKSON HOUSE
540-463-2552 • 540-463-4088 Fax
http://www.stonewalljackson.org
Michael A. Lynn
8 E Washington St
Lexington VA 24450-2529
The Confederate general's only home with restored garden & museum shop. Tours every half hour Mon-Sat 9-5, Sun 1-5; last tour 4:30PM. Open until 6PM June-August (last tour 5:30PM). Closed major holidays.

STONEWALL JACKSON SHRINE
804-633-6076
120 Chatham Ln
Fredericksburg VA 22405
Building where Jackson died. Open summers 9 AM-5 PM.

STRATFORD HALL PLANTATION
804-493-8038
State Route 3 • Stratford VA 22558
Robert E. Lee's birthplace. Visit rebuilt mill, slave quarters, spring house, stables, more. Tours available. Admission.

J.E.B. STUART BIRTHPLACE, INC.
540-251-1833
PO Box 240 • Ararat VA 24053-0240
Memberships to help preserve the birthplace of J.E.B. Stuart begin at $25.

TALLASSEE CHAMBER OF COMMERCE
334-283-5151
334-283-2940 Fax
301A King St
Tallassee AL 36078-1315
Oversees Confederate Armory (only one to have survived war) & Confederate Officers Quarters (believed to be only 2 houses ever built by CSA government).

TANNEHILL IRONWORKS HISTORICAL STATE PARK
205-477-5711 • 205-477-9400 Fax
12632 Confederate Pkwy
Mc Calla AL 35111-2620
Iron & Steel Museum depicting Confederate iron production. Period craftsmen.

ROBERT TOOMBS HOUSE
706-678-2226
PO Box 605 • 216 E Robert Toombs Ave
Washington GA 30673-0605
Confederate general & secretary of state's restored home.

U.S. NATIONAL PARK SERVICE CIVIL WAR PARKS
http://www.nps.gov/Architext/AT-NPSquery.html
Provides search for all national park sites relating to the Civil War.

VALENTINE RIVERSIDE
800-365-7272
550 E Marshall St
Richmond VA 23219-1852
Richmond's innovative history park at the falls of the James River. Civil War tours, sound/light show, vintage carousel, high-tech exhibits, African-American history/tours, archeological digs, living history.

VANISHING GLORY
601-634-1863
717 Clay St
Vicksburg MS 39180-2933
Historical, wide-screen, half-hour drama depicting Union's siege of Vicksburg, from writings of soldiers & civilians.

VICKSBURG CONVENTION & VISITORS BUREAU
800-221-3536
601-636-4642 Hayes Latham
http://www.vicksburg.org/cvb
PO Box 110
Vicksburg MS 39181-0110
Annual March "Run Through History" through Vicksburg NMP. 10K race, 5K walk, 1-mile run. Refreshments, music.

VICKSBURG NATL. MILITARY PARK
601-636-0583
3201 Clay St
Vicksburg MS 39180-3469

WEST VIRGINIA INDEPENDENCE HALL
304-238-1300
304-238-1302 Fax
1528 Market St
Wheeling WV 26003-3532
National Historic Landmark. Site of debates concerning secession & statehood. Tours & exhibits.

WILSON'S CREEK NATL. BATTLEFIELD
417-732-2662
6424 W Farm Rd 182
Highway ZZ
Republic MO 65738
Site of 1861 battle. Exhibits, tours, visitor's center with 13-min. film. Admission - $2/person or $4/car. Open year-round.

WINTER QUARTERS
318-467-9750
RR 1 Box 91
State Route 608
Newellton LA 71357-9709
Civil War relics & displays at site where Grant's troops were fed & quartered by Union sympathizer's wife.

LIBRARY BINDING COMPANY
800-792-3352
2900 Franklin Ave
Waco TX 76710-7315
Professional binding service with fast delivery for books, theses, magazines, newspapers, paperbacks, leather editions, Bibles, portfolios, etc. Free price list or advice.

JAMES MEYER BOOKBINDING CO.
315-258-3930
800-841-7797
26 E Genesee St
Auburn NY 13021-4006
Professional bookbinding & restoration - our full-time business. Leather, goldwork, edge gilding. Prices vary.

OLDE RIDGE BOOKBINDERY
800-635-3421
716-244-5510
274 Goodman St N
Rochester NY 14607-1154
Book repair & rebinding done by professional. Leather book binding, protective boxes, custom binding our specialty.

148TH NEW YORK
George Shadman
PO Box 64
Watkins Glen NY 14891-0064
They Marched on Richmond - story of the 148th NY Volunteers & the Army of the James. 300 pp. - $22 + $3 S&H.

ACADEMIC BOOK CENTER
503-287-6657 • 503-284-8859 Fax
5600 NE Hassalo St
Portland OR 97213-3699

CHARLES S. ADAMS
304-876-3533 Ph & Fax
201 Ryan Ct
Shepherdstown WV 25443-9443
Civil War books concerning operations in Md., W.Va. & the Shenandoah Valley.

AMAZON.COM BOOKS
http://www.amazon.com
Order from a list of more than a million titles, including all of Rockbridge Publishing's fine Civil War titles.

AMERICA'S NATL PARK MUSEUM STORE
215-597-2569
316 Chestnut St
Philadelphia PA 19106-2708

AMERICAN HISTORY CO.
540-371-6822
540-371-6897 Fax
AMHSTCO@ahoynet.com
701 Caroline St
Fredericksburg VA 22401-5903

AMERICAN OVERSEAS BOOK CO.
201-767-7600
201-784-0263 Fax
550 Walnut St
Norwood NJ 07648-1393

AMERICANA SOUVENIRS & GIFTS
http://www.americanagifts.com
302 York St
Gettysburg PA 17325-1930
Most complete line of Civil War souvenirs & memorabilia for both USA & CSA. Cannons, bullets, patches, toys, books, flags, videos, documents, insignias, & much more.

AMHERST COUNTY HISTORICAL MUSEUM
804-946-9860
PO Box 741
301 S Main St
Amherst VA 24521-0741

AMIRIAN'S FINE ART & FRAMING
919-735-9128
118 E Walnut St
Goldsboro NC 27530-3649

ANDERSONVILLE ANTIQUES
912-924-2558
912-924-1044
Peggy & Fred Sheppard
PO Box 26
Andersonville GA 31711-0026
Authentic Civil War guns, swords, buttons, documents; books on the Civil War.

ANTHEIL BOOKSELLERS
516-826-3101 Ph & Fax
2177 Isabelle Ct
North Bellmore NY 11710-1599
Naval, maritime, military aviation book catalogs. 1,500 book listings per catalog (quarterly). Catalog (1 yr subs.) - $6.

ANTIETAM BATTLEFIELD & BOOKSTORE
301-432-4329
Parks & History Association
PO Box 692
Highway 65 N
Sharpsburg MD 21782-0692

APPALACHIAN BOOKSTORE
706-276-1992
190 Old Orchard Sq
East Ellijay GA 30539-1929

THE ARCHIVE SOCIETY
800-257-3481
717-233-0561 Fax
PO Box 940
Hicksville NY 11802-0940
Union Leaders - a library of firsthand accounts by the men who led the Union to victory.

ARIZONA HISTORICAL SOCIETY
520-628-5774
Publications Division
949 E 2nd St
Tucson AZ 85719-4898
Confederate Pathway to the Pacific: Major Sherod Hunter and Arizona Territory, CSA, by L. Boyd Finch. $39.95 + S&H.

THE ARMCHAIR SOURCE
1959 Peace Haven Rd Ste 111
Winston Salem NC 27106
More than 2,500 titles of primary sources in the history of the Americas. Free catalog.

THE ARMCHAIR SUTLER
919-875-0111
1500 Seminole Trl
Raleigh NC 27609-7416

ASHLAWN HIGHLAND GIFT SHOP
804-293-5539
1941 Ashlawn Highland Dr
Charlottesville VA 22902-7549

ATLANTA CYCLORAMA
404-658-7625
800C Cherokee Ave SE
Atlanta GA 30315-1440

ATLANTIC BOOKS
843-723-4751 • 843-723-7654 (Bay St.)
310 King St
Charleston SC 29401-1441
2nd location: 191 E. Bay St., Charleston, SC.

B J'S BOOKS
703-347-4111
381 W Shirley Ave • Warrenton VA 20186

BARBARA'S BOOKSTORE
800-327-5471
817-335-5972 Ph & Fax
215 W 8th St
Fort Worth TX 76102-6150

BARNETTE'S FAMILY TREE BOOK CO.
barnette@neosoft.com
Mic Barnette
1001 North Loop W
Houston TX 77008-1766
Guide to tracing your Civil War ancestors - $12.50. Catalog - $1.

BATTLEZONE, LTD.
PO Box 266
Towaco NJ 07082-0266
Military patches, pins, decals, planes, books. 5,000+ items. Color catalog - $4.50 ppd. ($2 ref. w/ 1st order)

BE BOOKS
3712 Walnut Ave Ste 8135
Altoona PA 16601-1342
National Park handbooks: Gettysburg, Antietam, Fort Sumter, Vicksburg, etc. *Artillery Through the Ages*, *Fort Pulaski*, etc. Free catalog.

BEACHVIEW BOOKS
912-638-7282
215 Mallory St
Saint Simons Island GA 31522-4716

THE BEAUFORT BOOKSTORE
803-525-1066
2127 Boundary St
Beaufort SC 29902-3827

BECK'S ANTIQUES & BOOKS
540-371-1766
708 Caroline St
Fredericksburg VA 22401-5904

BELLE & BLADE
201-328-8488
201-442-0669 Fax
124 Penn Ave
Dover NJ 07801-5335
Send for catalog of war books, videos, toys, swords, knives, & gifts. Catalog - $3; free w/ order.

BERGMAN BOOKS
PO Box 28393
Columbus OH 43228-0393
Ohio in the War, by Whitelaw Reid. One of the most thorough state histories to come out of the Civil War. 2 vol., 2100 pp., hardcover. $99.00 ppd.

THE BEST SELLER
540-463-4647
540-463-3714 Fax
29 W Nelson St
Lexington VA 24450-2033

BLOUNT COUNTY GENEALOGICAL & HISTORICAL SOCIETY
ATTN: TC
PO Box 4986
Maryville TN 37802-4986
Loyal Mountain Troopers: The 2nd and 3rd Tenn. Vol. Cavalry in the Civil War. Details these largely ignored Southerners who served the Union. $32.50 ppd.

BLUE & GRAY BOOKS & PRINTS
919-441-5311
PO Box 1835
1700 S Virginia Dare Trl
Kill Devil Hills NC 27948-1835

BLUE PEACH
540-253-5536
PO Box 375
The Plains VA 20198-0375

THE BOOK CELLAR
804-979-7788 • 804-979-7787
316 E Main St
Charlottesville VA 22902-5234

THE BOOK CENTER
301-663-1222
1305 W 7th St
Frederick MD 21702-4152

THE BOOK CENTER
301-722-8344 Ph & Fax
301-722-2284
bkcenter@netbiz.net
15 N Centre St
Cumberland MD 21502-2305

THE BOOK CHASE
540-687-6874
PO Box 2258 • 102 W Washington St
Middleburg VA 20118-2258

THE BOOK DEPOT
919-527-9663
4109 W Vernon Ave • Kinston NC 28504

THE BOOK GALLERY
11400 W Huguenot Rd
Midlothian VA 23113-1193

BOOK KEEPERS, INC.
205-879-5741
PO Box 530862
Birmingham AL 35253-0862

BOOK PEOPLE
804-288-4346
536 Granite Ave
Richmond VA 23226-2148

THE BOOKERY
540-464-3377
107 W Nelson St
Lexington VA 24450-2035

BOOKMARK OF CHARLOTTE
704-377-2565
100 N Tryon St Ste 265
Charlotte NC 28202-4025

BOOKMASTERS DISTRIBUTION SERVICES
800-247-6553
1444 US Route 42
Mansfield OH 44903
The Irish Brigade & Its Campaigns as seen through the eyes of *New York Herald* war correspondent David Conyngham - $27.50.

BOOKS & COMPANY
PO Box 1046 • Dunkirk NY 14048-6046
Historical recipes & cooking info. from Civil War era. Recipes from notable figures & soldiers. History of some classic recipes. $7 ppd.

BOOKS OF THE SOUTH
205-854-2690
1269 Huffman Rd
Birmingham AL 35215-6314

THE BOOKSTACK
540-885-2665
1 E Beverley St
Staunton VA 24401-4322

THE BOOKSTORE
804-384-1746
4925 Boonsboro Rd
Lynchburg VA 24503-2260

BOOKWORLD
800-444-2524
1933 Whitfield Loop
Sarasota FL 34243
Leather and Soul, 513-pg novel based on the escape of a POW from Confederates - $21.89.

THE BOOKWORM
540-829-6209 Ph & Fax
214 N East St # A
Culpeper VA 22701-2738

BRASSEY'S
800-775-2518 • 800-428-5331
PO Box 960
Herndon VA 20172-0960
Books on history, including *Confederate Raider*, biography of Raphael Semmes, commander of CSS *Alabama*.

BREEDLOVE ENTERPRISES
PO Box 538 • Bolivar OH 44612-0538
Titles pertaining to women & the Civil War.

THE CANNONADE
PO Box 20601 • Rochester NY 14602-0601
Nice Boom: The American Civil War Artillery Reenactor's Handbook, Sean McAdoo, ed. 100+ pp., including drill, living history, tactics, NCO training & more. $10.95 + $3 S&H.

CEDAR CREEK BATTLEFIELD FOUNDATION, INC.
540-869-2064 • 540-869-1438 Fax
http://www.winchesterva.com/cedarcreek
Suzanne Lewis
PO Box 229
Middletown VA 22645-0229
Visitors Center & bookshop overlooking battlefield. Oct. reenactment. Ref. library, large CW book selection, flags, prints, maps & square foot certificates. All proceeds go to preservation of battlefield.

CHAMPLIN BOOKS, INC.
PO Box 782
Gulf Breeze FL 32562-0782
Military history, GeoPolitics, & Techno-Thrillers. All periods & conflicts. Free catalog.

CHOCTAW BOOKS
601-352-7281
926 North St • Jackson MS 39202-2614

CITADEL GIFT SHOP
803-953-5110
803-953-4802 Fax
MSC # 110
171 Moultrie St
Charleston SC 29409-0002

CIVIL WAR BOOK DISCUSSION GROUP
JPHA1982@aol.com (for more info.)
Peggy Vogtsberger
Discuss Civil War books with other AOL members, every other Wed., 8 PM EST. Keyword - CAFE BOOKA; held in Salon #2.

CIVIL WAR BOOKS ONLINE
http://members.aol.com/bookkritik/civilwar.html
Fritz Heinzen
Selection of the finest in Civil War publishing; features new & recent titles as well as the classics.

CIVIL WAR SOLDIERS MUSEUM
850-469-1900
850-469-9328 Fax
http://www.cwmuseum.org
info@cwmuseum.org
108 S Palafox Pl
Pensacola FL 32501
Explore the life of the Civil War soldier through exhibits of personal, religious, medical, musical, military, political & social aspects of the War. Tours available.

SUSAN LOTT CLARK
PO Box 2009
Waycross GA 31502-2009
Southern Letters & Life in the Mid-1800s. Hardbound, 472-pg. book based on 214 war-era family letters. Cloth - $40. Leather - $50.

CLARK'S GUN SHOP, INC.
540-439-8988
10016 James Madison Hwy
Warrenton VA 20186-7820
Retailer of books, Civil War relics, Kepis, flags, buttons, Confederate souvenirs, original Confederate money & state notes, Civil War prints.

COMMAND POST
201-627-6272
201-627-6627 Fax
PO Box 1015
Denville NJ 07834-0615
Books & videos on the Civil War, including the role of women. Free catalog.

CONFEDERATE BOOKSHELF
PO Box 1327
Harlem GA 30814-1327
New & reprinted books on the War for Southern Independence. Free price list.

CONFEDERATE DIRECTORY
915-446-4439
David Martin
PO Box 61
Roosevelt TX 76874-0061
Reference for vendors of Confederate currency, books, tapes, flags, stationery, memorabilia, reenactors' supplies, services, memorials, etc.; includes COMPLETE Confederate Constitution. $12 (ppd.).

CONFEDERATE MEMORIAL ASSOCIATION
202-483-5700
1917 N Utah St
Arlington VA 22207-2348

THE CONFEDERATE SHOPPE
205-942-8978
928 Delcris Dr
Birmingham AL 35226-1953
Books, audio & video tapes, flags, bumper stickers, auto tags; modern clothing & linens. What we don't have, we try to find.

CONSERVATIVE BOOK CLUB
33 Oakland Ave Ste 1
Harrison NY 10528-3739
Best books on history, politics, & other important issues together in one book club.

THE CORNER SHELF
540-825-4411
213 Southgate Shopping Ctr
Culpeper VA 22701-3833

CORTLAND COUNTY HISTORICAL SOCIETY, INC.
607-756-6071
25 Homer Ave • Cortland NY 13045-2056
Hosts Suggett House Museum & Kellogg Memorial Research Library. *A Regiment Remembered: 157th New York Volunteers* - Lt. William Saxton's diary, 157 pp. - $20 + $3.40 S&H. NYS - add 8% sales tax.

COTTON ROW BOOKSTORE
601-843-7083
333 Central Ave
Cleveland MS 38732-2647

COWLES HISTORY GROUP
http://www.thehistorynet.com
Attn: Military History Index
PO Box 3242 • Leesburg VA 20177-8111
Cross-referenced index of more than 3,000 entries, through 1000s of years of battle. Every subject addressed in *Military History* magazine's first decade of publication - $24.95.

JONATHAN CREEK BOOKS
PO Box 6
Lake Junaluska NC 28745-0006
Civil War Curiosities. Strange stories, oddities, events & coincidences - $9.95. Other titles available from Rutledge Hill Press.

COL. GROVER CRISWELL
352-685-2287 • 352-685-1014 Fax
PO Box 6000
Salt Springs FL 32134-6000
Buys/sells currency, stocks, bonds, money, slavery items, autographs. 51st year of business. *Comprehensive Catalog of Confederate Paper Money*, hardcover, 350 pp. - $35 (ppd.). 432-pp. price list of collectibles - $8 (ref.). Free book list.

CRITTENDEN SCHMITT ARCHIVES
http://www.erols.com/tyrannus/archives/csavideo.html
PO Box 4253 / Courthouse Station
Rockville MD 20849-4253
Technical & historical books & videotapes relating to weapons & ammunition of all types & eras.

CROSSROADS COUNTRY STORE
540-433-2084
Shenandoah Heritage Farmer's Market
Route 11 S
VA
Shenandoah Valley's premier Civil War store; books, flags, music, souvenirs, crafts, gifts, jewelry. Part of the Shenandoah Heritage Farmer's Market. Open Mon-Sat 10am-6pm.

CROWN RIGHTS BOOKS
http://members.aol.com/crwnrts/resource.htm
PO Box 769
Wiggins MS 39577-0769
The Real Lincoln - reprint, 1904 expose. 288 pp., softcover - $10 ea. Free catalog.

CW BATTLES
1943 N Grimes St Ste B229
Hobbs NM 88240-2722
Handbook of 230 major Civil War battles; when, where, who, what index. $9.95 + S&H.

D & B RUSSELL BOOKS
318-865-5198
129 Kings Hwy • Shreveport LA 71104-3402

ELIZABETH P. DARGAN
mdargan@erols.com
3257 Roman Mill Ct
Oakton VA 22124-2131
The Civil War Diary of Martha Abernathy, wife of Dr. C.C. Abernathy of Pulaski, Tennessee. $13.95 ppd.

JOHN H. DAVIS, JR.
9707 Old Georgetown Rd Apt 1423
Bethesda MD 20814-1751
Common Soldier Uncommon War, by Sidney Morris Davis. 526 pp., hardcover - $38 ppd.

DEE GEE'S GIFTS & BOOKS
919-726-3314
508 Evans St • Morehead City NC 28557

DENTON & ASSOCIATES
800-960-3003
L. M. Denton
PO Box 468 • Queenstown MD 21658-0468
A Southern Star for Maryland: MD & the Secession Crisis. Attempt to set the record straight as far as MD's role in the war. Hardcover, 256 pp. - $26 ppd.

DER TIER SHOPPE
800-520-3808
25907 54th Avenue Ct E
Graham WA 98338-9515
Extensive collection of Civil War & related books, including *The Killer Angels*, *N.B. Forrest*, *All for the Union*, etc.

THE DIXIE PRESS
615-831-0776 Ph & Fax
PO Box 110783 • Nashville TN 37222-0783
Publisher, wholesaler & retailer of Southern books & genealogy products. Free catalog.

DUBLIN BOOK CENTER
912-272-9255
Billie Tate, Mgr.
2001 Macon Rd # 29 • Dublin GA 31021
In business in central Georgia for 24 years. Complete line of books for men, women & children, many CW titles. Will special order.

EDISTO BOOKSTORE
803-869-1885
PO Box 420 • 547 Highway 174
Edisto Island SC 29438-0420

ELDEN EDITIONS
http://patriot.net/~crouch/rough.html
2111 Wilson Blvd Ste 550
Arlington VA 22201-3001
Rough Riding Scout: The Story of John W. Mobberly, Loudoun's Own Civil War Guerilla Hero, by Richard E. Crouch. Softcover, 50 pp. - $10 + $2 S&H.

FAMILY TREE BOOKSHOP
410-820-5252
410-820-5254 Fax
9B Goldsborough St
Easton MD 21601-3119

KENNETH B. FERGUSON
k4kxo@netside.com
204 Sailing Ct
Lexington SC 29072-7684
Defense of Charleston Harbor, by Capt. John Johnson. Reprint of the classic 1890 edition of Johnson's book. On top 100 list. $35.

FIRESIDE BOOKS
704-245-5188
2612 US Highway 74 Byp # 509
Tri-City Mall
Forest City NC 28043-6192

THE FLAG GUYS
914-562-0088 x307
http://www.flagguys.com
Flagguys@aol.com
283 Windsor Hwy Dept 307
New Windsor NY 12553-6909
Flags of all types & sizes. Books, Kepis, accessories, swords, cassettes, CDs, novelties. Free catalog. (See ad page 263)

FOUR SEASONS BOOKS
304-876-3486
116 W German St
Shepherdstown WV 25443

FRAME GALLERY OF STATESVILLE
704-873-6097 Ph & Fax
Carol Chappell
110 W Broad St
Statesville NC 28677-5256
Framed & unframed prints. Offering Mort Kuntsler & Troiani prints, Civil War accessories, encapsulation services utilizing current archival technology. Books.

FRANKLIN BOOK CO.
215-635-5252 • 215-635-6155 Fax
7804 Montgomery Ave Ste 3
Elkins Park PA 19027-2698

FRANKLIN BOOKSELLERS
615-370-5737 Publisher
615-790-1349 Store
118 4th Ave S
Franklin TN 37064-2622

FRONTIER PRESS
409-740-7988
409-740-0138 Fax
http://www.doit.com/frontier
kgfrontier@aol.com
Karen M. Green
PO Box 3715
Galveston TX 77552-0715
Bookstore specializing in historical & genealogical titles, incl. collection of nearly 350 books specifically dealing with the Civil War. Free catalog.

GALLERY 30
717-334-0335
30 York St
Gettysburg PA 17325-2337

GALLERY OF MOUNTAIN SECRETS
540-468-1900
Richard & Linda Holman
PO Box 370
Route 250 Main St
Monterey VA 24465-0370

GARRETT PRODUCTIONS
800-870-9626
Thomas A. Garrett
185A Newberry Commons
Etters PA 17319-9362
Insight to the Battle of Gettysburg, 28-pg book. Great for first-timers or refresher - $10.97 ppd. *The Monuments of Gettysburg* 40-min. videotape - $32 ppd.

THE GENERAL STORE
703-261-3860
2522 Beech Ave
Buena Vista VA 24416-3014

THE GENERAL'S BOOKS
800-CIVIL WAR
522 Norton Rd
Columbus OH 43228-2617
Affiliate of *Blue & Grey* magazine. 1,000+ Civil War titles. Fascinating & excellent reading. Call for catalog.

GETTYSBURG FRAME SHOP & GALLERY
717-337-2796 • 717-337-2481 Fax
Paul Selmer
25 Chambersburg St
Gettysburg PA 17325-1102
Limited prints by most noted Civil War artists. Originials by Rocco, Reeves, Gnatek, Bender, Umble, Wikoff, Prechtel, Forquer. Civil War books. Catalog - $1.

GETTYSBURG NMP BOOKSTORE
800-JULY 3 1863
717-334-1891 Fax
Robert Housch
Visitor Center Electric Map
95 Taneytown Rd
Gettysburg PA 17325-2804
Complete Civil War bookstore specializing in books, tapes, CDs & videos. Free catalog.

GIVENS BOOKS
804-385-5027
2345 Lakeside Dr
Lynchburg VA 24501-6730

THE GOOD OL' REBEL
706-553-2202
10105 White House Pkwy
Woodbury GA 30293-3101

GOODSON ENTERPRISES, INC.
970-923-0063 • 303-838-1357
PO Box 128 • Shawnee CO 80475
Georgia Confederate 7000, Part I - complete battle & CW history of Barton & Stovell's Georgia brigade ($20). *Part II: Letters & Diaries* ($15). Both titles - $30. Add $3 S&H.

GOSPEL TRUTH/CIVIL WAR ROOM
412-238-7991
228 W Main St
Ligonier PA 15658-1130
Full-service Christian bookstore & Civil War room. Kunstler calendars, patterns, pewter figurines, books, videos, music, hats, accessories, shirts, Woolrich wool & much more.

GRANT COUNTY HISTORICAL SOCIETY
608-723-2287 • 608-723-4925
129 E Maple St • Lancaster WI 53813-1765
Operates from Cunningham Museum. *Our Boys* - 64 stories of men & boys from Grant County, Wisc.; names of all 750 Grant Co. soldiers who died in the war. $25 + $3 S&H.
(See ad page 271)

THE GREENHOUSE
540-364-1959
PO Box 525
8393 W Main St
Marshall VA 20116-0525

GREYSTONE'S HISTORY EMPORIUM & GALLERY
717-338-0631
717-338-0851 Fax
http://www.GreystoneOnline.com
461 Baltimore St
Gettysburg PA 17325-2623
Producers of *CW Journal* have created a store, gallery & museum. Military miniatures, books, videos, collectibles, art, exhibits, story theatre. Unique merchandise.

GUIDON BOOKS
602-945-8811 • 602-946-0521 Fax
7117 E Main St
Scottsdale AZ 85251-4315

EDWARD R. HAMILTON, BOOKSELLER
5265 Oak
Falls Village CT 06031
Overstocks, remainders, imports & reprints. 1,000s of titles in more than 60 subject areas, including the Civil War. $20-$40 books as low as $1.95-$3.95. Free catalog.

HANNAH'S LETTERS
972-291-9266
560 Flower Ln
Cedar Hill TX 75104
Hannah's Letters, by Charles Finsley. 30 battlefield letters, history of 67th Ohio Inf. 101 pp., hardcover - $27 + $4 S&H.

HARPERS FERRY BOOKSTORE
304-535-6881
PO Box 197 • Shenandoah St
Harpers Ferry WV 25425-0197

HEARTHSTONE BOOKSHOP
703-960-0086 • 888-960-3300 Orders
703-960-0087 Fax
http://www.hearthstonebooks.com
info@hearthstonebooks.com
Stuart Nixon
5735A Telegraph Rd
Alexandria VA 22303-1205
Genealogical books, software, CDs & supplies, including listings on Civil War history & research. Catalog - $2 (ref.).

HERITAGE ANTIQUES
540-788-3274
8733 Old Dumfries Rd
Catlett VA 20119-1934

HERITAGE BOOKS, INC.
800-398-7709
301-390-7709
http://www.heritagebooks.com
1540 Pointer Ridge Pl Ste E
Bowie MD 20716-1800
Books on history, Americana, Civil War, & genealogy. Free catalog.

HERITAGE OF HONOR
703-751-1863
PO Box 22485
Alexandria VA 22304-9248

HISTORIC MIDWAY MUSEUM STORE
606-846-4214
PO Box 4592
124 E Railroad St
Midway KY 40347-4592
Civil War newspapers, books on Kentucky. Scale model cannons.

HISTORICAL BRIEFS, INC.
800-732-4746
Civil War Reports - most authentic reports available, written as events unfolded & published in *Harper's Weekly*. 232 pp. - $24.95 + $3.75 S&H.

HISTORY BOOK CLUB
Camp Hill PA 17012-0001
"The Best History Has to Offer." Today's finest selections in all areas of history, from ancient to modern, available at discount prices.

HISTORY BOOK SOCIETY
PO Box 2225
Williamsburg VA 23187-2225
Outstanding books at unbeatable prices. Broad selection of new titles. Free broadside catalog.

HOOKED ON HISTORY
708-255-2340
15 N Elmhurst Ave
Mount Prospect IL 60056-2400

HOOP & HAVERSACK SUTLERY
517-643-5368
PO Box 415
Merrill IL 48637-0415

HOWELL PRESS
800-868-4512 • 804-977-4006
howellpres@aol.com
1713-2D Allied Lane
Charlottesville VA 22903-5336
Civil War titles, as well as books on history, transportation, cooking & gardening. (See ad page 267)

IRISH BRIGADE GIFT SHOP
504 Baltimore St
Gettysburg PA 17325-2605
T-shirts, sweatshirts, jackets, books, flags, recruiting posters, photos, pins, stationery, prints, figurines & more - all relating to the Irish Civil War service. Detailed item list - send business-size SASE.

THE JOHNS HOPKINS UNIVERSITY PRESS
800-537-5487
http://jhupress.jhu.edu/home.html
Hampden Station
Baltimore MD 21211
The Long Roll (softcover - $15.95) and *Cease Firing* (softcover - $14.95), both by Mary Johnston, a Civil War novelist rediscovered.

JUNIATA COUNTY HISTORICAL SOCIETY
498B Jefferson St
Mifflintown PA 17059-1400
An Imperishable Fame: The Civil War Experience of George F. McFarland, by Michael Dreese - 210 pp., $20 (ppd.).

KONECKY & KONECKY
212-807-8230
156 5th Ave Ste 823
New York NY 10010-7002
Books on America's Civil War & other periods. Call/write for listing.

KRAINIK & WALVOORD
703-536-8045
PO Box 6206
Falls Church VA 22040-6206
A Collector's Guide to Photographic Cases. Definitive reference on plastic ("Gutta Percha") daguerreotype cases. Hardcover - 800 illus. & price guide - $90 ppd.

ROBERT LACOVARA
609-624-0608 Ph & Fax
2089 N Route 9
Cape May Court House NJ 08210-1163
Cumberland County and South Jersey During the Civil War, 9th New Jersey Regiment, Flags and History of New Jersey Volunteers During the Civil War - all reprints. Other titles.

LADIES' ISLAND BOOKSTORE
803-524-0444
2 Islands Cswy • Beaufort SC 29902-1737

THE LAST SQUARE
800-750-4401
http://www.lastsquare.com
questions@lastsquare.com
5944 Odana Rd
Madison WI 53719-1214
Dedicated to military history. Gaming supplies, miniatures, books, fine prints. Call for info.

GEORGE LAYMAN
55 Littleton Rd Apt 24F
Ayer MA 01432-1762
1866 Peabody Breech-Loading Rifle Catalog, new repro. *Rolling Block Rifle* and *A Guide to the Maynard Breech Loader.* Single shot books.

LEGENDS
913-242-5060
Matt & Susan Matthews
703 S Main St • Ottawa KS 66067-2803

LINCOLN LETTERS
PO Box 80821 • Lansing MI 48908-0821
Personal Reminiscences of Abraham Lincoln, by Smith Stimmel. Reprint of rare book; originally published in 1928. Ltd. quantities - $15. (See ad page 272)

LINCOLN PARK BOOKSHOP
312-477-7087
2423 N Clark St
Chicago IL 60614-2717

LITTLE WARS
504-924-6304 • 504-924-5307 Fax
3034 College Dr
Baton Rouge LA 70808-3117

LONGSTREET HOUSE
609-448-1501
David Martin
PO Box 730 • Hightstown NJ 08520-0730
Original & reprint titles on Gettysburg & unit histories from New Jersey, New York, Pennsylvania, Delaware, & South Carolina. Free catalog.

LOUDOUN MUSEUM SHOP
703-777-8331
14 Loudoun St SW • Leesburg VA 20175
Visit our shop located in restored 1767 log cabin. Unique gift items include historic maps, books & hand-crafted gifts by local artisans.

MAC MILLAN GENERAL REFERENCE
800-428-5331
201 W 103rd St
Indianapolis IN 46290-1093
The Atlas of the Civil War - puts the entire Civil War at your fingertips. At bookstores or order direct.

MAIN STREET BOOKS
704-892-6841
PO Box 1210
126 S Main St
Davidson NC 28036-1210

MAIN STREET BOOKS
703-628-1232
152 E Main St # 2-W
Abingdon VA 24210-2835

JOHN MAINOR
21493 Campbell Dr
Brooksville FL 34601-1408
Civil War Stories by E.H. Sutton, 1910. Firsthand account of 24th Georgia at Fredericksburg, Chancellorsville, Gettysburg, & life in POW camps. Reprints - $12 ppd.

MARY ELLEN & CO. TIMELESS TREASURES VICTORIAN SHOP
800-669-1860 Orders
219-656-3000 Fax
Mary Ellen Smith
100 N Main St
North Liberty IN 46554-9218
Historical sewing patterns, Victorian boots, parasols, hats, fans, hoops, petticoats, camisoles, etc. Variety of books. Victorian gifts, wedding accessories, etc. Retail/wholesale. New Victorian gift shop - call for hours. Catalog - $3 (ref.).

MC CAIN'S BOOKS
703-740-3354
PO Box 369 • 9400 S Congress St
New Market VA 22844-0369

HENRY V. MC CREA
PO Box 951 • Marianna FL 32447-0951
Red Dirt and Isinglass: A Wartime Biography of a Confederate Soldier - stirring account of infantryman Marion Hill Fitzpatrick's adventures with the ANV, 5/62-4/65. $34.45 ppd.

TIM MC KINNEY
RR 2 Box 300A • Fayetteville WV 25840-9570
Robert E. Lee & the 35th Star, R.E. Lee at Sewell Mountain: The West Virginia Campaign, & other titles.

MILITARY BOOK CATALOG
PO Box 4470
Cave Creek AZ 85327-4470
Military history, medals, uniforms, weapons, collectibles. More than 1,000 titles. Catalog - $2. Medals catalog - $1.

THE MILITARY BOOK CLUB
6550 E 30th St • PO Box 6357
Indianapolis IN 46206-6357
From ancient to modern history. Special deals with membership. Many Civil War titles.

MISSOURI HISTORICAL SOCIETY
PO Box 11940
Saint Louis MO 63112-0040
Civil War books. In *The Civil War in St. Louis, a Guided Tour,* Wm. C. Winter brings to life the monuments, markers, & memories of the Civil War in St. Louis. 192 pp. Paper - $22.95. Cloth - $32.95.

MONOCACY BATTLEFIELD & BOOKSTORE
301-662-3515
Parks & History Association
4801 Urbana Pike # B
Frederick MD 21704-7307

MONTGOMERY COUNTY HISTORICAL SOCIETY
212 S Water St
Crawfordsville IN 47933-2535
The Diary of Private Ambrose Remley & His Four Years in the Lightning Brigade - story of Wilder's mounted infantry & Spencer repeating rifle - $23.

W. M. MORRISON BOOKS
512-266-3381
morrisonbooks@worldnet.att.net
15801 La Hacienda Dr
Austin TX 78734-1431
Personal Civil War letters of Lawrence Sullivan "Sul" Ross, CSA. - $29.50 ppd.

JIM MUNDIE, BOOKS
281-531-8639
12122 Westmere Dr
Houston TX 77077-4022

R. L. MURRAY
315-594-2019
murrayrl@redcreek.net
13205 Younglove Rd
Wolcott NY 14590-9742
"Hurrah for the Ould Flag!" True story of Capt. Andrew Cowan & the 1st NY Independent Bty. at Gettysburg - $12. Other titles.

MUSEUM OF FRONTIER CULTURE
540-332-7850
PO Box 810
1250 Richmond Rd
Staunton VA 24402-0810

NEW DOMINION BOOK SHOP
804-295-2552
804-295-9986 Fax
404 E Main St
Charlottesville NC 22902-5236

NEW LEAF BOOKSTORE, LTD.
540-347-7323
43 Main St
Warrenton VA 20186-3420

NEW MARKET BATTLEFIELD MILITARY MUSEUM
540-740-8065
540-740-3663 Fax
John Bracken
9500 Collins Dr
PO Box 1131
New Market VA 22844-1131
Comprehensive museum shop featuring CW relics, flags, uniforms, bullets, buttons, swords, muskets, currency, personal items, memorabilia, etc. More than 1200 book titles. Open Mar. 15-Dec. 1.

MRS. A.C. NICHOLS
4048 Rectortown Rd
Marshall VA 20115-3241
The Little Fork Rangers, 1861-1865: A Sketch of Co. D, 4th Virginia Cavalry (Culpeper's only cavalry company) - 130 pp., hardcover - $21; softcover - $11. Add S&H.

NORTHERN VIRGINIA DAILY
540-465-5137
Civil War Book
PO Box 69 • Strasburg VA 22657-0069
Standing Ground - 18-part newspaper series on Civil War in the Shenandoah Valley compiled into unique new book. Softcover - $16 ppd.

OLD HISTORICAL VIEWS
803-723-7708
188 Meeting St
Charleston SC 29401-3155

ANDREW OREN MILITARY BOOKS
414-744-3927
3156 S Kinnickinnic Ave
Milwaukee WI 53207-2974
Civil War books. Booklist available.

P & L ENTERPRISE
301-449-5730
PO Box 518
Temple Hills MD 20757-0518
Buffalo Soldiers - ltd. ed. prints, statues, books. Color brochure - $2.

PAGE ONE
PO Box 4232 • Richmond VA 23220-8232
Guide to Virginia Civil War - all the Civil War trail sites.

PALMETTO BOOKWORKS
PO Box 11551
Columbia SC 28211-1551
The Gallant Gladden: The Life and Times of Gen. Addley Hogan Gladden, by Edith Anthony Purvis - $35 + $2 S&H.

PALMYRA TRADING CO.
703-984-8888
97 Franley Ln
Woodstock VA 22664-2653

PAPER TREASURES
703-740-3135
PO Box 1160
9595 S Congress St
New Market VA 22844-1160

JOHN M. PELLICANO
13829 Jewel Ave
Flushing NY 11367-1964
Conquer or Die: The 39th New York Volunteer Infantry - Garibaldi Guard, a military history. $14.95 + $3 S&H.

PICKET POST
717-337-2984
341 Baltimore St
Gettysburg PA 17325-2602

THE PIEDMONT ENVIRONMENTAL COUNCIL
540-347-2334
PO Box 460
Warrenton VA 20188-0460
Hallowed Ground: Preserving America's Heritage, by Rudy Abramson. Piedmont -- America's most historic land -- is captured in all its moods through words & pictures. $40.

PRAIRIE TRAVELER BOOKS
131 W Cavalier Rd
Scottsville NY 14546-1206
Books: Western American History, fur traders, Indian tribes, cavalry, cowboys, Custer, etc. Free catalog.

PROVISION MEDIA
901-668-4249
7046 Broadway # 318
Lemon Grove CA 91945-1406
The Gettysburg Experience, book - $10.95. Computer clip art. Civil War, anatomy, botany, earth science, IBM/Mac format - $19.95.

R B BOOKS
800-497-1427 • 717-232-7944
717-238-3280 Fax
Ruth Hoover Seitz
1006 N 2nd St • Harrisburg PA 17102-3121
Gettysburg: Civil War Memories, including color photos from renowned J. Howard Wert Gettysburg Collection. 64 pp. $9.95 + $3 S&H. (See ad page 260)

R. M. J. C., INC.
PO Box 684
Appomattox VA 24522-0684
CW-period New Testament, hardcover - $13 ppd. Choose Union (black) or Confederate (brown). Reprinted from original. Free quarterly, CW-related newspaper, *The Christian Banner*, deals with Christian aspect of the war.

R & R BOOKS
716-346-2577
3020 E Lake Rd
Livonia NY 14487
Books on weapons, featuring *The British Soldier's Firearm*, *Spencer Repeating Firearms*, *Confederate Edged Weapons*, etc.

R W BOOKS
703-257-7895
8657 Sudley Rd • Manassas VA 20110-4588

MORRIS RAPHAEL
318-369-3220
1404 Bayouside Dr
New Iberia LA 70563-2824
A Gunboat Named Diana (book) - $21.95 ppd. *The Battle in the Bayou Country* (5th printing) - $21.95 ppd. Brochure.

REALLY NEAT BOOKS
540-564-0688
182 Neff Ave • Harrisonburg VA 22801-3488

RED TIE MUSIC & BOOKS
7410 Brixworth Ct Unit 101
Baltimore MD 21244-5660
The Civil War Fifer - songbook featuring favorite & lesser-known melodies, lyrics, histories & artwork - $12.95 + $2.50 S&H. Other songbooks & collections of lyrics & poetry.

THE RICHMOND BOOKSHOP, INC.
804-644-9970
808 W Broad St • Richmond VA 23220-3807

RICHMOND NEWSPAPERS SUPPLEMENTARY PUBLICATIONS
800-422-4434
PO Box 85333 • Richmond VA 23293-5333
The Insider's Guide to the Civil War (Eastern Theater), Travel Guide - $9.95.

ROANOKE VALLEY HISTORY MUSEUM GIFT SHOP
540-342-5772
PO Box 1904 • 1 Market Sq
Roanoke VA 24008-1904

THE ROBERTS CIVIL WAR LIBRARY
800-520-3808
25907 54th Avenue Ct E
Graham WA 98338-9515
Many books dealing with the Civil War including *N.B. Forrest* - $15; *Gen. A.P. Hill* - $14; *Landscapes of the Civil War* - $40. Others.

ROYAL OAK BOOKSHOP
540-635-7070
207 S Royal Ave
Front Royal VA 22630-3205

RUFFIN FLAG COMPANY
706-456-2111 • 706-456-2112 Fax
http://www.mindspring.com/~micromgt/ruffin.htm
241 Alexander St NW
Crawfordville GA 30631-2804
Auto tags, bumper stickers, books, T-shirts, crew sweatshirts, polo shirts, regulation battle flags, etc. Jeff Davis, Dixie's Pride, N.B. Forrest, etc. Retail/wholesale. Catalog - $1.

RURAL CITIZEN BOOKSTORE, INC.
540-635-6673
http://ruralcitizen.com
rory@ruralcitizen.com
PO Box 286
370 Rome Beauty Dr
Markham VA 22643-0286
Specializes in books on Southern culture & heritage.

MIKE RUSSELL
401 Virginia Ave
Herndon VA 20170-5437
Quarterly catalog of Victorian artifacts & relics, emphasis on obsolete currency, bottles & pipes - $2. *The Collector's Guide to Clay Tobacco Pipes, Vol. I* - $20.45 ppd.

RUTH'S BOOKS & CARDS
703-879-9695
RR 1 Box 2-H
Dayton VA 22821-9801

SARATOGA SOLDIER SHOP
518-885-1497
518-885-0100 Fax
831 Route 67 Bldg 5
Ballston Spa NY 12020
1000 54mm pewter soldiers, cavalry & artillery kits. Civil War & other eras, paints, modelers' aids, & booklist. Catalog - $6.

SATISFIED MIND
540-665-0855
11 S Loudoun St
Winchester VA 22601-4719

SAUERS HISTORY SHOP
800-510-1108
3531 Martha Custis Dr
Alexandria VA 22302-2002
Eagerly awaited research guide to Civil War material in the *National Tribune*, 1877-1884. $19.95 ppd. (In KY, $20.97).

SAVANNAH HISTORY MUSEUM
912-238-1779
303 Martin Luther King Jr Blvd
Savannah GA 31401-4217

THE SCHOLAR'S BOOKSHELF
609-395-6933
609-395-0755 Fax
http://www.scholarsbookshelf.com
books@scholarsbookshelf.com
110 Melrich Rd
Cranbury NJ 08512-3511
A major book catalog company that produces three 88-pp. Military History catalogs each year. Catalogs feature a substantial variety of Civil War books & videos. Free catalog.

CARL SCIORTINO MILITARIA
PO Box 29809
Richmond VA 23242-0809
700-item catalog of Civil War militaria - $2 (ref.). Military books - 600 titles. Catalog - $2 (ref.).

SEAWEED'S SHIPS OF HISTORY
800-SEA-WEED
304-652-1525 Fax
PO Box 154, Dept M
Sistersville WV 26175-0154
Histories of U.S. naval, army transports, most Coast Guard, sunken ships, etc. $8 & up.

SECOND CHANCE BOOKS
703-948-3667
HC 3 Box 224
Rochelle VA 22738-9707

SECOND CORPS BOOKSHOP
804-861-1863
209 High St
Petersburg VA 23803-3241

SENECA RIDGE GALLERY
412-828-0240
426 Allegheny River Blvd
Oakmont PA 15139-1725
Civil War & 18th-century art, books, videos, games, music, more!

SHAMROCK HILL BOOKS
770-569-1802
770-569-1801 Fax
http://www.bookguy.com
HISTORYBKS@aol.com
Ed O'Dwyer
12725 Bethany Rd
Alpharetta GA 30004-1080
Books on the Civil War with specialty in Irish participation. Kepis, music & more. Email credit card accounts welcome. Catalog.

E. SHAVER, BOOKSELLER
912-234-7257
912-234-7258 Fax
326 Bull St
Savannah GA 31401-4517

THE SHENANDOAH ATTIC
540-464-8888
3 N Main St • Lexington VA 24450-2520

SHENANDOAH COUNTY LIBRARY STORE
540-984-8200
300 Stoney Creek Blvd
Edinburg VA 22824-9706

SHENANDOAH SEASONS
800-484-7745 code 0361
989 Black Bear Rd
Maurertown VA 22644-2839

SHENANDOAH TRADER
540-740-3735 • trader@m-c-b.com
Ross & Mary Smith
1988 Shipwreck Dr
New Market VA 22844-3408
Books for the collector of Civil War & earlier periods of American militaria. Manufacturer of quality artifact display cases of oak & walnut. Button cases. Catalog - $1 (ref.).

WILLIAM S. SMEDLUND
770-322-0544
1666 Glen Arm Dr
Lithonia GA 30058-5513
Campfires of Georgia's Troops, 1861-65. Encyclopedic history of 747 named Georgia camps. Includes locations, dates, sources, letters, maps, images. Indices, 322 pp., hardbound - $37 ppd.

SOLDIERS, ETC.
317-846-0156
317-573-9449 Fax
P0 Box 20276
Indianapolis IN 46220-0276
Books on the Civil War, including *The Story the Soldiers Wouldn't Tell: Sex in the Civil War*, and *Pulling the Temple Down.*

SOUTHERN GUN WORKS
757-934-1423 • 757-925-1177 Fax
109 Cherry St • Suffolk VA 23434-5306
Civil War prints, autographed military books, memorabilia. Art by Troiani, Spaulding, Kunstler, Gallon, others.

SOUTHERN HISTORICAL SHOWCASE
800-854-7832 • 615-321-0639
http://www.southernhistorical.com
southernhistorical@nashville.com
1907 Division St • Nashville TN 37203-2705
Southern military art & books, prints, original documents & autographs, photos, engravings. Prechtel, Reeves, Kunstler, Kidd, Gallon, Summers, Heron, Garner, Rocco. Cat. - $5.

STARS & BARS GIFT SHOP AT BEAUVOIR
601-388-9074 • 601-388-1313
2244 Beach Blvd
Biloxi MS 39531-5002

A. MARTIN STEPAK
954-401-0780
PO Box 10088 • Tampa FL 33679-0088
Book about the media's betrayal of the South. Fascinating reading. $24.95.

STONEWALL JACKSON MUSEUM AT HUPP'S HILL
540-465-5884 • 540-465-5999
540-465-8157 Fax
Babs Melton
33229 Old Valley Pike • US 11 North
Strasburg VA 22657-3715
Exhibits of Jackson's 1862 Valley Campaign with original artifacts & hands-on reproductions. Children's room has costumes, Civil War camp, & discovery boxes.

STRICTLY SOUTHERN
912-454-1860 • 912-453-8483 Fax
http://www.accucomm.net/~theSouth
PO Box 1945 • Milledgeville GA 31061
Confederate shop featuring books, T-shirts, souvenirs, Kunstler prints, jewelry. Mail orders available.

SURRATT HOUSE MUSEUM & GIFT SHOP
301-868-1121 • 301-868-8177 Fax
http://www.clark.net/pub/surratt/surratt.html
Laurie Verge, Director
PO Box 427 • 9118 Brandywine Rd
Clinton MD 20735-0427
1852 home of Surratt family. Served also as tavern, hostelry, post office & link in Confederate spy network. Played role in Lincoln assassination. Offsite bus tours. (See ad page 258)

TATTERED COVER BOOK STORE
303-322-7727
1628 16th St • Denver CO 80202-1162

ALBERTA TAYLOR
614-667-6087
4725 Security Dr Apt 208
Springfield OH 45503-5850
Hearts of Fire: ... Soldier Women of the Civil War. 2nd printing of this must-read details accounts of women who went to war disguised as men. $22.95 ppd.

L.B. TAYLOR, JR.
757-253-2636
108 Elizabeth Meriwether
Williamsburg VA 23185-5107
Civil War Ghosts of Virginia - 232 pp., softcover, $12 + $3 S&H. Author gathers legends, lore & happenings, matching them with historical fact, vignettes & anecdotes.

TAYLORMADE WRIGHT
812-866-3295
10630 W State Rd Ste 256
Lexington IN 47138
With Bowie Knives and Pistols by Dave Taylor. Morgan's Raid in Indiana. Experience the raid by those who lived it. 30 pix. $12 ppd.

TEMPEST BOOKS
519-736-8629 • 888-233-5666
519-736-8620 Fax
235 Dalhousie
Amherstburg, Ontario N9V 1W6 CANADA
New books for old ideas. Military, naval, costuming, fiction, reference. Maps for campaign planning.

TENNESSEE STATE MUSEUM
615-741-2692
5th & Deaderick Sts
Nashville TN 37243-1120
Civil War exhibits include largest depository of artifacts from war's Western Theater. *Civil War Drawings from the Tennessee State Museum* - book, $10.

THAT BOOKSTORE IN BLYTHEVILLE
870-763-3333 • 870-763-1125 Fax
http://www.bookweb.org/bookstore/blytheville
bookstbly@missconet.com
316 W Main St
Blytheville AR 72315-3318
Full service community bookstore: special orders, out-of-print searches, frequent buyer plan.

THEME PRINTS, LTD.
800-CIVL WAR
718-225-4067
PO Box 610123
Bayside NY 11361-0123
Books, antique arms, historic documents, photographs, letters & autographs from Revolutionary era to early Hollywood. Includes Civil War memorabilia. Fully illus. catalog - $5, or $12/yr. (5 issues).

CAROLE THOMPSON, FINE PHOTOGRAPHS
901-278-2741 • 901-726-5533 Fax
ctfp@ix.netcom.com
1515 Central Ave
Memphis TN 38104-4907
Gardner's Sketchbook of the Civil War, 100 museum quality albumen photos by Alexander Gardner & Timothy O'Sullivan. Buys/sells/appraises.

TIME-LIFE BOOKS
PO Box 85563 • Richmond VA 23285-5563
Civil War series covering many interesting facets of the war. Write for details.

TOOMEY'S BOOKSHOP
410-850-0831 Ph & Fax
PO Box 122 • Linthicum MD 21090-0122
Baltimore During the Civil War, by Scott S. Sheads & Daniel C. Toomey. Hardcover, 224 pp. - $24.95 + $3 S&H. Other titles.

TOTAL INFORMATION
716-254-0628 • 716-254-0209 Fax
robert%total_information@mcimail.com
844 Dewey Ave
Rochester NY 14613-1995

TSUNAMI, INC.
509-529-0813
509-527-3691 Fax
http://www.wwics.com/~tsunami
Tsunami@wwics.com
Charles Potts
PO Box 100
Walla Walla WA 99362-0204
How the South Finally Won the Civil War, and the Political Future of the United States. May change the way you read American History. 440 pp. Hardcover, sewn, dust jacket - $29 ppd.

TURN OF THE PAGE
803-425-5100
1671 Springdale Dr Ste 9
Camden SC 29020-2079

USA HISTORY STORE
508-947-8866
http://www.usahistorystore.com
PO Box 109
Middleboro MA 02346-0109
Authentic brass camp candlesticks perfect for 19th-century impression. Set of 2 - $13.95 + $3 S&H. Books, games, flags & period clothing.

VALOR ART & FRAME LTD.
540-372-3376
CWFugi@aol.com
Joe Fulginiti
718 Caroline St
Fredericksburg VA 22401-5904
Civil War artwork, artifacts & books. Featuring artwork of Don Troiani. Carry all major Civil War artists. Custom museum mount framing. 15 years of service. Free catalog.

VIRGINIA BORN & BRED
540-463-1832
16 W Washington St
Lexington VA 24450-2121

VIRGINIA HISTORICAL SOCIETY MUSEUM SHOP
804-342-9671
804-358-4901
PO Box 7311
428 North Blvd
Richmond VA 23221-0311

THE VIRGINIA SHOP AT CHARLOTTESVILLE
1047B Emmet St N
Charlottesville VA 22903-4834

PATRICIA VOLKMANN
2842 Cherry Point Ln
Maryland Heights MO 63043-1708
Missouri: Our Civil War Heritage. Covers 76 Missouri counties in the Civil War. 492 pp. Softcover - $25 ppd.

OPHELIA WADE
911 Osborn Ave
Kennett MO 63857-2154
Preacher from Liberty Hill - biographical novel of Joseph Richardson, who fought in Lee's ANV & was imprisoned in Fort Delaware. 365 pp. - $22 ppd.

WAYSIDE MUSEUM OF AMERICAN HISTORY
540-465-5884
540-465-5899 Fax
132 N Massanutten St
Strasburg VA 22657-2300

WELL-TRAVELED IMAGES
414-896-0555
http://www.globaldialog.com/~eicher/index.htm
eicher@globaldialog.com
Lynda Eicher
S60 W24160 Red Wing Dr
Waukesha WI 53186-9508
Color photos of CW battlefields, sites. Books. Matted color prints of 10,000+ CW-related images, also available for publication. Call or email for catalog. See internet home page for samples & info. on books.

WHEATON HISTORY CENTER
PO Box 373
Wheaton IL 60189-0373
Journal of Capt. Henry Whipple Chester: 2nd Ohio Volunteer Cavalry. Recollections of the War of the Rebellion. 200 pp., 97 illus., extensive index - $34.59 + $5 S&H.

WHITE'S ELECTRONIC, INC.
800-547-6911
1011 Pleasant Valley Rd
Sweet Home OR 97386-1098
Five different books on finding & detecting buried treasure, gold, etc., from $4.95.

WILLETT BOOKS
PO Box 5871
Kingsport TN 37663-0871
A Union Soldier Returns South - Civil War letters/diary of PR. Willett, 113th OVI. Details of battle, daily life, thoughts, photos, repros of some letters/diary. Hardcover - $14.95.

THE WINCHESTER BOOK GALLERY
540-667-3444
185 N Loudoun St
Winchester VA 22601-4789

WINCHESTER-FREDERICK CO. VISITORS CENTER
540-662-4135
1360 S Pleasant Valley Rd
Winchester VA 22601-4447

WISTERIA MANOR
540-722-0145
135 N Loudoun St
Winchester VA 22601-4717

GEORGE F. WITHAM
901-465-6722 Ph & Fax
155 Raspberry Cv
Eads TN 38028-3003
Catalog of Civil War Photographers - alphabetical listing by state of more than 5900 Civil War-era photographers. Softcover - $16.50 ppd.

WILLIAM P. ZUCCHERO BOOKS
804-974-7057
2105 Wisteria Dr
Charlottesville VA 22911-9047

20TH MAINE, INC.
207-865-4340
207-865-9575 Fax
Patricia Hodgdon
49 West St
Freeport ME 04032-1127
Specialized bookstore devoted to Civil War with new & old books, art, music, videos, antiques & much more.

ABERDEEN BOOKS
303-795-1890 Ph & Fax
http:2//www.sonic.net/~bstone:aberdeen/
Tom Petteys, Owner
1360 W Littleton Blvd
Littleton CO 80120
Wide range of new & used military books, including Civil War titles.

ABRAHAM LINCOLN BOOK SHOP
312-944-3085
312-944-5549 Fax
357 W Chicago Ave
Chicago IL 60610-3052
U.S. Military History, French & Indian War, Revolution, 1812, Mexican, Civil War, Indian Wars. Books, prints, autographs. Buy/sell. Catalog - $5.

AMERICAN MILITARY ANTIQUES
410-465-6827
Courtney B. Wilson & Assoc.
8398 Court Ave
Ellicott City MD 21043-4514
Appraisers & dealers in fine 19th-century military Americana. Civil War memorabilia, books, photos, swords, forearms, relics. Buys/sells.

AMERICANA MERCANTILE
PO Box 4066
Hastings MN 55033-7066
American History books, documents, maps, & more.

DR. C. E. BAKER
652 16th Ave NW
Birmingham AL 35215-5351
Books by great men. R. L. Dabney's works on Jackson, Defense of Virginia, etc. M. E. Bradford's, J. William Jones' works, etc. Write for more listings.

BATTLEFIELD BOOKSTORE
800-340-8268
236 New Bridge St
Jacksonville NC 28540-4708
Civil War books - new, used & reprints. Military books of all eras. Free catalog.

BAY STREET BOOKS
202-546-3893
1740 Bay St SE
Washington DC 20003-1646
Civil War books - out-of-print & some new titles.

MIKE BRACKIN
203-647-8620
PO Box 23
Manchester CT 06045-0023
Large assortment of Civil War & Indian War autographs, accoutrements, memorabilia, insignia, medals, buttons, GAR, documents, photos & books. Catalog - $6/yr for 5 issues.

BRANDY STATION BOOKSHELF
PO Box 1863
Harrah OK 73045-1863
Buys/sells Civil War books.Regimental, rare & out-of-print editions; also reprints & current titles. Want lists welcome. Free catalog.

BUTTERNUT AND BLUE
410-256-9220
410-256-8423 Fax
Jim McLean
3411 Northwind Rd
Baltimore MD 21234-1250
Offer 5 to 6 comprehensive book catalogs each year. Librarian from prestigious college proclaimed that ours was "the best CW catalog." Catalog - $2 ($5 outside US) - free after order or $10 for 1-yr. subs. with no order.

CAMP POPE BOOKSHOP
319-351-2407
319-339-5964 Fax
http://members.aol.com/ckenyoncpb
ckenyoncpb@aol.com
PO Box 2232
Iowa City IA 52244-2232
Largest selection of in-print titles, including reprints, on trans-Mississippi theater of the Civil War. Free catalog.

CIVIL WAR ANTIQUITIES
614-363-1862
http://www.civilwarantiquities.com
Todd Rittenhouse, Prop.
PO Box 1411
Delaware OH 43015-1411
Quality CW items. Guns, swords, letters, currency, books, prints. Buy/sell/trade. Full service custom framing & matting; specializing in conservation framing. Shop located at 13-1/2 N Sandusky St., Delaware, Ohio. Free catalog.

CIVIL WAR ASSOCIATES BOOKSTORE
313-586-2916
6200 Blanchett Rd
Newport MI 48166-9723
Civil War, Custer & Indian Wars books, new & used. Catalog.

CIVIL WAR LADY DRY GOODS
507-825-3182 Ph & Fax
622 3rd Ave SW
Pipestone MN 56164-1529
Repro Civil War gowns & accessories. Victorian jewelry & cameos. Wigs/hair pieces, 1860s dolls. Diaries & journals; 1860s fashion books. Catalog - $5.

STAN CLARK MILITARY BOOKS
717-337-1728 • 717-337-0581 Fax
915 Fairview Ave
Gettysburg PA 17325-2906
Buys/sells Civil War books, ltd. edition prints, autographs, letters, documents, postcards, soldiers' items; special interest in U.S. Marine Corps items.

CLIO'S HISTORY BOOKSHOP
703-777-1815 • ClioBooks@aol.com
Jason Duberman
PO Box 168 • 103 Loudoun St SW
Leesburg VA 20178-0168
Military & political history titles from ancient to modern times; Civil War a specialty. Cat. - $3.

COLUMBUS ARMORY
706-327-1424 Ph & Fax
David S. Brady
1104 Broadway
Columbus GA 31901-2429
Complete Civil War store featuring books, relics, art, muskets & supplies. Buy/sell/trade. Free price list.

THE CONFLICT BOOKSHOP
800-847-0911 • EPETE1731@aol.com
213 Steinwehr Ave
Gettysburg PA 17325-2801
Latest in Civil War titles, as well as fine collection of used & rare books, audio & video tapes & other memorabilia. Free flyer.

COPPERFIELD'S/CBC BOOKNETWORK
915-590-0602 • 915-590-7010 Fax
booknet@ix.netcom.com
2150 Trawood Dr Ste B200
El Paso TX 79935-3322
Discount history & genealogy books. Searches for out-of-print books at no cost or obligation. Free catalog.

DIXIE DEPOT
706-265-7533
706-265-3952 Fax
http://www.ilinks.net/~dixiegeneral
Dixie_Depot@stc.net
John Black
PO Box 1448
72 Keith Evans Rd
Dawsonville GA 30534-0027
Pro-Southern educational products: video/audio tapes, new/old books, bumper stickers, flags, wearables, lapel pins, exclusive Great Seal items. More than 600 items! Catalog. (See ad page 260)

DON'T KNOW MUCH ABOUT HISTORY
800-531-9173
http://members.aol.com/p20IL/index.html
P20IL@aol.com
Phil Lauricella, President
316 Franklin St
Geneva IL 60134-2639
More than 200 prints by well-known artists such as Kunstler, Rocco, Troiani & Stivers. Carry 300+ Civil War titles on our bookshelves & will research out-of-print or rare items. Free catalog.

DOSS BOOKS
PO Box 660194
Birmingham AL 35266-0194
Civil War books & maps. Many out-of-print or rare. List - $1.

THE EARLY AMERICAN HISTORY SHOPPE
603-772-7973
225 Water St
Exeter NH 03833-2417
Books (antiquarian & in-print), ephemera, prints, antique memorabilia & collectibles, T-shirts, CD-Rom, flags, games, tapes, maps, mugs, miniatures, genealogies & more. Specialize in the Civil War. Free catalogs.

THE EARLY WEST
800-245-5841
PO Box 9292
College Station TX 77842-9292
Books on Custer, the West, Indian Fighters, outlaws, lawmen, frontiersmen, etc. Free catalog.

EASTERN FRONT/WARFIELD BOOKS, INC.
540-338-1672 • 540-338-1910 Fax
36734 Pelham Ct
Philomont VA 20131
Great classic books of the American Civil War.

EDMONSTON PUBLISHING, INC.
315-824-1965
PO Box 38 • Hamilton NY 13346-0038
While My Country Is in Danger, 12th NJ. *No Middle Ground*, Union Artillery. $22.95 ea. *Memoirs of the 149th NYV* - $35.95. *Unfurl the Flags* - $4.95. S&H - $3.50/$1.50/$1.00. Other new & used titles. Free catalog.

FARNSWORTH HOUSE MILITARY GALLERY
717-334-8838
717-334-5862 Fax
farnhaus@mail.cvn.net
Loring H. Shultz
401 Baltimore St
Gettysburg PA 17325-2623
Large selection of Don Troiani art - Gettysburg's exclusive dealer for over 10 yrs. New, used & rare books on Civil & Indian wars. Buy/sell/trade. Catalog - $2. (See ad page 272)

FIRST CORPS BOOKS
803-798-5513
FirstCorps@msn.com
126 Silverhill Rd
Columbia SC 29210
Specializing in material concerning South Carolina in the Civil War. 100s of Civil War titles, both out-of-print & new. Want lists accepted. Catalogs - $2/yr.

JIM FOX - BOOKS
9 Precipice Rd
Camden SC 29020-4811
South Carolina Regimental Series. Autobiographies, biographies, stories, regimental history, & all kinds of books dealing with South Carolina & the Civil War.

FRIENDS OF NEW YORK STATE NEWSPAPER PROJECT
http://www.nysl.nysed.gov/nysnp
vweiss@mail.nysed.gov
PO Box 2402
Empire State Plaza Station
Albany NY 12220-0402
Maps & Letters from NY State's Civil War Newspapers, 1861-1863 - $22.

G W SPECIALTIES
816-356-7457
George Scheil
7311 Ditzler Ave
Raytown MO 64133-6439
Civilian reprints of magazines & schoolbooks from mid-1800s. Free catalog.

GAULEY RIVER BOOK COMPANY
http://www.cais.com/gauley/index.html
gauley@cais.com
37 Pidgeon Hill Dr
Sterling VA 20165-6102
Turn Them out to Die Like a Mule, by J.M. Priest. *Mosby's Confederacy*, *War Stories*, etc. INTERNET - check our website for listings of other books.

GWYN'S COLLECTIBLES & BOOKS
717-957-4141
717-957-9208 Fax
Gwyn L. Irwin
211 Front St
Marysville PA 17053-1413
Civil War books. Roster of soldiers in the "War of the Rebellion" from Monroe County, New York. 26 pp., 3 columns - $12 ppd.

S. A. HEARN - BOOKS
717-742-3737
Chet Hearn
PO Box 67
Potts Grove PA 17865-0067
Civil War books bought/sold. Want lists welcome. Free bi-monthly price list/catalog.

HERITAGE BOOKS
Dale Curry
313 Woodlawn Ave
Zanesville OH 43701-4939
Civil War books & gifts. Free catalog.

HIGGINSON BOOK COMPANY
508-745-7170 • 508-745-8025 Fax
higginsn@cove.com
148 Washington St
PO Box 778
Salem MA 01970-0778
Reprinters of regimental histories, American genealogies & local histories. Thousands of titles, mail or bookstore. Cat. - $4 (ref.).

HISTORY IN PRINT
800-816-3571 • 219-465-5778 Fax
PO Box 1295
Valparaiso IN 46384-1295
World's largest seller of Civil War books, videos, audio tapes, maps & fine art prints. Delivered to your door - select from 100s of titles! Free catalog.

INKLINGS BOOKSHOP
804-845-BOOK
1206 Main St • Lynchburg VA 24504-1818
New & used books, out-of-print searches. Civil War, South, Literature, History, Religion, etc.

KENNESAW MOUNTAIN MILITARY ANTIQUES
770-424-5225 • 770-424-0434 Fax
CANNONBALL@aol.com.
3017 Butler Creek Rd NW
Kennesaw GA 30152-3327
Civil War relics & complete list of books available. New, reprints, & reference books. Catalog subscription - $10.

LOG CABIN SHOP
800-837-1082
330-948-1082
330-948-4307 Fax
http://www.logcabinshop.com
logcabin@logcabinshop.com
8010 Lafayette Rd
PO Box 275
Lodi OH 44254-0275
Full line of muzzleloading guns, kits, components, supplies, accessories, books, cookware, blankets, etc. 200-pp. catalog - $5.

MAIL CALL JOURNAL
http://www.HistoryOnline.net
mcj@historyonline.net
PO Box 5031, Dept. B1
South Hackensack NJ 07606-4231
Actual letters & journals written by Civil War soldiers. Excerpts from books; original essays & poetry. 6 issues/yr. - $24.95. Sample - send SASE.

AL MASON - BOOKS
860-693-2708
5 Highledge Rd
Canton CT 06019-2226
Civil War books - used, out-of-print, new & rare. More than 350 listings; Confederate, Union, general & Lincoln sections. Free catalog.

BILL MASON BOOKS
919-247-6161
http://www.collectorsnet.com/mason/index.htm
bmasonbks@abaco.coastalnet.com
104 N 7th St
Morehead City NC 28557-3807
Rare, new, used, out-of-print Civil War, Western Americana, military & nautical, quality books, prints, & ephemera. Free catalog.

MAST LANDING BOOKS
207-865-6432
4 Flying Point Rd
Freeport ME 04032-6429
Civil War books bought/sold. Lists regularly issued.

NEWMAN RARE BOOKS
410 S Michigan Ave
Chicago IL 60605-1302
Your source for Civil War history.

OLD FAVORITES BOOKSHOP
3055 Lauderdale Dr
Richmond VA 23233-7800
Civil War, WWII, other military books, prints & maps. Free catalog on request.

OWENS & RAMSEY HISTORICAL BOOKSELLERS
804-272-8888
mramsey@mindspring.com
2728 Tinsley Dr
Richmond VA 23235-2448
Richmond's Civil War book headquarters. Buy/sell/trade new, used & rare books. Free monthly catalog.

WALLACE D. PRATT, BOOKSELLER
1801 Gough St Apt 304
San Francisco CA 94109-3345
Out-of-print, rare Civil War & other military & naval books. Free catalog.

TOM ROFFE
PO Box 266
Leicester NY 14481-0266
New & out-of-print Civil War-era military books. More than 200 bios, regimentals, weapons, etc. Annual listing - SASE.

J. M. SANTARELLI
215-576-5358
Civil War Books & Publishing
226 Paxson Ave
Glenside PA 19038-4612
Antique, reprint & out-of-print books. Also publishes new material. More than 300 Civil War titles. Catalog - $2.

SECOND STORY BOOKSHOP
540-463-6264
books@rockbridge.net
Nancy Coplai
College Square Shopping Ctr
Lexington VA 24450
New, used & rare books on the Civil War. Also offer mail order service - shipping daily!

SOUTHERN YANKEE VETERANS MEMORABILIA
409-264-1865 Dan Reed
409-852-2822 Mike Carter
Buy/sell/trade GAR & UCV relics, postcards, Civil War books. Catalogs - $10 (3 issues/yr.).

SPARTAN BOOKS OF MAINE
800-515-3113
PO Box 1645 • Presque Isle ME 04769-1645
Books from the originals by Gordan, Longstreet, Early, & historians plus reference works, etc.

TALL SHIPS BOOKS
319-396-2549
PO Box 8027
Cedar Rapids IA 52408-8027
Historical fiction from age of fighting sail. Catalog - $3 (ref. w/ 1st order).

C. CLAYTON THOMPSON - BOOKSELLER
510-462-5211 Ph & Fax
http://members.aol.com/Greatbooks
Greatbooks@aol.com
PO Box 5033 • Pleasanton CA 94566-8402
Civil War & military books - 1st editions. Catalog - $5 (ref.)

TOMES OF GLORY BOOKSHOP
610-935-9510 • PPODLICK@aol.com
845 Valley Forge Rd
Phoenixville PA 19460-2623
Carefully selected, gently read Civil War & military history books. Nearly 2,000 Civil War titles in stock. Open Wed-Sat, 10am-5pm.

TRANS-MISSISSIPPI MILITARIA
972-517-8111 Ph & Fax
http://www.collectorsnet.com/transmiss/index.html
charlucv@flash.net
Charles Brecheisen
1004 Simon Dr • Plano TX 75025-2501
UCV, GAR, Civil War & Indian War period relics, books & diaries, papers, letters, covers & records, medical instruments. Always buying. Catalogs - $10 (min. 3 large lists).

TRULY UNIQUE MILITARY SURPLUS & COLLECTIBLES
800-336-5225
2619 N University St
Peoria IL 61604-2667
Featuring 2 new books - *The Story the Soldiers Wouldn't Tell: Sex in the Civil War* and *Pulling the Temple Down: The Fire-Eaters and the Destruction of the Union*. Other titles.

WILDMAN'S CIVIL WAR SURPLUS
770-422-1785
2879 S Main St
Kennesaw GA 30144-5624
Rare & antique guns, books, & other Civil War collectibles. Price list - $2. (See ad page 258)

YANK & REB TRADER
740-345-4092
PO Box 4704
Newark OH 43058-4704
Civil War artifacts. Buy/sell. Large inventory of reference books not available in bookstores. Catalog - $5 for 6 issues (ref. w/ purchase).

YANKEE FORAGER
517-263-3925
137 Park St
Adrian MI 49221-2528
Civil War specialty books, documents, photos, relics, & more. Catalog - $2.

YE OLDE POST OFFICE
334-928-0108
17070 Scenic Hwy 98
PO Box 9
Point Clear AL 36564-0009
Dealer in antique & military collectibles, guns, swords, uniforms, books, etc.

AVID READER USED & RARE BOOKS
919-933-9585
462 W Franklin St
Chapel Hill NC 27516-2313

BLACK HORSE BOOKS
409-449-5712
Jim Synnott
118 Wick Willow Dr
Montgomery TX 77356-8242
Rare & out-of-print Confederate military history. Catalog - $3/3 issues.

BOHEMIAN BRIGADE BOOKSHOP
423-694-8227 • 423-531-1846 Fax
Ed Archer
7347 Middlebrook Pike
Knoxville TN 37909-3108
Specializing in 1st edition & out-of-print Civil War books, hard-to-find CW titles & popular reprints. Also, CW prints. Collection assistance. Catalog - $3.

BOOKS! BY GEORGE
205-323-6036 • 205-323-6014 Fax
Frank W. George
2424 7th Ave S
Birmingham AL 35233-3318
Retail sale of scarce, used & rare books. Appraisals.

BROADFOOT PUBLISHING COMPANY
910-686-4816
910-686-4379 Fax
http://broadfoot.wilmington.net
Tom Broadfoot
1907 Buena Vista Cir
Wilmington NC 28405-7892
Sell rare & out-of-print material, own publications by catalog. In-print catalog - $2. Out-of-print catalog - $5 (ref. w/ order).

C & W USED BOOKS
703-491-7323
14587 Potomac Mills Rd
Woodbridge VA 22192-6808

Q. M. DABNEY & CO.
PO Box 42026
Washington DC 20015-0626
Old & rare Civil War books. Catalog - $1.

DEEP SOUTH
PO Box 1184
Escatawpa MS 39552-1184
1863 CSA Almanac. Authentic, 98-pp., Constitution, CSA stats, battle diary, etc. $7.95 ppd.

DAVID E. DOREMUS, BOOKS
617-641-3308
100 Hillside Ave
Arlington MA 02174-7269
Used & rare regimental histories, biographies, & battle reports. Buys/sells. Catalog - $2, 8-10 issues/yr.

JOHN S. GIMESH, MD
910-484-2212
PO Box 53788 • Fayetteville NC 28305
Authentic Civil War-era medical, surgical, dental & apothecary items; Civil War-era medical texts. Buy/sell.

HISTORICAL AMERICANA
718-409-6407
Peter Hlinka
PO Box 310 • New York NY 10028-0017
Military & civilian decorations, medals, award certificates, insignia items, books, & other Americana collectibles. Free catalog.

HISTORICAL MILITARY ART & COLLECTIBLES
PO Box 1806
Lafayette CA 94549-8006
Collector books, limited edition military art, & military & political collectibles, including medals, flags, badges, pins, & patches. Free catalog.

HOFFMAN RESEARCH SERVICES
412-446-3374
http://www.abebooks.com/home/hoffsrch
hoffsrch@westol.com
Ralph Hoffman
PO Box 342 • Rillton PA 15678-0342
Free international book search. Professional bookfinders since 1965; members of Interloc, Advanced Book Exchange & Virtual Book Shop. Please send SASE w/ mail requests.

MURRAY HUDSON - ANTIQUARIAN BOOKS & MAPS
800-748-9946
901-836-9057
901-836-9017 Fax
mapman@usit.net
109 S Church St
PO Box 163
Halls TN 38040-0163
Large selection of Civil War authentic maps & prints. 1300+ items (priced $25-$7,500). Rare Forrest bust; large Lee print. Catalog - $10 (ref.).

HUGHES BOOKS
504-948-2427
PO Box 840237 • New Orleans LA 70184
Buy/sell rare books, documents, & autographs. Civil War, the South, Louisiana, New Orleans. 3 catalogs - $3.

KUBIK FINE BOOKS
937-294-0253
3474 Clar Von Dr
Dayton OH 45430-1708
Buy/sell rare & out-of-print books on British, French, European, & U.S. military history. Autographs & historical fiction. 1st editions of 19th-century Civil War books. Catalog - $3.

RICHARD A. LA POSTA
860-828-0921
154 Robindale Dr
Kensington CT 06037-2054
Civil War books. Regimental histories. First editions. Search service. Buy/sell/trade. Next 2 price lists - $1.

LEXINGTON HISTORICAL SHOP
540-463-2615
Bob Lurate
PO Box 1428 • Lexington VA 24450-1428
Civil War memorabilia. Buy/sell books, relics, flags, currency, ephemera. Appraisals. Visit shop Mon-Sat 10-6, College Square Shopping Center, Route 11N, Lexington, Va.

LOOK BACK IN TIME
803-986-9097 • 803-986-9297 Fax
PO Box 572
Port Royal SC 29935-0572
CW newspapers, engravings, books, relics, & much more. Want lists welcome. Free catalog.

MARCHER BOOKS
6204 N Vermont Ave
Oklahoma City OK 73112-1312
Rare & out-of-print American History books. Free catalog.

MC GOWAN BOOK CO.
919-968-1121
800-449-8406
919-968-1644 Fax
http://www.mcgowanbooks.com
mcgowanbooks@mindspring.com
R. Douglas Sanders
PO Box 4226 • 106 S Christopher Rd
Chapel Hill NC 27515
Always buying. Highest prices paid for fine & rare Civil War books, autographs, documents, photographs, etc. Catalog subs. - $3.

MERIDIAN STREET USED BOOKS
317-482-4882
126 S Meridian St • Lebanon IN 46052-2523
Buy/sell/trade used books on all subjects, including military history. Search service.

THE MILITARY BOOKMAN
212-348-1280
29 E 93rd St • New York NY 10128-0609
Military, naval & aviation history. Out-of-print & rare books. Cat. by subscription.

THE MT. STERLING REBEL
606-498-5821 • Terry Murphy
PO Box 481 • Mount Sterling KY 40353
Buy/sell since 1979 rare, out-of-print, & previously owned Civil War books. Limited inventory of Civil War paper items, ephemera, autographs & images. Catalog upon request.

THE OLD PAPERPHILES
401-624-9420 • 401-624-4204 Fax
PO Box 135 • Tiverton RI 02878-0135
Offering 100s of accurately described paper collectibles. Great variety, wide price range. Autographs, documents, books. Catalog - $8 for next 10.

OLDE SOLDIER BOOKS, INC.
301-963-2929 • 301-963-9556 Fax
Warbooks@erols.com
Dave Zullo
18779 N Frederick Ave Ste B
Gaithersburg MD 20879-3158
Largest selection of rare & hard-to-find books. Documents, letters, photographs, autographs, manuscripts. Buy/sell. Free catalog.

OUT-OF-STATE-BOOK-SERVICE
PO Box 3253
San Clemente CA 92674-3253
Books located, out-of-print free search service. No obligation.

PEMBROKE INK
PO Box 445 • Chesterfield VA 23832-0445
For the discriminating collector. Dealer of documents & rare books. Extensive list.

PROFILES IN HISTORY
800-942-8856 • 310-859-7701
310-859-3842 Fax
345 N Maple Dr Ste 202
Beverly Hills CA 90210-3859
Autographs wanted. Also buying original letters, documents, vintage photos, manuscripts, & rare books (signed). Illus. catalog - $45/yr. Sample - $10.

THE QUEEN'S SHILLING
703-779-4669
14 Loudoun St SE
Leesburg VA 20175-3011
Old, rare & antiquarian books, autographs on military history, all periods. Catalog - $3.

RED LANCER
PO Box 8056
Mesa AZ 85214-8056
Original 19th-century military art, rare books, Victorian-era campaign medals & helmets, toy soldiers. Catalog - $12 for 3-4 issues/yr.

STEPHEN M. ROWE
PO Box 19671
Raleigh NC 27619-9671
Rare & first editions.

PAUL SPERLING
160 E 38th St # 25
New York NY 10016-2651
Still looking for a book? Free search.

STAMPEDE INVESTMENTS
608-254-7751
1533 River Rd
Wisconsin Dells WI 53965-9002
Large inventory of original letters & documents from the most important people in U.S. History to fit every budget. Free catalog.

UHR BOOKS
207-929-5100
uhrbooks@mix-net.net
Old & rare books on women in the Civil War, especially nurses. Free list.

ABRAHAM'S LADY
609-853-6882 • abraham@comten.com
Donna Abraham
1402 Saint Matthew Dr
Verga NJ 08093
Trims, notions & accessories for sewing Civil War reproduction clothing; bone buttons, metal stays, hats, jewelry, soutache. Catalog - $1.

ALICE'S COUNTRY COTTAGE
301-766-7344
1010 McCauley Ct
Hagerstown MD 21740-7115
The "Jefferson Shirt," 100% cotton, wooden buttons, homespun look, period design - $24.95 + $3 S&H. Specify men's or women's. Call for additional info.

TIM ALLEN
410-549-5145
1429 Becket Rd • Eldersburg MD 21784-6114
Civilian slouch hats - handsewn, fully lined, stamped with period labels, handmade to order. Call or send SASE for more info.

ALTERYEARS
818-585-2994 • 818-432-4530 Fax
3749 E Colorado Blvd
Pasadena CA 91107-3808
Patterns, books, supplies & accessories to help you make your own historical clothing from Civil War & other eras. Visit our store! 200+-pg. catalog - $5 (4th cl.); $8 (priority).

AMAZON DRY GOODS
319-322-6800 • 319-322-4138
319-322-4003 Fax
J. Burgess, Pres.
407 Brady St
Davenport IA 52801-1510
Victorian apparel & accessories. Corsets, bonnets, hoop skirts, fans & snoods, hats, paper dolls, flags, books, patterns, shoes & boots. Sutlers' wholesale catalog. Retail catalogs (pattern, shoe, & general) - all 3 for $15.

AMERICAN STITCHES
28 Forest St
Danvers MA 01923-1571

ARTCAST
770-270-9659
PO Box 28561
Atlanta GA 30358-0561
1861 reproduction West Point class ring. Original reproductions of the May & June class. (Only year with 2 graduations.) Sterling - $59.95; gold - $169.95.

AUTHENTIC REPRODUCTIONS
717-437-9174
RR 2 Box 989 • Milton PA 17847-9314
Top selection of quality men, women, & children's repro clothing & accessories at unbeatable prices. Laidacker historical garments. Catalog - $3.

BAINBRIDGE TRADITIONAL BOOTMAKERS
01761-471430 Ph & Fax
The Square • Timsbury, Bath, BA 3 1 HY U.K.
Handmade to measure, historically accurate mehtods & materials. Incorporating Timefarer footwear. Free brochure.

BERMAN LEATHER
617-426-0870 • 617-357-8564 Fax
Robert S. Berman
25 Melcher St
Boston MA 02210-1516
Leather hides like CW era for belts, straps, clothing, bags, even footwear. Full catalog of hardware, tools, buckles & kits - $3 (ref.).

THE BLOCKADE RUNNER
931-389-6294
http://www.blockaderunner.com
103 Blackman Blvd • Wartrace TN 37183
18th-19th c. goods. Custom work & fitting, all types uniforms, civilian & ladies' wear; standard & custom tents. All work done in-house. Catalog - $2.

BONNET BRIGADE
Pat Wullenjohn
PO Box 28 • Fremont CA 94537-0028
Civil War-period clothing, equipment, weapons, accoutrements, & camping equipment. Catalog - $3.

C & C SUTLERY
208-388-0973 • 208-384-9523 Fax
CLOX@RMCI.NET
3353 Fuller Rd • Emmett ID 83617-9514
Full-service Civil War supplier. Uniforms, etc.

C & D JARNAGIN
601-287-4977 • 601-287-6033 Fax
http://www.jarnaginco.com
Robin Jarnagin
PO Box 1860 • 103 Franklin St
Corinth MS 38834-1860
Military & historical outfitters. Research, develop, & manufacture high quality uniforms, leather gear, footwear, & tinware for American troops, 1750-1865. 18th-century & CW catalogs - $3 each. (See ad page 257)

CANTRELL & CO.
513-667-3379
CAC309@aol.com
Charles A. Cantrell
933 N Westedge Dr
Tipp City OH 45371-1527
Historically accurate, museum-quality Confederate uniforms & clothing. Catalog & fabric samples - $2.

CAPS & KEPIS
302-994-6428
2665 Longfellow Dr
Wilmington DE 19808-3733
Custom-made officers' & enlisted Confederate provisionals, standard Federal, Rebel caps, extensive insignia, state buttons, haversacks, shirts, pants, coats, jackets, overcoats. Catalog - $2.

CARRICO'S LEATHERWORKS
316-922-7222
316-922-3311 Fax
David Carrico
811 5000 Rd
Edna KS 67342
Authentic reproduction Civil War cavalry equipment & accoutrements. Saddles, bridles, holsters, belts, etc. Free price list.

CASTLE KEEP, LTD.
630-801-1696
630-801-1910 Fax
http://www.Reenact.com
ernie@Smartgate.com
Ernest Klapmeier
83 S La Salle St
Aurora IL 60505-3331
Reenactor supplies; clothing & equipment to put man or woman into the field. Owner has 20 yrs. reenacting experience & understands concept of authenticity.

CAVALRY REGIMENTAL SUPPLY
806-798-8867 Fax
PO Box 64394
Lubbock TX 79464-4394
Custom, handmade, obsolete military footwear (c.1500-1943). 7 styles of Civil War boots & shoes. Catalog - $2 + SASE (ref.).

THE CAVALRY SHOP
804-266-0898
T.E. Johnson, Jr.
9700 Royerton Dr
Richmond VA 23228-1218
Civil War leather goods, buckles; horsegear. Catalog - $2. (See ad page 259)

CIVIL WAR DESIGNS
303-424-6414 Ph & Fax
PO Box 646
Arvada CO 80001-0646
Custom embroidery of Civil War designs, incl. flags, personalities, campaign names, etc.

CIVIL WAR LADY DRY GOODS
507-825-3182 Ph & Fax
622 3rd Ave SW
Pipestone MN 56164-1529
Repro Civil War gowns & accessories. Victorian jewelry & cameos. Wigs/hair pieces, 1860s dolls. Diaries & journals; 1860s fashion books. Catalog - $5.

MICHAEL D. CLARK
513-724-3167
PO Box 641
Williamsburg OH 45176-0641
Authentic key-wind watches. Completely restored. Fine running condition. Open & hunting style cases. Price list - send large SASE.

CONFEDERATE YANKEE
203-453-9900 Ph & Fax
Dennis Semrau & Terry Brettman-Semrau
PO Box 192
Guilford CT 06437-0192
Custom clothing based on originals. Reproduction fabrics used. Catalog & sample - $3. (See ad page 257)

CRESCENT CITY SUTLER
812-983-4217
17810 Highway 57
Evansville IN 47711-9318
Reproduction & original Civil War uniforms & equipment. Catalog - $3.

DIFFERENT DRUMMER
704-669-0097
704-669-5191 Fax
UnreConfed@aol.com
Kirk D. Lyons
1112 1/2 Montreat Rd Ste 1
PO Box 1411
Black Mountain NC 28711-1411
Men's & women's reproduction clothing. Original Victorian clothing & photos; consultation service.

DINUNZIO'S SHOE REPAIR
717-273-5854 • 717-283-7079 Fax
118 S 8th St 0149 Lebanon PA 17042-5213
Civil War boots repaired to authenticity, with fine workmanship giving careful attention to every detail. Estab. 1916.

DIRTY BILLY'S HATS
410-775-1865 Orders
717-334-3200 Shop
7574 Middleburg Rd
Detour MD 21757-8781
Military & civilian hats, caps & accessories; exact reproductions. Visit our shop at 430A Baltimore St, Gettysburg, Pa. Catalog - send 32¢ stamp.

DIXIE FASHIONS
804-527-2028
George Dunn
11300 Cedar Hill Ct • Richmond VA 23233
Confederate & Union exact reproduction uniforms, made to fit, museum-quality work, including all leather accessories, shell jackets, sashes, frocks, trousers, Kepis, shirts. Cat. $3.

DIXIE GUN WORKS, INC.
800-238-6785 Orders only
901-885-0700 • 901-885-0440 Fax
PO Box 130
Union City TN 38281-0130
The source for firearms, parts, shooting supplies, leather goods, uniforms, books, patterns & cannons. 600-pg catalog with more than 8,000 items - $5.

DONNA'S STITCHES BACK IN TIME
800-808-7685
We stitch for sutlers. High-quality muslin shirts - $13.50 wholesale. Also sell retail. Price list on request.

MRS. DUBERVILLE DRESSES & MILLINERY
Celeste Burrell
Old Gettysburg Village • 777 Baltimore St
Gettysburg PA 17325-2600
Authentic, handmade period fashions.

DYESTONE CO.
615-796-7364
320 Dyestone Springs Rd
Hohenwald TN 38462-5565
Resoles & restores cavalry boots & brogans using original process. All kinds of leather repair.

AN EARLY ELEGANCE
717-338-9311
61 Steinwehr Ave
Gettysburg PA 17325-2811
American-made items & authentic reproductions. CW-era writing box, fabrics. Gifts at reasonable prices. Product guide - business-size SASE. Fabric swatch book - $2.50.

MRS. EDDINS' FINE SEWING EMPORIUM
770-389-1470
186 Hayes Cir • Rex GA 30273-1546
Union & Confederate uniforms, women's clothing & accessories. Custom sewing & hand-knitting. Catalog - $2 (ref. w/ purchase).

ELIZABETH ANN & CO.
216-632-9808
PO Box 716 / 15960 E High St
Middlefield OH 44062-0716
Top quality wool, 23 colors - $15.50/yd. + S&H. Custom tailoring. Sack coats, shell jackets, pants, officers' frocks; ladies' & children's clothing. Wool sample - send SASE.

THE EMPORIUM
417-683-2764
Ed & Maryln Peterka
RR 1 Box 363 • Ava MO 65608-9726
Supplies for the muzzleloader & living history participant. Patterns, hosiery, ladies' straw hats. Catalog - $3 (ref.).

PETER EVANS PIPES
305-361-5589
285 W Mashta Dr • Dept F
Key Biscayne FL 33149-2419
Custom-made period pipes, reproductions, clays, quality pipe accessories. For smokers, reenactors, collectors, historians. Free brochure.

FAIR OAKS SUTLER, INC.
540-972-7744 Noon-9 PM
540-972-3256 24-hr Fax
9905 Kershaw Ct • Spotsylvania PA 22553
High-quality replica Civil War uniforms, accoutrements, equipment & muskets; Kepi & bummer caps our specialty. Satisfaction guaranteed. Catalog - 2 stamps.

FAIRMOUNT SUTLERY
717-864-3335 • 717-256-3081 Daytime
Janice Hilley, Prop.
RR 1 Box 271B • Benton PA 17814-9681
Reproduction CW-period uniforms & civilian clothing for men & women. Cat. free w/ SASE.

FALL CREEK SUTTLERY
765-482-1861 • 765-482-1848 Fax
http://fcsutler.com • Andy Fulks
AJF5577@aol.com or fcsutler@aol.com
PO Box 92 • Whitestown IN 46075-0092
Authentic reproduction Civil War & mid-19th-century uniforms, leather goods, weapons, shoes, tents, insignia, reference books & more. 32-pg catalog - $3. (See ad page 271)

FAMILY HEIRLOOM WEAVERS
717-246-2431 Ph & Fax
familyheirloom@mindspring.com
775 Meadowview Dr
Red Lion PA 17356-8608
Reproduction fabrics - historically accurate ingrain carpets & jacquard coverlets. Uniforms, shirtings, etc. Brochure & swatches - $4.

FARMHOUSE FABRICS
414-622-4884 • 414-622-5207 Fax
PO Box 188 • Pine River WI 54965-0188
CW dress fabric - authentic reproductions of Civil War-era cotton fabric. 10 patterns, 3 colors ea. $6.99/yd. Swatch set & cat. - $2 ppd.

FOOTWEAR
320 Dyestone Springs Rd
Hohenwald TN 38462-5565
All period footwear repaired to original condition, pegged, sewn, nailed. Soles & heels - $29.50. Boots - $48.

FRANKLY MY DEAR
777 Baltimore St • Gettysburg PA 17325-2600
Gone with the Wind dress patterns, incl. green drapery dress, barbeque dress & burgundy dress.

FRAZER BROTHERS' 17TH REGIMENT
214-696-1865 • 214-426-4230 Fax
5641 Yale Blvd Ste 125
Dallas TX 75206-5026
Uniforms & equipment, artillery hardware, & side arms. Civilian clothing (men only). Handmade leather goods. Large supply of tinware. Boots. American products.

FREDERICKSBURG MONOGRAMMING & EMBROIDERY
540-373-3937 • 540-373-4006 Fax
525 Caroline St
Fredericksburg VA 22401-6013
Custom embroidery of favorite Civil War designs. Casual clothing, fast delivery; quantity orders/dealers welcomed. All work on-site, from artwork to finished garment.

GENTEEL ARTS ACADEMY
717-337-0283 • 717-337-0314 Fax
http://www.cvn.net/~cschmitt
cschmitt@mail.cvn.net
CarolAnn Schmitt
PO Box 3014 • Gettysburg PA 17325-0014
Offers workshops, lectures & seminars on period clothing, construction & fitting techniques. Classes offered frequently. Call/write for details & brochure. Free catalog.

GOSPEL TRUTH/CIVIL WAR ROOM
412-238-7991
228 W Main St
Ligonier PA 15658-1130
Full-service Christian bookstore & Civil War room. Kunstler calendars, patterns, pewter figurines, books, videos, music, hats, accessories, shirts, Woolrich wool & much more.

GRAND ILLUSIONS
302-366-0300 • 302-738-1858 Fax
705 Interchange Blvd
Newark DE 19711-3594
Manufacturers of fine Civil War uniforms & civilian clothing for men, women & children. Uniform research & manufacturer for miniseries on *Andersonville*. Catalog - $3.

THE GRAND SPECTACLE
607-732-7500
607-732-6045 Fax
Richard S. Buchanan, Optician
528 W Water St
Elmira NY 14905-2524
Authentic 19th-century oval spectacles with time-period cases. Free brochure.

GREEN RIVER TRADING CORP.
502-531-3115 Ph & Fax
ekelle@scrtc.net
PO Box 2
Bonnieville KY 42713-0002
Original & repro Civil War relics, clothing, weapons.

GREY OWL INDIAN CRAFT SALES CORP.
718-341-4000
718-527-6000 Fax
Wes Cochrane
13205 Merrick Blvd
PO Box 340468
Jamaica NY 11434-0468
Green River knives, powder flasks, military buttons, buckskin, leathers, dags, strikers, books, tapes, videos, recordings, etc. 200 custom kits/4000+ items. Catalog - $3.

HARRIET'S TCS
540-667-2541
540-722-4618 Fax
http://www.harriets.com
PO Box 1363
Winchester VA 22604-7863
185 patterns ca.1690-1945. Rentals, fabric, kits, supplies, hoops, parasols, lace. *Harriet's Then & Now* - 19th-century magazine, $6/issue. Annual subscription - $30. Color, photo-illus. catalog - $12.

THE HEIRLOOM EMPORIUM
216-437-8563
24 Leffingwell Dr
Orwell OH 44076-9522
Free catalog.

HERITAGE DRUM CO.
256-533-5498
http://fly.hiwaay.net/~tpalmer/heritage2.htm
ropedrum@juno.com
Terry Cornett
4021 Apollo Dr SW
Huntsville AL 35805-5601
Custom order, period repro snare & bass drums. Hand-crafted.

HILLBILLY SPORTS, INC.
410-378-4533
PO Box 70
Conowingo MD 21918-0070
Leather goods, period firearms, uniform items, camp items & much more. Catalog - $3.

HIS LADY & THE SOLDIER SUTLERY
517-435-3518 Summer
352-583-4627 Winter
851 Kaypat Dr
Hope MI 48628-9615
Period hair goods & accessories for the lady & gentleman reenactor. Catalog - $2.

THE HORSE'S MOUTH HISTORICAL CLOTHIER
760-737-9548
760-737-9714 Fax
http://home.pacbell.net/costumes
costumes@pacbell.net
131 S Orange St
Escondido CA 92025-4124
Uniforms, living history, period wedding attire. Custom-made to your specifications. 45 yrs. of professional experience in design, tailoring & pattern drafting.

THE HOUSE OF TIMES PAST
864-834-0061
634 W Darby Rd
Greenville SC 29609-7121
Period shop with authentic clothing, rifles, muzzleloading supplies & accessories for living historians & reenactors. Catalog - $2.

I. C. MERCANTILE
122 E Jewell Dr
Republic MO 65738-2202
Boots - $185. Group discount available. Additional information - send SASE.

JAMES COUNTRY MERCANTILE
816-781-9473
816-781-1470 Fax
JAMESCNTRY@aol.com
Del Warren or Michael Gooch
111 N Main St
Liberty MO 64068-1639
For your military & civilian reenacting needs - weapons, accoutrements, clothing, patterns. Illus. catalog - $6 ppd.

THE JEWELER'S DAUGHTER
301-733-3200
301-733-5076 Fax
24 W Washington St
Hagerstown MD 21740-4804
1860 VMI (Virginia Military Institute) class ring. Repro from original museum piece. 10K gold, wax seal style, "Let Virginia Choose" - $259.95.

JOHNNIE O'S
401-781-0725 • 401-941-7932 Fax
PO Box 25083
Providence RI 02905-0596
Pocket watch chains. Ideal for reenactors. Manufacturers of American-made watch chains in 14 kt. gold, sterling silver, gold-filled, layered gold. Free catalog.

K & P WEAVER
kpweaver@aol.com • Ken & Paula Weaver
PO Box 1131, Dept J
Orange CT 06477-7131
Historically accurate repro men's clothing for military or civilian impression. Custom-made with handsewn buttonholes. Quality accessories; cherry dominoes, checkers with canvas board. Early leather baseballs, bats, uniforms & books. Catalog with swatches - $1.

KATI'S KLASSICS & SUTLERY
334-774-1254 • Kathryn Nugent
RR 5 Box 78 • Ozark AL 36360-9209
Ladies', men's & children's attire. Handmade vests, ball gowns, 1800-present.

LA BONNETERIE FINE 19TH C. MILLINERY
732-928-9335
http://www.webtvmagic.com/LaBonneterie.htm
LABONNETERIE1@webtv.net; millinery-one@webtv.net
Susan Pescatore
599 Hyson Rd • Jackson NJ 08527-4410
Fine 19th c. millinery. Bonnets, hats, day caps & headpieces specifically for the female reenactor. Catalog - $3 (ref. w/ purchase).

THE LADIES' PARLOR
660-727-3592
660-727-2086 Fax
http://www.nemr.net/~lparlor/
lparlor@nemr.net
Patricia Mullenix
PO Box 274
Kahoka MO 63445
Ladies' clothing & accessories. Best source for HAIR. Available for workshops. 1863 on-line *Petersons* magazine.

LEVI LEDBETTER, SUTLER
704-485-4746 Orders
Frank Lanning, Prop.
7032 Mineral Springs Rd
Oakboro NC 28129-8855
Uniforms are our specialty. Tentage, knapsacks, accoutrements, canteens, tinware, blankets, buttons, buckles & brogans. Price list - send long SASE.

W.W. LUNNSFORD
Adler@radiks.net
29601 Highway 275
Valley NE 68064-7415
Reproduction Richmond Depot Type I, II, & III jackets (sizes 38-46); trousers (size 28-42); U.S. sack coat & kersys. Brochure - send SASE.

MAGGIE DESIGNS
703-830-3640
Kathy Moffitt
13704 Springstone Dr
Cifton VA 20124-2350
Civil War scarves/panels. History on silk for women & men. The 69th Regt. Irish Brigade design hand-painted on 33" square hand-rolled silk. $83.90 ppd.

HEIDI MARSH PATTERNS
3494 N Valley Rd
Greenville CA 95947-9604
Authentic patterns & how-to books of the CW era (1855-1865) for all ages. Ballgowns, blouses, undergarments, hoops, boning, etc. Playing cards & other sundries; books. Catalog - $3.

MRS. MARTIN'S MERCANTILE & MILLINERY
419-474-2093 Ph & Fax
4566 Oakhurst Dr
Sylvania OH 43560-1736
Historically correct, custom-made period clothing from 1850-1865 for the discriminating woman. Catalog - $4.50.

MARY ELLEN & CO. TIMELESS TREASURES VICTORIAN SHOP
800-669-1860 Orders
219-656-3000 Fax
Mary Ellen Smith
100 N Main St
North Liberty IN 46554-9218
Historical sewing patterns, Victorian boots, parasols, hats, fans, hoops, petticoats, camisoles, etc. Variety of books. Victorian gifts, wedding accessories, etc. Retail/wholesale. New Victorian gift shop - call for hours. Catalog - $3 (ref.).

MC KECHNIE-LID DESIGN & RESEARCH
1146 N Central Ave # 110
Glendale CA 91202-2506
Museum-quality 19th-century clothing at reasonable 20th-century prices. Authentic clothing for the discriminating woman of fashion. Catalog - $2. (See ad page 263)

MENDELSON'S LEATHER
501 Short St
Grants Pass OR 97527-5443
Master leather craftsman makes moccasin boots, full spectrum of custom goods you can't find anywhere else.

MERCURY SUPPLY CO.
409-327-3707
101 Lee St • Livingston TX 77351-4226
Civil War uniforms, reproduction equipment, tents, accoutrements, leather goods, firearms military & civilian. Catalog - $2.

MICHAELS & PERRIN
717-922-1065 • 717-922-1245
tperrin@sunlink.net
414 Main St • PO Box 29
Hartleton PA 17829-0029
Uniforms & period clothing for men & women. Equipment for reenactors. Catalog.

MJN BOOT & LEATHER SHOP
605-368-2922
Mick Nesseim
PO Box 351 • 27210 468th Ave.
Tea SD 57064-0351
Custom-made, fine officers' boots, 1859 light artillery boot & brogans. Catalog - $2.

JOSEPH MONASTRA
2332 21st St NE
Canton OH 44705-2408
Spectacles reproduced from originals, prescription or clear poly carb. Lenses may be added by most large vision centers. $35 ppd.

MYSTICAL MOON
207-845-2098 • 207-845-2023 Fax
http://www.midcoast.com/~mystical
mystical@midcoast.com
113 Liberty Rd
Washington ME 04574-3809
Full line of 18th-19th-century military & civilian clothing. Hand-stitching by request. Price list - free.

NASHVILLE DEPOT
615-833-2275
141 Neese Dr • 500 Zodiac Bldg
Nashville TN 37211-2750
Authentically reproduced carpetbag in colorful period designs. Lined interior with pockets & enclosed rigid bottom. Leather handles & straps. 18"Lx18"Dx"8"W - $79.50 + $6.75 S&H.

NEEDLE & THREAD
717-334-4011
Darlene Grube
2215 Fairfield Rd
Gettysburg PA 17325-7214
Offering beautiful line of fabrics. 100% wool, cotton, silk, linen, homespun, hooping - steel bones, Heidi Marsh, Folkwear, Past Patterns. Call/write. (See ad page 263)

NEW WAY BOOT SHOP
800-334-1484
120 S Keeneland Dr
Richmond KY 40475-3278
Officers' military coats, c.1862. Researched for authenticity. Military buttons, detachable cape, wool blend, satin lining, blue or gray - $219.95.

NINETEENTH CENTURY MERCANTILE
508-398-1888 Ph & Fax
Barbara A. Amster
2 N Main St
South Yarmouth MA 02664-3151
Hard-to-find goods recreated in ca.1800s fashion. Housewares, dry goods, toiletries, remedies, hardware, fashion accessories, etc. All presented in 19th-century mercantile atmosphere. Hundreds of items.

PETTICOAT JUNCTION
716-549-4998
307 Lakeside Rd • Angola NY 14006-9551
100% cotton or silk underpinnings, flounced petticoats, corset covers, 4- & 5-bone hoops, chemise, drawers. Men's civilians & uniforms, much more. Authenticity guaranteed. Catalog - SASE.

QUARTERMASTER SHOP
810-367-6702
810-367-6514 Fax
5565 Griswold Rd
Kimball MI 48074-1906
Authentic reproduction men's Civil War clothing. Union, Confederate, civilian impressions. Large inventory & custom tailoring. Catalog - $5.

R & K SUTLERY
217-732-8844
1015 1200th St
Lincoln IL 62656-5047
Complete line of military uniforms & civilian clothing for both men & women; coats, pants, skirts, blouses, dresses, etc. Top quality tents, Officer's Wall, A-frames, dog tents & sibley. Catalog - send SASE.

R.L. SHEP PUBLICATIONS
707-964-8662 Ph & Fax
fsbks@mcn.org
Fred Struthers
PO Box 2706
Fort Bragg CA 95437-2706
Publishes reprints of important sewing & tailoring manuals as an aid to accurate reproduction of period dress.

REENACTMENT EYEWARE
717-322-9849
RR 4 Box 62
Williamsport PA 17701-9551
Prescription lenses placed in your period frames by a certified optician. Frames repaired.

S & S SUTLER OF GETTYSBURG
717-677-7580 • 717-337-0438 Fax
Tim Sheads
PO Box 218
Bendersville PA 17306-0218
Reproduction Civil War uniforms, leather goods, insignia, tinware, & more. Free catalog.

SERVANT & CO. / CENTENNIAL GENERAL STORE
717-334-9712
800-GETTYS-1 Orders
717-334-7482 Fax
http://www.servantandco.com
230 Steinwehr Ave
Gettysburg PA 17325-2814
Quality Civil War uniforms & period clothing. Patterns, Kepis, leather goods, accessories, hats. Catalog - $6.

NANCY SHAW
716-894-2538
37 Westchester Dr
Cheektowaga NY 14225-4531
Authentic Civil War-period design unbleached muslin shirts with gathered back, dropped shoulders, & 4 wooden buttons - $18-$20.Unbleached muslin poke bags.

SPECTACLE ACCOUTREMENTS
410-281-6069
Gregg Crockett, Optician
2918 N Rolling Rd • Baltimore MD 21244
Reenactor eyewear, eyeglass prescriptions filled. Buy/sell/trade.

STALEY'S SUNDRIES
540-899-6464 • 540-373-2469 Fax
710 Caroline St • Fredericksburg VA 22401
Largest collection of Civil War music anywhere. Military insignia, flags, hats, clothing, patterns, buttons, buckles, miniatures, books, magazines & gift items.

A STITCH IN TIME
505-847-0360 • 505-847-0140 Fax
PO Box 766 • Mountainair NM 87036-0766
Day, camp & evening wear; ball gowns & outerwear; Scottish Highlander & Zouaves; civilian & military uniforms. Catalog.

STONY BROOK HISTORICAL UNIFORMERS
609-825-7307
Chris Sullivan
50 Porreca Dr • Millville NJ 08332-4840
Manufacturers of Federal uniform trousers. Also supply NY State Seal buttons in stamped brass. Free catalog.

SUTLERS OF THE SIXTEEN
905-338-9427
Lorne & Nancy Weller
1359 White Oaks Blvd #906
Oakville Ontario L6H 2R8 CANADA
Period footwear, 19th-century historical clothing, pine boxes & more.

TARA HALL, INC.
800-205-0069 • 212-802-6423 Fax
http://www.fighting69th.com
tarahall@earthlink.net
Vic Olney
PO Box 2069 • Beach Haven NJ 08008-0109
Meagher's Irish Brigade, Fighting 69th, Corcoran's Irish Legion memorabilia, shirts, jackets, hats, sweaters, steins, pins, flags, books, miniatures, poster, belt buckles, NINAs, etc. Free catalog. (See ad page 272)

TIMELESS TEXTILES
717-930-0201
Mary Harkless
321 N Union St • Middletown PA 17057-1442
Historically correct fabric, retail & wholesale, for reenactors of all eras. Carry both civilian & military, ladies' & men's fabrics.

JAMES TOWNSEND & SON, INC.
219-594-5852
http://www.jastown.com/
PO Box 415 • Pierceton IN 46562-0415
Large selections of reenactment supplies, 1740-1840. Clothing, blankets, eyeglasses, cookware, trade silver, shoes, hats, lanterns, tentage, knives, kegs, etc. Catalog - $2.

TREASURES OF THE PAST
Co. 64 H 256
Riceville TN 37330
Confederate & Union uniforms. High quality. Low prices. List - $2.

TURKEY FOOT TRADING CO.
419-832-1109
Allen & Colleen Schroll
PO Box 58 • Grand Rapids OH 43522-0058
18th- & 19th-century merchandise: beads, clothing, iron work, tinware, more. Catalog.

TURTLE RUN MERCANTILE
601-638-3573
turtlemerc@aol.com
Mava Collard
714 Newit Vick Dr
Vicksburg MS 39180-8746
Exquisite, handmade hairnets of silk, fine wool, chenille, and "plain twist" from a period pattern - $15 & up + S&H. Beading & special orders welcome. Silk bonnets; cape & bonnet sets made to order. Send SASE for info.

UNIFORMS OF ANTIQUITY
501-389-6308
p.bradley@cswnet.com
122 Sweetgum Ln • Mena AR 71953-3845
Uniforms recreated for collectors, historians, & skirmishers. Catalog - $2.

UPPER MISSISSIPPI VALLEY MERCANTILE CO
319-322-0896 • 319-383-5549 Fax
1607 Washington St
Davenport IA 52804-3613
Top quality goods & supplies for Civil War reenactors; uniforms, tinware, tents, leather goods, muskets, books, weapons, patterns, more. 100-pp., illus. catalog - $3.

USA HISTORY STORE
508-947-8866
http://www.usahistorystore.com
PO Box 109
Middleboro MA 02346-0109
Authentic brass camp candlesticks perfect for 19th-century impression. Set of 2 - $13.95 + $3 S&H. Books, games, flags & period clothing.

WHISKEY RUNNER
605-232-9552
PO Box 304
North Sioux City SD 57049-0304
Boots & clothing from American Colonial to the 1900 Western frontier. Catalog - $3 (ref.).

WHISTLING SWAN
814-796-6654
100% cotton muslin shirt, 1-button style. L/XL - $28 + S&H.

THE WINCHESTER SUTLER, INC.
540-888-3595
540-888-4632 Fax
270 Shadow Brook Ln
Winchester VA 22603-2071
Reproduction Civil War firearms, uniforms, camp gear, accessories, shoes, boots, hats, etc. Catalog - $4.

WOMEN'S NATION
908-726-1716 Ph & Fax
325 Avenel St
Avenel NJ 07001-1534
Fine jewelry in the Victorian style for the lady reenactor. Brooches, earrings, lockets, pendants, crosses, bracelets & rings. Free catalog.

ANTEBELLUM COVERS
301-869-2623 Ph & Fax
888-ANTEBEL (268-3235)
http://www.antebellumcovers.com
antebell@antebellumcovers.com
PO Box 3494 • Gaithersburg MD 20885-3494
Civil War & 19th-century U.S. paper collectibles incl. soldiers' letters, images, general orders, patriotic envelopes, autographs, slavery documents & advertising paper; CD-ROMs of Civil War & historical titles. Free catalog. Internet customers can be notified by email each time auction is posted.

ARCHIVE ARTS
760-723-2119 Ph & Fax
http://www.archivearts.com
George@primemail.com
PO Box 2455 • Fallbrook CA 92088-2455
Clip art, 62 editions for Mac & PC; 8 Civil War editions. More than 450 CW images - $25/edition or CD with 3600 images - $99. Free cat.

ART RESTORATION SERVICES
804-974-1726
PO Box 6701 • Charlottesville VA 22906-6701
Document CW objects & their associated stories with this unique new system. War book - $14.95; w/ diskettes: DOS - 3.5" or 5.25" - $39.95; Mac/Windows - $89.95. Visa/MC accepted.

BOYD PUBLISHING CO.
800-452-4035 • 912-452-4020 after 6pm EST
tignall@accucomm.net
PO Box 367 • Milledgeville GA 31061-0367
100s of new historical publications & genealogical references. Computer software, incl. *Official Record of the War of the Rebellion* - all 127 vols. on CD-ROM, $89.95 + $5 S&H.

BRODERBUND
39500 Stevenson Pl Ste 204
Fremont CA 94539-3103
Family Tree Maker CD-Rom - solid starting point for genealogical research. PC compatible with Windows programs, 386 or higher, 4MB RAM (8MB recommended).

CD-RAP
PO Box 3552 • Richmond VA 23235-7552
"The Civil War Chronicles" - 1st in series of 6 CD-ROMs featuring a complete collection of *Harper's Weekly* newspapers, 1860-1865. Eyewitness accounts, battle sketches & illustrations. 800+ documents. $49.99 + S&H.

COMPUTER ARCHIVE TECHNOLOGY
800-787-1355
PO Box 54
Boyds MD 20841-0054
"Civil War Originals," CD-ROM, Vol. 1. Electronic repro of historic publications recounting original descriptions of the war. Lee, Grant, etc.

CONFEDERATE DESK
812-948-5057 • rebeldesk@aol.com
201 Virginia Ct 0149
New Albany IN 47150-5076
New online research service. Most major archives & manuscript depositories accessed immediately. Call, write or access e-mail.

GENEALOGICAL PUBLISHING CO.
800-296-6687
1001 N Calvert St
Baltimore MD 21202-3897
Publishers of the *Index to the Roll of Honor*, an incredible guide to the 228,639 Union dead listed in the *Roll*'s 27 vols. 1164 pp. $75. On CD-ROM, incl. entire Roll of Honor - $49.99. Free catalog.

GRACE TECHNOLOGIES
800-778-6629
1476 Glenmore Ct
Apopka FL 32712-2046
Antietam/Sharpsburg - study the battlefield by computer. Computer-based learning for DOS-PCs, Windows - $33.95. Other subjects.

GRAFICA MULTIMEDIA, INC.
800-867-5563
415-358-5555
415-358-5556 Fax
http://www.graficamm.com
info@graficamm.com
Lisa Padilla
1777 Borel Pl Ste 500
San Mateo CA 94402-3514
Award-winning multimedia publishing & production company since 1988. Interactive solutions for business communication, marketing, sales, & education. CD/ROM - $49.95.

GROLIER INTERACTIVE, INC.
http://www.grolier.com
90 Sherman Tpke
Danbury CT 06816-0002
Battle of the Ironclads - CD-ROM. Accurate, riveting simulation of the CW battle between the *Monitor* & the *Merrimac*. Multiple modes of play.

GUILD PRESS OF INDIANA
317-848-6421 • 800-913-9563 Orders
http://www.guildpress.com
435 Gradle Dr
Carmel IN 46032-2535
The Civil War CD-Rom; *Iron Men, Iron Will*;*The Road to Glory*; *Rebel Sons of Erin*; *Field Surgeon at Gettysburg*. Other titles.

H-BAR ENTERPRISES
800-432-7702 • 205-622-3040 Fax
http://www.hbar.com • hbar@oakman.tds.net
1422 Davidson Loop
Oakman AL 35579-5820
Official Records - every word indexed, both reports & correspondence included. Custom CDs available - choose your books. Create own computer databases, add personal notes. Call for info.

HAFPAN PRODUCTIONS
518-346-3563
EDLE31A@prodigy.com
PO Box 9274 • Niskayuna NY 12309-0274
Best selection of board & computer wargames. Free catalog.

HEARTHSTONE BOOKSHOP
703-960-0086 • 888-960-3300 Orders
703-960-0087 Fax
http://www.hearthstonebooks.com
info@hearthstonebooks.com
Stuart Nixon • 5735A Telegraph Rd
Alexandria VA 22303-1205
Genealogical books, software, CDs & supplies, including listings on Civil War history & research. Catalog - $2 (ref.).

HISTORICAL IMPRESSIONS
888-603-0100
970-256-0157 Fax
lskaf@iti2.net
PO Box 60323
Grand Junction CO 81506-8758
PC & Mac standard & multimedia Civil War screensavers for Union, South or mixed versions. Limited ed. art, posters, bookmarks, magnets, postcards. Dealer inquiries welcome. Catalog. (See ad page 264)

HISTORICAL STUDIES GROUP
612-774-9405
1235 Reaney Ave
Saint Paul MN 55106-4011
Series of regimental-level Civil War board & computer games. Accurate, realistic, detailed. Each includes 2 major battles, 2 learning scenarios & a 24-pp. historical analysis.

HUDSON'S HOBBY GAMES
817-461-0126 • HudsonGame@aol.com
PO Box 121503 • Arlington TX 76012-1503
CW board games & computer software. Free catalogs.

INFINET OP
800-816-4774 • jameson@whytel.com
PO Box 934 • Frisco TX 75034-0934
Screen savers for your PC. "Leaders & Generals" or "Confederate Flags" - 20+ images/disk. Windows 3.1 or 95, 486 with 4+ MB RAM rqd.

INFO CONCEPTS, INC.
800-747-1861 • 505-298-1528 Fax
11024 Montgomery Blvd NE Ste 284
Albuquerque NM 87111-3962
CW Regimental Info. System - computer-based information source detailing 2,550 Confederate units, 50 orders of battle, 6,000 officers' names, maps, portraits, flags, etc. $99.95 + $7 S&H. Call for info.

INTERACTIVE MAGIC
888-646-2442 (N. Am.) • 919-461-0722
http://www.imagicgames.com
"American Civil War: From Sumter to Appomattox" - Strategy game on 2 CDs. Face the challenge of refighting & rethinking the war. Bonus Historical Tapes CD.

ISIS INTERACTIVE
800-417-4747 • 7910 Woodmont Ave Ste 327
Bethesda MD 20814-3015
Interactive CDs - one for Lee, one for Grant. Meet the generals, up close & personal. $24.95 ea. + $3.95 S&H. Both - $39.95 + $3.95 S&H.

JUNCTION SOFTWARE
970-256-0194 • 751 Horizon Ct Ste 244
Grand Junction CO 81506-8718
ArtCollector for Windows. Track your art collection, invoices, inventory, for-sale lists & much more. Living history Civil War screensavers by Historical Impressions.

MULTI EDUCATOR, INC.
800-866-6434
914-235-4340 • 914-235-4367 Fax
http://www.multied.com • multied@multied.cpm
244 North Ave • New Rochelle NY 10801
2 CD-Rom set, Windows/Macintosh. Featuring complete chronology of war events, in-depth coverage of every major battle, 3,000 photos, more than 1,000 pgs of text. Print/export all photos & text. $79.95.

THE PRESTON BROOKS SOCIETY
800-820-1860
PO Box 13012 • James Island SC 29422
Largest & best 100% Confederate Clip Art, Vol. 1. PC & MAC versions - more than 125 images on 5 disks, incl. flags, battles, soldiers, ships, weapons, stamps, forts, & much more!

PROVISION MEDIA
901-668-4249
7046 Broadway # 318
Lemon Grove CA 91945-1406
The Gettysburg Experience, book - $10.95. Computer clip art. Civil War, anatomy, botany, earth science, IBM/Mac format - $19.95.

RESEARCH DATABASE
http://www.civilwardata.com/acw
Don't miss the Civil War again! Visit the largest, most in-depth, & fully searchable research database of U.S. Civil War history. See website for free demonstration.

SIERRA IMPRESSIONS
800-757-7707
http://www.sierra.com
"Robert E. Lee: Civil War General" - true-to-life CD-ROM game. Relive battles, lead troops through 7 historic engagements. In-depth multimedia presentation, reenactment footage, evocative illustrations.

STOKES IMAGING SERVICES
800-856-4498 • 512-458-2201
7000 Cameron Rd • Austin TX 78752
Selected Civil War photographs, 1861-1865. Tapes CD-ROM for IBM or PC compatible - $79.95.

STRATEGIC SIMULATIONS, INC.
800-601-PLAY
Wargame Construction Set III: Age of Rifles, 1846-1905, PC-DOS CD-ROM. Includes 3 Civil War campaigns, 25 CW scenarios. Available in retail stores.

TALONSOFT
410-933-9191
800-211-6504 Orders only
http://www.talonsoft.com
Talonsoft1@aol.com
75162.373@compuserve.com
PO Box 632 • Forest Hill MD 21050-0632
"Battleground 7: Bull Run" - CD-ROM computer game for Windows. Play head-to-head via modem, e-mail or internet. Also in the Battleground series: Antietam, Gettysburg, Shiloh.

TARGET AUCTIONS
816-965-0013 Orders
http://www.usbusiness.com/target/us.htm
PO Box 17841 • Kansas City MO 64134-0141
"Tattered Flags" - the most fun you'll ever have fighting the Civil War! Original game for the PC, $14.95 + $3 S&H. CW games, stamps.

TDC INTERACTIVE
310-937-6090 • 310-937-1771 Orders
310-937-0210 Fax
http://www.loop.com/~samp
samp@loop.com
PO Box 219 • Manhattan Beach CA 90267
Twelve Roads to Gettysburg, comprehensive CD-ROM for PC or Mac - $29.95.

TEKNOVATION
540-548-4128
660 Montei Dr • Earlysville VA 22936-9690
Images of the Civil War, Vol. 1. Selected Civil War photographs 1861-1865. Interactive PC images. Use as screensaver, with printout capability. $24.95.

TROUBADOUR INTERACTIVE
800-497-0042
trubador@crocker.com
PO Box 12 • Northfield MA 01360-0012
Windows CD-ROM - *Fateful Lightning: A Narrative History of the Civil War.* 40+ animated campaign & battle maps. Era songs, video clips, modern color photos of battlefields. $34.95 + $2 S&H.

TWELVE ROADS TO GETTYSBURG
800-832-0032 • 310-452-6722 Fax
Historically accurate, updated version of the fully interactive CD-ROM. Experience Gettysburg in such detail you can almost smell the gunpowder. Works on both Mac & PC. $24.95 + $5 S&H.

WALDEN FONT
800-519-4575 • http://www.waldenfont.com
PO Box 871 • Winchester MA 01890-8171
Originial typefaces, graphics & ornaments to create authentic fliers, newsletters & broadsides. Works with word processing & graphics software - $39 + $3 S&H. For PC or Mac.

ZIGZAG MULTIMEDIA
800-561-2765
100 professional quality photos on CD-ROM, with extensive text history to print into your own documents & presentations. Heritage of America series, incl. Civil War Battlefields. $49.95/CD.

BLACKJACK TRADING COMPANY
Chuck Hanselmann
PO Box 707
Blythewood SC 29016-0707
Buyer of family Confederate paper, stamps, letters, autographs, currency, slave documents, slave tags, & estates.

BNR PRESS
800-793-0683 Orders & Fax
419-732-NOTE (6683)
http://www.dcache.net/~bnrpress
bnrpress@dcache.net
Fred Schwan
132 E 2nd St
Port Clinton OH 43452-1115
Publisher of the *Comprehensive Catalog of Confederate Paper Money* by Grover Criswell & other titles of interest to collectors. Hardcover - $35; dealer discounts. Advertising opportunities.

C & N COINS & COLLECTIBLES
908-845-0045
2301 Route 9
Howell Station Track 3
Howell NJ 07731-3374
Buy/sell paper Americana, currency, stocks & bonds. Civil War & period images.

CALIFORNIA COIN COMPANY
800-370-COIN
PO Box 578128
Modesto CA 95357-8128
U.S. Morgan silver dollars & other rare collectible coins guaranteed to grade "very fine." Call/write for list.

CAROLINA GOLD & SILVER, INC.
803-736-0540
8502 Two Notch Rd
Columbia SC 29223-6307
1864 Confederate $5, $10, or $20 bills - $30.

CIVIL WAR ANTIQUITIES
614-363-1862
http://www.civilwarantiquities.com
Todd Rittenhouse, Prop.
PO Box 1411
Delaware OH 43015-1411
Quality CW items. Guns, swords, letters, currency, books, prints. Buy/sell/trade. Full service custom framing & matting; specializing in conservation framing. Shop located at 13-1/2 N Sandusky St., Delaware, Ohio. Free catalog.

CIVIL WAR COMMEMORATIVE COINS
kaykay@injersey.com • Kathleen Ellerbusch
3587 Highway 9 Ste 512
Freehold NJ 07728-3288
1995 Civil War Battlefield Commemorative Coins - Proof Silver Dollars. Designer of obervse - Troiani; reverse - Mercanti. Limited number with certif. of authenticity - $32 ppd.

CIVIL WAR STORE
504-522-3328
212 Chartres St • New Orleans LA 70130
Mail order catalog - weapons, currency, bonds, stamps, letters, diaries, CDVs, prints, slave broadsides & bills of sale, autographs, photos. Catalog - $4.

CLARK'S GUN SHOP, INC.
540-439-8988
10016 James Madison Hwy
Warrenton VA 20186-7820
Retailer of books, Civil War relics, Kepis, flags, buttons, Confederate souvenirs, original Confederate money & state notes, CW prints.

CLUB'S COLLECTIBLES
10029 243rd Pl SW
Edmonds WA 98020-5751
Museum-quality framed prints, produced from archive negatives, & authentic Confederate currency mounted & framed. Many generals.

THE CONFEDERATE TREASURY
800-632-2383 • 615-721-4155 Fax
http://www.ConfederateTreasury.com
1100 N Main St • Tennessee Ridge TN 37178
Confederate States Currency 1861-1865. Complete 70-note, full-color set of currency issued by Confederate government. Exact in detail, protected in album. $139.95.

PETER CRANE RARE COINS
721 Cheriwood Ct
Youngstown OH 44512-1725
Fractional currency of the Civil War; coins.

COL. GROVER CRISWELL
352-685-2287 • 352-685-1014 Fax
PO Box 6000 • Salt Springs FL 32134-6000
Buys/sells currency, stocks, bonds, money, slavery items, autographs. 51st year of business. *Comprehensive Catalog of Confederate Paper Money*, hardcover, 350 pp. - $35 (ppd.). 432-pp. price list of collectibles - $8 (ref.). Free book list.

CSA CURRENCY PAGE
http://www.CSAcurrency.com
Homepages providing info. on authentic Confederate currency, bonds, coins, & stamps.

CSA SILVER DOLLAR
1156 Sledge Ave
Memphis TN 38104-4657
Ltd. ed. Nathan Bedford Forrest commemorative coin, .999 fine silver, mirror finish. $29.95 + $3 S&H.

GEORGE ESKER
PO Box 100 • La Place LA 70069-0100
Civil War memorabilia (especially Confederate), currency, images, relics, bullets, buttons, projectiles, documents. Catalog - $9 for 3 issues.

FIRST NATIONAL RESERVE
800-321-8700 • 409-866-7536 Fax
6520 College St
Beaumont TX 77707-3305
Collectible coins. *Insider's Guide to U.S. Coin Values* - 200-pg.

GETTYSBURG COIN CO.
39 N Washington St # 233
Gettysburg PA 17325
Genuine Civil War era coins, pre-1866.

GIBSON'S CIVIL WAR COLLECTIBLES
423-323-2427 • 423-323-8123 Fax
Paul, Linda & Bryan Gibson
PO Box 948
Bristol TN 37621-0948
Autographs, CSA bonds & currency, diaries, flags, letter groups, newspapers, photos, slave items, uniforms, any other paper items.

GREAT AMERICAN COINS, INC.
800-622-3330
1 Odell Plz
Yonkers NY 10701-1402
Original U.S. govt.-minted "New Orleans" Morgan silver dollars. Mint condition. $35/coin. Write for extensive listing of other coins.

BRIAN & MARIA GREEN, INC.
336-993-5100
336-993-1801 Fax
http://www.collectorsnet.com/bmg/index.shtml
bmgcivilwar@webtv.net
PO Box 1816J
Kernersville NC 27285-1816
Civil War autographs, letters, documents, diaries, CSA stamps, covers, currency, etc. Catalog - $5/yr for 4 issues.

MAJ. ARTHUR HENRICK - PAYMASTER
http://acwa.org/pay.html
PayCall@aol.com or MajorAWH@aol.com
PO Box 61075
Sunnyvale CA 94088-1075
High quality facsimiles of Civil War notes. Mix of 30+ notes, such as 1862 Greenbacks, CSA & state/local notes - $3 (cash, check or stamps). Member of ACWA.

THE HISTORICAL SHOP
504-467-2532 • 504-464-7552 Fax
Yvonne & Cary Delery
PO Box 73244
Metairie LA 70033-3244
Photos, documents, autographs, CSA currency, letters, slavery ads & items, relics, framed displays & other collectibles. Buys/sells. Illus. catalogs - $8/yr.

INTERNATIONAL COINS & CURRENCY, INC.
800-451-4463
62 Ridge St # 218
Montpelier VT 05602-3136
Sets of CSA currency & historic U.S. mint first issues.

JPL ANTIQUES
914-896-6006
211 Main St
Fishkill NY 12524-2209
CSA currency, bonds, documents, letters, CDVs, newspapers, accoutrements, CSA/Union imprints. Price list - $1.

PHILLIP B. LAMB, LTD.
504-899-4710
800-391-0115 Orders
504-891-6826 Fax
http://www.LambRarities.com
lambcsa@aol.com
PO Box 15850
2727 Prytania St
New Orleans LA 70175-5850
Buy/sell Confederate memorabilia; CDVs, currency, documents, photos, art, bonds, slave items, swords, buttons, bullets, autographs, & much more.

LEXINGTON HISTORICAL SHOP
540-463-2615
Bob Lurate
PO Box 1428 • Lexington VA 24450-1428
Civil War memorabilia. Buy/sell books, relics, flags, currency, ephemera. Appraisals. Visit shop Mon-Sat 10-6, College Square Shopping Center, Route 11N, Lexington, Va.

HARDIE MALONEY
504-522-3328
212 Chartres St
New Orleans LA 70130-2215
Civil War store. Confederate currency, bonds, stamps, covers, CDV.s, letters, diaries, documents, autographs, pistols & swords.

JOHN MASON ENTERPRISES
6878 Immokalee Rd
Keystone Heights FL 32656-8993
Authentic Confederate war bond coupons, with informative history - $8.

N.F.C.C.
912-382-0554
1436 Tift Ave N • PO Box 1388
Tifton GA 31794-1388
Offering Battle of Gettysburg US Commemorative coins & 1861 Confederate half-dollar replicas. Both in .999 silver & crisply struck. From $29.95.

NATIONAL COLLECTOR'S MINT, INC.
800-936-MINT x443
4401 Connecticut Ave NW
Washington DC 20008-2322
Original US Morgan Silver Dollars - some of the last in the world. $19.40 ea. + $3 S&H. Independent distributor of US coins & currency, replicas, rarities, etc.

NOLES CONFEDERATE STATES TREASURE
PO Box 1134 • Calena AL 35040-1134
Civil War coins. Robert E. Lee 1-oz. silver coin, 1st in series. $24.95 ea.

HOWARD L. NORTON
PO Box 22821 • Little Rock AR 72221-2821
Buy/sell/appraise. Autographs, Civil War items, Americana, historical documents, photographs, coins, currency, stamps, postal history. All transactions confidential. Catalog.

OLD MILL COIN CO.
PO Box 425 • New Boston NH 03070-0425
Copper-nickel Indian cent, 2-cent piece, 3-cent piece. All 3 - $21.95. Confederate currency - $27.95 ea. All currency dated 1861-65.

MIKE RUSSELL
401 Virginia Ave
Herndon VA 20170-5437
Quarterly catalog of Victorian artifacts & relics, emphasis on obsolete currency, bottles & pipes - $2. *The Collector's Guide to Clay Tobacco Pipes, Vol. I* - $20.45 ppd.

BRAD SAWYER
804-482-1725
PO Box 15543
Chesapeake VA 23328-5543

HUGH SHULL
803-432-8500 • 803-432-9958 Fax
PO Box 761 • Camden SC 29020-0761
Confederate notes, bonds, obsolete currency (1700s-1900). US paper money (prior to 1930). Buy/sell. Catalog - $3 (ref. on order). Annual subscription - $10. (See ad page 267)

STONEWALLS
810-231-2417
PO Box 218
Lakeland MI 48143-0218
Buy/sell/trade Confederate currency, U.S. coins. Genuine, collectible condition. Free price sheet.

TWO COLONELS ENTERPRISES
330-745-2888 Ph & Fax
http://www.webchamps.com/twocolonels
twocolonels@webchamps.com
Daniel P Sens
1287E Sevilla Ave
Akron OH 44314-1457
Patriotic reproduction stamps & stationery. Many designs. Union & Confederate. Genuine stamps, covers, & paper. Prices on request. Wholesale & retail catalogs - free.

URE PRESS
636 Piney Forest Rd
Danville VA 24540-2800
Confederate Treasure in Danville - documented, clues to 196,000 silver dollars buried in Danville, Va. Hardcover - $26.07 ppd.

VICTORIAN RARE COIN
617-665-9739
617-665-0922 Fax
numismat@aol.com
Andrew N. Seminerio
PO Box 151
Melrose MA 02176-0002
Civil War coinage. Specimens ranging from cents through $20 gold pieces, both circulated & uncirculated condition. Free price list of more than 4,500 different U.S. coins.

B. H. VINSON, JR.
804-794-5751
13205 Lady Ashley Rd
Midlothian VA 23113-4563
Commemorative coins.

WAR BETWEEN THE STATES MEMORABILIA
717-337-2853
Len Rosa
PO Box 3965
Gettysburg PA 17325-0965
Buy/sell soldiers' letters, envelopes, documents, CDVs, photos, autographs, newspapers, badges, ribbons, relics, framed display items, currency, & more. Estab. 1978. Illus. catalogs - $10/yr for 5 issues. Active buyers receive future subscriptions free.

WORLD EXONUMIA
815-226-0771
815-397-7662 Fax
http://www.exonumia.com
Rich Hartzog
PO Box 4143BWX
Rockford IL 61110-0643
Civil War & sutler tokens, medals, slave tags, Civil War dog tags, corps badges, sutler paper, GAR reunion badges, etc. Buy/sell; mail bid sales. Publisher of *Sutler Paper Money*.

BLUEGRASS CASE COMPANY
606-663-9871
800-668-9871
606-663-6369 Fax
272 Airport Rd
PO Box 386
Stanton KY 40380-0386
Display frames, collectors' frames, lined, unlined, velvet or foam inserts, stands for frames. Ideal for guns, knives, badges, all collectibles. Call for sizes.

COLLECTORS SERVICES
419-884-1377
PO Box 742
Westerville OH 43086-0742
1/35 scale figurines, dioramas. Oak display cases - custom sizes available.

D & M WOODCRAFTS
800-498-7820
716-625-8530
http://www.localnet.com/~dmgerber
dmgerber@localnet.com
5363 Oakwood Dr
North Tonawanda NY 14120-9619
Keepsake relic cases made of oak, cherry or walnut. Comes complete with double strength glass, brass hinges, lock & key. Color brochure - $2.

R. ANDREW FULLER COMPANY
PO Box 2071
Pawtucket RI 02861-0071
Award cases: all sizes, hardwood, lined, glass top. Free catalog.

GDR ENTERPRISES
803-889-6360
PO Box 807
Hollywood SC 29449-0807
Wooden ammunition crates; shipping containers, chests, officer's desk, & more. Handcrafted reproductions for military historians since 1982. Photo-illus. catalog - $2.

PERSONAL TREASURES
770-431-1689
4980 Oakdale Rd SE
Smyrna GA 30080-7132
Wide variety of display cases from chip board mounts to high quality hardwood finish & polished brass hardware. Glass panel tops. Price list - SASE.

PRESERVATION PRODUCTS
608-839-4038
preservprod@yahoo.com
Jeffery C. Remy
3813 Bass Ln
Cottage Grove WI 53527
Wooden ammunition boxes, shipping containers, traveling chests, offiers' & regimental desks, & more. Historically accurate reproductions of Civil War & Indian War. Photo-illus. catalog - $2 (ref.).

REMEMBRANCE ART
Ray Helmicki
1481 N Creek Rd
Lake View NY 14085-9516
Art gallery-quality Civil War shadow boxes in solid oak. Ltd. ed. of *Country Divided*, 30"x16" - $375. For more info, send SASE. Dealer inquiries welcome. Catalog - $3 (ref.).

SHENANDOAH TRADER
540-740-3735
trader@m-c-b.com
Ross & Mary Smith
1988 Shipwreck Dr
New Market VA 22844-3408
Books for the collector of Civil War & earlier periods of American militaria. Manufacturer of quality artifact display cases of oak & walnut. Button cases. Catalog - $1 (ref.).

VETERAN'S DISPLAY CASES
Paul Hammonds
S67W29308 Hawks Rest Ct
Mukwonago WI 53149-9015
Hardwood display cases made of either oak or walnut. Also custom-made sword & gun cases.

AMERICAN CIVIL WAR INSTITUTE
whittm@campbellsvil.edu
Kent Masterson Brown, Dir.
Campbellsville University
1 University Dr
Campbellsville KY 42718-2799

AMERICAN MILITARY UNIVERSITY
703-330-5398 • 703-330-5109 Fax
http://www.amunet.edu/
amugen@amunet.edu
9104 Manassas Dr Ste P
Manassas Park VA 20111-5211
Degree programs in military history, warfare studies & defense management. "*Civil War Studies*" concentration in M.A. in Military Studies degree. 250+ courses in curriculum. Three 15-week semesters beginning in January, May & September.

ASSOCIATION FOR THE PRESERVATION OF CIVIL WAR SITES
888-606-1400 • http://www.apcws.com
11 Public Sq Ste 200
Hagerstown MD 21740-5510
Not-for-profit membership organization that preserves Civil War sites for educational & recreational uses. Website: organizational news & membership info.

BLUE & GRAY EDUCATION SOCIETY
804-797-4535
416 Beck St • Norfolk VA 23503-5302
Non-profit organization which interprets battlefields for public visitation. North Anna is most recent achievement. More than 600 members via tax-exempt donation. Seminars, tours, symposiums & debates.

CELEBRATE HISTORY
800-748-9901
http://www.celebratehistory.com
PO Box 70332
Port Richmond CA 94807-0332
Held annually every President's Day holiday weekend (Feb. 13-15, 1998) at South San Francisco Conference Center. Includes complete Civil War round table & symposium.

CIVIL WAR CONFERENCE
919-515-3184
Ann Coughlin
NC State Univ. Col. of Forest Resources
PO Box 8001
Raleigh NC 27695
Conference featuring speakers & tours. Hosted by NC Civil War Tourism Council & NC State Univ. Annual event - April.

CIVIL WAR DRUM & FLAG SHOWS
830-966-3480 • nyclay@swtexas.net
Nancy Clayton
PO Box 153 • Utopia TX 78884-0153
Drum & flag storytelling performance for school assemblies, history & music classes (grades PK-college), teachers' meetings, conventions & living history events. Brochure - send SASE.

CIVIL WAR EDUCATION ASSOCIATION
800-298-1861
540-667-2339 Fax
21 N Loudoun St
Winchester VA 22601-4715
Non-profit organization presenting the finest seminars, symposia, & tours. Develops educational materials, publishes/distributes Civil War books. Contact for extensive calendar of events.

CIVIL WAR EDUCATION ASSOCIATION SYMPOSIUM
800-298-1861 • 540-678-8598
PO Box 78 • Winchester VA 22604-0078
Civil War Symposium. Special speakers. Annual September event.

CIVIL WAR EDUCATION CENTER
308 W College Blvd
Roswell NM 88201-5165
Offering series of tests leading to certification as an expert, senior expert & master expert in Civil War knowledge.

CIVIL WAR INSTITUTE
215-637-5016
Holy Family College Cont. Ed Office
Grant & Frankford Aves
Philadelphia PA 19114
Certificate awarded upon completion of 8 non-credit courses over 2-yr. period. Brochure.

CIVIL WAR LADY MAGAZINE
507-825-3182 Ph & Fax
622 3rd Ave SW • Pipestone MN 56164-1529
Quarterly magazine about women's civilian issues of the 1860s. Fashion news, feature articles, reenacting tips, etiquette. $21/yr. (4 issues). Annual August Natl. Conference for Women.

CIVIL WAR PRESERVATION CONFERENCE
540-786-2470
Rappahannock Valley CWRT
PO Box 7632 • Fredericksburg VA 22404
Conference & tours, banquet. Annual event - March.

CIVIL WAR SOCIETY
800-247-6253 • 540-955-1176
540-955-2321 Fax
cwmag@mnsinc.com
PO Box 770
Berryville VA 22611-0770
Membership includes award-winning *Civil War Magazine*, calendar, newsletters, membership cert., preservation & education activities, ancestors research guide, tours, seminars, discounts & camaraderie. Call for brochure & free sample magazine.

CONFERENCE ON WOMEN & THE CIVIL WAR
800-473-3943
roslin@nfs.com
12728 Martin Rd
Smithsburg MD 21783-9337
Through lectures on various topics, recognizes & honors the services performed by women for their country & its people during the 1860s.

GENTEEL ARTS ACADEMY
717-337-0283
717-337-0314 Fax
http://www.cvn.net/~cschmitt
cschmitt@mail.cvn.net
CarolAnn Schmitt
PO Box 3014
Gettysburg PA 17325-0014
Offers workshops, lectures & seminars on period clothing, construction & fitting techniques. Classes offered frequently. Call/write for details & brochure. Free catalog.

HARRISBURG CIVIL WAR EXPOSITION & SEMINARS
717-780-2587
vlgentze@hacc01b.hacc.edu
Harrisburg Area Community College
1 HACC Dr • Harrisburg PA 17110-2903
Showcases reenactor demonstrations, living historians, historical societies' displays, merchants. Seminars feature many topics, guest speakers. Advance registration required. Annual March-April event. Call to be placed on mailing list.

HARTFORD CIVIL WAR SYMPOSIUM
800-298-1861
540-667-2339 Fax
Civil War Education Association
PO Box 78
Winchester VA 22604-0078
Annual May symposium in Hartford, Ct., with several Civil War historians.

LIVING HISTORY ASSOCIATES, INC.
804-788-1493
804-788-1489 Fax
PO Box 4914
Richmond VA 23227
Providing history-related services to clients; Richmond-area tours, 1860s speakers bureau, special events, living history workshops, film & TV project consultants.

LIVING HISTORY ASSOCIATION, INC.
PO Box 1389
Wilmington VT 05363-1389
Reenactors' Liability Insurance, covering reenactments, encampments, black powder, cavalry, artillery; personal injury, equipment insurance. Educational programs, workshops, full historical museum. Newsletter, events & info - $3.

MID-ATLANTIC CONFERENCE OF CIVIL WAR ROUND TABLES
610-262-1614
CWRT of Eastern PA
PO Box 333
Allentown PA 18105-0333
Special speakers. Annual conference - April.

MIDWEST CWRT CONFERENCE
Cincinnati CWRT
PO Box 1336
Cincinnati OH 45201-1336
Annual April conferences with several speakers, book sales, raffles, tours.

MINERVA CENTER ON WOMEN & THE MILITARY
410-437-5379
http://www.MinervaCenter.com
mouseminer@aol.com
20 Granada Rd
Pasadena MD 21122-2708
Non-profit education foundation & publisher presents the 3rd printing of *An Uncommon Soldier: The Civil War Letters of Sarah Rosetta Wakeman, alias Pvt. Lyons Wakeman*. $25.

MISSISSIPPI IN THE CIVIL WAR CONFERENCE
804-797-4535
BGES
PO Box 129
Danville VA 24543-0129
CW Symposium co-sponsored by BGES & MS Dept. of Archives & History in Jackson, MS. Guest speakers. Annual event - November.

GEORGE TYLER MOORE CENTER FOR THE STUDY OF THE CIVIL WAR
304-876-5399
304-876-5429
304-876-5079 Fax
Shepherd College
Shepherdstown WV 25443
For continuing study/education of the most pivotal time in American History - the Civil War. Research being compiled on CW soldiers through a sophisticated database.

MULTI EDUCATOR, INC.
800-866-6434
914-235-4340
914-235-4367 Fax
http://www.multied.com
multied@multied.cpm
Marc Schulman
244 North Ave
New Rochelle NY 10801
2 CD-Rom set, Windows/Macintosh. Featuring complete chronology of war events, in-depth coverage of every major battle, 3,000 photos, more than 1,000 pgs of text. Print/export all photos & text. $79.95.

MUSEUM OF AMERICAN FINANCIAL HISTORY
212-908-4519
212-908-4601 Fax
http://www,mafh.org
mafh1@pipeline.com
26 Broadway
New York NY 10004-1703
America, Money and War: Financing the Civil War. 42-pg illus. catalog of exhibit - $14.25 ppd. Education kit with slides - $49.95 ppd.

NATIONAL CIVIL WAR ARTILLERY & INFANTRY SCHOOL
315-483-9284
Frank Cutler
6343 Kelly Rd
Sodus NY 14551-9502
Training & classes in Youngstown, NY, under top instructors from around the country. Live & train inside historic fort. $6 fee. Annual event - May.

NATIONAL CIVIL WAR ASSOCIATION
PO Box 70084
Sunnyvale CA 94086-0084
Union & Confederate units involved in reenactments, educational presentations. Open to all interested reenactors. Individ. membership - $35.

NATIONAL CONGRESS OF CWRTs
501-225-3996
jlrussell@civilwarbuff.com
CWRTA
PO Box 7388
Little Rock AR 72217-7388
Speakers & tours. Annual October conference sponsored by Civil War Round Table Associates.

NATIONAL MUSEUM OF CIVIL WAR MEDICINE
301-695-1864 0149 800-564-1864
301-695-6823 Fax
http://www.civilwarmed.org
LauraM@civilwarmed.org
JaNeen M. Smith, Ex. Dir.
48 E Patrick St " PO Box 470
Frederick MD 21705-0470
Center for study & interpretation of Civil War medical history. Medical artifacts, manuscripts, books & materials. 1861-1865. Museum store. Memberships available. Annual conference 1st weekend in August.

NEVADA CIVIL WAR VOLUNTEERS
http://pw2.netcom.com/baugh1/index.html
PO Box 11033 • Reno NV 89510-1033
Living history & other programs devoted to Civil War study, such as "Soldier for an Hour." Educational presentations. Union, Confederate & civilian groups. Annual membership - $15 (individ.); $25 (family).

NORWICH UNIVERSITY
800-336-6794
Unique, off-campus history program at nation's first private military college. BA/MA degrees from home. Accredited.

OHIO CIVIL WAR ASSOCIATION
419-586-5294 • 419-586-6763 Fax
106 Haig St • Celina OH 45822-2708
Hosts annual CW conference & other events.

JOHN PELHAM HISTORICAL ASSOCIATION, INC.
757-838-1685
http://members.aol.com/JPHA1982
JPHA1982@aol.com • Peggy Vogtsberger
7 Carmel Ter • Hampton VA 23666-2807
Bi-monthly newsletter, "The Cannoneer." Annual convention & tour of Fredericksburg; commemorative ceremony at Kelly's Ford. Supports preservation; active in erecting monuments. Archives located at Jacksonville Public Library, Jacksonville, Ala.

PENN STATE ALUMNI ASSN.
814-865-7679
Mary Jane Stout
105 Old Main • Pennsylvania State University
University Park PA 16802-1501
Penn State-sanctioned lecturers & battlefield walking tours by leading historians/authors. Also available over the Internet. A continuing & distance education service.

SARASOTA CIVIL WAR SYMPOSIUM
800-298-1861
CW Education Assn.
PO Box 78 • Winchester VA 22604-0078
Well-known authors & speakers on the Civil War. Annual event: January-February.

SCHOOL OF THE PIECE
David V. Medert
600 W 5th St Apt 21
Chillicothe OH 45601-2217
School for artillery at Camp Sherman's rifle range. Also, school of the soldier for infantry. Modern & period camping. Annual May event.

SCHOOL OF THE SOLDIER & SWAP MEET
Steven C. Huddleston
12 Bow St • Danvers MA 01923-3520
Programs on military manual of arms, marching maneuvers, camp life, tent setup, period engineering, medicine, ladies' & civilian topics. Modern facilities. Annual event - April.

SLIDE-A-FACT
PO Box 66085
Saint Petersburg FL 33736-6085
101 Civil War battles & facts listed in chronological order in a "slide-rule" format. Informative & fun. $6.95 ppd.

TOMAHAWK GAMES
330-539-6413
bu958@yfn.ysu.edu
Jim Schmalzried
720 Churchill Rd
Girard OH 44420-2121
"Civil War Command," more than 1,200 multiple-choice trivia questions. 52-photo ID page, pawns, flags, objectives. Ideal for families & teachers. $25 check or MO. 10-day guarantee.

TRAVEL AMERICA, INC.
800-225-2553
131 Dodge St Ste 5
Beverly MA 01915-1861
Seminars & trips on such topics as the American Revolution, the Old West, the Civil War, American History. Contact for info.

THE UNITED STATES CIVIL WAR CENTER
504-388-3156
504-388-4876 Fax
http://www.cwc.lsu.edu
David Madden, Director
Louisiana State University
Baton Rouge LA 70803-0001
Facilitates the creation of a database encompassing *all* Civil War interests; promotes CW studies from multiple perspectives. Website: best comprehensive index to historic & Civil War-related websites.

WEST PALM BEACH CIVIL WAR SYMPOSIUM
800-298-1861
540-667-2339 Fax
Civil War Education Association
PO Box 78
Winchester VA 22604-0078
Annual February symposium with many renowned Civil War historians.

WEST VIRGINIA REENACTORS ASSOCIATION
304-472-5964
PO Box 2133
Buckhannon WV 26201-7133
Participates in reenactments & educational presentations; sponsors special events.

MIKE WOSHNER
412-884-9299
mwoshner@bellatlantic.net
2306 Spokane Ave
Pittsburgh PA 15210-4414
Author of reference book & historical presentations on "India-rubber & gutta-percha in the Civil War era," encompassing history, patents, military trials & award-winning display of rare artifacts.

STEVEN J. WRIGHT
7644 Burholme Ave
Philadelphia PA 19111-2411
Civil War & Plains Indian Wars historian.

ANTEBELLUM COVERS
301-869-2623 Ph & Fax
888-ANTEBEL (268-3235)
http://www.antebellumcovers.com
antebell@antebellumcovers.com
PO Box 3494
Gaithersburg MD 20885-3494
Civil War & 19th-century U.S. paper collectibles incl. soldiers' letters, images, general orders, patriotic envelopes, autographs, slavery documents & advertising paper; CD-ROMs of Civil War & historical titles. Free catalog. Internet customers can be notified by email each time auction is posted.

BLACKJACK TRADING COMPANY
Chuck Hanselmann
PO Box 707
Blythewood SC 29016-0707
Buyer of family Confederate paper, stamps, letters, autographs, currency, slave documents, slave tags, & estates.

C & N COINS & COLLECTIBLES
908-845-0045
2301 Route 9
Howell Station Track 3
Howell NJ 07731-3374
Buy/sell paper Americana, currency, stocks & bonds. Civil War & period images.

CARDS WITH MY PARDS (TM)
877-443-1863 (toll free)
cardswithmypards@yahoo.com
Tony & Pat Fantilli
PO Box 6186
Clearwater FL 33758-6186
Buys & sells CW playing card decks; repro CW card decks. Historically accurate, colorful & informative "Civil War Playing Cards" newsletter. (See ad page 263)

CIVIL WAR CATALOG
Bob & Pat Bartosz
PO Box 226 • Wenonah NJ 08090-0226
Attention Civil War Collectors - $3 for next 3 issues. Letters, documents, slave papers, hires, etc. Historical documents, ephemera.

CIVIL WAR STORE
504-522-3328
212 Chartres St
New Orleans LA 70130-2215
Mail order catalog - weapons, currency, bonds, stamps, letters, diaries, CDVs, prints, slave broadsides & bills of sale, autographs, photos. Catalog - $4.

CLASS COLLECTIBLES
2005 Route 35 N Ste 124
Oakhurst NJ 07755
Repros of death certificates.

COHASCO, INC.
914-476-8500
914-476-8573 Fax
E. Snyder
Postal 821
Yonkers NY 10702
Semi-annual mail/phone auction catalogs containing varied CW memorabilia: generals, maps, letters, photos, ephemera, etc. Our 50th year in business. Catalog - $5.

CONFEDERATE POSTMASTER
PO Box 1864
Middletown CT 06457-8364
Repro stamps, 60 different envelopes. Regimental envelopes on special order. 2 stamps, stationery available to match: U.S. Corps w/ division stationery; framed C.S. stamps. Finest quality now available. Catalog - $2 (credit on order); send SASE.

CSA
PO Box 570060
Whitestone NY 11357-0060
Confederate passports. Accurate, historical, might-have-beens. $4.

THE EARLY AMERICAN HISTORY SHOPPE
603-772-7973
225 Water St
Exeter NH 03833-2417
Books (antiquarian & in-print), ephemera, prints, antique memorabilia & collectibles, T-shirts, CD-Rom, flags, games, tapes, maps, mugs, miniatures, genealogies & more. Specialize in the Civil War. Free catalogs.

EBN COMMUNICATIONS
PO Box 1395
Des Plaines IL 60017-1395
"Abraham Lincoln, 1865. Death of the President!" Front-page replica of the *New York Herald*, one of premier newspapers of the day, dated April 15, 1865. $12.50.

FEDERAL HILL ANTIQUITIES
410-584-8185 / 8329
14 Glen Lyon Ct
Phoenix MD 21131-1212
Purveyors of fine autographs & collectibles. Letters & documents, photos, relics & artifacts, ephemera. Buy/sell/trade.

GIBSON'S CIVIL WAR COLLECTIBLES
423-323-2427
423-323-8123 Fax
Paul, Linda & Bryan Gibson
PO Box 948
Bristol TN 37621-0948
Autographs, CSA bonds & currency, diaries, flags, letter groups, newspapers, photos, slave items, uniforms, any other paper items.

STEPHEN A. GOLDMAN HISTORICAL NEWSPAPERS
410-357-8204
410-343-3507 Fax
http://www.historicalnews.com
SAGHNOLDNEWS@msn.com
PO Box 359
Parkton MD 21120-0359
Historical newspapers bought/sold - 16th-20th centuries. Bound volumes or single issues. Military, political, wild west, gangsters, Civil War, many more! Extensive catalog - $2. (See ad page 268)

BRIAN & MARIA GREEN, INC.
336-993-5100
336-993-1801 Fax
http://www.collectorsnet.com/bmg/index.shtml
bmgcivilwar@webtv.net
PO Box 1816J
Kernersville NC 27285-1816
Civil War autographs, letters, documents, diaries, CSA stamps, covers, currency, etc. Catalog - $5/yr for 4 issues.

GARY HENDERSHOTT
501-224-7555
PO Box 22520
Little Rock AR 72221-2520
Autographs, photographs, imprints, flags & memorabilia of the Civil War era. Catalog - $3.

HISTORICAL BRIEFS, INC.
800-732-4746
Civil War Reports - most authentic reports available, written as events unfolded & published in *Harper's Weekly*. 232 pp. - $24.95 + $3.75 S&H.

HISTORICAL COLLECTIBLE AUCTIONS
336-570-2803 • 336-570-2748 Fax
PO Box 975
Burlington NC 27215
Quarterly auctions of Civil War collectibles including photography, manuscripts, autographs, weapons, etc. Consignments encouraged. Catalog - $20/issue; next 3 for $45.

THE HISTORICAL SHOP
504-467-2532
504-464-7552 Fax
Yvonne & Cary Delery
PO Box 73244
Metairie LA 70033-3244
Photos, documents, autographs, CSA currency, letters, slavery ads & items, relics, framed displays & other collectibles. Buys/sells. Illus. catalogs - $8/yr.

THE HISTORY WORKS
800-717-7359
vjackson@select.net
2788 Loker Ave W
Carlsbad CA 92008-6612
Reproductions of Muster Roll forms, stationery, art, & Regimental Action Reviews. Call/write for complete details. Free catalog.

HUGHES
717-326-1045
717-326-7606 Fax
tim@rarenewspapers.com
PO Box 3636
Williamsport PA 17701-8636
Newspapers; rare, historic - 1600s-1985. Extensive catalog of genuine issues - $2.

THE INDIAN SHOP
606-441-0773
Von Hilliard
PO Box 246
Independence KY 41051-0246
Authentic Civil War newspapers - $10 ea. Indian relics. Catalog - $5 (ref.).

LOWELL JERENS
715-834-3938
639 Putnam Dr
Eau Claire WI 54701-3304
Civil War-era sheet music.

JPL ANTIQUES
914-896-6006
211 Main St
Fishkill NY 12524-2209
CSA currency, bonds, documents, letters, CDVs, newspapers, accoutrements, CSA/Union imprints. Price list - $1.

DEBORAH LAMBERT
1945 Lorraine Ave
Mc Lean VA 22101-5331
Slavery documents, Civil War newspapers, prints, letters, autographs, battle maps. List - $1.

LEXINGTON HISTORICAL SHOP
540-463-2615 • Bob Lurate
PO Box 1428 • Lexington VA 24450-1428
Civil War memorabilia. Buy/sell books, relics, flags, currency, ephemera. Appraisals. Visit shop Mon-Sat 10-6, College Square Shopping Center, Route 11N, Lexington, Va.

LOOK BACK IN TIME
803-986-9097 • 803-986-9297 Fax
PO Box 572 • Port Royal SC 29935-0572
Civil War newspapers, engravings, books, relics, & much more. Want lists welcome. Free catalog.

M.J.M. COLLECTIBLES
879 W Park Ave # 244
Ocean NJ 07712-7205
Reproduced copy of Lee's death certificate, suitable for framing. $10.

HARDIE MALONEY
504-522-3328
212 Chartres St
New Orleans LA 70130-2215
Civil War store. Confederate currency, bonds, stamps, covers, CDV.s, letters, diaries, documents, autographs, pistols & swords.

BILL MASON BOOKS
919-247-6161
http://www.collectorsnet.com/mason/index.htm
bmasonbks@abaco.coastalnet.com
104 N 7th St
Morehead City NC 28557-3807
Rare, new, used, out-of-print Civil War, Western Americana, military & nautical, quality books, prints, & ephemera. Free catalog.

MEEHAN MILITARY POSTERS
212-634-5683
PO Box 477 • New York NY 10028-0018
Genuine war posters. Catalog - $10 (ref.).

MENIG'S MEMORABILIA
708-258-9487
517 S Manor Dr • Peotone IL 60468-9129
Authentic Civil War autographs, newspapers, and documents. Free catalog.

THE MT. STERLING REBEL
606-498-5821
Terry Murphy
PO Box 481 • Mount Sterling KY 40353-0481
Buy/sell since 1979 rare, out-of-print, & previously owned Civil War books. Limited inventory of Civil War paper items, ephemera, autographs & images. Catalog upon request.

SUSAN A. NASH
304-876-3772
PO Box 1011
Shepherdstown WV 25443-1011
Paper conservation. Specialist in historic documents, photographs, prints, drawings, maps, letters, broadsides. Cleaning, mending, deacidification, museum matting. By appt.

NORTHERN CO. ARCHIVES/ACQUISITIONS
800-432-8777
18640 Mack Ave
PO Box 36793
Grosse Pointe Woods MI 48236-0793
Buyers of autographs, documents, photo collections, stock certificates, letters, contracts, etc. Lifetime member MS&D Society. Top $ paid.

THE OLD PAPERPHILES
401-624-9420
401-624-4204 Fax
PO Box 135
Tiverton RI 02878-0135
Offering 100s of accurately described paper collectibles. Great variety, wide price range. Autographs, documents, books. Catalog - $8 for next 10.

OLDE SOLDIER BOOKS, INC.
301-963-2929
301-963-9556 Fax
Warbooks@erols.com
Dave Zullo
18779 N Frederick Ave Ste B
Gaithersburg MD 20879-3158
Largest selection of rare & hard-to-find books. Documents, letters, photographs, autographs, manuscripts. Buy/sell. Free catalog.

PALMETTO PRESENCE
803-641-2382
http://www.21mall.com/ppresence.htm
jarnett@seescape.net
Jim Arnett
PO Box 527
Montmorenci SC 29839-0527
Confederate relics, ephemera. Online catalog.

PROFILES IN HISTORY
800-942-8856 • 310-859-7701
310-859-3842 Fax
345 N Maple Dr Ste 202
Beverly Hills CA 90210-3859
Autographs wanted. Also buying original letters, documents, vintage photos, manuscripts, & rare books (signed). Illus. catalog - $45/yr. Sample - $10.

STEVEN S. RAAB AUTOGRAPHS
800-977-8333 • 610-446-4514 Fax
http://www.raabautographs.com
raab@netaxs,com
PO Box 471
Ardmore PA 19003-0471
Serious collectors, respected dealers. Top dollars paid for collection & quality individual autographs, documents, manuscripts, signed photos, & interesting letters. Catalog sample - $5; $15/yr.

REB ACRES
540-377-2057
rebacres@cfw.com
57 Steeles Fort Rd
Raphine VA 24472-2503
Specializing in Civil War artifacts. Priced right for beginning collectors. Comprehensive, 32-pg catalog - send 3 first-class stamps.

REBEL STAND
PO Box 4972
Falls Church VA 22044-0972
Hand-lettered reproduction of authentic Confederate Officer's Commission/Appointment - $25 ea. Include name, officer rank, & CS unit desired on your frameable document with order.

JEFFEREY M. RIGBY, CONSERVATOR
518-828-5929 Ph & Fax
167 County Route 25
Hudson NY 12534-3263
Preservation of paper documents - letters, muster rolls, maps, broadsides, etc. Satisfaction guaranteed. AIC guidelines followed by professional associate with more than 20 yrs. experience. Free catalog.

DALE W. ROSE
302-239-3120 evenings
104 Tern Ct
Wilmington DE 19808-1966
Harpers Weekly specialist. Original engravings: Civil War through 1897. Send want list.

SHARPSBURG ARSENAL
301-432-7700
301-432-7440 Fax
101 W Main St • PO Box 568
Sharpsburg MD 21782-0568
Purveyors of fine Civil War militaria; firearms, edged weapons, buttons, bullets, leather accoutrements, battlefield relics, books, flags, personal & camp items, paper, letters, framed prints. Buy/sell. (See ad page 264)

HUGH SHULL
803-432-8500
803-432-9958 Fax
PO Box 761
Camden SC 29020-0761
Confederate notes, bonds, obsolete currency (1700s-1900). US paper money (prior to 1930). Buy/sell. Catalog - $3 (ref. on order). Annual subscription - $10. (See ad page 267)

R.M. SMYTHE & CO., INC.
800-622-1880
212-943-1880
212-908-4047 Fax
http://www.rm-smythe.com
26 Broadway Ste 271
New York NY 10004-1701
Where historic paper collections of the world are researched, auctioned, bought & sold. Est. 1880.

DALE S. SNAIR
660-747-0341
904 Deer Run Apt C
Warrensburg MO 64093-8633
Civil War images, paper items, weapons, accoutrements. $4 for next 4 price lists.

SOUTHERN HISTORICAL SHOWCASE
800-854-7832
615-321-0639
http://www.southernhistorical.com
southernhistorical@nashville.com
1907 Division St
Nashville TN 37203-2705
Southern military art & books, prints, original documents & autographs, photos, engravings. Artists: Prechtel, Reeves, Kunstler, Kidd, Gallon, Summers, Heron, Garner, Rocco. Catalog - $5.

STAMP OF APPROVAL
800-808-0567
10 Kendall Green Dr
PO Box 2157
Milford CT 06460-3068
Original Battle of Gettysburg decorated envelope, postmarked the first day the Gettysburg stamp was issued - 7/1/1963. Call for details.

STAMPEDE INVESTMENTS
608-254-7751
1533 River Rd
Wisconsin Dells WI 53965-9002
Large inventory of original letters & documents from the most important people in U.S. History to fit every budget. Free catalog.

STRATFORD'S NOVELTY, LTD
843-797-8040
Kent Stratford
PO Box 1860
Goose Creek SC 29445-1860
Civil War-related novelties & gifts. Confederate flag imprinted products & merchandise. Large selection. Bumper stickers. Free list & pricing.

TRANS-MISSISSIPPI MILITARIA
972-517-8111 Ph & Fax
http://www.collectorsnet.com/transmiss/index.html
charlucv@flash.net
Charles Brecheisen
1004 Simon Dr • Plano TX 75025-2501
UCV, GAR, Civil War & Indian War period relics, books & diaries, papers, letters, covers & records, medical instruments. Always buying. Catalogs - $10 (min. 3 large lists).

UNIVERSITY ARCHIVES
Matthew McGarry, Dir. of Advertising
1406 Overlook Dr
Mount Dora FL 32757-3769
Buy/sell. Letters, documents, clipped signatures, 1400-present. Annual subscription of $29.95 yields at least 4 of the best catalogs in the industry.

WAR BETWEEN THE STATES MEMORABILIA
717-337-2853
Len Rosa
PO Box 3965
Gettysburg PA 17325-0965
Buy/sell soldiers' letters, envelopes, documents, CDVs, photos, autographs, newspapers, badges, ribbons, relics, framed display items, currency, & more. Estab. 1978. Illus. catalogs - $10/yr for 5 issues. Active buyers receive future subscriptions free.

JOHN WILLS
410-574-0771
3323 Berlin Ct
Abingdon MD 21009-2806
Complete selection of original Civil War-dated issues of *Harper's Weekly.*

YESTERDAY'S NEWS, USA
612-721-5526
5344 34th Ave S
Minneapolis MN 55417-2167
Civil War autographs, books, documents, images, militaria, & identified items. 19th & 20th-cent. newspapers & magazines. Catalogs.

AMERICAN AFGHAN COMPANY
410-744-5470
1074 Craftswood Rd
Baltimore MD 21228-1312
50" x 60" cotton weave Confederate battle flag afghan. $49.95 ea. Other products.

AMERICAN FLAG & GIFT
800-448-3524 • 805-473-0126 Fax
http://www.anyflag.com
flags@anyflag.com
John Solley
737 Manuela Way
Arroyo Grande CA 93420-6108
Discount prices on quality American-made flags, banners & flagpoles, too! Catalog - $2 (ref. on 1st order).

ANCIENT AMERICAN ART
601-566-2778 • 601-566-4925
http://www.pointsouth.com/aaa.htm
aaart@dixie-net.com
PO Box 1745
Verona MS 38879-1745
Handmade reproductions of battle & regimental flags of the Civil War. T-shirts $20. Prints $25. Wholesale discounts.

C. BRENNER
540-778-1811
343 Kite Hollow Rd
Stanley VA 22851-4713
Authentic reproduction flags - Union & Confederate, national colors, brigade & corps, company, state, guidons, etc.

CALDWELL STUDIOS
618-747-2655
RR 2 Box 160
Tamms IL 62988-9605
Professional reproductions of regimental flags constructed & hand-painted. Reasonable prices. Reenactment tested. Call Zac for free information.

CATAWBA FLAG DEPOT
800-467-0082
206 N College Ave
Newton NC 28658-3256

CAVALIER SHOPPE
800-227-5491
Rex Jarrett, Owner
PO Box 511
Bruce MS 38915-0511
Confederate flag apparel - 100% cotton. Shirts, slacks, shorts, skirts, boxers, belts, ties, watches, flags. Free catalog.

CIVIL WAR DRUM & FLAG SHOWS
830-966-3480
nyclay@swtexas.net
Nancy Clayton
PO Box 153 • Utopia TX 78884-0153
Drum & flag storytelling performance for school assemblies, history & music classes (grades PK-college), teachers' meetings, conventions & living history events. Brochure - send SASE.

CLARK'S GUN SHOP, INC.
540-439-8988
10016 James Madison Hwy
Warrenton VA 20186-7820
Retailer of books, Civil War relics, Kepis, flags, buttons, Confederate souvenirs, original Confederate money & state notes, Civil War prints.

COLLECTOR'S ARMOURY
800-544-3456 x515 • 703-684-6111
703-683-5486 Fax
James W. Hernly
PO Box 59, Dept CWB
Alexandria VA 22313-0059
Full line of "non-firing" reproduction pistols, rifles, cannons, Civil War swords, knives, bayonets, canteens, cap boxes, bugles & flags. Free catalog.

THE COLONIAL CONNECTION
757-229-1499 Ph & Fax
colconx@webtv.net • Eric Grosfils
226 Warehams Pt
Williamsburg VA 23185-8923
Hinchliffe 25mm & 15mm Museum Miniatures, historically accurate flags & military miniatures, painted or unpainted - imported from England. Free catalog.

CONFEDERATE ENTERPRISES
800-996-8883
Flags, jackets, bumper stickers. Keep it flying!

THE CONFEDERATE SHOPPE
205-942-8978
928 Delcris Dr • Birmingham AL 35226-1953
Books, audio & video tapes, flags, bumper stickers, auto tags; modern clothing & linens. What we don't have, we try to find.

CONFEDERATE SUPPLY CO.
PO Box 2012
Murfreesboro TN 37133-2012
Confederate flag souvenirs - bandanas, license plates. Conf. battleflag - $15 + $2.50 S&H. Catalog - $1.

THE CORPORAL'S COLOURS
106 Haig St
Celina OH 45822-2708
Confederate Commemorative Series Battleflag T-shirts. Designs based on solid research. Portion of proceeds earmarked for flag preservation. $15. Free list.

CROSSROADS COUNTRY STORE
540-433-2084
Shenandoah Heritage Farmer's Market
Route 11 S
VA
Shenandoah Valley's premier Civil War store; books, flags, music, souvenirs, crafts, gifts, jewelry. Part of the Shenandoah Heritage Farmer's Market. Open Mon-Sat 10am-6pm.

DER DIENST
PO Box 221
Lowell MI 49331-0221
Confederate officer's hat insignia, exact full-size repros - $21.50. More than 400 authentic metal & badge replicas. Catalog - $5 (free w/ order).

DIXIE DEPOT
706-265-7533 • 706-265-3952 Fax
http://www.ilinks.net/~dixiegeneral
Dixie_Depot@stc.net
John Black
PO Box 1448 • 72 Keith Evans Rd
Dawsonville GA 30534-0027
Pro-Southern educational products: video/audio tapes, new/old books, bumper stickers, flags, wearables, lapel pins, exclusive Great Seal items. More than 600 items! Catalog. (See ad page 260)

DRUMMER BOY AMERICAN MILITARIA
717-296-7611
Christian Hill Rd
RR 4 Box 7198
Milford PA 18337-9713
Civil War repro goods: uniforms, buttons, leather goods, insignia, firearms, tinware, canteens, flags, books, blankets, sabers, etc. Catalog - $1.

DUPAGE FLAG CO.
617-720-3294
ill13@aol.com
Steven W. Hill
20 Chester Ave
Dedham MA 02026-6104
Museum-quality reproductions, made from unit's originals. Silk flags, hardwood staffs, cords & tassels, finials cast from originals.

THE FLAG GUYS
914-562-0088 x307
http://www.flagguys.com
Flagguys@aol.com
283 Windsor Hwy Dept 307
New Windsor NY 12553-6909
Flags of all types & sizes. Books, Kepis, accessories, swords, cassettes, CDs, novelties. Free catalog. (See ad page 263)

FRANKLIN FLAG & BANNER
800-891-5599
Many U.S. & Confederate flags. Custom-made flags.

FRONTIER FLAGS
888-432-4324 • 307-867-2551
307-867-2523 Fax
David G. Wallace-Menard
1761 Owl Creek Rd
Thermopolis WY 82443-9119
Makers of finely replicated historical flags specializing in silk, wool or cotton. Camp colors, company flags, regimental, guidons - all eras. Free research & quotes. Museum, movie & reenactor acclaimed. Free catalog. (See ad page 268)

GIBSON'S CIVIL WAR COLLECTIBLES
423-323-2427 • 423-323-8123 Fax
Paul, Linda & Bryan Gibson
PO Box 948
Bristol TN 37621-0948
Autographs, CSA bonds & currency, diaries, flags, letter groups, newspapers, photos, slave items, uniforms, any other paper items.

GRANNIE'S ATTIC SHURT HAUS
800-827-5127 • 717-337-8704
922 Johns Ave
Gettysburg PA 17325-2901
Souvenirs, printed & embroidered T-shirts, including Gnatek color portrait shirts. Flags & accessories. 2nd shop located at 13 Steinwehr Ave., Gettysburg.

GARY HENDERSHOTT
501-224-7555
PO Box 22520 • Little Rock AR 72221-2520
Autographs, photographs, imprints, flags & memorabilia of the Civil War era. Catalog - $3.

HISTORIC SPORTSWEAR
615-754-4334
611 Oakwood Ter • Mount Juliet TN 37122
Beautiful silk necktie! Show your pride with Southern Banners, crafted with Southern pride of the finest silk. Free brochure & dealer list.

IRISH BRIGADE GIFT SHOP
504 Baltimore St
Gettysburg PA 17325-2605
T-shirts, sweatshirts, jackets, books, flags, recruiting posters, photos, pins, stationery, prints, figurines & more - all relating to the Irish Civil War service. Detailed item list - send business-size SASE.

ISI PRINTS
2821 Minot Ln
Waukesha WI 53188-4525
Limited ed. prints of Civil War battle flags, by J.B. Collins.

JKG HANDCRAFTS
PO Box 667
Glade Spring VA 24340-0667
Handmade Confederate battle flag quilts - $150-$350. Others flag quilts available - send SASE for descriptions.

LEE-GRANT, INC.
804-352-5234 • Harry A. Lillie
RR 4 Box 102 • Appomattox VA 24522-8916
Limited ed. prints. Dug & undug artifacts from in & around Appomattox, Va. Flags of all sorts.

LEXINGTON HISTORICAL SHOP
540-463-2615 • Bob Lurate
PO Box 1428 • Lexington VA 24450-1428
Civil War memorabilia. Buy/sell books, relics, flags, currency, ephemera. Appraisals. Visit shop Mon-Sat 10-6, College Square Shopping Center, Route 11N, Lexington, Va.

JOSEPH L. MARTIN
1125 Kennesaw Springs Ct
Kennesaw GA 30144
Buying, selling, trading fine Civil War swords, guns, uniforms, flags, etc. Over 35 yrs of experience in dealing military items. Competent appraisals available.

THE MILITARY COLLECTION
PO Box 830970M
Miami FL 33283-0970
Helmets, uniforms, field gear, awards, medals, flags, weapons, swords, photos, etc. Cat. $8.

MUSEUM OF AMERICAN CAVALRY
540-740-3959
Peter & Jane Comtois
298 Old Cross Rd • New Market VA 22844
History of the Horse Soldier from colonial times through Vietnam & modern times. Gift shop with books, flags, weapons, relics, other items. Formerly Indian Hollow Antiques.

NESHANIC DEPOT
610-847-5627
610-847-8618 Fax
283 Durham Rd
PO Box 367
Ottsville PA 18942-0367
Historic artifacts, muzzleloading guns & supplies, originals, reproductions, & historic flags.

OLDE SOUTH, LTD.
T. R. Meetze
PO Box 11302
Columbia SC 29211-1302
Classic check design - Confederate flag background. Send void check & deposit slip with $13.95 (incl. S&H) for 200. Script lettering & personal message available.

PIEDMONT FLAG COMPANY
800-467-0082
704-466-3765 Fax
PO Box 685
Maiden NC 28650-0685
Standards & colors of the USA & CSA. 100% sewn cotton custom historical flags.

PYRAMID AMERICA
901-452-1323
800-737-1323
Quality USA, Texas or Confederate flags & flag apparel. Jackets, shorts, T-shirts, bandanas, backpacks, knives, framed/unframed prints, more. Call for more info.

RBM ENTERPRISES
502-893-5057
PO Box 6374, Dept A
Louisville KY 40206-0374
Updated version of our classic necktie. Confederate battle flags with red stripes on navy or gray background - $18.50.

REGIMENTAL FLAG & BANNER
919-496-2888 • 919-496-7720 Fax
rebelflags@aol.com
1909 Seven Paths Rd
Louisburg NC 27549-7015
Flags - historical to modern. Civil War theme shirts, caps. Free catalog.

RICHMOND ARSENAL
804-272-4570 Ph & Fax
7605 Midlothian Tpke
Richmond VA 23235-5223
100% authentic Civil War antiques, from common bullets & buttons to museum quality weapons, accoutrements, uniforms, drums & flags. Photo-illus. catalog - $10 for 3 issues.

RUFFIN FLAG COMPANY
706-456-2111 • 706-456-2112 Fax
http://www.mindspring.com/~micromgt/ruffin.htm
241 Alexander St NW
Crawfordville GA 30631-2804
Auto tags, bumper stickers, books, T-shirts, crew sweatshirts, polo shirts, regulation battle flags, etc. Jeff Davis, Dixie's Pride, N.B. Forrest, etc. Retail/wholesale. Catalog - $1.

SHARON & JEFF'S WORKSHOP
914-735-2418 Ph & Fax
Jeff Rodriguez
205 Cardean Pl • Pearl River NY 10965-1828
Museum-quality, custom-made flags at reasonable prices.

SHARPSBURG ARSENAL
301-432-7700 • 301-432-7440 Fax
101 W Main St • PO Box 568
Sharpsburg MD 21782-0568
Purveyors of fine Civil War militaria; firearms, edged weapons, buttons, bullets, leather accoutrements, battlefield relics, books, flags, personal & camp items, paper, letters, framed prints. Buy/sell. (See ad page 264)

SOUTHERN HERITAGE PRINTS
256-539-3358
George Mahoney, Jr.
PO Box 503 • Huntsville AL 35804-0503
Civil War flags, memo pads, envelopes, bookmarks, paperweights, chronology chart/map, prints. *Last Charge at Brandy Station*, ltd. ed. print by C.E. Monroe, Jr. - $135 inc. S&H. Portion of proceeds goes to APCWS.

STRATFORD'S NOVELTY, LTD
843-797-8040
Kent Stratford
PO Box 1860 • Goose Creek SC 29445-1860
Civil War-related novelties & gifts. Confederate flag imprinted products & merchandise. Large selection. Bumper stickers. Free list & pricing.

TARA HALL, INC.
800-205-0069
212-802-6423 Fax
http://www.fighting69th.com
tarahall@earthlink.net
Vic Olney
PO Box 2069 • Beach Haven NJ 08008-0109
Meagher's Irish Brigade, Fighting 69th, Corcoran's Irish Legion memorabilia, shirts, jackets, hats, sweaters, steins, pins, flags, books, miniatures, poster, belt buckles, NINAs, etc. Free catalog. (See ad page 272)

UNITED STATES FLAG SERVICE
800-USA-FLAG
5741 Elmer Derr Rd
Frederick MD 21703-7411
Largest historic collection of repros in the nation. All kinds & types, USA & CSA unit regiments, state & foreign country flags. Made in USA. List - $3.

USA HISTORY STORE
508-947-8866
http://www.usahistorystore.com
PO Box 109
Middleboro MA 02346-0109
Authentic brass camp candlesticks perfect for 19th-century impression. Set of 2 - $13.95 + $3 S&H. Books, games, flags & period clothing.

VILLAGE SURPLUS
PO Box 530931
Mountain Brook AL 35253-0931
Confederate flag magnets - $5 ppd.

BASKET TREATS
2316 Delaware # 177
Buffalo NY 14216-2606
Civil War cards & American History decks. $9.95 ea. ppd. Set - $17.76.

CHATHAM HILL GAMES, INC.
518-392-5022 • 518-392-3121 Fax
http://www.regionnet.com/colberk/chgames.html
CHGames@taconic.net • Ray Toelke
PO Box 253 • Chatham NY 12037-0253
"Gettysburg, The Battlefield Game." Board game, in full color, incorporating many events, detailed descriptions, questions & answers of the 3-day battle - $24.95.

COLUMBIA GAMES, INC.
800-636-3631
http://www.columbiagames.com/
questions@columbiagames.com
PO Box 3457 • Blaine WA 98231-3457
"Dixie" - a tactical CW card game consisting of collectible cards - $7.95/deck of 60 random cards. 1 for each regiment, battery & brigade officer at Bull Run, Shiloh, Gettysburg. Free catalog.

R. P. DARRAH
5954 Coca Cola Blvd
Columbus GA 31909-5531
Civil War board games, master tactician level, & kits. From $12 up. Write for details.

DEER VALLEY GAME CO.
http://www.getnet.com/~dvgc
PO Box 31661 • Mesa AZ 85275-1661
Squares - Civil War battle game of maneuvers & attack - $24.95 + $3.50 S&H.

EDUCATIONAL MATERIALS ASSOCIATES, INC.
804-293-GAME
PO Box 7385 • Charlottesville VA 22906-7395
Civil War game with FREE poster - $14.95 ppd! From Civil War Heartland...America's #1 "family-type" map games & national best-sellers. Ages 8-adult. Dealers welcome. Free catalog. (See ad page 265)

HAFPAN PRODUCTIONS
518-346-3563
EDLE31A@prodigy.com
PO Box 9274
Niskayuna NY 12309-0274
Best selection of board & computer wargames. Free catalog.

HISTORICAL STUDIES GROUP
612-774-9405
1235 Reaney Ave
Saint Paul MN 55106-4011
Series of regimental-level Civil War board & computer games. Accurate, realistic, detailed. Each includes 2 major battles, 2 learning scenarios & a 24-pp. historical analysis.

HUDSON'S HOBBY GAMES
817-461-0126
HudsonGame@aol.com
PO Box 121503
Arlington TX 76012-1503
Civil War board games & computer software. Free catalogs.

INTERACTIVE MAGIC
888-646-2442 (N. America)
919-461-0722
http://www.imagicgames.com
"American Civil War: From Sumter to Appomattox" - Strategy game on 2 CDs. Face the challenge of refighting & rethinking the war. Bonus Historical Tapes CD.

THE JOHNNY REB GAME COMPANY
http://www.erinet.com/bp/johnreb.html
HillJhn@aol.com
7599 Chrisland Cove
Falls Church VA 22042-7558
"Johnny Reb" is 64-page set of tactical wargame rules that enable the refighting of Civil War battles with miniature soldiers of any size.

K & P WEAVER
kpweaver@aol.com
Ken & Paula Weaver
PO Box 1131, Dept J
Orange CT 06477-7131
Historically accurate repro men's clothing for military or civilian impression. Custom-made with handsewn buttonholes. Quality accessories; cherry dominoes, checkers with canvas board. Early leather baseballs, bats, uniforms & books. Catalog with swatches - $1.

MABELS CARD SHOP
203-698-0029
http://www.mabels.com
mabels@futuris.net
PO Box 331
Old Greenwich CT 06870-0331
Play Cards with History. Outstanding selection of Civil War & American History playing cards. Catalog.

P.S.I.
909-652-2568 • 909-652-0497
PO Box 568 • Winchester CA 92596-0568
"The Campaign of '63 Begins." Join this sophisticated, multi-player, play-by-mail simulation of the Gettysburg campaign. Call/write for info.

SLIDE-A-FACT
PO Box 66085
Saint Petersburg FL 33736-6085
101 Civil War battles & facts listed in chronological order in a "slide-rule" format. Informative & fun. $6.95 ppd.

SPEERIT STRATEGY GAMES
800-831-1155 • 704-849-7777 Ph & Fax
10612 Providence Rd # 325
Charlotte NC 28277-0233
"Gettysburg: Three Days in July" - turning point of the war is in your hands. $44.95 ppd.

STARMASTER
http://www.iboutique.com/starmaster/index.html
2500 Laurelhill Ln • Fort Worth TX 76133
Playing cards featuring Civil War generals, battles, armaments & trivia. 3 decks - $18. Free catalog.

STRATAMAX, INC.
6238 Raintree Ln
Oaklandon IN 46236-2933
Rebs & Yanks, 2-player Civil War card game - $18 + $2 S&H.

STRATEGIC SIMULATIONS, INC.
800-601-PLAY
Wargame Construction Set III: Age of Rifles, 1846-1905, PC-DOS CD-ROM. Includes 3 Civil War campaigns, 25 CW scenarios. Available in retail stores.

STUEMPFLE'S MILITARY MINIATURES
717-762-0825
13190 Scott Rd • Waynesboro PA 17268
Over 200 resin kits, bunkers & conversions in 1/7s & 1/76. Leva, B P Cast, Crusader, Revell, 54mm kits, war games, etc. Catalog - $3.

TALONSOFT
410-933-9191 • 800-211-6504 Orders only
http://www.talonsoft.com
Talonsoft1@aol.com
75162.373@compuserve.com
PO Box 632 • Forest Hill MD 21050-0632
"Battleground 7: Bull Run" - CD-ROM computer game for Windows. Play head-to-head via modem, e-mail or internet. Also in the Battleground series: Antietam, Gettysburg, Shiloh.

TARGET AUCTIONS
816-965-0013 Orders
http://www.usbusiness.com/target/us.htm
PO Box 17841 • Kansas City MO 64134-0141
"Tattered Flags" - the most fun you'll ever have fighting the Civil War! Original game for the PC, $14.95 + $3 S&H. Other Civil War games, stamps.

TOMAHAWK GAMES
330-539-6413
bu958@yfn.ysu.edu • Jim Schmalzried
720 Churchill Rd • Girard OH 44420-2121
"Civil War Command," more than 1,200 multiple-choice trivia questions. 52-photo ID page, pawns, flags, objectives. Ideal for families & teachers. $25 check or MO. 10-day guarantee.

TRI-J COMMUNICATIONS
PO Box 542227
Houston TX 77254-2227
Recreate famous battles with the "Phantasy Civil War Alliance." Play General & make battle plans in play-by-mail action. Win medals & other prizes. $5 for rules & free challenge.

U.S. GAMES SYSTEMS, INC.
203-353-8400 • 203-353-8431 Fax
USGames@aol.com • Lee Stockwell
179 Ludlow St • Stamford CT 06902-6900
Heavily illustrated, informative & entertaining CW playing cards & card games. Facsimile decks of cards originally published in the 1860s. Award-winning Civil War series. Catalog - $2. (See ad page 264)

USA HISTORY STORE
508-947-8866
http://www.usahistorystore.com
PO Box 109 • Middleboro MA 02346-0109
Authentic brass camp candlesticks perfect for 19th-century impression. Set of 2 - $13.95 + $3 S&H. Books, games, flags, period clothing.

WINSOME GAMES
412-244-0599
412-486-3157 Fax
http://fyi.net/~winsome
winsome@fyi.net
515 W Hutchinson Ave Ste 6
Pittsburgh PA 15218-1347
Damn the Torpedoes, Civil War card game based on naval battles, 114-card deck - $25 + $5 S&H. Free catalog.

HUDSON ALEXANDER
911 Velma Ln
Murfreesboro TN 37129-2367
Will research your soldier/unit from Tennessee.

BARNETTE'S FAMILY TREE BOOK CO.
barnette@neosoft.com • Mic Barnette
1001 North Loop W
Houston TX 77008-1766
Guide to tracing your Civil War ancestors - $12.50. Catalog - $1.

BATTLEFIELDS REVISITED
BattRev@aol.com • Patricia Watt
PO Box 231
New Cumberland PA 17070-0231
Research Civil War soldiers, sailors - all nationalities. Reports, records, histories.

BLOUNT COUNTY GENEALOGICAL & HISTORICAL SOCIETY
ATTN: TC
PO Box 4986
Maryville TN 37802-4986
Loyal Mountain Troopers: The 2nd and 3rd Tenn. Vol. Cavalry in the Civil War. Details these largely ignored Southerners who served the Union. $32.50 ppd.

BOYD PUBLISHING CO.
800-452-4035
912-452-4020 after 6pm EST
tignall@accucomm.net
PO Box 367
Milledgeville GA 31061-0367
100s of new historical publications & genealogical references. Computer software, incl. *Official Record of the War of the Rebellion* - all 127 vols. on CD-ROM, $89.95 + $5 S&H.

BRODERBUND
39500 Stevenson Pl Ste 204
Fremont CA 94539-3103
Family Tree Maker CD-Rom - solid starting point for genealogical research. PC compatible with Windows programs, 386 or higher, 4MB RAM (8MB recommended).

BROWN PUBLICATIONS
BrianB1578@aol.com
PO Box 25501 • Little Rock AR 72221-5501
In the Footsteps of the Blue & Gray - $24.95 + $2 S&H. Describes CW-related research sources in state archives, National Archives & LDS collection. History of ea. corps & hard-to-find technical information.

THE CIVIL WAR GARRISON
PO Box 1681
Springfield IL 62705-1681
Will research the veteran you designate & write his personal story in the War Between the States, or produce a Civil War plaque of his experiences.

CIVIL WAR RESEARCH
219-483-0640
PO Box 8355
Fort Wayne IN 46898-8355
Will research your Civil War soldier through the official records. Provides brief report & extracts from the official records - $34.95.

THE DIXIE PRESS
615-831-0776 Ph & Fax
PO Box 110783
Nashville TN 37222-0783
Publisher, wholesaler & retailer of Southern books & genealogy products. Free catalog.

JOHN EMOND
PO Box 44625
Washington DC 20026-4625
Will research military & pension records at National Archives. Reasonable fees - no charge until found.

FRONTIER PRESS
409-740-7988
409-740-0138 Fax
http://www.doit.com/frontier
kgfrontier@aol.com
Karen M. Green
PO Box 3715
Galveston TX 77552-0715
Bookstore specializing in historical & genealogical titles, incl. collection of nearly 350 books specifically dealing with the Civil War. Free catalog.

GENEALOGICAL PUBLISHING CO.
800-296-6687
1001 N Calvert St
Baltimore MD 21202-3897
Publishers of the *Index to the Roll of Honor*, an incredible guide to the 228,639 Union dead listed in the *Roll*'s 27 vols. 1164 pp. $75. On CD-ROM, incl. entire Roll of Honor - $49.99. Free catalog.

E. GREISSER
771D E Main St • Bridgewater NJ 08807-3339
Civil War soldiers from Philadelphia & New Jersey. Pension, family & church records when available.

THE HANDLEY LIBRARY ARCHIVES
540-662-9041 x22
PO Box 58 • Winchester VA 22604-0058
Contain numerous historical documents & personal records.

HAUK DATA SERVICES
1885 Arrowhead Trl
Huntington IN 46750-1382
"The Virginia Ancestor Series," indexed reports on the descendants of prominent Virginia families. Many with Civil War participants: Lee, Taylor, etc. Brochure - legal-size SASE.

HEARTHSTONE BOOKSHOP
703-960-0086
888-960-3300 Orders
703-960-0087 Fax
http://www.hearthstonebooks.com
info@hearthstonebooks.com
Stuart Nixon
5735A Telegraph Rd
Alexandria VA 22303-1205
Genealogical books, software, CDs & supplies, including listings on Civil War history & research. Catalog - $2 (ref.).

HEIRLINES
800-570-4049
James W. Petty, Genealogist
PO Box 893
Salt Lake City UT 84110-0893
Will help you find your ancestors & begin learning about your genealogy. Search censuses, church, court, & land records, military files, etc., in America & other countries.

HERITAGE BOOKS, INC.
800-398-7709
301-390-7709
http://www.heritagebooks.com
1540 Pointer Ridge Pl Ste E
Bowie MD 20716-1800
Books on history, Americana, Civil War, & genealogy. Free catalog.

HIGGINSON BOOK COMPANY
508-745-7170
508-745-8025 Fax
higginsn@cove.com
148 Washington St
PO Box 778
Salem MA 01970-0778
Reprinters of regimental histories, American genealogies & local histories. Thousands of titles by mail or in our bookstore. Catalog - $4 (ref.).

INSTITUTE FOR CIVIL WAR RESEARCH
ICWRJohn@aol.com
7913 67th Dr
Middle Village NY 11379-2908
Histories of more than 7,500 Civil War units, Union & Confederate. Organizational data, engagement lists, maps, etc. $15/unit. Other services.

TED JONES, CIVIL WAR VETERANS
tedjones@epix.net
RR 1 Box 1317
Little Meadows PA 18830-9730
Let me find your CW ancestors. Write for info.

LOTZ HOUSE WAR BETWEEN THE STATES MUSEUM
615-791-6533
http://www.phoenix.w1.com/lotz
Lotzrebel@aol.com
Ronny Mangrum, Dir.
1111 Columbia Ave • Franklin TN 37064-3616
Area's most comprehensive Civil War collection. Tours of Lotz House, which was used as hospital after Battle of Franklin; genealogy services.

MARY LOU PRODUCTIONS
800-774-8511
PO Box 17233 • Minneapolis MN 55417-0233
"Gift of Heritage" - how-to video showing you the process of creating your own family documentary, including tips on researching, organizing, & combining info. - $32.95. Call for more info.

JAMES MEJDRICH
630-668-0384
128 N Knollwood Dr
Wheaton IL 60187-4731
Will check the register of Confederate graves in Mississippi for $1/name & SASE.

MELTINGPOINT
716-875-8158
220 Delaware Ave Ste 204
Buffalo NY 14202-2107
Family crests & shields. Authentic, researched, hand-crafted jewelry & gift items relating to your family surname. Free brochure.

MERTIN RESEARCH SERVICES
888-248-7166
PO Box 1323 • Summit NJ 07902-1323
Experienced genealogist will research Civil War ancestors. Pensions, service records, Union or Confederate.

NATIONAL GENEALOGICAL SOCIETY
703-525-0050 Office
703-841-9065 Library
703-525-0052 Fax
http://www.genealogy.org/~ngs
ngslibe@wizard.net OR 76702.2417@compuserve.com
4527 17th St N
Arlington VA 22207-2399

OLD FAVORITES BOOKSHOP
3055 Lauderdale Dr
Richmond VA 23233-7800
Civil War, WWII, other military books, prints & maps. Free catalog on request.

PHOTOGRAPHY OF YESTERYEAR
423-510-9306
cwphotogpr@aol.com
Frank or Rita Harned
1 Prior Dr
Chattanooga TN 37421-2168
Photograph birthplaces, churches, cemeteries, landmarks. Photograph CW battlefields of approximate location of your ancestor's unit. Limited unit research available for TN, GA, KY.

PONDER BOOKS
Janice Ponder
PO Box 792 • Mason TX 76856-0792
Publisher of books on Civil War, history & genealogy. Trans-Mississippi region. Free booklistAugust 18, 1997.

H. J. POPOWSKI
614-276-4993 • 614-274-4110 Fax
PBFV68A@prodigy.com
158 N Chase Ave
Columbus OH 43204-2603
Capsule histories of any US Army unit, 1861-1865. Volunteers, regulars & USCT. Plus sources. $10 ea.

CLAUDE V. REICH, PhD
1516 N 14th St
Reading PA 19604-1850
Open-ended database of more than 35,000 Pa. Volunteers at the Battle of Gettysburg.

THE REPRINT COMPANY, PUBLISHERS
PO Box 5401
Spartanburg SC 29304-5401
4-volume set contains alphabetical roll of 90,000 Louisiana Confederate army members. In-depth, many vital statistics. Call/write.

S. SCHUMACHER
425-259-1641
103505.1733@compuserve.com
4027 Rucker Ave Ste 747
Everett WA 98201-4839
CW pension & bountyland packets researched - $20/name. Send name, state mustered in, wife's name, & regiment (if known). Union soldier's burial place researched; 200,000+ names - $10/name. Send details & SASE.

THE SOUTHERN ARMY ALBUM!
John Mills Bigham
4833 Arcadia Rd
Columbia SC 29206-1307
Christopher Memminger's homeplace. 4 families share Confederate oral histories & images. Military headstones 1776+ recorded in 3 antebellum churchyards. Lasting regional 1992 video production. $21.95.

SOUTHERN LION BOOKS, INC.
770-963-6776
solionbook@aol.com
J. H. Segars
PO Box 347163
Atlanta GA 30334-7163
Fine books about Southern history, 1861-1865. *In Search of Confederate Ancestors: The Guide*. Critically acclaimed by SCV & UDC. 112 pp., illus. - $10 + $1.50 S&H.

STATE HISTORICAL SOCIETY OF MISSOURI
573-882-7083
1020 Lowry St
Missiouri University
Columbia MO 65201
Research libraries; historical & genealogical materials.

GEOFF WALDEN
35197 23 Mile Rd # 4
New Baltimore MI 48047-3639
Will research your ancestor who served with the Kentucky Infantry or Artillery for $3/name. Capsule unit histories for $8/regt. or battery.

JAMES & KAREN WARD
9906 Warson Ct
Richmond VA 23237-3908
Virginia Confederates. Photocopies of your ancestors' military records from the Virginia State Archives. Send soldier's name, county or brigade & $40.

19TH ALABAMA INFANTRY REGT., ARMY OF TENN.
http://fly.hiwaay.net/~dsmart/index.html
Reenactment organization. Website provides many links to pages of related topics.

2ND MARYLAND INFANTRY, CO. A, CSA
http://www.sutler.com/2ndMD/2ndMD.htm

AMAZON.COM BOOKS
http://www.amazon.com
Order from a list of more than a million titles, including all of Rockbridge Publishing's fine Civil War titles.

AMERICAN BATTLEFIELD PROTECTION PROGRAM
http://www2.cr.nps.gov/abpp/abpp_t.html
U.S. government's leading battlefield preservation program.

THE AMERICAN CIVIL WAR
http://mirkwood.ucs.indiana.edu/acw
Links to sites with many Civil War topics.

AMERICAN CIVIL WAR
http://pages.prodigy.com/NJ/schwalbe/schwalbe.html
Limited battlefield travelogue, links to national groups.

AMERICAN CIVIL WAR HOMEPAGE
http://sunsit.utk.edu/civil-war
User-friendly general index to Civil War websites.

THE AMERICAN CIVIL WAR INFORMATION ARCHIVE
http://www.access.digex.net/~bdboyle/cw.html
Index to general-interest Civil War sites.

AMERICAN FLAG & GIFT
http://www.anyflag.com
flags@anyflag.com
Discount prices on quality American-made flags, banners & flagpoles, too!

ANCIENT AMERICAN ART
http://www.pointsouth.com/aaa.htm
aaart@dixie-net.com
Handmade reproductions of battle & regimental flags of the Civil War. T-shirts $20. Prints $25. Wholesale discounts.

ANTIETAM BATTLEFIELD INFO.
http://www.antietam.com
Sponsored by APCWS; info. on Antietam, including archives.

ANTIQUE FIREARMS
http://www.antiqueguns.com
robles@best.com
Buy/sell/trade antique firearms, swords & collectibles. Info. on weapons & gun shows designed for serious collectors.

ANTIQUE MILITARIA & COLLECTORS NETWORK
http://www.collectorsnet.com/index.html
Provides links to services, periodicals, dealers, & events.

ASSOCIATION FOR THE PRESERVATION OF CIVIL WAR SITES
http://www.apcws.com
Not-for-profit membership organization that preserves Civil War sites for educational & recreational uses. Website: organizational news & membership info.

BARRY'D TREASURE
http://www.iglou.com/btreasure
Civil War accoutrements, books, bullets, cartridges, dug items, other relics & artifacts. Extensive, illustrated catalog.

BATTLE OF GETTYSBURG HOMEPAGE
http://www.mindspring.com/~murphy11/getty
Strives to be the most comprehensive & professional study of the battle of Gettysburg.

BATTLE SUMMARIES
http://www2.cr.nps.gov/abpp/battles/tvii.htm
Maintained by the Civil War Sites Advisory Committee of the ABPP.

THE BLUE & GRAY TRAIL
http://ngeorgia.com/travel/bgtrail.html
Civil War sites & stories from North Georgia & Chattanooga.

BUFFALO SOLDIERS ON THE WESTERN FRONTIER
http://www.imh.org/imh/exh1.html
Exhibit of the famed African-American soldiers.

CAMP CHASE GAZETTE
http://nemesis.cybergate.net/~civilwar/index.html
Peruse a sample of this publication devoted to the coverage of Civil War reenacting.

CENSUS BUREAU
http://www.census.gov
U.S. census information.

CIVIL WAR @ CHARLESTON
http://www.awod.com/gallery/probono/cwchas/
Guide to events, local CWRT, other resources in attempt to preserve history & heritage of the Civil War in & around Charleston, S.C.

CIVIL WAR ARTILLERY
http://cwartillery.org/artillery.html
Basic info. & suggestons for further viewing & reading about artillery in the Civil War; focus on field artillery.

CIVIL WAR ARTILLERY HOMEPAGE
http://www.geocities.com/Athens/1862
Includes glossary, tables, bibliography relating to Civil War artillery.

CIVIL WAR BOOK DISCUSSION GROUP
JPHA1982@aol.com (for more info.)
Discuss Civil War books with other AOL members, every other Wed., 8 PM EST. Keyword - CAFE BOOKA; held in Salon #2.

CIVIL WAR BOOKS ONLINE
http://members.aol.com/bookkritik/civilwar.html
Selection of the finest in Civil War publishing; features new & recent titles as well as the classics.

CIVIL WAR CIRCUIT
http://members.tripod.com/~Chubbles/circuit/cwc.html
Webring of Civil War sites.

CIVIL WAR COMMEMORATIVE COINS
kaykay@injersey.com
1995 Civil War Battlefield Commemorative Coins - Proof Silver Dollars. Designer of obervse - Troiani; reverse - Mercanti. Limited number with certificate of authenticity - $32 ppd.

THE CIVIL WAR HOMEPAGE
http://www.civil-war.net
Links to Civil War pages on the internet; calendar of events.

CIVIL WAR LESSON PLAN
http://www.smplanet.com/civilwar/civilwar.html
Teaches upper elementary school students the central issues of the Civil War.

CIVIL WAR LIST
http://www.public.usit.net/mruddy
Table of Civil War links & information.

CIVIL WAR MALL
http://www.CivilWarMall.com
Online shopping mall for Civil War enthusiasts. Space available to Civil War retailers.

CIVIL WAR MASTER LINKS & RESOURCES COLLECTION
http://www.autonomy.com/civilwar.htm
Alphabetical listing of Civil War sites on the web.

CIVIL WAR READER
http://www.civilwarreader.com
"Home for those with a passion for Civil War literature." Thomas Publications.

CIVIL WAR ROUND TABLE OF GREATER BOSTON
http://k12.oit.umass.edu/masag/1092o.html
Monthly meetings on the last Friday of each month. Field trips. 37th year.

CIVIL WAR VIRTUAL ARCHIVE RING
http://www.geocities.com/Athens/Forum/1867/cwring.html
Ring of websites with primary reference material. "Virtual library" designed for researchers.

CIVIL WAR WOMEN
http://scriptorium.lib.duke.edu/collections/civil-war-women.html
Manuscript sources in the Special Collections Library at Duke University.

CONFEDERATE CIPHER WHEEL
http://members.aol.com/ubchi2/cipher.htm
Picture & history of cipher wheel used by the South during the Civil War.

THE CONFEDERATE NETWORK
http://www.confederate.net
Links to several sites of Southern interest, including reenactments & merchants.

CONFEDERATE PENSION RECORDS (TEXAS)
http://link.tsl.state.tx.us/c/compt/pension.html
Search of more than 54,000 pension records in Texas State Archives, providing name, pension number & county.

THE CONFEDERATE TREASURY
http://www.ConfederateTreasury.com
Confederate States Currency 1861-1865. Complete 70-note, full-color set of currency issued by Confederate government. Exact in detail, protected in album. $139.95.

COWLES HISTORY GROUP
http://www.thehistorynet.com
Cross-referenced index of more than 3,000 entries, through 1000s of years of battle. Every subject addressed in *Military History* magazine - $24.95.

CROSSROADS OF THE CIVIL WAR
http://www.civilwarsites.com
APCWS-sponsored. Describes Civil War attractions in & around Washington County, MD. Day-by-day accounts of battles of Antietam & Gettysburg.

CSA CURRENCY PAGE
http://www.CSAcurrency.com
Homepages providing info. on authentic Confederate currency, bonds, coins, & stamps.

CSA NET
http://www.pointsouth.com
Southern heritage page with directory for each of its several topics.

DAUGHTERS OF UNION VETERANS OF THE CIVIL WAR
http://suvcw.org/duv.htm
DUVCW@aol.com
Organization for female lineal descendants of Union veterans.

DIXIE MART
http://www.pointsouth.com
The Virtual Southern Mall. Links with various merchants & services of interest to Southerners.

DIXIELAND RING
http://www.geocities.com/BourbonStreet/2757/index.html
Webring designed to bring Confederate sites together.

DIXIENET
http://www.dixienet.org
Official national web site of the Southern League. Several links with other sites. Application to join can be downloaded.

E-MAIL AMERICAN CIVIL WAR
http://www.blarg.net/~dhhill/Research.html
Links to Civil War research & resource sites.

FRANKLIN COUNTY, PA, IN THE CIVIL WAR
http://www.pa.net/franklin/warcount.htm
Civil War activities in the county by area: Chambersburg, Greencastle, Mercersburg, Waynesboro.

FREDERICKSBURG & SPOTSYLVANIA NMP
http://www.nps.gov/frsp/frspweb.htm
Visit the largest military park in the world without leaving home.

GAULEY RIVER BOOK COMPANY
http://www.cais.com/gauley/index.html
gauley@cais.com
Turn Them out to Die Like a Mule, by J.M. Priest. *Mosby's Confederacy*, *War Stories*, etc. INTERNET - check our website for listings of other books.

GENERAL OFFICERS OF THE CIVIL WAR
http://people.delphi.com/yatsuo/go_main.htm
Picture gallery of Union & Confederate generals.

GETTYSBURG DISCUSSION GROUP
http://www.arthes.com/gdg/
Discussion group focusing on Battle of Gettysburg - scholarly & informative.

GETTYSBURG GUIDE
http://www.GettysburgGuide.com
Unofficial guide & index to anything & everything relating to Gettysburg.

GODEY'S LADY'S BOOK
http://www.uvm.edu/~hag/godey/
Portions of & commentary on this most famous 19th-century women's magazine.

GRAND ARMY OF THE POTOMAC
http://pages.prodigy.com/CGBD86A/garhp.htm
Homepage of the GAR - CW vets org.

U.S.GRANT NETWORK
http://www.saints.css.edu/mkelsey/gppg.html
usglady@excel.net
Organization commemorating Gen. Grant. Join us to learn more about this often misunderstood Civil War hero. Website: articles, images, & other links associated with Ulysses S. Grant.

H-BAR ENTERPRISES
http://www.hbar.com • hbar@oakman.tds.net
Official Records - every word indexed, both reports & correspondence included. Custom CDs available - choose your books. Create own computer databases, add personal notes.

H-NET CIVWAR
http://h-net2.msu.edu/~civwar
Online discussion list concerning Civil War-era culture & history. Book reviews, links.

HERITAGE PRESERVATION ASSOCIATION
http://www.hpa.org
HPA@america.net
National non-profit organization protects & preserves history, symbols & culture of the American South. Reg. membership - $40.

HISTORIC CARLISLE BARRACKS
http://carlisle-www.army.mil/usamhi
Traces 200-yr. history of one of our nation's oldest military garrisons.

HISTORY BUFF'S HOMEPAGE
http://www.historybuff.com/index.html
Devoted to newspaper press coverage of events in U.S. history, incl. the Civil War era.

THE HISTORY CHANNEL
http://www.historychannel.com/index2.html
Homepage & index of A&E's cable History Channel.

THE HISTORY PLACE
http://www.historyplace.com/civilwar/index.html
Timeline of major Civil War events; photos of major players in the war.

THE HORSE'S MOUTH HISTORICAL CLOTHIER
http://home.pacbell.net/costumes
costumes@pacbell.net
Uniforms, living history, period wedding attire. Custom-made to your specifications. 45 yrs. of professional experience in design, tailoring & pattern drafting.

HOUSTON CIVIL WAR ROUND TABLE
http://members.aol.com/Houstcwrt/index.html
reyork@ibm.net
Website: information, programs & schedule of events.

HOWITZERS ONLINE
http://www.novagate.net/~howitzers
Designed to educate & entertain those wishing to learn more about the 2nd Richmond Howitzers. Includes "research center."

ILLINOIS IN THE CIVIL WAR
http://www.outfitters.com/illinois/history/civil
Histories of Illinois companies; general history relating to Illinois' role in the war.

IMAGES OF BATTLE
http://ils.unc.edu/civilwar/civilwar.html
Selected letters of soldiers on both sides of the conflict; from the Southern Historical Collection.

INDIANA IN THE CIVIL WAR
http://www.thnet.com/~liggetkw/incw/cw.htm
Details the Hoosier State's contribution to the war effort.

INTERNET CIVIL WAR EXPO
http://www.bmark.com/cw.show
World's 1st Civil War Expo on the Internet, 24 hrs./day, 365 days/yr. Many major dealers. One month ads available for your extra relics, books, & other items.

JEWS IN THE CIVIL WAR
http://www.geocities.com/Athens/Forum/1867/jewish.htm
Articles & letters from & about Jewish Civil War participants, both Yankee & Rebel. Includes link to genealogy database.

KENNESAW CIVIL WAR MUSEUM
http://www.ngeorgia.com/history/kcwm.html
Authentic cotton gin; home of "The General," famous Civil War locomotive. Website: Directions & contact info.; brief history of "the General."

THE LADIES' PARLOR
http://www.nemr.net/~lparlor/
lparlor@nemr.net
Ladies' clothing & accessories. Best source for HAIR. Available for workshops. 1863 on-line *Petersons* magazine.

LIBRARY OF CONGRESS PHOTO COLLECTION
http://rs6.loc.gov/cwphome.html
Selected Civil War photos.

ABRAHAM LINCOLN ONLINE
http://www.netins.net/showcase/creative/lincoln.html
Anything & everything Lincoln, including website links, books & other resources.

THE MARKS COLLECTION
http://www.markscollection.com
Resurrection Morn - ltd. ed. 1250 - $95. *Honor in Darkest Hour* - ltd. ed. 2000 - $95.

MILES OF HISTORY (CIVIL WAR AUCTION)
http://www.collectorsnet.com/miles
huskey@usit.net
Buy/sell/trade Civil War items. Images, buttons, weapons, documents, personal items, & authentic period jewelry available through internet auction on website.

THE MUSEUM OF THE CONFEDERACY
http://www.moc.org/
Maintains most comprehensive collection of military, political & domestic artifacts & art associated with the Confederacy. Adjacent to White House of the Confederacy, restored to its CW appearance.

NATIONAL GENEALOGICAL SOCIETY
http://www.genealogy.org/~ngs
ngslibe@wizard.net OR
76702.2417@compuserve.com

NATIONAL PARKS & CONSERVATION ASSN.
http://npca.org/
Provides info. regarding this non-profit organization & its dedication to preserving national parks.

NATIONAL REGISTER OF HISTORIC PLACES (NPS)
http://www.cr.nps.gov/nr/nrhome.html
Info. on how to nominate property to the National Register & benefits of registration. Lists currently registered historic properties.

NATIONAL TRUST FOR HISTORIC PRESERVATION
http://www.nthp.org
Non-profit organization committed to preserving the heritage & livability of America's communities. Operates historic house museums, publishes monthly magazine & newsletter. Memberships welcome.

NAVAL HISTORICAL CENTER
http://www.history.navy.mil
Mission statement: "To enhance the Navy's effectiveness by preserving, analyzing & interpreting its hard-earned experience & history..."

OHIO IN THE CIVIL WAR
http://www.infinet.com/~lstevens/a/civil.html
Info. & sources on units, prison camps, war stories, round tables, etc.

PALMETTO PRESENCE
http://www.21mall.com/ppresence.htm
jarnett@seescape.net
Confederate relics, ephemera.

PAMPLIN PARK: NATL. MUSEUM OF THE CIVIL WAR SOLDIER
http://www.pamplinpark.org
pamplinpark@mindspring.com
Site of 1865 battle - preserved fortifications, walking trails, guided tours, living history, gift shop, restaurant. New high-tech museum (May 1999) focuses on common soldier. Website features museum gift shop.

PAPERS OF JEFFERSON DAVIS
http://www.ruf.rice.edu/~pjdavis
Complete edition of Davis' works & papers.

JOHN PELHAM HISTORICAL ASSOCIATION, INC.
http://members.aol.com/JPHA1982
JPHA1982@aol.com
Bi-monthly newsletter, "The Cannoneer." Annual convention & tour of Fredericksburg; commemorative ceremony at Kelly's Ford. Supports preservation; active in erecting monuments. Archives located at Jacksonville Public Library, Jacksonville, Ala.

POETRY & MUSIC OF THE CIVIL WAR
http://www.erols.com/kfraser/
Lyrics to poems & music of the Civil War, both Union & Confederate.

REENACTOR RING
http://www.geocities.com/soho/6546/ring.html
Webring formulated to bring world of Civil War reenacting, both North & South, together.

REENACTOR'S WEB MALL
http://rampages.onramp.net/~lawsonda/mall
Links to directories of sutlers, basic 19th-century supplies, etc.

REENACTORS HOMEPAGE
http://www.cwreenactors.com
"Dedicated to the brave souls, North & South, who fought & died in the War Between the States."

RESEARCH DATABASE
http://www.civilwardata.com/acw
Don't miss the Civil War again! Visit the largest, most in-depth, & fully searchable research database of U.S. Civil War history. See website for free demonstration.

REWEP ASSOCIATES
http://rewep.simplenet.com
Organization striving to preserve Southern heritage.

RURAL CITIZEN BOOKSTORE, INC.
http://ruralcitizen.com
rory@ruralcitizen.com
Specializes in books on Southern culture & heritage.

SELECTED CIVIL WAR PHOTOGRAPHS
http://rs6.loc.gov/cwphome.html
Resource providing views of 1,118 historic photos.

SHAMROCK HILL BOOKS
http://www.bookguy.com
HISTORYBKS@aol.com
Books on the Civil War with specialty in Irish participation. Kepis, music & more. Email credit card accounts welcome.

SONS OF CONFEDERATE VETERANS (NATL. OFFICE)
http://www.scv.org
Dedicated to preserving & defending history & principles of the Old South. Recruiting male descendants of those who fought in the Confederacy. Contact for membership info.

SONS OF UNION VETERANS
http://suvcw.org/
Organization for the descendants of Union veterans.

SOUTHERN HISTORICAL SHOWCASE
http://www.southernhistorical.com
southernhistorical@nashville.com
Southern military art & books, prints, original documents & autographs, photos, engravings. Artists: Prechtel, Reeves, Kunstler, Kidd, Gallon, Summers, Heron, Garner, Rocco.

TENNY'S CIVIL WAR PAGE
http://www.mebbs.com/tenny/civilwar.htm
Extensive links to Civil War websites.

C. CLAYTON THOMPSON - BOOKSELLER
http://members.aol.com/Greatbooks
Greatbooks@aol.com
Civil War & military books - 1st editions.

TIME LINE OF THE CIVIL WAR
http://rs6.loc.gov/ammem/timeline.html
Time line drawn largely from the work of Richard B. Morris.

U.S. NPS CIVIL WAR PARKS
http://www.nps.gov/Architext/AT-NPSquery.html
Provides search for all national park sites relating to the Civil War.

THE UNITED STATES CIVIL WAR CENTER
http://www.cwc.lsu.edu
Facilitates the creation of a database encompassing *all* Civil War interests; promotes CW studies from multiple perspectives. Website: best comprehensive index to historic & Civil War-related websites.

THE VALLEY OF THE SHADOW
http://jefferson.village.virginia.edu/vshadow2
Info. regarding the Shenandoah Valley in the Civil War, gleaned from the "Valley Archive."

VIRGINIA DIVISION OF TOURISM
http://www.VIRGINIA.org
Call for free Civil War brochure, "Virginia Is for Lovers" travel guide & state highway map.

VIRGINIA TECH LIBRARIES CIVIL WAR COLLECTION
http://scholar2.lib.vt.edu/spec/civwar/cwhp.htm
Provides descriptions & excerpts of manuscripts from Va. Tech's archives, as well as links to other sites.

VMI ARCHIVES & CIVIL WAR RESOURCES
http://www.vmi.edu/~archtml/cwsource.html
Full-text examples of Civil War-era collections found in VMI's archives.

VMI ARCHIVES GUIDE TO MANUSCRIPTS
http://www.vmi.edu/~archtml/msguide2.html
Civil War collections.

WARR ART GALLERY
http://www.websun.com/warr/
Confederate-themed prints for viewing & purchase.

WELCOME TO NORTH GEORGIA
http://ngeorgia.com
Links to people, places & events of North Georgia's Civil War history.

BELLINGER'S MILITARY ANTIQUES
770-992-5574
Bill Bellinger
PO Box 76371-SB • Atlanta GA 30358-1371
FULL-TIME DEALER of antique firearms, edged weapons, belt plates, leather goods, books & miscellaneous from the 17th-19th century. Civil War a specialty. Catalog - $3; 4 issues - $10 (overseas - $20).

BERMAN LEATHER
617-426-0870 • 617-357-8564 Fax
Robert S. Berman
25 Melcher St
Boston MA 02210-1516
Leather hides like Civil War era for belts, straps, clothing, bags, even footwear. Full catalog of hardware, tools, buckles & kits - $3 (ref.).

BORDER STATES LEATHERWORKS
501-361-2642
501-361-2851 Fax
1158 Apple Blossom Ln
Springdale AR 72762-9762
Civil War collectibles, original weapons & equipment. Reproduction cavalry saddles & equipment. Custom hand-forged bits.

KEN BROWN
614-498-8379
17261 Sligo Rd
Kimbolton OH 43749-9604
Quality, handmade, reproduction cavalry tack, equipment & accoutrements. Free brochure.

WALTER BUDD
3109 Eubanks Rd
Durham NC 27707-3622
Finest selection of US military antiques, firearms, swords, uniforms, head gear, cavalry equipment, McClellan saddles, mess gear, horse-drawn army wagons & rolling stock, etc. Subscription rate - $5 for 8 issues.

C & D JARNAGIN
601-287-4977
601-287-6033 Fax
http://www.jarnaginco.com
Robin Jarnagin
PO Box 1860
103 Franklin St
Corinth MS 38834-1860
Military & historical outfitters. Research, develop, & manufacture high quality uniforms, leather gear, footwear, & tinware for American troops, 1750-1865. 18th-century & CW catalogs - $3 each. (See ad page 257)

CARRICO'S LEATHERWORKS
316-922-7222
316-922-3311 Fax
David Carrico
811 5000 Rd
Edna KS 67342
Authentic reproduction Civil War cavalry equipment & accoutrements. Saddles, bridles, holsters, belts, etc. Free price list.

THE CAVALRY SHOP
804-266-0898
T.E. Johnson, Jr.
9700 Royerton Dr
Richmond VA 23228-1218
Civil War leather goods, buckles; horsegear. Catalog - $2. (See ad page 259)

DIXIE GUN WORKS, INC.
800-238-6785 Orders only
901-885-0700
901-885-0440 Fax
PO Box 130
Union City TN 38281-0130
The source for firearms, parts, shooting supplies, leather goods, uniforms, books, patterns & cannons. 600-pg catalog with more than 8,000 items - $5.

DIXIE LEATHER WORKS
502-442-1058
800-888-5183 Orders only
502-448-1049 Fax
PO Box 8221
Paducah KY 42002-8221
Military & civilian museum-quality repros. 60+ hard-to-find leather items. Documents, maps, printed labels & stationery. Swords, firearms, & hats. Handmade chairs, desks; leather medical cases & bottle roll-up kits. Photo- illus. catalog - $6.

DRUMMER BOY AMERICAN MILITARIA
717-296-7611
Christian Hill Rd • RR 4 Box 7198
Milford PA 18337-9713
Civil War repro goods: uniforms, buttons, leather goods, insignia, firearms, tinware, canteens, flags, books, blankets, sabers, etc. Catalog - $1.

DYESTONE CO.
615-796-7364
320 Dyestone Springs Rd
Hohenwald TN 38462-5565
Resoles & restores cavalry boots & brogans using original process. All kinds of leather repair.

FALL CREEK SUTTLERY
765-482-1861 • 765-482-1848 Fax
http://fcsutler.com
AJF5577@aol.com or fcsutler@aol.com
Andy Fulks
PO Box 92
Whitestown IN 46075-0092
Authentic reproduction Civil War & mid-19th-century uniforms, leather goods, weapons, shoes, tents, insignia, reference books & more. 32-pg catalog - $3. (See ad page 271)

FRAZER BROTHERS' 17TH REGIMENT
214-696-1865
214-426-4230 Fax
5641 Yale Blvd Ste 125
Dallas TX 75206-5026
Uniforms & equipment, artillery hardware, & side arms. Civilian clothing (men only). Handmade leather goods. Large supply of tinware. Boots. American products.

FRENCH'S STORE & TRADING COMPANY
717-530-5037
PO Box 454
Shippensburg PA 17257-0454
Authentic Civil War reproductions of trade goods, 17th-19th century. Specializing in cavalry & leather goods & saddles. Catalog - $1.

FRONTIER SADDLE
941-322-2560
Gabriel Libraty
5530 Juel Gill Rd
Myakka City FL 34251-9234
Replica saddles of the Old West & military; from mountain man to Civil War to classic Western saddles. Free catalog.

HEARTLAND HOUSE
540-672-9267
540-672-4963 Fax
neocelt@earthlink.net
Nick Nichols
Old Blue Ridge Tpke
Rochelle VA 22738
Troiani calls us "the *Stradivarius* of historical leather craftsmen." Full line of Victorian-era saddlery, tack & equestriana (U.S., C.S., British military, & civilian). Illus. catalog - $4 (ref.).

HILLBILLY SPORTS, INC.
410-378-4533
PO Box 70
Conowingo MD 21918-0070
Leather goods, period firearms, uniform items, camp items & much more. Catalog - $3.

J.K. LEATHER
540-955-0301
Dave Allen
RR 2 Box 3026
Berryville VA 22611-9501
Repairs & restoration of all leather goods, esp. antique saddles & tack. Custom-made leather products. Handmade saddles.

MENDELSON'S LEATHER
501 Short St
Grants Pass OR 97527-5443
Master leather craftsman makes moccasin boots, full spectrum of custom goods you can't find anywhere else.

MERCURY SUPPLY CO.
409-327-3707
101 Lee St
Livingston TX 77351-4226
Civil War uniforms, reproduction equipment, tents, accoutrements, leather goods, firearms military & civilian. Catalog - $2.

MJN BOOT & LEATHER SHOP
605-368-2922
Mick Nesseim
PO Box 351
27210 468th Ave.
Tea SD 57064-0351
Custom-made, fine officers' boots, 1859 light artillery boot & brogans. Catalog - $2.

NAVY ARMS CO.
201-945-2500
689 Bergen Blvd
Ridgefield NJ 07657-1499
Finest in quality replica firearms. Revolvers, Sharps rifles & carbines, Enfields, leather goods.

NMC ENTERPRISES
800-591-2999 (24 hrs.)
913 18th St Apt 2
Santa Monica CA 90403-3251
Civil War blackpowder accessories; fine, handcrafted leather. Holsters, belts, pouches, bags, buckles. Free catalog.

OLD SUTLER JOHN
607-775-4434 Ph & Fax
Westview Station
PO Box 174
Binghamton NY 13905-0174
Full line of quality reproduction Civil War guns, bayonets, swords, uniforms, leather items, & other collectibles. Catalog - $3. (See ad page 260)

OLD WEST SADDLE SHOP
307-577-1356
http://www.trib.com/SADDLESHOP
mattsee@trib.com
6584 Hummingbird Ln
PO Box 4300 • Casper WY 82604
Selection of period saddles.

PECARD ANTIQUE LEATHER CARE
541-937-3348
R.S. Dorsey
PO Box 263
Eugene OR 97440-0263
Finest antique leather care. Moisturizes, softens, preserves - absolutely safely. Colorless, odorless, long-lasting. 6 oz. tub - $9.50 ppd. 16 oz. tub - $17 ppd. 32 oz. tub - $28 ppd.

REB'S TRADING POST
3608 Alta Vista Dr
Waco TX 76706-3741
Canvas goods, lodges, tents, flys, bags, etc. Blanket rifle sheaths, antler products, leather products, belt blanks, holsters, etc. Catalog - $1.

S & S SUTLER OF GETTYSBURG
717-677-7580
717-337-0438 Fax
Tim Sheads
PO Box 218
Bendersville PA 17306-0218
Reproduction Civil War uniforms, leather goods, insignia, tinware, & more. Free catalog.

SERVANT & CO. / CENTENNIAL GENERAL STORE
717-334-9712
800-GETTYS-1 Orders
717-334-7482 Fax
http://www.servantandco.com
230 Steinwehr Ave
Gettysburg PA 17325-2814
Quality Civil War uniforms & period clothing. Patterns, Kepis, leather goods, accessories, hats. Catalog - $6.

SHARPSBURG ARSENAL
301-432-7700
301-432-7440 Fax
101 W Main St
PO Box 568
Sharpsburg MD 21782-0568
Purveyors of fine Civil War militaria; firearms, edged weapons, buttons, bullets, leather accoutrements, battlefield relics, books, flags, personal & camp items, paper, letters, framed prints. Buy/sell. (See ad page 264)

TOM SMITH
716-337-0181
12101 New Oregon Rd
Springville NY 14141-9619
US Cavalry Horse Equipment, 1859-1917. Custom work. Correct hardware & leather spec's (no harness leather). Color catalog - $7.

TWIN OAKS SADDLERY
407-790-2461
11580 46th Pl N
Royal Palm Beach FL 33411-9141
American-made Civil War goods/reproductions. Cartridge box plates, carbine box, cap box, sword belts, sashes, holsters, saddlebags, saddles & parts, belts & buckles, tinware. Catalog - $2.

UPPER MISSISSIPPI VALLEY MERCANTILE CO
319-322-0896
319-383-5549 Fax
1607 Washington St
Davenport IA 52804-3613
Top quality goods & supplies for Civil War reenactors; uniforms, tinware, tents, leather goods, muskets, books, weapons, patterns, more. 100-pp., illus. catalog - $3.

YESTERYEAR
615-893-3470
Larry W. Hicklen
3511 Old Nashville Hwy
Murfreesboro TN 37129-3094
Quality dug & non-dug Civil War artifacts of all types. Buckles, buttons, swords, guns, paper, leather, etc. Mail order subscription - $5/yr.

1837 B&B/TEA ROOM
803-723-7166
126 Wentworth St
Charleston SC 29401-1737
Within walking distance of historic Charleston sites. Private baths, other amenities; full breakfast.

ANTIETAM OVERLOOK FARM B&B
800-878-4241
PO Box 30
Keedysville MD 21756-0030
95 acres of tranquility with a 4-state view at the battlefield in Sharpsburg, MD. AC suites, private screened porches, garden tubs, fireplaces & bath. Country-style breakfast & hospitality.

B&B RESERVATON SERVICE (MO & IL)
314-771-1993
Represents quality B&B inns in Missouri & eastern IL. Gift certificates available.

BALADERRY INN
717-337-1342
40 Hospital Rd
Gettysburg PA 17325-7798
Served as hospital during battle of Gettysburg. Private baths, many amenities; full country breakfast.

BASIN PARK HOTEL
501-253-7837
800-643-4972
12 Spring St
Eureka Springs AR 72632-3105
Near Pea Ridge NMP. 55 rooms, suites, & jacuzzi suites.

THE BATTERY CARRIAGE HOUSE INN
803-727-3100
800-775-5575
803-727-3130 Fax
20 S Battery St
Charleston SC 29401-2727
11 rooms, private baths; continental breakfast.

BATTLEFIELD BED & BREAKFAST
717-334-8804
Charlie & Florence Tarbox
2264 Emmitsburg Rd
Gettysburg PA 17325-7114
Where hospitality & history come together. Daily CW demonstrations. Each room has theme dedicated to units which fought on grounds; private bathrooms. Carriage rides, weather permitting.

BECHTEL VICTORIAN MANSION B&B INN
800-550-1108 • 717-259-7760
http://www.bbonline.com/pa/bechtel
Charles E. Bechtel
400 W King St
East Berlin PA 17316
Charming restored Victorian mansion in East Berlin National Historic District, 18 mi. east of Gettysburg. Private baths, full candlelight breakfasts. Perfect for Civil War, history & architecture buffs. Brochure.

BEECHMONT INN
800-553-7009
315 Broadway
Hanover PA 17331-2505
Elegant, ca.1834 house with 7 guest rooms & suites, antiques, grand staircase, fireplaces, whirlpool, A/C, private baths, gourmet breakfast & refreshments. Quiet courtyard & gardens. AAA/Mobil approved.

BELLEVUE B&B
573-335-3302 • 800-768-6822
312 Bellevue St
Cape Girardeau MO 63701-7233
Fully restored Hunze Home. Private baths, off-street parking; full breakfast. Visit nearby Civil War sites.

BEVERLY HILLS INN
404-233-8520
65 Sheridan Dr NE • Atlanta GA 30305-3101
Within minutes of Atlanta's numerous Civil War sites. 18 rooms w/ kitchen & private baths; continental breakfast.

BLUFF VIEW INN
615-265-5033
412 E 2nd St • Chattanooga TN 37403-1105
Rooms & suites, private baths; full gourmet breakfast.

BRAEHEAD B&B
540-899-3648
123 Lee Dr • Fredericksburg VA 22401
1859 house within Fredericksburg Battlefield Park. Gen. Lee breakfasted here before the battle. 3 guest rooms; continental breakfast.

BRAFFERTON INN
717-337-3423
Sam & Jane Back
44 York St • Gettysburg PA 17325-2301
Experience the adventure & charm of historic Gettysburg in this 1786 National Registry home. Antiques, elaborate stenciling throughout. 10 rooms, private baths, full breakfasts.

THE CAPTAIN'S QUARTERS
706-858-0624 • 800-710-6816
706-861-4053 Fax
13 Barnhardt Cir
Fort Oglethorpe GA 30742-3601
On northern border of Chickamauga NMP. 5 rooms & 2 suites, private baths; 3-course breakfast.

CEDAR MOUNTAIN CAMPGROUND
800-234-0968
http://www.civil-war.net/cedar.html
bemerson@hs.gemlink.com
20114 Camp Rd • Culpeper VA 22701-7404
Central to 8 battlefields. Tent sites, RV full hook-up, fishing pond, rec room. Groups welcome.

CEDARCROFT FARM B&B
816-747-5728 • 800-368-4944
http://www.cedarcroft.com
Bill Wayne
431 SE Y Hwy
Warrensburg MO 64093-8316
Many amenities. Visit nearby battlefields & other Civil War sites.

CLASSIC QUESTS
800-458-5394
2 Federal St • Saint Albans VT 05478-2035
Escorted tours, many with multi-night stays in fine hotels/inns. Quality historic & scenic tours. Escorted rail tours. Free catalog.

COTTONWOOD INN
304-725-3371
800-868-1188
http://www.mydestination.com/cottonwood
travels@mydestination.com
Barbara Sobol, Owner
RR 2 Box 61S
Charles Town WV 25414-9616
Antietam/Harpers Ferry area. Country setting. Large guest rooms, private baths, TV/AC. Fireplaces, full breakfasts. Farmhouse B&B, 6 quiet acres with stream.

COUNTRY ESCAPE B&B
800-484-3244 code 4371
717-338-0611
717-334-5227 Fax
Merry V. Bush
275 Old Route 30
Mc Knightstown PA 17343
Just outside Gettysburg. Rates $65-80. Full breakfast. Children & families welcome; outside children's play area. Hot tub under the stars. Call for reservations or brochure.

CREEK CROSSING FARM AT CHAPPELLE HILL B&B
540-338-7550
Barbara Barody
PO Box 18 • Lincoln VA 20160

DAYS INN
301-739-9050
900 Dual Hwy • Hagerstown MD 21740-5913
Conveniently located near several major battlefields: Gettysburg, Antietam, Harpers Ferry. Outdoor pool & playground. Full service restaurant.

THE DOUBLEDAY INN
717-334-9119
http://www.bbonline.com/pa/doubleday
Charles & Ruth Anne Wilcox, Innkeepers
104 Doubleday Ave
Gettysburg Battlefield PA 17325-8519
Fine country inn directly on Gettysburg Battlefield. Panoramic views from atop Oak Ridge. CW memorabilia, antiques, central air, full breakfast. Presentations by historians. Call for rates & brochure.

EDGEWOOD PLANTATION
804-829-2962
4800 John Tyler Memorial Hwy
Charles City VA 23030-3300
8 rooms in house rich with Civil War history; full candlelight breakfast. Hosts special events.

FARLEY PLACE B&B
502-442-2488
166 Farley Pl • Paducah KY 42001-1442
Home of Aunt Em Jarrett, who saved local Confederate flag from destruction by Union gunboats. Single & double occupancy rooms; full or continental breakfast. Period antiques.

FARNSWORTH HOUSE INN
717-334-8838
401 Baltimore St
Gettysburg PA 17325-2623
"Showplace of the Civil War." Daily house tours, fine dining. Bed & breakfast - Victorian elegance, private baths. Tavern, bookstore.

FEDERAL CREST INN B&B
804-845-6155
800-818-6155
804-845-1445 Fax
1101 Federal St
Lynchburg VA 24504-3018
Elegant historic home, private baths, central air, antiques, full country breakfast. Civil War sites nearby, including Appomattox.

FLAHERTY HOUSE
800-217-0618
1888 Victorian B&B convenient to Gettysburg battlefield. Warm hospitality, casual elegance; hearty breakfast. Walk to 300 antique dealers. $60-$135.

FORT EARLY B&B
804-846-3628
3629 Fort Ave
Lynchburg VA 24501-3817
Rooms with private baths. Visit nearby Civil War sites & attractions.

FORT LEE INN
800-941-3752
http://www.Altoona.NET/fortlee/
PO Box 92
Marsteller PA 15760-0092
Journey back to the Civil War era in this secluded mountain hideaway on 100 acres of woods & farmland. Hiking & mountain biking trails, many activities, spectacular view.

FREDERICKSBURG COLONIAL INN
540-371-5666
1707 Princess Anne St
Fredericksburg VA 22401
30-room inn, private baths; rooms furnished with antiques. Continental breakfast.

THE GASLIGHT INN
404-875-1001
404-876-1001 Fax
http://www.gaslightinn.com
1001 Saint Charles Ave NE
Atlanta GA 30306-4221
6 rooms, suites; private baths. Continental breakfast. Minutes from Atlanta's Civil War attractions.

THE GENERALS' QUARTERS
601-286-3325
601-287-8188 Fax
924 N Fillmore St
Corinth MS 38834-4125
In historic downtown Corinth, close to several Civil War attractions. Rooms w/ private baths. Tour maps.

GETTYSBURG HOTEL
717-337-2000
717-337-2075 Fax
1 Lincoln Sq
Gettysburg PA 17325-2205
Reconstructed hotel in the heart of the historic district. Call/write for more info.

GETTYSTOWN INN
717-334-2100
89 Steinwehr Ave
Gettysburg PA 17325-2811
5 rooms, private baths; full country breakfast served at Dobbin House Tavern next door. Ballroom available for parties & other events.

GORDON-LEE MANSION
706-375-4728 • 800-487-4728
217 Cove Rd
Chickamauga GA 30707-1408
Rosecrans' headquarters & Civil War hospital now offers 6 rooms w/ private baths; full breakfast. Artifacts museum. Within minutes of Chickamauga battlefield & other Civil War-related sites.

GRACE HALL B&B
334-875-5744 • 334-875-9967 Fax
506 Lauderdale St
Selma AL 36701-4527
Mayor's home occupied by Union forces in 1865. 6 rooms. Tours available.

HAGERSTOWN/SNUG HARBOR KOA
301-223-7571 • 800-562-7607
11759 Snug Harbor Ln
Williamsport MD 21795-3153
Camp with us on the Conococheague Creek; fish, canoe, or just relax. 15 min. from Antietam, 30 min. from Harpers Ferry & Gettysburg. Civil War discounts!

HAMPTON INN OF FREDERICK
301-698-2500 • 800-HAMPTON
5311 Buckeystown Pike
Frederick MD 21704-9404
Minutes away from noted Civil War museums & sites. Ask about the special Frederick Historian Rate.

HARPERS FERRY GUEST HOUSE
304-535-6955
PO Box 1079 • 800 Washington St
Harpers Ferry WV 25425-1079
Large rooms; off-street parking. Close to Harpers Ferry & Antietam.

HERITAGE MOTOR LODGE
717-334-9281
64 Steinwehr Ave • Gettysburg PA 17325
Convenient, clean, comfortable; AAA approved. Handicapped accessible rooms. Restaurant, meeting facilities; battlefield tours/package plans available. Shopping next door at Old Gettysburg Village.

HIGHPOINT
800-283-4099
215 Linton Ave
Natchez MS 39120-2315
Large Victorian home ca.1890. Three guestrooms, private baths. Full plantation breakfast. Tour antebellum mansions in Natchez & the Vicksburg battlefield. 1997 B&B Property of the Year.

HILLCREST FARM B&B
540-752-9341
1487 Garrisonville Rd
Stafford VA 22554
4 rooms with in-suite baths; Civil War theme. Outdoor pool.

HISTORIC CASHTOWN INN
800-367-1797 • 717-334-9722
PO Box 103
Cashtown PA 17310-0103
Fine dining/cocktails. Four rooms, private baths, & luxury suites. Headquarters for generals A.P. Hill & Imboden. Appears in the *Gettysburg* movie.

THE EMMANUEL HUTZLER HOUSE
804-353-6900
http://www.bensonhouse.com
be.our.guest@bensonhouse.com
2036 Monument Ave
Richmond VA 23220-2708
Spacious, antique-furnished rooms; off-street parking. At center of 3-mile historic district along Monument Ave. featuring statues of Confederate heroes.

INNS OF GETTYSBURG
800-496-2216
Adams Apple
3 Lincoln Way W • New Oxford PA 17350
Gracious hospitality at 15 historic inns. Wineries, museums, tours, golf, biking, antiquing nearby. Brochure.

JAMES PLACE B&B
910-251-0999 • 800-303-9444
9 S 4th St
Wilmington NC 28401-4534
3 rooms; central AC. Civil War attractions in surrounding area.

KEHR'S CORNER CUPBOARD
717-624-3054
New Oxford PA
Quiet, serene B&B, ca.1810. 8 mi. east of Gettysburg. Full breakfast, private baths, A/C, fireplaces, off-street parking.

KEYSTONE INN B&B
717-337-3888
http://www.virtualcities.com
231 Hanover St • Gettysburg PA 17325-1913
Great 3-story house with 5 rooms, all with private baths. Comfortable beds & wonderful breakfasts.

KILLAHEVLIN B&B
800-847-6132 • 540-636-7335
540-636-8694 Fax
http://www.vairish.com
KLLHVIN@shentel.com
1401 N Royal Ave
Front Royal VA 22630-3625
Located on Civil War encampment hilltop & site of Mosby's Rangers' hangings. Landmarks register. Luxurious accommodations, fireplaces, whirlpools, views; full breakfast, private Irish pub.

LA VISTA PLANTATION B&B
540-898-8444 • 800-529-2823
540-898-9414 Fax
http://www.bbonline.com/va/lavista
LAVISTABB@aol.com
4420 Guinea Station Rd
Fredericksburg VA 22408-8850
Circa 1838 home in countryside south of Fredericksburg. Room or 2-bedroom apartment, private baths. Fireplaces. Full breakfast. Home to Jackson's deathbed, 1865-1900. Close to Jackson shrine.

LIGHTNER FARMHOUSE B&B
717-337-9508
Gettysburg PA 17325
19 country acres just 3 miles from Cemetery Hill on Baltimore Street. Used as hospital during the battle.

LINDEN ROW INN
804-783-7000 • 800-348-7424
804-648-7504 Fax
100 E Franklin St
Richmond VA 23219-2108
Antique-furnished rooms; continental breakfast. Local Civil War attractions close by.

THE MADISON HOUSE B&B
800-828-6422 • 804-528-1503
Dale & Irene Smith
413 Madison St • Lynchburg VA 24504-2435
Lee surrendered here. Longstreet recuperated here. Early, Dearing, Garland, Rodes buried here. Elegant accommodations. "Dedicated to Yesterday's Charm with Today's Convenience." Civil War Library. Tour packets.

MAGNOLIA HOUSE B&B
919-633-9488 • 800-601-9488
315 George St • New Bern NC 28562-5681
3 rooms, private baths; full breakfast. Civil War Museum, other attractions within walking distance.

MANSFIELD PLANTATION
800-355-3223
1776 Mansfield Rd
Georgetown SC 29440-6923
Historic bed & breakfast combining the best of the old & the new South. $75-$95/night, double occupancy. Guided tours for groups of 12 or more with advance registration - $6/person.

MC MECHEN HOUSE INN
304-538-7173
109 N Main St • Moorefield WV 26836-1154
Served as both Union & Confederate headquarters. 7 rooms, amenities; breakfast, afternoon tea. Restaurant & gift shop.

MULBERRY FARM B&B
717-334-5827
Minutes from Gettysburg battlefield; ca.1817 home in orchard country setting. Private baths, full breakfast.

NORTH BEND PLANTATION B&B
804-829-5176
12200 Weyanoke Rd
Charles City VA 23030-3632
Brimming with Civil War history. 5 rooms, private baths; full country breakfast.

OLD APPLEFORD INN
800-275-3373 • 717-337-1711
Gettysburg PA 17325
Victorian mansion, 10 guest rooms, private baths, full breakfast. AAA approved.

OLDE HARDING HOUSE INN
717-338-0151
PO Box 246 • Cashtown PA 17310-0246
Built in 1803, used as tavern & inn during & after Battle of Gettysburg. Eventually became Col. Harding's home.

PAGE HOUSE INN
804-625-5033
800-599-7659
804-623-9451 Fax
323 Fairfax Ave
Norfolk VA 23507-2215
Rooms with private baths. Visit nearby Hampton Roads Naval Museum & other attractions.

THE PATHWAY INN
912-928-2078
800-889-1466
501 S Lee St
Americus GA 31709-3919
3 rooms, private baths & whirlpools; evening reception, full breakfast. Near Andersonville.

PIPER FARM HOUSE B&B
301-797-1862
Antietam National Battlefield
PO Box 100
Sharpsburg MD 21782-0100
Antietam National Battlefield, Sharpsburg, MD, next to Bloody Lane. Headquarters of Gen. J. Longstreet. Fully restored; period antiques. Three guest rooms, private baths.

A PLACE AWAY B&B
912-924-2558 • 912-924-1044
Peggy & Fred Sheppard
PO Box 26 • Andersonville GA 31711-0026
Bed & breakfast in historic village of Andersonville, Ga.

RANSON-ARMORY HOUSE
304-535-2142
690 Washington St
Harpers Ferry WV 25425
Rooms with private baths. Area rich with Civil War history.

ROBBINS' NEST B&B
601-286-3109
1523 E Shiloh Rd
Corinth MS 38834-3632
3 rooms; off-street parking. Complimentary afternoon tea & refreshments.

SELBY HOUSE
540-373-7037
226 Princess Anne St
Fredericksburg VA 22401-6039
Four spacious rooms, private bath, full breakfasts. Official tour guide for battles of Fredericksburg, Chancellorsville, Wilderness, and Spotsylvania Court House. Member of APCWS.

SKI LIBERTY HOTEL
717-642-8288 x301
Pat Custer
Carroll Valley PA
10 mi. from Gettysburg, within 1/2 hour of Antietam, Harpers Ferry & Frederick. 40 rooms. Perfect for exhibitions, receptions, reunions, & Civil War balls. Seating for up to 300 people, ample parking.

SOUTH MOUNTAIN RECREATION AREA
301-791-4767
21843 National Pike
Boonsboro MD 21713-1640
MD State Park with camping, swimming, boating fishing. Reservations accepted. Call about our Civil War camping package; short drive to several major CW battlefields.

STONE SOUP GALLERY & SOLDIERS HAUNT INN
540-722-3976 • HAUNTINN@aol.com
107 N Loudoun St
Winchester VA 22601-4717
Original etchings, antique (1800s) furniture & quilts, antique reproductions. Bed & breakfast in building built in 1760. Showcase of regional talents.

SUNDAY'S B&B
800-221-4828
39 Broadway
Hagerstown MD 21740-4019
Minutes from Antietam. Victorian elegance. Personalized service. Full breakfasts. Afternoon tea, wine & cheese, fruit basket.

TAYLOR HOUSE INN
910-763-7581 • 800-382-9982
14 N 7th St • Wilmington NC 28401-4645
5 rooms, private baths; candlelight breakfast.

WALNUT STREET INN
417-864-6346 • 417-864-6184 Fax
900 E Walnut St
Springfield MO 65806-2603
14 rooms, private baths & porches. Close to Wilson's Creek.

WELBOURNE
540-687-3201
Nathaniel & Sherry Morison
22314 Welbourne Farm Ln
Middleburg VA 20117-3939
Bed & breakfast - home of Col. Richard H. Dulany, 7th Va. Cavalry, where Mosby, Pelham, Stuart & von Borcke stayed! Traditional Southern breakfast & beautiful countryside.

WHITE ELEPHANT B&B INN
901-925-6410
http://www.bbonline.com/tn/elephant
Sharon & Ken Hansgen
304 Church St • Savannah TN 38372-2014
Victorian home, 10 miles to Shiloh battlefield. Full breakfasts, private baths. Owner leads guided tours of Shiloh & nearby CW sites.

WOODSTOCK INN
816-833-2233
800-276-5202
http://www.independence-missouri.com
1212 W Lexington St
Independence MO 64050
11 rooms, private baths; full breakfast; no smoking, handicap accessible. Civil War trench lines nearby.

AMERICA'S CIVIL WAR
703-771-9400
AmericasCivilWar@thehistorynet.com
741 Miller Dr SE Ste D2
Leesburg VA 20175-8994
Bi-monthly magazine - $24/yr. Back issues - $5 ea.

THE ARTILLERYMAN
800-777-1862 • 802-889-3500
802-889-5627 Fax
firetec@firetec.com attn.artilleryman
RR 1 Box 36, Monarch Hill Rd
Tunbridge VT 05077-9707
Quarterly magazine dealing with artillery, 1750-1898. Safety, places to visit, history, workshops, & more. $18/yr. Sample - $2.

AUTOGRAPH TIMES
1125 W Baseline Rd # 2-153
Mesa AZ 85210-9501
The only monthly newspaper for autograph collectors. Sample copy - $2 S&H.

BACKWOODSMAN MAGAZINE
719-783-9028 Ph & Fax
Lynne Richie
PO Box 627 • Westcliffe CO 81252-0627
The voice of the 19th century. Features 19th-century crafts, muzzleloading, homestead-how-to, leather projects, trapping, etc. 1 year - $16.

BATTLE CRY
810 Gales Ave
Winston-Salem NC 27103-3704
Multi-period reenacting publication covering Civil War & others. $8/yr. for 4 issues.

BLUE & GRAY MAGAZINE
614-870-1861 Ph & Fax
800-CIVIL WAR
PO Box 28685 • Columbus OH 43228-0685
Excellent bi-monthly magazine covering variety of Civil War subjects, campaigns, profiles of famous soldiers. Interesting side bits, etc. 1 yr - $19. 2 yrs - $35. 3 yrs - $46.

CARDS WITH MY PARDS (TM)
877-443-1863 (toll free)
cardswithmypards@yahoo.com
Tony & Pat Fantilli
PO Box 6186
Clearwater FL 33758-6186
Buys & sells CW playing card decks; repro CW card decks. Historically accurate, colorful & informative "Civil War Playing Cards" newsletter. (See ad page 263)

THE CITIZENS' COMPANION
614-373-1865
Camp Chase Publishing
PO Box 707
Marietta OH 45750-0707
Magazine for civilian side of reenacting. Info. on clothing, behavior, living history impressions & more. $20/yr. for 6 issues.

THE CIVIL WAR BRIGADIER
johnn6yy@aol.com
A & B Historical Productions
7448 Brous Ave.
Philadelphia PA 19152-4404
Reenactor's newspaper for Delaware Valley. 11 monthly issues - $18.65/yr.

CIVIL WAR BULLET COLLECTOR NEWSLETTER
oma00077@mail.wvnet.edu
Chuck Haislip
66 W Main St Apt 3
White Sulphur Springs WV 24986-2437
Newsletter with classified section distributed by Civil War Bullet Collector Association. $10/yr. for 6 issues.

THE CIVIL WAR COURIER
800-418-1861 0149 716-873-2594
716-873-0800 Fax
galprint@localnet.com
2503 Delaware Ave
Buffalo NY 14216-1712
Newspaper published 10 times/yr. Many items of interest to Civil War buffs. 11th year of publication. Subscriptions - $20/yr.

CIVIL WAR HISTORY
330-672-7913 • 330-672-3104 Fax
Sandy Clark
Kent State University Press
307 Lowry Hall / PO Box 5190
Kent OH 44242-0001
Scholarly journal featuring studies of mid-19th century U.S. history. Book reviews. Quarterly publication - $21/yr. individ. subs.; $32/yr. institutional subs. & libraries. Add $6/yr. for foreign subs.

CIVIL WAR LADY MAGAZINE
507-825-3182 Ph & Fax
622 3rd Ave SW • Pipestone MN 56164-1529
Quarterly magazine about women's civilian issues of the 1860s. Fashion news, feature articles, reenacting tips, etiquette. $21/yr. (4 issues). Annual August Natl. Conference for Women.

CIVIL WAR MAGAZINE
800-247-6253
540-955-1176
540-955-2321 Fax
cwmag@mnsinc.com
PO Box 770
Berryville VA 22611-0770
Official magazine of the Civil War Society - bi-monthly, full-color, devoted to Civil War history. Scholarly, balanced representation of people & ideas behind the war. Call for subscription, society membership or ad info.

THE CIVIL WAR NEWS
800-777-1862
802-889-3500
802-889-5627 Fax
http://www.civilwarnews.com
firetec@firetec.com attn.cwn
RR 1 Box 36
Monarch Hill Rd
Tunbridge VT 05077-9707
96+ pg current events newspaper: news, photos, features, columns, letters, reenactments, collecting, firearms, calendar, book reviews, ads. 11 issues - $27. Free sample issue. (See ad pg 267)

CIVIL WAR ROUND TABLE ASSOCIATES
501-255-3996
jlrussell@civilwarbuff.com
PO Box 7388
Little Rock AR 72217-7388
Est. 1968; oldest national CW battlefield preservation organization. Publishes *CWRT Digest*, newsletter devoted to news of contemporary activities, inspired by interest in CW history & historic preservation. $12.50/yr.

CIVIL WAR TIMES ILLUSTRATED
800-435-9610
Cowles History Group
602 S King St Ste 300
Leesburg VA 20175-3919
Another excellent bi-monthly magazine from Cowles covering many aspects of the Civil War & related materials. Subscriptions - $21/yr.

COLUMBIAD
PO Box 8200
Harrisburg PA 17105
Quarterly review of the War Between the States. Appeals to well-informed generalists, amateur scholars & professional historians alike. Subs. - $34.95/yr.

CONFEDERATE DIRECTORY
915-446-4439
David Martin
PO Box 61
Roosevelt TX 76874-0061
Reference for vendors of Confederate currency, books, tapes, flags, stationery, memorabilia, reenactors' supplies, services, memorials, etc.; includes COMPLETE Confederate Constitution. $12 (ppd.).

CONFEDERATE HISTORICAL INSTITUTE
501-225-3996
jlrussell@civilwarbuff.org
PO Box 7388
Little Rock AR 72217-7388
Est. 1979 to promote study of Confederate history. Speakers & tours, annual institute - April. Newsletter. Membership - $20/yr.

THE CONFEDERATE MBR NEWSLETTER
770-270-0542
Peter Bertram, Editor
PO Box 451421
Atlanta GA 31145-9421
6-pg illustrated newsletter cataloging UCV, SCV Reunion Medals, badges & ribbons. $12/yr. ($17 outside USA), 4 issues. Free sample copy - large SASE.

CONFEDERATE VETERAN
8506 Braesdale Ln
Houston TX 77071-1118
Bi-monthly periodical focusing on Confederate soldier. Articles & Southern heritage for the unreconstructed Southerner. $14/yr.

COWLES HISTORY GROUP
http://www.thehistorynet.com
Attn: Military History Index
PO Box 3242
Leesburg VA 20177-8111
Cross-referenced index of more than 3,000 entries, through 1000s of years of battle. Every subject addressed in *Military History* magazine's first decade of publication - $24.95.

COWLES HISTORY GROUP CALENDARS
800-358-6327
PO Box 921
North Adams MA 01247-0921
1998 Civil War & Military History calendars. Perfect gifts for history buffs - $14.95.

DEPARTMENT OF THE SOUTH, INC.
352-394-7206
PO Box 680784 • Orlando FL 32868-0784
"Hilton Head Dispatch" - official newsletter for reenactment community. Latest info. on events, book reviews, battle reports, unit history, life in trenches & on home front. $17/yr. for 6 issues.

G W SPECIALTIES
816-356-7457
George Scheil
7311 Ditzler Ave • Raytown MO 64133-6439
Civilian reprints of magazines & schoolbooks from mid-1800s. Free catalog.

GETTYSBURG MAGAZINE
800-648-9710 • 937-461-4260 Fax
http://www.morningsidebooks.com
msbooks@erinet.com
Bob Younger
PO Box 1087
Dayton OH 45401-1087

STEPHEN A. GOLDMAN HISTORICAL NEWSPAPERS
410-357-8204 • 410-343-3507 Fax
http://www.historicalnews.com
SAGHNOLDNEWS@msn.com
PO Box 359
Parkton MD 21120-0359
Historical newspapers bought/sold - 16th-20th centuries. Bound volumes or single issues. Military, political, wild west, gangsters, Civil War, many more! Extensive catalog - $2. (See ad page 268)

THE GUN REPORT
309-582-5311
309-582-5555 Fax
John Mullen
PO Box 38
Aledo IL 61231-0038
The new *Gun Report Index* - your guide to 35 years of collectible firearm history. 128 pp., $24.95 + $3.50 S&H.

HARRIET'S TCS
540-667-2541 • 540-722-4618 Fax
http://www.harriets.com
PO Box 1363
Winchester VA 22604-7863
185 patterns ca.1690-1945. Rentals, fabric, kits, supplies, hoops, parasols, lace. *Harriet's Then & Now* - 19th-century magazine, $6/issue. Annual subscription - $30. Color, photo-illus. catalog - $12.

HERITAGE PRESERVATION ASSOCIATION
800-86-DIXIE
770-928-2714
770-928-2719 Fax
http://www.hpa.org
HPA@america.net
PO Box 98209
Atlanta GA 30359-1909
National non-profit organization protects & preserves history, symbols & culture of the American South. Reg. membership - $40. Call for more detailed information.

HILTON HEAD DISPATCH
407-295-7510
7214 Laurel Hill Rd
Orlando FL 32818-5233
Publication indicating where to find reenactments, shows, & book fairs dealing in history. Covering the Southeast. $15/yr. for 6 issues.

HISTORIC MIDWAY MUSEUM STORE
606-846-4214
PO Box 4592
124 E Railroad St
Midway KY 40347-4592
Civil War newspapers, books on Kentucky. Scale model cannons.

HISTORIC TRAVELER MAGAZINE
717-657-9555
102430.410@compuserve.com
6405 Flank Dr
Harrisburg PA 17112-2750
Bi-monthly magazine guide to historic sites. Travel, routes, background, etc. $11.97/yr.

HISTORICAL BRIEFS, INC.
800-732-4746
Civil War Reports - most authentic reports available, written as events unfolded & published in *Harper's Weekly*. 232 pp. - $24.95 + $3.75 S&H.

JD PUBLISHING
PO Box 386
Crystal Lake IL 60039-0386
Monthly newsletter, *Lincoln in the 20th Century* - $5/issue.

JM COMICS
PO Box 56982
Jacksonville FL 32241-6982
First & only historically accurate Civil War comic series. "Southern Blood" takes you from Fort Sumter to Appomattox. 1 yr/12 issues - $22.50.

K & P VALLEY COLLECTIBLES
540-635-8564
499 Osprey Ln
Front Royal VA 22630-8336
Original, Civil War excavated relics & artifacts, incl. weapons & newspapers. Specialize in original Harper's Weekly issues. List available.

KENTUCKY CIVIL WAR JOURNAL
502-866-5513
PO Box 628
Russell Springs KY 42642-0628
Monthly publication featuring the Civil War in Kentucky. Subs. - $24.

THE LADIES' PARLOR
660-727-3592
660-727-2086 Fax
http://www.nemr.net/~lparlor/
lparlor@nemr.net
Patricia Mullenix
PO Box 274
Kahoka MO 63445
Ladies' clothing & accessories. Best source for HAIR. Available for workshops. 1863 on-line *Petersons* magazine.

MAIL CALL JOURNAL
http://www.HistoryOnline.net
mcj@historyonline.net
PO Box 5031, Dept. B1
South Hackensack NJ 07606-4231
Actual letters & journals written by Civil War soldiers. Excerpts from books; original essays & poetry. 6 issues/yr. - $24.95. Sample - send SASE.

MILITARY HISTORY MAGAZINE
703-771-9400
MilitaryHistory@thehistorynet.com
741 Miller Dr SE Ste D2
Leesburg VA 20175-8994
Excellent bi-monthly magazine covering the spectrum of military history - $24/yr. Back issues available.

MILITARY ILLUSTRATED
Wise Owl Worldwide Publication
4314 W 238th St
Torrance CA 90505-4509
Offers unrivaled reputation among military historians, enthusiasts, & modelers. Authoritative articles, research, photographs, etc. 12 issues - $80. From ancient to modern, excellent reference sources.

MILITARY IMAGES
http://www.civilwar-photos.com
milimage@csrlink.net
RR 1 Box 99A
Henryville PA 18332-9726
Estab. 1979. Publication presenting great photographs of Yanks, Rebs & Indian War soldiers. Subscriptions - $24/yr. for 6 issues.

MUZZLE BLASTS
812-667-5131
812-667-5137 Fax
Natl. Muzzleloading Rifle Assn.
PO Box 67
Friendship IN 47021-0067
Represents all aspects of muzzleloading. More than 25,000 members/300 charter clubs throughout the country. Subscription with $30 membership.

NORTH SOUTH TRADERS CIVIL WAR
540-67-CIVIL
540-672-7283 Fax
nstcw@msn.com
PO Box 631
Orange VA 22960-0370
Illustrated, bi-annual *Civil War Collectors' Price Guide* - $25 + $3 S&H. Bi-monthly magazine, heavily illustrated - $25/yr.

OWEN & OWEN PUBLICATIONS
Jim Owen
PO Box 6745
Columbia SC 29260-6745
Publish an "American History Quarterly" historical newsletter - with lots of Civil War stuff. Free sample copy.

THE PROFESSIONAL TREASURE HUNTERS HISTORICAL SOCIETY
603-357-0607
800-447-6014 (New England)
603-352-1147 Fax
George Streeter
14 Vernon St • Keene NH 03431-3440
Info. about treasure hunting in US. Metal detecting info. Treasure club activities in US. Newsletter - *Treasure Hunter's Gazette.*

R.M.J.C., INC.
PO Box 684
Appomattox VA 24522-0684
CW-period New Testament, hardcover - $13 ppd. Choose Union (black) or Confederate (brown). Reprinted from original. Free quarterly, CW-related newspaper, *The Christian Banner*, deals with Christian aspect of the war.

REBELLION CONSTITUTION
PO Box 45
Guysville OH 45735-0045
Journal on Civil War homefront life. Printed letter press, archival paper, original wood engravings. Sample copy - $6. Next 4 issues - $22.

RECREATING HISTORY
http://www.recreating-history.com
PO Box 487 • Groveland CA 95321-0487
Magazine of hands-on living history. Historic crafts, cooking & clothing from pre-medieval to gaslight eras. 6 issues/yr.

REENACTOR'S JOURNAL
309-463-2123 • 309-463-2188 Fax
PO Box 1864
Varna IL 61375-1864
For the "Who, what, where, when and how-to" of Civil War Reenacting. 12 issues - $24. Sample issue - $3.

DALE W. ROSE
302-239-3120 evenings
104 Tern Ct
Wilmington DE 19808-1966
Harpers Weekly specialist. Original engravings: Civil War through 1897. Send want list.

SAVAS PUBLISHING CO.
800-848-6585
1475 S Bascom Ave Ste 204
Campbell CA 95008-0629
Original books. Features battles & campaigns, unit histories, & quarterly journal - *Civil War Regiments*. Distributed by Stackpole Books (800-732-3669). Free catalog.

SIGNAL CORPS ASSOCIATION
410-768-3162
Lisa Christofich, Editor; Walt Mathers
13 Beach Rd
Glen Burnie MD 21060-7506
Publish monthly, multi-page newsletter - $9/yr. Sample copy - 70¢.

THE SINGLE SHOT EXCHANGE MAGAZINE
803-628-5326 Ph & Fax
singleshotex@earthlink.net
Dept B
PO Box 1055
York SC 29745-1055
Monthly magazine for black powder cartridge, silhouette & Schuetzen shooters, & antique gun collectors. Buy/sell/trade, historical & how-to articles. Antique & classic firearms only - $27.50/yr. V/MC accepted.

SMOKE & FIRE CO.
800-766-5334
419-832-0303
419-832-5008 Fax
http://www.smoke-fire.com
dmeyers@smoke-fire.com
PO Box 166
Grand Rapids OH 43522-0166
Monthly newspaper lists upcoming living history events, all time periods. Good Civil War section. Fine articles, news & great cartoons. $18/yr. Sample - $2.

SOUTHERN PARTISAN CORP.
PO Box 11708
Columbia SC 29211-1708
Quarterly magazine dedicated to renewing sectional consciousness among Southerners. Interesting reading from the Southern view. $18/yr.

TOY SOLDIERS & COLLECTIBLES
301-898-7686 evenings
Larry Riggles
PO Box 301
Libertytown MD 21762-0301
Full-color quarterly magazine for plastic toy soldier collectors. Annual subscription - $18.95 ppd. Overseas & Canadian rates available. Sample copy - $5.95 ppd.

JOHN WILLS
410-574-0771
3323 Berlin Ct
Abingdon MD 21009-2806
Complete selection of original Civil War-dated issues of *Harper's Weekly*.

WOMEN'S HISTORY MAGAZINE
800-435-9610
PO Box 1776
Mount Morris IL 61054-0398
Magazine from Cowles History Group, focusing on women in history.

ZACH'S PUBLICATION CO.
92 Woodside Ave
Winthrop MA 02152-2901
Letters of the Civil War - quarterly publication. Letters describe camp life, battles, & engagements. Subscription - $18/yr. Also "Massachusetts During the Civil War" monthly newsletter. Subscription $6/yr.

AMERICANA MERCANTILE
PO Box 4066
Hastings MN 55033-7066
American History books, documents, maps, & more.

ANTIQUE AMERICANA
PO Box 389
Whitman MA 02382-0389
CW documents, books, autographs, maps.

THE APS COMPANY
301-963-0141 • yorkst@aol.com
Gregg Clemmer
14513 Brookmead Dr
Germantown MD 20874
USGS Topo maps - $4 ea. + $3 S&H (free on orders over $100). Complete US coverage.
(See ad page 272)

ARMISTEAD CIVIL WAR COLLECTIONS LTD.
310-280-3507
310-472-6081 Fax
8306 Wilshire Blvd Ste 684
Beverly Hills CA 90211-2382
Authentic 19th-century CW map engravings - extremely rare. Civil War-related art.

BENNETT'S
800-825-8622
3914 Broadway St
Galveston TX 77550-3822
Hand-carved granite campaign maps of Vicksburg, Gettysburg, & Shenandoah.

CHARTIFACTS
804-272-7120
PO Box 8954
Richmond VA 23225-0654
Antique historic coast survey maps of the 1800s. Most U.S. sea ports, shores. Reprints. Illus. lists - $1. Specify area.

CIVIL WAR MAP CO.
888-745-5762
22892 Cobb House Rd
Middleburg VA 20117-3022
Reproduction map of "Battlefield of Antietam" - 17"x19". $25 (unframed) ppd.; $120 (framed) ppd. Left corner inscription - "... presented to Gen RoELee by J.E.B. Stuart."

COLLIER MAPPING
113 Mirandy Ct
Bridgewater VA 22812-9567
Detailed maps of battles/engagements in the Shenandoah Valley. Free catalog.

DOSS BOOKS
PO Box 660194
Birmingham AL 35266-0194
Civil War books & maps. Many out-of-print or rare. List - $1.

FULCRUM PUBLISHING
303-277-1623
303-279-7111 Fax
fulcrum@concentric.net
Promotions Mgr.
350 Indiana St Ste 350
Golden CO 80401-5093
Publisher of books & calendars including *Mapping the Civil War*, collection of rare maps from the Library of Congress. Free catalog.
(See ad page 270)

GETTYSBURG NMP BOOKSTORE
800-JULY 3 1863
717-334-1891 Fax
Robert Housch
Visitor Center Electric Map
95 Taneytown Rd
Gettysburg PA 17325-2804
Complete Civil War bookstore specializing in books, tapes, CDs & videos. Free catalog.

THE HISTORIAN'S GALLERY
770-522-8383
770-522-8388 Fax
history@atl.mindspring.com
3232 Cobb Pkwy Ste 207
Atlanta GA 30339-3896
Brokers & dealers in maps, autographs, selected relics.

HISTORIC PRINT & MAP CO.
888-824-5777
http://www.civilwarprints.com
85 Riberia St
Saint Augustine FL 32084
Famous historic lithographs; repros.

HISTORIC URBAN PLANS, INC.
607-272-MAPS
PO Box 276
Ithaca NY 14851
Repros of historic maps, plans & birds-eye views. Free catalog.

HISTORY IN PRINT
800-816-3571 • 219-465-5778 Fax
PO Box 1295 • Valparaiso IN 46384-1295
World's largest seller of Civil War books, videos, audio tapes, maps & fine art prints. Delivered to your door - select from 100s of titles! Free catalog.

MURRAY HUDSON - ANTIQUARIAN BOOKS & MAPS
800-748-9946
901-836-9057
901-836-9017 Fax
mapman@usit.net
109 S Church St
PO Box 163
Halls TN 38040-0163
Large selection of Civil War authentic maps & prints. 1300+ items (priced $25-$7,500). Rare Forrest bust; large Lee print. Catalog - $10 (ref.).

KIRCHNER PRINTS
615-376-8144
615-376-8145 Fax
http://www.csamap.com
PO Box 2224
Brentwood TN 37024-2224
Historically accurate Map of the Confederacy hand-drawn by George B. Kirchner.

DEBORAH LAMBERT
1945 Lorraine Ave
Mc Lean VA 22101-5331
Slavery documents, CW newspapers, prints, letters, autographs, battle maps. List - $1.

LOUDOUN MUSEUM SHOP
703-777-8331
14 Loudoun St SW
Leesburg VA 20175-2907
Visit our shop located in restored 1767 log cabin. Unique gift items include historic maps, books & hand-crafted gifts by local artisans.

MAPS OF ANTIQUITY
PO Box 569P
Montclair NJ 07042-0569
19th-century historical & decorative authentic antique maps. Catalog - $3.

MC ELFRESH MAP CO.
716-372-8801
Earl & Michiko McElfresh
309 N Union St • PO Box 565
Olean NY 14760-0565
Detailed watercolor maps showing crops, orchards, fences, farms, residences, ground cover & woodlands. Pea Ridge, Antietam, Shiloh, Gettysburg, Chancellorsville (incl. Fredericksburg & Salem Church), Manassas & Cedar Mountain. From $8.95. Free product & price list.

JOHN S. MOSBY HERITAGE AREA
540-687-6681
PO Box 1178
Middleburg VA 20118-1178
Maps of Mosby Heritage Area - $20. Audiotape driving tour "Prelude to Gettysburg" - $17. Free "Drive Through History" brochure.

SUSAN A. NASH
304-876-3772
PO Box 1011
Shepherdstown WV 25443-1011
Paper conservation. Specialist in historic documents, photographs, prints, drawings, maps, letters, broadsides. Cleaning, mending, deacidification, museum matting. By appt.

NORTHERN MAP CO.
800-314-2474
PO Box 129
Dunnellon FL 34430-0129
Maps from the Civil War. Old state, city, railroad, & county maps, 70-120 years old, & map kits. Free catalog.

OLD FAVORITES BOOKSHOP
3055 Lauderdale Dr
Richmond VA 23233-7800
Civil War, WWII, other military books, prints & maps. Free catalog on request.

DON PITCHER
75 Washington Ave Unit 7-204
Hamden CT 06518-6403
Offering original wood engravings as removed from Civil War-period newspapers. Locations, battles, leaders, maps, etc. Free catalog/list. (See ad page 260)

JEFFEREY M. RIGBY, CONSERVATOR
518-828-5929 Ph & Fax
167 County Route 25
Hudson NY 12534-3263
Preservation of paper documents - letters, muster rolls, maps, broadsides, etc. Satisfaction guaranteed. AIC guidelines followed by professional associate with more than 20 yrs. experience. Free catalog.

DAVID B. ROBINSON
PO Box 35926
Richmond VA 23235-0926
Complete listing of every engagement in Virginia referenced to the Official Records. 79 pp. - $12 ppd.

TEMPEST BOOKS
519-736-8629
888-233-5666
519-736-8620 Fax
235 Dalhousie
Amherstburg, Ontario N9V 1W6 CANADA
New books for old ideas. Military, naval, costuming, fiction, reference. Maps for campaign planning.

TRAILHEAD GRAPHICS, INC.
800-390-5117
303-766-7015
303-766-7108 Fax
trlhead@dimensional.com
PO Box 472991
Aurora CO 80047-2991
Full-color, detailed Civil War battlefield maps. Show all monuments, markers & tablets; essential visitor information. Custom mapping available.

WRITE-TO-PRINT
245 East St Apt 203
Honeoye Falls NY 14472-1236
Extensive photos of men & battles. Maps showing placement of the regiments in battles, 24th, 81st, 110th, 147th, 184th NYV Infantry & 24th Cavalry, their stories - $20.

A TO Z HOBBY CENTER
718-486-5390
543 Bedford Ave Ste 163
Brooklyn NY 11211-8511

ALTUS INTERNATIONAL, LTD.
612-922-6948
5609 Interlachen Cir
Edina MN 55436-1331
Civil War chess set - wooden, hand-carved, painted, lacquered. Historically accurate. Board is plate glass with beveled edges. Ea. player stands 6-1/2" tall.

AMERICA'S COVERED BRIDGES
PO Box 516 • Lightfoot VA 23090-0516
22-piece collection of replicas, incl. "Old Humpback Bridge," a covered bridge saved from destruction by a negotiated agreement between Union & Confederate forces. $45 ea. Write for complete list.

AMERICAN REMEMBERS
1019 24th St
Portsmouth OH 45662-2821
54mm miniature sets mounted on oak base. More info. - send SASE.

ARMIES IN MINIATURE
1745 Tradewinds Ln
Newport Beach CA 92660-4313

BONNIE'S GIFT WORLD OF PRODUCTS
800-650-5350 • 619-789-6485
619-789-1551 Fax
Bgwhp@aol.com
Keith Bonney
117 Los Banditos Dr
PO Box 1978
Ramona CA 92065-1978
Complete line of 54mm soldiers & sets as well as sculptures, casting molds, kits, corgi vehicles, ships, prints, etc. Catalog - $3.

BUSSLER MINIATURES
PO Box 188
Hanover MA 02339-0188
Unpainted Civil War metal soldiers. 54mm scale shown in a 10 pp., illus. catalog - $3.

CENTRAL GEORGIA CASTING
3445 Osborne Pl
Macon GA 31204-1843
Hand-painted/unpainted miniatures. Fast service, custom work. Reenactor miniatures from photograph. Sample infantry figure, brochure & $5 credit - send $5.75 for 25 mm or $9.75 for 54 mm. Brochure only - $2.

CLASSIC TOY SOLDIERS, INC.
913-451-9458
413-533-5266 (Jim McGough)
913-451-2946 Fax
David Payne
11528 Canterbury Cir
Leawood KS 66211-2917
Accurate Civil War sets, Union & Confederate. Many other items. America's leading manufacturer & distributor of fine quality toy soldiers. Complete list of all playsets - $2.

COASTAL ENTERPRISES
PO Box 1053
Brick NJ 08723-0108
Create an army - molds & casting supplies. Mold catalog - $3. Metal casting catalog - $3. Russian figure catalog - $2.

DAVID COEN, LTD.
318-345-5450
508 McCain Dr
Monroe LA 71203-4054
Hand-painted Civil War miniatures & historical dioramas, museum quality. Catalog - $3 + large SASE.

COLLECTORS SERVICES
419-884-1377
PO Box 742 • Westerville OH 43086-0742
1/35 scale figurines, dioramas. Oak display cases - custom sizes available.

THE COLONIAL CONNECTION
757-229-1499 Ph & Fax
colconx@webtv.net • Eric Grosfils
226 Warehams Pt
Williamsburg VA 23185-8923
Hinchliffe 25mm & 15mm Museum Miniatures, historically accurate flags & military miniatures, painted or unpainted - imported from England. Free catalog.

THE DUNKEN CO.
409-364-2020
PO Box 95 • Calvert TX 77837-0095
Lead soldier molds, Civil War, WWI & II. Cannons, ancients, fantasy, Britains, 1776, etc. Molds $7-$15. Kits $19-$35. Include $2 S&H. Free catalog.

DUTKINS' COLLECTIBLES
609-428-9559 • 609-428-9640 Fax
http://www.dutkins.com
1019A Route 70 W
Cherry Hill NJ 08002-3530
Molds to cast 25 mm & 54 mm figures. Civil War, Indian Army, British, Zulu, etc. Cat. $5.

F. J. AUTHENTICS
703-361-0925
9514 Country Roads Ln
Manassas VA 20112-2779
Custom, hand-painted Civil War figures. 90 mm pewter. Small diorama setting on wooden plaque. Free catalog.

ANTHONY FERRAGAM
1574 N Jerusalem Rd
Merrick NY 11566-1210
54mm metal toy soldiers. Civil War, Napoleonic, Rev. War, Zulus, Indians, Cavalry, Bengal Indians, WW II, Knights, etc.

FORPRIN ENTERPRISES, INC.
PO Box 371 • Nashua NH 03061-0371
Finest hand-painted historical miniatures from Russia. 54mm/90mm. Ancient Greeks to U.S. Civil War. Painted/unpainted. Color catalog - $3.

FRASER INTERNATIONAL
800-878-5448
5990 N Belt E Ste 606 • Humble TX 77396
Detailed miniature sculpture of Stone Mountain memorial. Hand-crafted in Scotland, licensed by the state of Georgia. $39.50 + $4.50 S&H.

G & H STERLING INC., LTD.
8362 Pines Blvd Ste 290
Pembroke Pines FL 33024-6600
Precision molded figurines, hand-finished with antique pewter.

THE GENERAL'S ARMORY
61 Debbie Dr • South Windsor CT 06074
1/10 to 1/2 scale miniature black powder & decorative cannon. Civil War dioramas. List - $3 (ref. w/ purchase).

GHQ
800-BUY-1945
28100 Woodside Rd • Excelsior MN 55331
Infantry, cavalry, artillery, siege guns, mortars, etc. 10mm by Rebellion, pewter. Free catalog.

GREYSTONE'S HISTORY EMPORIUM & GALLERY
717-338-0631 • 717-338-0851 Fax
http://www.GreystoneOnline.com
461 Baltimore St • Gettysburg PA 17325-2623
Producers of *CW Journal* have created a store, gallery & museum. Military miniatures, books, videos, collectibles, art, exhibits, story theatre. Unique merchandise.

HISTORICAL MINIATURES BY GEORGE GRASSE
760-944-7877
760-481-7550 Fax
http://histomin.com
histomin@cts.com
1573 Pacific Ranch Dr
Encinitas CA 92024-5509
Professional, hand-painted, museum-quality, military miniatures - 54mm & up. Civil War catalog - $4.

IMRIE-RISLEY MINIATURES, INC.
518-885-6054
518-885-0100 Fax
PO Box 89
Burnt Hills NY 12027-0089
Celebrating 50th year of model-making. 54mm pewter kits of Civil War soldiers, leaders, cavalry & artillery. Catalog - $6.

J & B, INC.
910-674-2999
520 Hwy 62 E
Pleasant Garden NC 27313
Fine quality, hand-painted resin Civil War figurines. List - $1 (ref.).

J & L MINIATURES
269 W Gates Ave
Lindenhurst NY 11757-4536
CW 54mm metal figures, painted or unpainted. Among the finest available. Free photo-illus. catalog.

MR. K PRODUCTS
Michael G. Kovacevich
Dept B
PO Box 5234
Fairlawn OH 44334-0234
CIVIL WAR SOLDIERS! 1/32 & 1/72 scale soft plastic, infantry, cavalry, artillery, accessories. Catalog - $2.

DENNIS KATALLO
4610 Wolverhampton Way
Missouri City TX 77459-2722
Handpainted Civil War figures - individual pieces to dioramas. Brochure - send large SASE.

LANDMARK CREATIONS, INC.
621 NW 53rd St Ste 240
Boca Raton FL 33487-8291
Official Fort Sumter model kit. Realistic, full color. Assembles to 2.5'x2'x 8". Pre-cut & pre-scored. $14.95 + $3 S&H.

THE LAST SQUARE
800-750-4401
http://www.lastsquare.com
questions@lastsquare.com
5944 Odana Rd
Madison WI 53719-1214
Dedicated to military history. Gaming supplies, miniatures, books, fine prints. Call for info.

MAGNUM CREATION
310-659-3077
835 S Wooster St Apt 315
Los Angeles CA 90035-1758
Original sculptured soldiers, 6"-12" tall, Civil War & WWI. Certificate with ea. $39.95.

MARCH THROUGH TIMES
702-972-4022 Fax
1530 Pass Dr
Reno NV 89509-3157
Toy soldiers, new & old. Color catalog - $5.

MARK MINIATURES
PO Box 683
Rehoboth MA 02769-0683
Miniatures from ancient times to WWI. Military, wheeled vehicles, hand-painted 54mm metal. Catalog - $3 w/ SASE.

MICHIGAN TOY SOLDIER CO.
248-586-1022
248-398-6367 Fax
http://www.michtoy.com
otr@mich.com
Rick Berry
401 S Washington Ave
Royal Oak MI 48067-3823
World's best selection of Civil War toy soldiers & figure kits. Buy/sell old toy soldiers, too! 92+ pp. catalog - $5 (ref.).

MILITARY MINIATURES
219-347-1565
The Pyles
PO Box 132
Kendallville IN 46755-0132
Hand-painted, exquisite miniatures. All wars available; CW specialists, Indian Wars included. List & pictures - send SASE.

MILITARY MITES
301-770-1135
301-778-6254 Fax
17557 Ashbourne Ln # A
Boca Raton FL 33496-2462
Civil War action miniatures, plastic, hand-painted, Union & Confederate. Catalog - $3.

MILITARY SHOPPE
308 Westwoods
Amherst OH 44001-2051
Bicorne miniatures, 25mm. Include Zouave in Kepis, Union Infantry, Limbers, Louisiana Tigers, etc. 30 figures/pack - $21. Sample/list - $2.

MR. MINIATURE
4096 Pavia Ln
Spring Hill FL 34606-2263
Supplies wargaming needs from pre-painted armies to painting the figures you don't have time for. Books, rules, figures & accessories. Catalog - $2.

MODEL EXPO, INC.
PO Box 229140
Hollywood FL 33022-9140
Video catalog of historic ship model kits. Video & color catalog - $5.

MODELERS MART
800-223-5260
http://www.pageworld.com/modelersmart
1555 Sunshine Dr
Clearwater FL 33765-1315
15 & 25 mm Civil War & other era metal figures. Catalog - $5 (with $5 on 1st order of $50 or more).

MUSKET MINIATURES, LLC
Dept. BJ
PO Box 1976
Broomfield CO 80038-1976
15mm & 22mm cast metal infantry, cavalry, artillery, & wagons. Also, camp, hospital, headquarters & army sets. Buildings, tents, fortifications, & wide range of scenery & accessories. Illus. catalog - $3 (ref.).

NORTHCOAST MINIATURES
707-443-8915
http://www.54mmtoysoldier.com/info/
oconnell@humboldt1.com
Bob & Judiann O'Connell
311 Boyle Dr • Eureka CA 95503-6403
Hand-painted 54mm metal Civil War wagons, cannons, and figures, Victorian & Napoleonic figures, Victorian wagons. Catalog - $1.

OZARK ARTS ASSOCIATION
OzarkArts@aol.com
PO Box 165 • Rogers AR 72757-0165
Join our collectors' club to purchase hand-crafted & painted 8" sculptures of Civil War soldiers. Illus. brochure - $1 (ref. w/ purchase).

THE POTOMAC GALLERY
800-882-1861 • 703-771-8085
703-771-8161 Fax
17 S King St
Leesburg VA 20175-2903
Hand-painted pewter Civil War chess set. Limited editions by Stivers, Kunstler, Gallon, Strain, Troiani & more. Custom framing done on site. (See ad page 258)

REGIMENTAL COLLECTIBLES
801-947-9100
PO Box 685 • Sandy UT 84091-0685
CW 54mm metal miniatures. Complete line of infantry, Zouaves, cavalry, artillery, gens., mortars, cannons, limbers, caissons. Various action poses, incl. casualties. Painted & unpainted. Catalog - $3.

ROCHESTER CHESS CENTER
800-ON-CHESS
Civil War chess sets. Grant & Lee 5" tall! Choose from various styles.

RORY'S REGIMENTS
412-347-3153
Rory Biggins
3950 Windsor Ct • Hermitage PA 16148-5302
54mm cast military figures, custom painted to your branch or regiment.

ROUND TOP MINIATURES
301-330-3552
7766 Epsilon Dr • Rockville MD 20855-2555
Painted miniatures 15mm-120mm. Custom, shadow box & museum dioramas - realistic & historically accurate; ea. is unique with custom-designed figures. Catalog - $2 (ref.).

SARATOGA SOLDIER SHOP
518-885-1497 • 518-885-0100 Fax
831 Route 67 Bldg 5
Ballston Spa NY 12020
1000 54mm pewter soldiers, cavalry & artillery kits. Civil War & other eras, paints, modelers' aids, & booklist. Catalog - $6.

SCENIC EFFECTS, INC.
510-235-1955 • 510-235-9901 Fax
Wendy Schuldt
PO Box 70332 • Port Richmond CA 94807
Ltd. ed. of historically accurate buildings, ea. handmade. Some include figures & are hand-painted; unpainted available. Catalog/listing - send SASE.

SCOTTY'S SCALE SOLDIERS
517-892-6177
1008P Adams St
Bay City MI 48708-5812
Miniatures from more than 50 manufacturers. 6mm to 30mm catalog - $6. 54mm to 125mm catalog - $5. Both catalogs - $10.

JACK SCRUBY'S TOY SOLDIERS
805-927-3805
PO Box 1809
Atascadero CA 93423-1809
54mm & 40mm traditional toy soldiers. Tru-craft, Britains & Eriksson repros, painted & unpainted. Catalog - $1.

SHAMROCK & THISTLE
1119 San Francisco St NE
Olympia WA 98506-4133
High-quality Civil War 54mm figures. Painted & unpainted. Catalog - $2.

SHENANDOAH MINIATURES
011-61-3-9534-1443 Ph & Fax
Paul Clarke
12 Holywood Grove
Carnegie Vic 3163 Australia
54mm ACW metal model soldier kits. World-wide mail order. Catalog - $7.50.

SHIPS & SOLDIERS
603-742-1886
PO Box 912
Dover NH 03820-0912
Antique-toy-style toy soldiers, boats, etc. Brochure - $2.

R.J. SIMARD
PO Box 514
Bristol RI 02809-0514
Custom-made ornamental 6" Civil War dolls made to your specifications. $10 ea. (send detailed description or snapshot). Civil War drum pins, enameled red, white & blue - $10 ea. Catalog - $2 (deductible).

SLAVIN'S GALLERY
800-448-9517
910-346-4105
http://slavin.onslowonline.net
201 Country Club Rd
Jacksonville NC 28546-6400
Finest illustrated Civil War history available. Fine art prints; original & ltd. eds. Sculptures; 1/8 & 1/4 scale model CS Artillery.

SPITZ MOUNTAIN ENTERPRISES
Steven Spitz
3013 S Washington St
Naperville IL 60540
Great generals & legendary heroes. Wooden military collectibles. Hand-carved & crafted. Authentically detailed. Grant, Lee, Jackson, Custer, Stuart, many more. $49.95 ea. Color brochure. Catalog - $2.50 (ref.).

STAD'S
905 Harrison St
Allentown PA 18103-3188
Original figures by Airfix, Marx, Tim Mee, BMC, etc. Catalog - $2 for 3 mo.

STONE MOUNTAIN MINIATURES, INC.
303-654-7989 • 303-659-9024 Fax
StonMtnMin@aol.com
PO Box 675
Brighton CO 80601-0675
Variety of 6mm, 15mm & 54mm pewter Civil War miniatures. Catalog - $4.

STUEMPFLE'S MILITARY MINIATURES
717-762-0825
13190 Scott Rd
Waynesboro PA 17268-9023
Over 200 resin kits, bunkers & conversions in 1/7s & 1/76. Leva, B P Cast, Crusader, Revell, 54mm kits, war games, etc. Catalog - $3.

TARA HALL, INC.
800-205-0069
212-802-6423 Fax
http://www.fighting69th.com
tarahall@earthlink.net
Vic Olney
PO Box 2069
Beach Haven NJ 08008-0109
Meagher's Irish Brigade, Fighting 69th, Corcoran's Irish Legion memorabilia, shirts, jackets, hats, sweaters, steins, pins, flags, books, miniatures, poster, belt buckles, NINAs, etc. Free catalog. (See ad page 272)

THOMAS' TIN SOLDIERS
152 W 26th St Apt 36
New York NY 10001-6825
Hand-painted pewter figurines in 54mm, flag bearers, gloss finish - $42.95 ea.

THOROUGHBRED FIGURES
3833 Buckhorn Pl
Virginia Beach VA 23456-4927
Ship models (1/600 scale) - antiques, assembled on walnut base. Send SASE for more info.

TOMTE TOWNE
717-337-3717
22 Baltimore St
Gettysburg PA 17325-2305
I/R military miniatures. Full-line dollhouse & miniature collectable shop.

THE TOY SOLDIER CO.
201-433-2370
201-433-0909 Fax
100 Riverside Dr
New York NY 10024-4822
Largest mail order resource of old & new plastic & lead toy soldiers. Illus., 90-pp. catalog - $3 ea., $12/yr. (6 issues).

TOY SOLDIERS & COLLECTIBLES
301-898-7686 evenings
Larry Riggles
PO Box 301
Libertytown MD 21762-0301
Full-color quarterly magazine for plastic toy soldier collectors. Annual subscription - $18.95 ppd. Overseas & Canadian rates available. Sample copy - $5.95 ppd.

TRADITION, USA
Miriam
12924 Viking Dr • Burnsville MN 55337-3524
World's largest range of figures, 25mm to 110mm. Traditional model soldiers cast in white metal. Available in kit form or painted. 250-pg catalog - $10.

RON WALL MINIATURES
800-445-0544 • 601-388-1707
601-388-0114 Fax
http://www.RonWall.com
768 Sharon Hills Dr • Biloxi MS 39532-4314
Est. 1975; oldest American toy soldier company. Historically accurate, 54mm, hand-painted, original pewter figures depicting the CW era.

WARWICK MINIATURES, LTD.
603-431-7139 Ph & Fax
PO Box 1498 • Portsmouth NH 03802-1498
Toy soldiers, solid cast 54mm metal, hand-painted in historically accurate color. More than 100 different sets from the Revolution to Civil War to Prussian, etc. Catalog - $4.

YOST ENTERPRISES
419-869-7082
276 State Route 42
Polk OH 44866
Hand-painted pewter miniatures, Union & Confederate, 15mm. Other time periods. Complete list - $1 + SASE.

THE CIVIL WAR GARRISON
PO Box 1681
Springfield IL 62705-1681
Will research the veteran you designate & write his personal story in the War Between the States, or produce a Civil War plaque of his experiences.

CONFEDERATE ARTS
8301 Alvord St Dept. C
Mc Lean VA 22102-1736
Great Seal of the Confederacy minted in exact detail in solid bronze. Limited ed. - $69.95.

ERIE LANDMARK COMPANY
800-874-7848 • 703-818-2157 Fax
4449 Brookfield Corporate Dr
Chantilly VA 20151-1692
Bronze & aluminum markers for indoor & outdoor use. National register plaques, custom worded. From medallions to roadside markers. Free brochure.

NESTA HARPER
PO Box 12
Rapidan VA 22733-0012
19th-century engravings of Civil War leaders & battle scenes. Hand-tinted & signed by artist. 9x12 - $11.95 ea. + $3.60 S&H. Price list - send SASE.

HRM & COMPANY, INC.
800-511-3864
http://www.apex-ephemera.com
hrmco@praxis.net
PO Box 775
Silver Springs FL 34489-0775
Civil War engravings - more than 1,000 original hand-colored newspaper engravings - $55 & up.

W. E. JACKSON & COMPANY
401-232-3570 Fax
PO Box 3842
North Providence RI 02911-0042
Civil War engravings, awards. Series of 3D embossed notecards from handcut dies. Lee, Jackson, Meade, artillery action, etc. 10 cards & envelopes per box.

LOOK BACK IN TIME
803-986-9097
803-986-9297 Fax
PO Box 572
Port Royal SC 29935-0572
Civil War newspapers, engravings, books, relics, & much more. Want lists welcome. Free catalog.

MOUNTAIN MAGIC IN METAL
719-486-8166
517 W Chestnut St
Leadville CO 80461-3903
Pictures engraved on zinc plates, taken from original photos. Lincoln, Grant, Lee ($295 ea.) or Gettysburg Address ($375). S&H - $25. Custom photographic engraving.

ORIGINAL FRAMEWORKS
800-654-1861
540-953-1655
http://ptiweb.com/civilwar
civilwar@nrv.net
Jay Rainey
Gables Shopping Center
1300 S Main St
Blacksburg VA 24060-5526
All Civil War artists at discount; signatures, documents, 19th-century steel engravings, relics. Will find any artwork. Always looking to purchase. Also at 4 E Washington St, Lexington, Va. (See ad page 259)

MICHAEL PINCUS
PO Box 839
Chesterland OH 44026-0839
Custom engraving by N-SSA Metal Engraver. Civil War patterns, slogans, names, etc. On your repro knives, swords. $25-$50 most pieces.

DON PITCHER
75 Washington Ave Unit 7-204
Hamden CT 06518-6403
Offering original wood engravings as removed from Civil War-period newspapers. Locations, battles, leaders, maps, etc. Free catalog/list. (See ad page 260)

POWDER HORNS
PO Box 397
Fletcher OH 45326-0397
Make powder horns from start to finish, including engraving them for your use, gifts, display, or sale - $12.95.

THE ABRAHAM LINCOLN MUSEUM
423-869-6235 • 423-869-6350 Fax
Box 2006 • Lincoln Memorial Univ.
Harrogate TN 37752
Exhibits include one of the largest Lincoln & Civil War collections.

ALABAMA CONSTITUTION VILLAGE
205-535-6564
109 Gates Ave SE
Huntsville AL 35801-4212
19th-century living history museum. Specialty shops.

ALABAMA STATE ARCHIVES & HISTORY DEPTARTMENT
334-242-4363 • 334-242-4435
334-240-3433 Fax
http://www.asc.edu/archives/agis.html
Reference Room
624 Washington Ave • PO Box 300100
Montgomery AL 36130-0100

AMHERST COUNTY HISTORICAL MUSEUM
804-946-9860
PO Box 741 • 301 S Main St
Amherst VA 24521-0741

ATLANTA HISTORY CENTER
404-814-4000
http://www.atlhist.org
Gordon Jones / Myers Brown
130 W Paces Ferry Rd NW
Atlanta GA 30305-1366
We Keep History from Getting Old -
Southeast's Most comprehensive CW exhibition, with more than 1,400 objects in 9,200 sq. ft. Artifacts, photos, videos & environments tell war's story through eyes of soldiers & civilians. (See ad page 269)

AUGUSTA-RICHMOND COUNTY MUSEUM
706-722-8454
560 Reynolds St
Augusta GA 30901-1430
Civil War exhibits comprised of Confederate display rooms.

BALTIMORE CIVIL WAR MUSEUM
410-385-5188
410-385-5189 Fax
601 S President St
Baltimore MD 21202-4339
Occupies 1850 President Street Station of the Philadelphia, Wilmington & Baltimore RR. Interprets Baltimore's role in the Underground RR, Pratt Street Riot of 1861 & the Civil War as a whole.

BARDSTOWN CIVIL WAR MUSEUM
502-349-0291
502-348-5204
310 E Broadway St
Bardstown KY 40004-1566
Hundreds of authentic artifacts of the Civil War.

THE BATTLE OF CARTHAGE CIVIL WAR MUSEUM
417-358-6643
205 Grant St
Carthage MO 64836-1604
Exhibits featuring Civil War history of Carthage. Open year-round; free admission.

THE BATTLES FOR CHATTANOOGA MUSEUM
615-821-2812
3742 Tennessee Ave
Chattanooga TN 37409-1240
Displays featuring Civil War history of Chattanooga. Admission.

BELLE BOYD HOUSE
304-267-4713
Berkeley Co. Historical Society
126 E Race St
Martinsburg WV 25401-4310
Hosts the Boyd Mason Civil War Museum.

BOONSBOROUGH MUSEUM OF HISTORY
Doug Bast
113 N Main St
Boonsboro MD 21713-1007
Civil War artifacts & displays, many from local battlefields. Admission.

CAMP MOORE CONFEDERATE MUSEUM & CEMETERY
504-229-2438
70640 Camp Moore Rd • PO Box 25
Tangipahoa LA 70465-0025
440 of Camp Moores soldiers buried in cemetery. Museum contains artifacts from the camp, which was destroyed by Union forces in 1864. Walking tours offered.

THE CARTER HOUSE
615-791-1861 • 615-794-1327 Fax
julep19@mail.idt.net
Thomas Cartwright, Dir.
1140 Columbia Ave. • Franklin TN 37065
Restored museum house; new museum, gift shop complex. House was Union headquarters & in center of fighting during Battle of Franklin, Nov. 1864. Youth programs, living history, tours, etc.

CASEMATE MUSEUM
757-727-3391
757-727-3886 Fax
PO Box 51341
Bernard Rd, Building 20
Fort Monroe VA 23651-0341
Civil War displays in museum housed in series of casemates. Guided tours for groups. Free.

CHARLES COUNTY
800-766-3386
PO Box B • La Plata MD 20646-0167
Historic inn with visitors like John Wilkes Booth. Dr. S.A. Mudd's house. Rolling meadows, forests, coastline, & Maryland seafood. Bird watching guide available.

THE CHARLESTON MUSEUM
803-722-2996
360 Meeting St
Charleston SC 29403-6297
Harbor & land tours, reenactments. Nationally recognized speakers. Period music. Call or write for upcoming events, exhibits, tours, & more. Free brochure.

CHATTANOOGA REGIONAL HISTORY MUSEUM
423-265-3247
423-266-9280 Fax
400 Chestnut St
Chattanooga TN 37402-4903
Artifacts, photos, uniforms, etc., from campaigns of Chattanooga & Chickamauga.

CIVIL WAR LIBRARY & MUSEUM
215-735-8196
215-735-3812 Fax
Steven J. Wright, Curator
1805 Pine St
Philadelphia PA 19103-6601
America's oldest chartered Civil War institution. 3 floors of exhibits, including uniforms, flags, weapons, & fine art, as well as special exhibits. Open Wed-Sun 11am-4:30pm. Small admission fee.

CIVIL WAR SOLDIERS MUSEUM
850-469-1900
850-469-9328 Fax
http://www.cwmuseum.org
info@cwmuseum.org
108 S Palafox Pl
Pensacola FL 32501
Explore the life of the Civil War soldier through exhibits of personal, religious, medical, musical, military, political & social aspects of the War. Tours available.

CONFEDERATE MEMORIAL HALL
423-522-2371
3148 Kingston Pike
Knoxville TN 37919-4627
Site of Longstreet's headquarters in 1862, now a Confederate museum & memorial.

CONFEDERATE MEMORIAL PARK
205-755-1990
437 County Road 63
Marbury AL 36051-3338
Cemetery w/ more than 300 Confederate soldiers & their widows. Civil War museum.

THE CONFEDERATE MUSEUM
713-342-8787
PO Box 179
2740 Farm Rd # 359
Richmond TX 77406-0179
Variety of Confederate artifacts, art, memoirs, & more.

CONFEDERATE MUSEUM
504-523-4522
Louisiana Historical Assn.
929 Camp St
New Orleans LA 70130-3907
Civil War artifacts & other items, many donated by veterans who used them.

THE CONFEDERATE RESEARCH CENTER & MUSEUM
817-582-2555
Hill College
PO Box 619
Hillsboro TX 76645-0619
Exhibits include flags, artillery pieces, ephemera & other items. Research center contains capsule histories of all CSA regiments & special units, as well as ships; other research material.

THE CONFEDERATE STATES ARMORY & MUSEUM
717-337-2340
529 Baltimore St
Gettysburg PA 17325-2607
Confederate weapons & artifacts. Admission.

THE CORINTH CIVIL WAR CENTER
601-287-9501
http://www.corinth.org/
civilwar@tsixroads.com
PO Box 45
Corinth MS 38835-0045
Offers 12-minute video of Corinth's role in the Civil War. Walking/driving tour maps available. Small gift shop.

CORTLAND COUNTY HISTORICAL SOCIETY, INC.
607-756-6071
25 Homer Ave • Cortland NY 13045-2056
Hosts Suggett House Museum & Kellogg Memorial Research Library. *A Regiment Remembered: 157th New York Volunteers* - Lt. William Saxton's diary, 157 pp. - $20 + $3.40 S&H. NYS - add 8% sales tax.

DAUGHTERS OF UNION VETERANS OF THE CIVIL WAR
217-544-0616
http://suvcw.org/duv.htm
DUVCW@aol.com
503 S Walnut St • Springfield IL 62704-1932
Organization for female lineal descendants of Union veterans.

DRUM BARRACKS CIVIL WAR MUSEUM
310-548-7509 • 310-548-2946 Fax
1052 N Banning Blvd
Wilmington CA 90744-4604
Displays army camp life in 1860s, role of California's soldiers during Civil War.

EXCHANGE HOTEL CIVIL WAR MUSEUM
540-832-2944
PO Box 542 • 400 S Main St
Gordonsville VA 22942-0542
Civil War museum featuring medical & railroad artifacts. Admission.

FORD'S THEATRE NHS
202-426-6924
511 10th St NW
Washington DC 20004-1499
Photos, art & other memorabilia relating to Pres. Abraham Lincoln, housed in museum in theater's basement.

FORT DELAWARE SOCIETY
302-834-1630
Bill Robelen, Pres.
PO Box 553 • Delaware City DE 19706-0553
Co-sponsors reenactments, operates museum & gift shop. Involved in research & fund-raising. Membership - $12/yr.

FORT DODGE CIVIL WAR DAYS
515-573-4231
http://www.fort.org • thefort@frontiernet.net
David Parker
Fort Museum
PO Box 1798 • Fort Dodge IA 50501-1798
Annual reenactments at Fort Museum & Fort Dodge. Military ball, civilian impressions, family activities. Call for dates.

FORT MC ALLISTER STATE HISTORIC PARK
912-727-2339
3894 Fort McAllister Rd
Richmond Hill GA 31324-4862
Civil War museum; best preserved Confederate earthworks.

FORT MIFFLIN ON THE DELAWARE
215-492-3395
Fort Mifflin Rd • Philadelphia PA 19153
Revolutionary fort which served as prison during the Civil War; reenactments held. Museum.

FORT WARD MUSEUM & HISTORIC SITE
703-838-4848
4301 W Braddock Rd
Alexandria VA 22304-1008
Museum in pattern of Union headquarters building, w/ various exhibits; tours. Research library available. Free admission. Closed Mon.

FREDERICKSBURG AREA MUSEUM
540-371-3037
PO Box 922 • 907 Princess Anne St
Fredericksburg VA 22401-0922
Exhibits pertaining to Fredericksburg's rich historical history. Admission fee.

THE GALENA-JO DAVIESS COUNTY MUSEUM
815-777-9129 • 815-777-9131 Fax
Galena-Jo Daviess Co Historical Society
211 S Bench St • Galena IL 61036-2203
Honors town's 9 residents who became Union generals, incl. Grant. Original Civil War weapons, tools, ephemera, art & more. Admission. Gift shop with books, prints, etc.

GAR MUSEUM & LIBRARY
215-289-6484
GARMUSLIB@aol.com
4278 Griscom St
Philadelphia PA 19124-3954
Museum opens 1st Sundays ea. month or by appt. GAR records, CW artifacts, extensive library. Admission - free. Inquiries welcome. Memberships - $15/yr.

GORDON-LEE MANSION
706-375-4728 • 800-487-4728
217 Cove Rd
Chickamauga GA 30707-1408
Rosecrans' headquarters & Civil War hospital now offers 6 rooms w/ private baths; full breakfast. Artifacts museum. Within minutes of Chickamauga battlefield & other Civil War-related sites.

GREYSTONE'S HISTORY EMPORIUM & GALLERY
717-338-0631
717-338-0851 Fax
http://www.GreystoneOnline.com
461 Baltimore St
Gettysburg PA 17325-2623
Producers of *CW Journal* have created a store, gallery & museum. Military miniatures, books, videos, collectibles, art, exhibits, story theatre. Unique merchandise.

HARPERS FERRY NHP
304-535-6298
PO Box 65
Route 340
Harpers Ferry WV 25425-0065
Museums, information center, hiking trails. Living history presentations & special events, 19th-cent. historic exhibits. Admission.

HILL COLLEGE CONFEDERATE RESEARCH CENTER & MUSEUM
PO Box 619
Hillsboro TX 76645-0619
Civil War displays & exhibits; extensive collection of research material.

HISTORIC HAMPTON
800-800-2202
757-727-1102
http://www.hampton.va.us/tourism
710 Settlers Landing Rd
Hampton VA 23669-4035
Historic reenactments, world-class museums, Chesapeake Bay seafood, Fort Wool, Casemate Museum at Fort Monroe, new site on the Va. Civil War Trail. Minutes from Williamsburg. Free guide.

HISTORIC HUNTSVILLE DEPOT
205-535-6028
320 Church St
Huntsville AL 35801
Original 1860s train depot with Civil War exhibits & original wartime graffiti on wall. Specialty shop.

JEFFERSON DAVIS STATE HISTORIC SITE
912-831-2335
912-831-2060 Fax
338 Jeff Davis Park Rd
Fitzgerald GA 31750-6343
Confederate memorial & museum, containing relics from a Ga. battle flag to rare uniforms. Davis family's capture at this site on May 10, 1865, marked official end of the Confederacy.

KATE GALLERY
652 Great Plain Ave
Needham MA 02192-3305
18th-20th century architecture, furniture & decorative art prints. Framed & unframed. Fine notecards. Illus. catalog - $2.

KENNESAW CIVIL WAR MUSEUM
770-427-2117 • 770-429-4538 Fax
http://www.ngeorgia.com/history/kcwm.html
2829 Cherokee St
Kennesaw GA 30144-2823
Authentic cotton gin; home of "The General," famous Civil War locomotive. Website: Directions & contact info.; brief history of "the General."

SGT. KIRKLAND'S MUSEUM & HISTORICAL SOCIETY, INC.
540-899-5565 • 540-899-7643 Fax
Civil-War@msn.com
912 Lafayette Blvd
Fredericksburg VA 22401-5617
Non-profit museum, association & press devoted to preservation of historical documents, artifacts, & texts; education; publication of meritorius books; & research & recovery of CW soldiers' records. Free catalog.

KURTZ CULTURAL CENTER
2 N Cameron St
Winchester VA 22601-4728
Welcome center for historic Winchester Civil War Information Center, Patsy Cline display, rotating exhibits. Open daily.

SIDNEY LANIER COTTAGE
912-743-3851
Middle Georgia Historical Society
PO Box 13358 • 935 High St
Macon GA 31208-3358
Birthplace of beloved Southern poet who served in the CSA & was imprisoned at Fort Lookout. Museum & gift shop.

LEE'S GETTYSBURG HEADQUARTERS
401 Buford Ave
US 30 W • Gettysburg PA 17325-1140
Civil War displays; period furnishings, original kitchen.

LEXINGTON HISTORICAL MUSEUM
660-259-6313
112 S 13th St
Lexington MO 64067
Exhibits relating to 1861 Battle of Lexington, town's history. Open weekdays, June-Sept.; weekends, May / Oct. Minimal admission fee.

THE LINCOLN MUSEUM
219-455-3864 • 219-455-6922 Fax
http://www.TheLincolnMuseum.org'
200 E Berry St
Fort Wayne IN 46802-2706
Extensive collection of memorabilia pertaining to Lincoln, incl. CW period artifacts; books.

THE LINCOLN ROOM MUSEUM
717-334-8188
12 Lincoln Sq • Gettysburg PA 17325-2205
Historic Will House hosts room where Lincoln completed his Gettysburg Address. Museum contains collection of Lincoln & Gettysburg related artifacts.

LIVING HISTORY ASSOCIATION, INC.
PO Box 1389 • Wilmington VT 05363-1389
Reenactors' Liability Insurance, covering reenactments, encampments, black powder, cavalry, artillery; personal injury, equipment insurance. Educational programs, workshops, full historical museum. Newsletter, events & info - $3.

LONE JACK CIVIL WAR MUSEUM
816-566-2272
Lone Jack MO 64070
Site of 1862 Battle of Lone Jack. Open daily, Apr.-Sept.; weekends, Oct.-Mar.

LOTZ HOUSE WAR BETWEEN THE STATES MUSEUM
615-791-6533
http://www.phoenix.w1.com/lotz
Lotzrebel@aol.com
Ronny Mangrum, Dir.
1111 Columbia Ave
Franklin TN 37064-3616
Area's most comprehensive Civil War collection. Tours of Lotz House, which was used as hospital after Battle of Franklin; genealogy services.

LOUDOUN MUSEUM SHOP
703-777-8331
14 Loudoun St SW
Leesburg VA 20175-2907
Visit our shop located in restored 1767 log cabin. Unique gift items include historic maps, books & hand-crafted gifts by local artisans.

MABRY-HAZEN HOUSE
423-522-8661
1711 Dandridge Ave
Knoxville TN 37915-1905
Museum includes Mrs. Mabry's sketches of surrounding trenches; other memorabilia.

THE MANASSAS MUSEUM
703-368-1873
703-257-8406 Fax
9101 Prince William St
Manassas VA 20110
CW & other historical exhibits. Closed Mon.

MANASSAS MUSEUM ASSOCIATES
703-368-1873
http://xroads.virginia.edu/~VAM/MAN/vam-intro.html
janemriley@aol.com
PO Box 560
9101 Prince William St
Manassas VA 20108-0560
Non-profit organization dedicated to the support of the Manassas Museum System & its mission to preserve the rich heritage of the Northern Virginia Piedmont area.

MANSFIELD STATE COMMEMORATIVE AREA
318-872-1474
15149 Highway 175
Mansfield LA 71052-4774
Civil War museum housing weapons, uniforms, ephemera, etc.

THE MARINERS' MUSEUM
800-581-7245
100 Museum Dr
Newport News VA 23606-3759
Chosen by NOAA as the official repository for items recovered from the *Monitor* wreck. Many other Civil War attractions less than an hour away.

MC COOK HOUSE MUSEUM
216-627-3345
Carroll Co Historical Society
PO Box 174
Carrollton OH 44615-0174
Memorial to the "Fighting McCooks," family who sent 14 members to fight for the Union. Artifacts & memorabilia.

MISSISSIPPI RIVER MUSEUM AT MUD ISLAND
901-576-7241
125 N Front St • Memphis TN 38103-1713
5 Civil War-related galleries. Displays include model of lower Mississippi River & life-size replica of ironclad.

MONTANA HISTORICAL SOCIETY MUSEUM
406-444-4710
225 N Roberts St
Helena MT 59601-4514

MOTTS MILITARY MUSEUM
614-836-5781
Warren Motts, Director
5761 Ebright Rd
Groveport OH 43125-9744
Civil War items & exhibits.

MUSEUM OF AMERICAN CAVALRY
540-740-3959
Peter & Jane Comtois
298 Old Cross Rd • New Market VA 22844
History of the Horse Soldier from colonial times through Vietnam & modern times. Gift shop with books, flags, weapons, relics, other items. Formerly Indian Hollow Antiques.

MUSEUM OF AMERICAN FINANCIAL HISTORY
212-908-4519 • 212-908-4601 Fax
http://www,mafh.org
mafh1@pipeline.com
26 Broadway • New York NY 10004-1703
America, Money and War: Financing the Civil War. 42-pg illus. catalog of exhibit - $14.25 ppd. Education kit with slides - $49.95 ppd.

MUSEUM OF FRONTIER CULTURE
540-332-7850
PO Box 810 • 1250 Richmond Rd
Staunton VA 24402-0810

MUSEUM OF HISTORIC NATCHITOCHES
318-357-0070
840 Washington St
Natchitoches LA 71457-4728
The Forgotten March: the Red River Campaign. Video documenting the largest campaign west of the Mississippi. $22.50 ppd. (Proceeds benefit museum)

THE MUSEUM OF THE CONFEDERACY
804-649-1861 • 804-644-7150 Fax
http://www.moc.org/
Janene Charbeneau
1201 E Clay St • Richmond VA 23219-1615
Maintains most comprehensive collection of military, political & domestic artifacts & art associated with the Confederacy. Adjacent to White House of the Confederacy, restored to its CW appearance.

NATIONAL CIVIL WAR WAX MUSEUM
717-334-6245 • 717-334-9686 Fax
Tammy Myers
297 Steinwehr Ave • Gettysburg PA 17325
Civil War museum appealing to young & old alike. Features causes & effects of war. Gift shop offers wide variety of CW memorabilia.

NATIONAL MILITARY HERITAGE MUSEUM
816-233-4321
701 Messanie St
Saint Joseph MO 64501
Exhibits spanning Civil War days to present; oral history. Open year-round. Admission - $2.

NATIONAL MUSEUM OF CIVIL WAR MEDICINE
301-695-1864 • 800-564-1864
301-695-6823 Fax
http://www.civilwarmed.org
LauraM@civilwarmed.org
JaNeen M. Smith, Ex. Dir.
48 E Patrick St
PO Box 470
Frederick MD 21705-0470
Center for study & interpretation of Civil War medical history. Medical artifacts, manuscripts, books & materials. 1861-1865. Museum store. Memberships available. Annual conference 1st weekend in August.

NEW BERN CIVIL WAR MUSEUM
919-633-2818
301 Metcalf St
New Bern NC 28562-5687
Award-winning collection of Union & Confederate weaponry & uniforms.

NEW MARKET BATTLEFIELD MILITARY MUSEUM
540-740-8065
540-740-3663 Fax
John Bracken
9500 Collins Dr
PO Box 1131
New Market VA 22844-1131
Comprehensive museum shop featuring CW relics, flags, uniforms, bullets, buttons, swords, muskets, currency, personal items, memorabilia, etc. More than 1200 book titles. Open Mar. 15-Dec. 1.

NEWPORT NEWS, VA
888-493-7386
Battlefield tours, historic houses, harbor tours, museum exhibits & living history events. Free visitor guide & Civil War tour brochure.

OAKLANDS HISTORIC HOUSE MUSEUM
615-893-0022
900 N Maney
PO Box 432
Murfreesboro TN 37133-0432
Antebellum home, alternately occupied by Union & Confederate armies; visited by Pres. Davis. Admission fee.

PAMPLIN PARK: NATL. MUSEUM OF THE CIVIL WAR SOLDIER
804-861-2408
804-861-2820 Fax
http://www.pamplinpark.org
pamplinpark@mindspring.com
6523 Duncan Rd
Petersburg VA 23803-7449
Site of 1865 battle - preserved fortifications, walking trails, guided tours, living history, gift shop, restaurant. New high-tech museum (May 1999) focuses on common soldier. Website features museum gift shop.

PEJEPSCOT HISTORICAL SOCIETY/ JOSHUA L. CHAMBERLAIN MUSEUM
207-729-6606 • 207-729-6012 Fax
http://www.curtislibrary.com/pejepscot.htm
pejepscot@curtislibrary.com
159 Park Row
Brunswick ME 04011-2005
Historical Society operates the Joshua Chamberlain Museum located in his former home. Also maintains the most comprehensive Chamberlain research collection available anywhere. Free catalog.

PERRYVILLE CIVIL WAR RELICS & MUSEUM
Ken Hamilton & Dr. Craig Knox
302 S Buell St
Perryville KY 40468-1026
Authentic Civil War artifacts & collectibles, 1861-1865. Guns, swords, photographs, belt buckles, buttons, dug relics, etc.

POPE'S TAVERN MUSEUM
205-760-6439
203 Hermitage Dr
Florence AL 35630-4667
Civil War artifacts & memorabilia; antiques. Admission.

PORT HUDSON STATE COMMEMORATIVE AREA
504-654-3775
756 W Plains Port Hudson Rd
Zachary LA 70791-8701
View Civil War displays, original breastworks. Living history & weapons demonstrations.

RAY CO. HISTORICAL SOCIETY & MUSEUM
816-776-2305
901 W Royle
Richmond MO 64085
Civil War exhibits, genealogy library. Open Wed-Sat. Admission - $1.

ROANOKE VALLEY HISTORY MUSEUM GIFT SHOP
540-342-5772
PO Box 1904
1 Market Sq
Roanoke VA 24008-1904

SAVANNAH HISTORY MUSEUM
912-238-1779
303 Martin Luther King Jr Blvd
Savannah GA 31401-4217

SHENANDOAH VALLEY FOLK ART & HERITAGE CENTER
540-879-2681
540-879-2616 Fax
Harrisonburg-Rockingham Hist. Soc.
382 High St
Dayton VA 22821
Civil War exhibit, electric map of Jackson's famous Valley Campaign; history exhibits.

SIEGE MUSEUM
804-733-2404
15 W Bank St
Petersburg VA 23803-3213
Museum depicting Petersburg life under Union siege.

SOLDIERS & SAILORS MEMORIAL HALL
412-621-4253
4141 5th Ave
Pittsburgh PA 15213-3547
Military history museum centering on Civil War, emphasizing Allegheny County. Uniforms, weapons, flags, GAR, more! Maintains library; gift shop. Open Mon-Fri 9 AM-4 PM; Sat-Sun 1-4 PM. Free admission.

SOLDIERS NATIONAL MUSEUM
717-334-4890
777 Baltimore St
Gettysburg PA 17325-2600
Gen. Howard's headquarters during Battle of Gettysburg; later became orphanage. Exacting, detailed dioramas of major CW battles, using 5,000+ miniatures, actual headgear & weapons. Artifacts & sculptures.

SOUTH CAROLINA CONFEDERATE RELIC ROOM & MUSEUM
803-734-9813 • 803-734-9823 Fax
bmoffat@oir.state.sc.us
Bonnibel G. Moffat
920 Sumter St • Columbia SC 29201-3919
SC military history from the Revolution through Desert Storm, with emphasis on the Confederate era.

SOUTH CAROLINA STATE MUSEUM
803-737-4921
PO Box 100107 • 301 Gervais St
Columbia SC 29202-3107
Civil War displays relating to SC among 4 floors of exhibits. Admission.

STARS & STRIPES MUSEUM/LIBRARY
573-568-2055
State Highway 25 • Bloomfield MO 63825
1861 birthplace of U.S.'s military newspaper.

A.H. STEPHENS STATE HISTORIC PARK
706-456-2602
PO Box 283
Crawfordsville GA 30631-0283
Site of Liberty Hall, home to Vice-President of the Confederacy Stephens; Confederate Museum.

GEN. STERLING PRICE MUSEUM
660-288-3204
412 Bridge St • Keytesville MO 65261
Exhibits relating to the Confederate general. Open May 15-Oct. 15. Free admission; donations accepted.

STONEWALL JACKSON HEADQUARTERS MUSEUM
540-667-3242 • WFCH@shentel.com
Todd Kern
415 N Braddock St
Winchester VA 22601-3921
Gen. Jackson used this home during the winter of 1861-62.

STONEWALL JACKSON HOUSE
540-463-2552 • 540-463-4088 Fax
http://www.stonewalljackson.org
Michael A. Lynn
8 E Washington St • Lexington VA 24450
The Confederate general's only home with restored garden & museum shop. Tours Mon-Sat 9-5, Sun 1-5; last tour begins 4:30PM. Open until 6PM June-August (last tour begins 5:30PM). Closed major holidays.

STONEWALL JACKSON MUSEUM AT HUPP'S HILL
540-465-5884 • 540-465-5999
540-465-8157 Fax
Babs Melton
33229 Old Valley Pike • US 11 North
Strasburg VA 22657-3715
Exhibits of Jackson's 1862 Valley Campaign with original artifacts & hands-on reproductions. Children's room has costumes, Civil War camp, & discovery boxes.

STRATFORD HALL PLANTATION
804-493-8038
State Route 3 • Stratford VA 22558
Robert E. Lee's birthplace. Visit rebuilt mill, slave quarters, spring house, stables, more. Tours available. Admission.

SURRATT HOUSE MUSEUM & GIFT SHOP
301-868-1121 • 301-868-8177 Fax
http://www.clark.net/pub/surratt/surratt.html
Laurie Verge, Director
PO Box 427
9118 Brandywine Rd
Clinton MD 20735-0427
1852 home of Surratt family. Served also as tavern, hostelry, post office & link in Confederate spy network. Played role in Lincoln assassination. Offsite bus tours. (See ad page 258)

GENERAL SWEENEY'S CIVIL WAR MUSEUM
417-732-1224 Ph & Fax
http://www.civilwarmuseum.com
TSweeney@alltel.net
Dr. Tom & Karen Sweeney
5228 S State Hwy ZZ • Republic MO 65738
Professionally designed museum of the Civil War in the Trans-Mississippi.

TANNEHILL IRONWORKS HISTORICAL STATE PARK
205-477-5711 • 205-477-9400 Fax
12632 Confederate Pkwy
Mc Calla AL 35111-2620
Iron & Steel Museum depicting Confederate iron production. Period craftsmen.

TENNESSEE RIVER MUSEUM
901-925-2364 • 800-552-3866
901-925-8069 Fax
teamhardin@centuryinter.net
507 Main St • US Route 64
Savannah TN 38372-2039
Exhibits presenting role of the Tennessee River in the Civil War. Located in downtown Savannah. Open Mon-Sat 9 AM-5 PM; Sun 1-5 PM. Adult admission - $2; children & students - free.

TENNESSEE STATE MUSEUM
615-741-2692
5th & Deaderick Sts
Nashville TN 37243-1120
Civil War exhibits include largest depository of artifacts from war's Western Theater. *Civil War Drawings from the Tennessee State Museum* - book, $10.

UNITED STATES CAVALRY MUSEUM
PO Box 2160
Fort Riley KS 66442-0160
Relive the history of America's mounted soldiers. Fine art gallery, period & topical exhibits, dioramas, AV shows, limited edition prints, books. Gift shop, free admission. Catalog.

USS CAIRO MUSEUM
601-636-2199
3201 Clay St • Vicksburg MS 39180-3469

VALENTINE RIVERSIDE
800-365-7272
550 E Marshall St
Richmond VA 23219-1852
Richmond's innovative history park at the falls of the James River. Civil War tours, sound/light show, vintage carousel, high-tech exhibits, African-American history/tours, archeological digs, living history.

VICKSBURG CIVIL WAR MUSEUM, INC.
301-368-4759
3327 Clay St • Vicksburg MS 39180-3423
5,000+ Civil War-related artifacts.

VIRGINIA HISTORICAL SOCIETY MUSEUM SHOP
804-342-9671 • 804-358-4901
PO Box 7311 • 428 North Blvd
Richmond VA 23221-0311

VIRGINIA WAR MUSEUM
757-247-8523
Huntington Park
9285 Warwick Blvd
Newport News VA 23607-1537
Discover America's military heritage. More than 60,000 artifacts from the Revolutionary War to Desert Storm. Galleries feature permanent exhibit on the Peninsula Campaign. Open daily - 9-5; Sunday - 1-5.

WARREN RIFLES CONFEDERATE MUSEUM
540-636-6982
540-635-2219
95 Chester St
Front Royal VA 22630-3368
Hours 9-4 Mon-Sat, 12-4 Sun. Open April 15-October 31. Admission fee.

WASHINGTON HISTORICAL MUSEUM
706-678-1776
308 E Robert Toombs Ave
Washington GA 30673-2038
Contains one of South's finest collections of Civil War relics & artifacts.

WAYSIDE MUSEUM OF AMERICAN HISTORY
540-465-5884
540-465-5899 Fax
132 N Massanutten St
Strasburg VA 22657-2300

WHEATON HISTORY CENTER
PO Box 373
Wheaton IL 60189-0373
Journal of Capt. Henry Whipple Chester: 2nd Ohio Volunteer Cavalry. Recollections of the War of the Rebellion. 200 pp., 97 illus., extensive index - $34.59 + $5 S&H.

WILDERNESS ROAD REGIONAL MUSEUM
540-674-4835
540-639-0351
PO Box 373
Newbern VA 24126-0373
Collection of Civil War artifacts & ephemera. Hosts Civil War events.

WINTER QUARTERS
318-467-9750
RR 1 Box 91
State Route 608
Newellton LA 71357-9709
Civil War relics & displays at site where Grant's troops were fed & quartered by Union sympathizer's wife.

WISCONSIN VETERANS MUSEUM & STORE
608-264-6086
608-266-1680
http://badger.state.wi.us/agencies/dva/museum/wvmmain.html
30 W Mifflin St
Madison WI 53703-2558
Authentic reproduction tinware from originals in our collection. Coffeepot, tin cups, canteens, etc. Blankets. Museum - 2 main galleries & various displays.

2ND MARYLAND FIFES & DRUMS
PO Box 172
Willow Hill PA 17271-0172
It's Those Marylanders Again!: Field Music of the Civil War - Cassette $10, CD $15; S&H $3. Group seen & heard in movie *Gettysburg*.

2ND SOUTH CAROLINA STRING BAND
717-337-3785 • J. Ewers
1820 Old Harrisburg Rd
Gettysburg PA 17325-8119
Favorite campfire songs of the Civil War, North & South.

37TH GEORGIA BAND
706-543-4559
766 Riverhill Dr
Athens GA 30606-4050
5 brass-band recordings - hymns, quicksteps, ballads, fife & drum music - all played on antique instruments in authentic 1860s style.

3RD FLORIDA REGIMENTAL BAND
904-824-6715
jej@aug.com / togans@aug.com
John Joline, Bandmaster
318 San Marco Ave
Saint Augustine FL 32084-1625
Florida's one & only Confederate brass band. Nationally famous group performs at reenactments, balls, civic functions, fund-raisers & private functions. CDs & tapes available.

52ND TENNESSEE STRING BAND
901-685-6678
5088 Helene Rd
Memphis TN 38117-7218
Authentic, professional 5-piece Civil War string band; variety of music for dances, balls, etc. Complete entertainment. *Voices of the Shiloh* - recent cassette.

5TH MICHIGAN REGT. BAND
http://www.mi5th.org
PO Box 170 • Novi MI 48376-0170
Civil War field band available for reenactments, concerts, educational programs, parades, etc. Cassettes - $12 ea. ppd.; CDs - $17 ea. ppd.

97th REGIMENTAL STRING BAND
813-391-4565
PO Box 2208
Largo FL 33779-2208
Cassettes & CDs of the 80 most popular Civil War songs. Many vols. Coffee cups, T-shirts, & spoken history cassettes. Catalog - SASE.

ACLAMON MUSIC
716-654-9637
716-654-6613 Fax
singerdon@aol.com
PO Box 10098
Rochester NY 14610-0098
Battle Cry of Freedom. 20 favorite Civil War songs available on CD - $15, cassette - $10. *Grandfather's Clock* on cassette - $10.

BRIGADE BUGLER
609-589-3901
George Rabbai
PO Box 165
Pitman NJ 08071-0165
Civil War infantry bugle calls, book & cassette, $19.95 ppd. for set. *Teach Yourself How to Play the Bugle* - for all levels of buglers, includes exercises, tonguing & lip flexibility. $8 ppd.

CAMELOT RECORDS
800-537-3839
cwsongbird@aol.com
Jan Kurtis or Susan Jacobson
6006 Barr Rd • Ferndale WA 98248-8747
Original & period Civil War music of Dave Mathews & Susan Jacobson set to spectacular reenactment footage. 3 soundtracks - cassettes $8, CDs $12; 4 videos - $15. S&H $3. Free catalog.

THE CAMP CHASE FIFES & DRUMS, INC.
PBFV68A@prodigy.com
Tom Kuhn
PO Box 461 • Groveport OH 43125-0461
150 years of US martial field music (1750-1900). 2 vols of Civil War music - $10 ea. ppd., $16 for both ppd.

DAN CHEATUM RECORDINGS
618-529-3038
616 Bakersfield Rd • Carbondale IL 62901
90-min. cassettes recorded with 1850s Martin guitar, vocals, harmonica, mandolin, fiddle. Accompanying songbooks with guitar chords. Catalog.

CIVIL WAR DRUM & FLAG SHOWS
830-966-3480
nyclay@swtexas.net
Nancy Clayton
PO Box 153 • Utopia TX 78884-0153
Drum & flag storytelling performance for school assemblies, history & music classes (grades PK-college), teachers' meetings, conventions & living history events. Brochure - send SASE.

THE CIVIL WAR MUSIC STORE
805-589-5544
13621 Powder River Ave
Bakersfield CA 93312-9022
Wide selection of Union & Confederate music. CDs or cassettes.

CONFEDERATE GRAY
615-320-1715 • 615-320-3272 Fax
http://www.dixienet.org/conf_gray/default.htm
congray@home.com
Meeks Booker
PO Box 121984 • Nashville TN 37212-1984
Hand-carved music boxes that play "Dixie" when opened; other tunes available. Named for great Southern leaders or battles. Refer to Source Book for 10% discount. Cat. $2 (ref.).

DAL PRODUCTIONS, LTD.
212-496-7677
Presenting Clamma Dale, an award-winning singing actress who has researched & reacquaints her listeners with CW songs, spirituals & poetry. *Unforgotten* - CD $15.98.

ELECTRIC QUILT MUSIC
http://www.equilt.com
PO Box 1314
Norcross GA 30091-1314
19 -song cassette, by David Ray Skinner, chronicles the wartime career of Conf. general John Hunt Morgan. $10 + $2 S&H.

FIFE & DRUM TRADING CO.
378 N Lakeview Ave
Winter Garden FL 34787-2715
Authentic Civil War fife & drum tunes played non-stop to a steady beat. Essential for marching drills & parade use. Catalog - $3. (See ad page 257)

HERITAGE DRUM CO.
256-533-5498
http://fly.hiwaay.net/~tpalmer/heritage2.htm
ropedrum@juno.com
Terry Cornett
4021 Apollo Dr SW
Huntsville AL 35805-5601
Custom order, period repro snare & bass drums. Hand-crafted.

HERITAGE MILITARY MUSIC FOUNDATION, INC.
504 S 4th St
Watertown WI 53094-4528
First Brigade Band recordings of Civil War music. Cassettes & CDs. Write for complete listing.

HISTORIC IMAGES
606 Glenbrook Rd
Savannah GA 31419-2444
Confederate, minstrel music by James Lord Pierpont, including "Strike for the South," "Our Battle Flag." Original "Jingle Bells," etc. Cassette - $6 ppd.

BOBBY HORTON
http://bizweb.lightspeed.net/~cwms
3430 Sage Brook Ln
Birmingham AL 35243-2046
Authentic music of the Civil War by Bobby Horton. Cassette - $10/volume. CD - $15. Write for list.

LOWELL JERENS
715-834-3938
639 Putnam Dr
Eau Claire WI 54701-3304
Civil War-era sheet music.

NATIVE GROUND MUSIC
800-752-2656 • 704-298-5607 Fax
http://www.circle.net/nativeground
banjo@circle.net
Wayne Erbsen
109 Bell Rd
Asheville NC 28805-1521
Civil War music performed in traditional style on old-time instruments. Cassettes, CDs, & songbooks focusing on 19th-century American themes. Instruction books. Free catalog.

NORD-DISC RECORD COMPANY
517-631-4151 • 517-631-5571 Fax
W. Buechner
4407 Gladding Ct Ste 102
Midland MI 48640-3383
American Civil War, trilogy; *Flight of the American Eagle*; *The Blue & the Gray*; & other patriotic works - all symphony orchestra, highest quality cassettes ($12.50 ref.) & CDs ($14.95 ref.). Catalog.

OLD DRUMS MADE NEW
301-824-5223 • Tom Law
62 W Water St • Smithsburg MD 21783-1643
Authentic Civil War-style rope drums. Men/boys - $250-$375. Old drums restored; new drums made. Parts to fit any drum.

POPE MUSIC
800-469-4767
82 E Allendale Rd • Saddle River NJ 07458
Clamma Dale, award-winning diva, sings songs, hymns, spirituals, & poetry, both North & South. CD or cassette.

POTOMAC THUNDER
410-549-7470 • RLather@aol.com
Tom & Rosemary Lather
5081 Amantea Way
Sykesville MD 21784-9319
Professional musicians will perform Civil War music for reenactments, dances, weddings, etc. Period music, fiddle & banjo tunes, & classical music. 20+ yrs. experience; references.

PUBLISHERS MARKETING
216 Roberts Ave
Bellmawr NJ 08031-2712
Treasury of Civil War songs. 25 of the best songs, North & South, sung by balladeer Tom Glazer. Cassette - $8.98, CD - $11.98 ppd.

THE REBELAIRES
912-285-8191
Dave Griffin
950 Sunset Ln • Waycross GA 31503-8030
Cassettes/CDs. *Carry the Memories On, For the Cause*, and *Confederate Man*. Original songs, old standards. $11/tape. Call for CD prices. Ball, banquet, convention bookings.

RED DRAGON MUSIC DEN
304-267-0411
http://www.reddragonmusic.com
reddragn@reddragonmusic.com
J. T. Foultz
PO Box 1776 • Martinsburg WV 25402-1776
Field drums, bagpipes, fifes, music tapes, CDs, books, & more. Free catalog.

RED TIE MUSIC & BOOKS
7410 Brixworth Ct Unit 101
Baltimore MD 21244-5660
The Civil War Fifer - songbook featuring favorite & lesser-known melodies, lyrics, histories & artwork - $12.95 + $2.50 S&H. Other songbooks & collections of lyrics & poetry.

RETURNING HEROES BALL
Patri & Barbara Pugliese
39 Capen St • Medford MA 02155-5824
Annual March ball featuring contra-dances, quadrilles, waltzes, polkas, & schottisches.

ROSE OF EL-A-NOY MINSTRELS
618-529-3038 • Dan Cheatum
616 Bakersfield Rd
Carbondale IL 62901-0641
Authentic Historic String Band recordings, 4 vols, cassettes. Live performances & period military balls. Dan Cheatum recordings - 2 cassettes, 2 songbooks. Cassettes - $9.95 ppd. Catalog.

RSV PRODUCTS
johnson@net-info.com
Mark Johnson
PO Box 26
Hopkins MN 55343-0026
Buglers! Collections of printed music, recordings on cassette/CD, & authentic brass bugles. Free info. Try Basic Bugler package - book & cassette $9.99 ppd. Free catalog.

SHAMROCK HILL BOOKS
770-569-1802
770-569-1801 Fax
http://www.bookguy.com
HISTORYBKS@aol.com
Ed O'Dwyer
12725 Bethany Rd
Alpharetta GA 30004-1080
Books on the Civil War with specialty in Irish participation. Kepis, music & more. Email credit card accounts welcome. Catalog.

SOUTHERN HORIZON
804-320-4680
minstral@aol.com
John Robison
2207 Wrens Nest Rd
Richmond VA 23235-3667
Camp & parlor music of the Civil War, dance & vocal, 2 cassettes $10 ea. Nationally known music ensemble.

SPARX ECHO PRODUCTIONS
800-ECHOES-1
PO Box 880
Pasadena MD 21123-0880
In Spite of Reason, Pop Rock Opera, based on the life of Abraham Lincoln during the Civil War. 2 CDs & libretto - $29.95.

SPRING RIVER MUSIC
212-879-8424
Robert Trentham
Lenox Hill Station
PO Box 1408
New York NY 10021-0041
Epitaph: A Collection of Civil War Songs. Tenor Robert Trentham sings 14 heartfelt songs. CDs - $14.98 ea. + $2 S&H (ref.).

STALEY'S SUNDRIES
540-899-6464 • 540-373-2469 Fax
710 Caroline St
Fredericksburg VA 22401-5904
Largest collection of Civil War music anywhere. Military insignia, flags, hats, clothing, patterns, buttons, buckles, miniatures, books, magazines & gift items.

AL VASONE
PO Box 2252
Darien CT 06820-0252
Civil War songs, sung by Al Vasone. 6 cassettes - $9.50 ea.

THE WILDCAT REGIMENT BAND
167 Route 85
Home PA 15747-9301
"Brass Band Music of the American Civil War," 70+ minutes of music, much never previously recorded. Cassette - $11.95, CD - $15.95; $1.75 S&H.

BRYAN WRIGHT
PO Box 07355
Detroit MI 48207-0355
CD, musical works dedicated to the 200,000 colored troops who fought for the restoration of the Union. "We go deal with the system." $18 ppd.

1ST WEST VA. LIGHT ARTILLERY, BATTERY D
304-242-2490
Capt. Joe Johnson
57 Greenwood Ave
Wheeling WV 26003-1448
Participate in reenactments, living history, encampments. Experience thrill of "booming" cannon. Recruits sought; receive training on full-scale artillery pieces.

4TH NORTH CAROLINA REGT., CSA, INC.
410-795-6282
joep@schmitzpress.com
Recruiter: Joe Pearson
4473 Bartholow Rd • Sykesville MD 21784
Authentic infantry unit with members in Md., Va., & Pa. Living history emphasized. Reenactments, talks, displays, etc. Well-researched unit with uniform documentation. Registered 501.C nonprofit corporation.

5TH NEW YORK, DURYEE'S ZOUAVES
http://www.zouave.org/index.html
PO Box 1601
Alexandria VA 22313-1601
Enlist in the 5th NY for authentic living history & reenacting.

7TH REGIMENT, TEXAS VOLUNTEER BRIGADE
303-221-3099
Capt. E. Roy Jordan
300 E Harmony Rd
Fort Collins CO 80525-3237
Civil War gun club to promote family fun through black powder shooting & safety.

8TH REGT. NJ VOLUNTEER INFANTRY
609-654-5561 Days
609-654-7168 Nights
Capt. Earl Aversano
226 Sunny Jim Dr
Medford NJ 08055-9249
Honorary reactivated NJ unit which participates in reenactments & historical events throughout the eastern U.S.

13TH VIRGINIA INFANTRY, CO. H
540-877-2483
Capt. David Melton
128 Susquehanna Trl
Winchester VA 22602-1735
Members participate in battle reenactments, living history, camp & drill demonstrations, memorials/ceremonies/dedications & help preserve historical sites & Confederate battle flags. Recruits welcome & encouraged.

17TH CONNECTICUT VOL. INFANTRY
407-295-7510
Maj. Jeff H. Grzelak
7214 Laurel Hill Rd • Orlando FL 32818-5233
Retrace the steps of the 17th Conn.; after 135 years, the regiment is once again on the march. Enlist today & see a part of U.S. history firsthand.

AMERICAN BATTLEFIELD PROTECTION PROGRAM
202-343-3941
http://www2.cr.nps.gov/abpp/abpp_t.html
Natl. Park Service
PO Box 37127
Washington DC 20013-7127
U.S. government's leading battlefield preservation program.

AMERICAN CIVIL WAR ASSOCIATION
http://www.acwa.org
CSA contact: AdjCSAACWA@aol.com ; Union contact: MajorAWH@aol.com
Arthur Henrick
PO Box 61075 • Sunnyvale CA 94088-1075
Private, non-profit educational organization & reenactment society which uses living history to help the public gain better understanding of the Civil War. 350 current members. More info - send SASE.

AMERICAN CIVIL WAR HISTORICAL REENACTMENT SOCIETY
andydesjardins@sympatico.ca
1013 Logan Ave
Toronto Ontario M4K 3E6 CANADA
Group seeking to preserve history of the more than 50,000 Canadians who fought in the U.S. Civil War.

AMERICAN SINGLE SHOT RIFLE ASSOCIATION
709 Carolyn Dr
Delphos OH 45833-1316
Association dedicated to the shooting of old black powder cartridge rifles.

ARMIES OF TENNESSEE
317-548-2594
PO Box 91 • Rosedale IN 47874-0091
Confederate & Union reenactors. Also involved in preservation. Annual memb. - $20.

ARMY OF THE PACIFIC
http://chaos.alchemy.net/AOP/
PO Box 1863 • Santa Barbara CA 93116
Infantry reenactors, specifically Union. "Authenticity and Pardships."

ASMIC
526 Lafayette Ave
Palmerton PA 18071-1621
Oldest military collecting club in the nation. Dedicated to collection & preservation of U.S. cloth & metal military insignia. Publishes quarterly *Trading Post* & newsletter.

ASSOCIATION FOR THE PRESERVATION OF CIVIL WAR SITES
888-606-1400
http://www.apcws.com
11 Public Sq Ste 200
Hagerstown MD 21740-5510
Not-for-profit membership organization that preserves Civil War sites for educational & recreational uses. Website: organizational news & membership info.

BERKELEY COUNTY HISTORICAL SOCIETY
304-267-4713 • Don C. Wood, Pres.
126 E Race St • Martinsburg WV 25401
Childhood home of Belle Boyd, famous Confederate spy. Civil War & military history museum; archives & genealogy section. Headquarters of historical society & landmarks commission. Free adm. Mon.-Sat., 10-4 PM.

BLOUNT COUNTY GENEALOGICAL & HISTORICAL SOCIETY
ATTN: TC • PO Box 4986
Maryville TN 37802-4986
Loyal Mountain Troopers: The 2nd and 3rd Tenn. Vol. Cavalry in the Civil War. Details these largely ignored Southerners who served the Union. $32.50 ppd.

BLUE & GRAY EDUCATION SOCIETY
804-797-4535
416 Beck St • Norfolk VA 23503-5302
Non-profit organization which interprets battlefields for public visitation. North Anna is most recent achievement. More than 600 members via tax-exempt donation. Seminars, tours, symposiums & debates.

CENTRAL MARYLAND HERITAGE LEAGUE
301-371-7090
PO Box 721 • Middletown MD 21769-0721
Dedicated to preserving the South Mountain battlefield area. Offering MD Campaign Afghan with scenes from South Mountain, Antietam & Harpers Ferry.

CIVIL WAR EDUCATION ASSOCIATION
800-298-1861
540-667-2339 Fax
21 N Loudoun St
Winchester VA 22601-4715
Non-profit organization presenting the finest seminars, symposia, & tours. Develops educational materials, publishes/distributes Civil War books. Contact for extensive calendar of events.

THE CIVIL WAR PLYMOUTH PILGRIMS DESCENDANTS SOCIETY
Scott W. Holmes
4910 Grape Tree Ln
Roanoke VA 24018-4106
Info. exchange concerning the Battle of Plymouth, NC, & its participants, namely the 3,000 Union prisoners dubbed the "Plymouth Pilgrims." Annual membership - $15.

CIVIL WAR SOCIETY
800-247-6253
540-955-1176
540-955-2321 Fax
cwmag@mnsinc.com
PO Box 770
Berryville VA 22611-0770
Membership includes award-winning *Civil War Magazine*, calendar, newsletters, membership cert., preservation & education activities, ancestors research guide, tours, seminars, discounts & camaraderie. Call for brochure & free sample magazine.

CIVIL WAR SONS
1725 S Farmer Ave
Tempe AZ 85281
Ancestors' records information, 3 stamps. Membership - $3; pin available.

THE CIVIL WAR TRUST
703-516-4944
800-CWTRUST
703-516-4947 Fax
civilwar@ari.net
Danielle McMahon
2101 Wilson Blvd Ste 1120
Arlington VA 22201-3062
Promotes appreciation & stewardship of our nation's cultural heritage through preservation of historic CW battlefields and through related education & preservation programs. Memberships start at $25.

CONFEDERATE HERITAGE BRIGADE
540-338-7907
PO Box 1224
Purcellville VA 20134-1224
Defend the Confederate right by joining our growing group for flag marches & commemorations. No dues.

CONFEDERATE HISTORICAL INSTITUTE
501-225-3996
jlrussell@civilwarbuff.org
PO Box 7388
Little Rock AR 72217-7388
Est. 1979 to promote study of Confederate history. Speakers & tours, annual institute - April. Newsletter. Membership - $20/yr.

CONFEDERATE MEMORIAL ASSOCIATION
202-483-5700
1917 N Utah St
Arlington VA 22207-2348

THE CONFEDERATE NAVY
8351 Roswell Rd Ste 363
Atlanta GA 30350-2810
Nation's fastest growing boat club. Membership card, official boat decal, bi-monthly newsletter, membership discounts, etc. A real boat club. $25.

CONFEDERATE SOCIETY OF AMERICA
PO Box 713
Plaquemine LA 70765-0713
"Action Arm" of the Confederate Movement. Subjects include gun control, immigration, moral breakdown, etc. Annual Membership, incl. bi-monthly newsletter - $20.

THE CORINTH CIVIL WAR CENTER
601-287-9501
http://www.corinth.org/
civilwar@tsixroads.com
PO Box 45
Corinth MS 38835-0045
Offers 12-minute video of Corinth's role in the Civil War. Walking/driving tour maps available. Small gift shop.

CORTLAND COUNTY HISTORICAL SOCIETY, INC.
607-756-6071
25 Homer Ave
Cortland NY 13045-2056
Hosts Suggett House Museum & Kellogg Memorial Research Library. *A Regiment Remembered: 157th New York Volunteers* - Lt. William Saxton's diary, 157 pp. - $20 + $3.40 S&H. NYS - add 8% sales tax.

DAUGHTERS OF UNION VETERANS OF THE CIVIL WAR
217-544-0616
http://suvcw.org/duv.htm
DUVCW@aol.com
503 S Walnut St
Springfield IL 62704-1932
Organization for female lineal descendants of Union veterans.

DIXIANA
800-272-3589
Private Southern Pride Airline club for weekend getaways. Affordable air transportation for members only. Call for more info. on membership requirements & application.

FORT DELAWARE SOCIETY
302-834-1630
Bill Robelen, Pres.
PO Box 553
Delaware City DE 19706-0553
Co-sponsors reenactments, operates museum & gift shop. Involved in research & fund-raising. Membership - $12/yr.

FRIENDS OF MONOCACY BATTLEFIELD, INC.
301-845-6241
FOMB@erols.com
PO Box 4101
Frederick MD 21705-4101
Non-profit, all-volunteer organization serving as independent advocate for the battlefield & working to preserve, protect & restore the site of the "battle that saved Washington."

FRIENDS OF NEW YORK STATE NEWSPAPER PROJECT
http://www.nysl.nysed.gov/nysnp
vweiss@mail.nysed.gov
PO Box 2402
Empire State Plaza Station
Albany NY 12220-0402
Maps & Letters from NY State's Civil War Newspapers, 1861-1863 - $22.

FRIENDS OF SHILOH NATL. MILITARY PARK
901-925-6410
Ken Hansgen, Sect.
PO Box 100
Shiloh TN 38376
Non-profit, all-volunteer organization serving as independent advocate for the battlefield & working to promote & preserve Shiloh NMP. Annual dues - $10.

FRIENDS OF THE MANASSAS NATL BATTLEFIELD PARK
703-330-1965
http://members.aol.com/manapark/friendhp.html
fit2prnt@erols.com • Karen Fojt
PO Box 141 • Catharpin VA 20143-0141
Supports the park to preserve its historic significance, cultural importance & natural values; encourages community involvement; provides a forum for community outreach.

FRIENDS OF THE NATIONAL PARKS AT GETTYSBURG
717-334-0772 • 717-334-3118
PO Box 4622
Gettysburg PA 17325-4622
National organization with purpose of preserving & restoring Gettysburg NP land, promoting educational resources & programs, & establishing a definitive Civil War museum.

GENERAL STAFF OF THE ARMY OF THE POTOMAC
301-845-7363
Joe Shelton, Pres.
PO Box 266 • Walkersville MD 21793-0266
Personalities from Civil War past. Civil War living history group & nonprofit organization.

GENERAL STAFF OF THE CONFEDERACY
301-845-7363
Joe Shelton, Pres.
PO Box 266 • Walkersville MD 21793-0266
Personalities from Civil War past. Civil War living history group & nonprofit organization.

GETTYSBURG BATTLEFIELD PRESERVATION ASSOCIATION
717-337-0031
Dr. Walter L. Powell, Pres.
PO Box 1863
Gettysburg PA 17325
Bi-annual newsletter "Battle Lines" (for $10 annual membership). Various Civil War books & prints available for donations. Annual Civil War Book Show.

GRANT COUNTY HISTORICAL SOCIETY
608-723-2287
608-723-4925
129 E Maple St
Lancaster WI 53813-1765
Operates from Cunningham Museum. *Our Boys* - 64 stories of men & boys from Grant County, Wisc.; names of all 750 Grant Co. soldiers who died in the war. $25 + $3 S&H. (See ad page 271)

U.S.GRANT NETWORK
http://www.saints.css.edu/mkelsey/gppg.html
usglady@excel.net
Diane Meives
W3547 Playbird Rd
Sheboygan Falls WI 53085-2017
Organization commemorating Gen. Grant. Join us to learn more about this often misunderstood Civil War hero. Website: articles, images, & other links associated with Ulysses S. Grant. Quarterly newsletter - $12.

HARRISONBURG-ROCKINGHAM HISTORICAL SOCIETY
PO Box 716
Dayton VA 22821
Sponsor Shenandoah Valley Folk Art & Heritage Center.

HERITAGE EMBROIDERY
402-488-7913
402-488-8167 Fax
http://WWW.CivilWarMall.com/Image.htm
Heritage@navix.net
Tom & Dorothy Rivett
PO Box 22424
Lincoln NE 68542-2424
Exclusive Mort Kunstler art images embroidered on quality American-made garments. Personalization available for reenactors, round tables, museums & galleries. Visit our online catalog.

HERITAGE PRESERVATION ASSOCIATION
800-86-DIXIE • 770-928-2714
770-928-2719 Fax
http://www.hpa.org
HPA@america.net
PO Box 98209
Atlanta GA 30359-1909
National non-profit organization protects & preserves history, symbols & culture of the American South. Reg. membership - $40. Call for more detailed information.

HERITAGEPAC
501-225-3996
heritagepac@aristotle.net
Jerry L. Russell, Director
PO Box 7281 • Little Rock AR 72217-7281
Non-profit lobbying group/action committee devoted to battlefield preservation.

THE INDEX PROJECT, INC.
2525 10th St N Apt 621
Arlington VA 22201-1966
Non-profit group preparing computerized index of 100,000 Union court-martials.

IRISH BRIGADE ASSOCIATION
201-694-7792 • laverty@crusoe.com
PO Box 3495 • Wayne NJ 07474-3495
Explores Irish dimension of U.S. military, with emphasis on Civil War. Membership - $25.

IRON BRIGADE ASSOCIATION
Milwaukee CWRT
Inst for CW Studies / Carroll College
100 N East Ave • Waukesha WI 53186-3103
Dedicated to the memory of the Iron Brigade in the West. Lifetime membership with lapel pin - $5; with medal replica - $15. Send full name, address & phone number with check.

JACKSON'S FOOT CAVALRY
804-780-3373 • 800-833-5522
B. Brenner Wood
Now mustering "F" Company, 21st Regt., Virginia Volunteer Cavalry. We are historians who interpret the Civil War by authentically portraying the common soldier.

JUNIATA COUNTY HISTORICAL SOCIETY
498B Jefferson St
Mifflintown PA 17059-1400
An Imperishable Fame: The Civil War Experience of George F. McFarland, by Michael Dreese - 210 pp., $20 (ppd.).

KENTUCKIANA ARMS COLLECTORS ASSN., INC.
PO Box 1776 • Louisville KY 40201-1776
Sponsors annual gun show in July; has resurrected John Hunt Morgan show. 200 tables, weapons, relics, accoutrements, displays, photos, memorabilia.

KERNSTOWN BATTLEFIELD ASSOCIATION
540-678-8598 • 800-298-1861
http://www.kernstownbattle.org
jridings@mnsinc.com
PO Box 1327 • Winchester VA 22604-7827
Non-profit organization endeavoring to acquire, maintain & interpret the Kernstown Battlefield. Primary goal is acquisition of 342-acre Grim Farm.

SGT. KIRKLAND'S MUSEUM & HISTORICAL SOCIETY, INC.
540-899-5565 • 540-899-7643 Fax
Civil-War@msn.com
912 Lafayette Blvd • Fredericksburg VA 2240
Non-profit museum, association & press devoted to preservation of historical documents, artifacts, & texts; education; publication of meritorius books; & research & recovery of CW soldiers' records. Free catalog.

LADIES OF THE GRAND ARMY OF THE REPUBLIC
http://suvcw.org/lgar.htm
Mrs. Elizabeth Koch, Natl. Sect.
119 N Swarthmore Ave Apt H1
Ridley Park PA 19078-2118
Organization for female descendants of Union veterans.

LADIES' SOLDIER'S FRIEND SOCIETY
Donna Wilson, Pres.
PO Box 150223
Nashville TN 37215
Living history participation. Publish "The Ladies' Companion" bi-monthly. Annual dues - $15.

LAWRENCE CIVIL WAR MEMORIAL GUARD, INC.
240 Andover St
Lawrence MA 01843-2246
Non-profit organization dedicated to preservation of Lawrence, Mass.'s Civil War history, its monuments & its graves.

LINCOLN CLUB OF TOPEKA
Dale Jirik
1331 SW Caledon St
Topeka KS 66611-2411

LITTLE BIG HORN ASSOCIATES
105 Bartlett Pl
Brooklyn NY 11229-6361
Join with us & learn more about the life and times of Gen. George A. Custer & his contemporaries.

LIVING HISTORY ASSOCIATION, INC.
PO Box 1389
Wilmington VT 05363-1389
Reenactors' Liability Insurance, covering reenactments, encampments, black powder, cavalry, artillery; personal injury, equipment insurance. Educational programs, workshops, full historical museum. Newsletter, events & info - $3.

GENERAL LONGSTREET MEMORIAL FUND
919-258-6966
919-775-5214 Fax
thomas.ils@mhs.unc.edu
Robert C. Thomas
112 Offset Farm Rd
Sanford NC 27330-9723
Non-profit fund to publish the *Longstreet Book of Honor*. Dedicated equestrian monument to Gen. James Longstreet at Gettysburg National Military Park in 1998. Newsletter.

THE LONGSTREET SOCIETY
770-531-0100
770-531-7956 Fax
PO Box 191
Gainesville GA 30503-0191
Formed to honor the life of Lt. Gen. James Longstreet. Dedicated to preserving landmarks & memorabilia. Currently restoring Longstreet's old Piedmont Hotel. Memberships accepted.

MANASSAS MUSEUM ASSOCIATES
703-368-1873
http://xroads.virginia.edu/~VAM/MAN/vam-intro.html
janemriley@aol.com
PO Box 560
9101 Prince William St
Manassas VA 20108-0560
Non-profit organization dedicated to the support of the Manassas Museum System & its mission to preserve the rich heritage of the Northern Virginia Piedmont area.

MILITARY ORDER OF THE LOYAL LEGION OF THE UNITED STATES (MOLLUS)
517-694-9394
http://suvcw.org/mollus.htm
YJNW42A@prodigy.com
Keith G. Harrison
4209 Santa Clara Dr
Holt MI 48842-1868
Founded in 1865 for direct or collateral descendants of commissioned officers of the Union army.

MILITARY ORDER OF THE STARS & BARS
615-380-1844
Sons of Confederate Veterans
PO Box 59
Columbia TN 38401-0059
Descendants of Confederate officers & government officials.

MINERVA CENTER ON WOMEN & THE MILITARY
410-437-5379
http://www.MinervaCenter.com
mouseminer@aol.com
20 Granada Rd
Pasadena MD 21122-2708
Non-profit education foundation & publisher presents the 3rd printing of *An Uncommon Soldier: The Civil War Letters of Sarah Rosetta Wakeman, alias Pvt. Lyons Wakeman*. $25.

MISSOURI CIVIL WAR REENACTORS ASSOCIATION
PO Box 417 • Fayette MO 65248-0417
Annual individual membership - $8; family - $12.

MISSOURI HISTORICAL SOCIETY
PO Box 11940 • Saint Louis MO 63112-0040
Civil War books. In *The Civil War in St. Louis, a Guided Tour,* Wm. C. Winter brings to life the monuments, markers, & memories of the Civil War in St. Louis. 192 pp. Paper - $22.95. Cloth - $32.95.

MONTGOMERY COUNTY HISTORICAL SOCIETY
212 S Water St
Crawfordsville IN 47933-2535
The Diary of Private Ambrose Remley & His Four Years in the Lightning Brigade - story of Wilder's mounted infantry & Spencer repeating rifle - $23.

MORGAN'S MEN ASSOC., INC.
Samuel Flora
1691 Kilkenny Dr
Lexington KY 40505-2316
Non-profit organization seeking to perpetuate the memory of Gen. John Hunt Morgan & his men. Write for more information.

NATIONAL CIVIL WAR ASSOCIATION
PO Box 70084 • Sunnyvale CA 94086-0084
Union & Confederate units involved in reenactments, educational presentations. Open to all interested reenactors. Individ. memb. $35.

NATIONAL GENEALOGICAL SOCIETY
703-525-0050 Office • 703-841-9065 Library
703-525-0052 Fax
http://www.genealogy.org/~ngs
ngslibe@wizard.net OR
76702.2417@compuserve.com
4527 17th St N • Arlington VA 22207-2399

NATIONAL MUSEUM OF CIVIL WAR MEDICINE
301-695-1864 • 800-564-1864
301-695-6823 Fax
http://www.civilwarmed.org
LauraM@civilwarmed.org
48 E Patrick St • PO Box 470
Frederick MD 21705-0470
Center for study & interpretation of Civil War medical history. Medical artifacts, manuscripts, books & materials. 1861-1865. Museum store. Memberships available. Annual conference 1st weekend in August.

NATIONAL MUZZLELOADING RIFLE ASSOCIATION
812-667-5131
812-667-5137 Fax
PO Box 67 • Friendship IN 47021-0067
Represents all aspects of muzzleloading. More than 25,000 members/300 charter clubs throughout the country. Subscription to *Muzzle Blasts* with $30 membership.

NATIONAL TRUST FOR HISTORIC PRESERVATION
202-673-4000
800-944-6847 to join
202-673-4038 Fax
http://www.nthp.org
1785 Massachusetts Ave NW
Washington DC 20036-2117
Non-profit organization committed to preserving the heritage & livability of America's communities. Operates historic house museums, publishes monthly magazine & newsletter. Memberships welcome. Brochures.

NATIONAL WOMAN'S RELIEF CORPS
217-522-4373
629 S 7th St
Springfield IL 62703-1636
Woman's auxiliary to the GAR.

NEVADA CIVIL WAR VOLUNTEERS
http://pw2.netcom.com/baugh1/index.html
PO Box 11033
Reno NV 89510-1033
Living history & other programs devoted to Civil War study, such as "Soldier for an Hour." Educational presentations. Union, Confederate & civilian groups. Annual membership - $15 (individ.); $25 (family).

NORTH-SOUTH SKIRMISH ASSOCIATION
http://mh004.infi.net/~nssa/
Phil Spaugy
501 N Dixie Dr
Vandalia OH 45377-2011
Team competition in high-level marksmanship with original or approved reproduction muskets, carbines, revolvers, & artillery at breakable targets in a timed match. Period regimental uniforms worn.

OHIO CIVIL WAR ASSOCIATION
419-586-5294
419-586-6763 Fax
106 Haig St
Celina OH 45822-2708
Hosts annual Civil War conference & other events.

ORDER OF SOUTHERN GRAY, INC.
540-955-3980
540-955-4126 Fax
cwpub@visuallink.com
Katherine Tennery, President
PO Box 351
Berryville VA 22611-0351
Virginia women dedicated to preserving Southern heritage. Free brochure.

OZARK ARTS ASSOCIATION
OzarkArts@aol.com
PO Box 165
Rogers AR 72757-0165
Join our collectors' club to purchase handcrafted & painted 8" sculptures of Civil War soldiers. Illus. brochure - $1 (ref. w/ purchase).

PEJEPSCOT HISTORICAL SOCIETY/ JOSHUA L. CHAMBERLAIN MUSEUM
207-729-6606
207-729-6012 Fax
http://www.curtislibrary.com/pejepscot.htm
pejepscot@curtislibrary.com
159 Park Row
Brunswick ME 04011-2005
Historical Society operates the Joshua Chamberlain Museum located in Chamberlain's former home. Also maintains the most comprehensive Chamberlain research collection available anywhere. Free catalog.

JOHN PELHAM HISTORICAL ASSOCIATION, INC.
757-838-1685
http://members.aol.com/JPHA1982
JPHA1982@aol.com
Peggy Vogtsberger
7 Carmel Ter
Hampton VA 23666-2807
Bi-monthly newsletter, "The Cannoneer." Annual convention & tour of Fredericksburg; commemorative ceremony at Kelly's Ford. Supports preservation; active in erecting monuments. Archives located at Jacksonville Public Library, Jacksonville, Ala.

POINT LOOKOUT POW DESCENDANTS ORGANIZATION
http://members.tripod.com/~PLPOW/pointlk.htm
plpow@erols.com
3587 Windmill Dr • Virginia Beach VA 23456
Bi-monthly newsletters, medals, bumper stickers, prison grounds meetings, POW reenactors. Programs provided. For membership application - send SASE.

POTOMAC ARMS COLLECTOR'S ASSN.
301-921-9673
PO Box 1812
Wheaton MD 20915-1812
Sponsors of annual October gun show, Frederick, MD. Guns, knives, & related items. Donation - $4.

THE PROFESSIONAL TREASURE HUNTERS HISTORICAL SOCIETY
603-357-0607
800-447-6014 (New England)
603-352-1147 Fax
George Streeter
14 Vernon St
Keene NH 03431-3440
Info. about treasure hunting in US. Metal detecting info. Treasure club activities in US. Newsletter - *Treasure Hunter's Gazette*.

REENACTORS OF THE AMERICAN CIVIL WAR
PO Box 1248
Magalia CA 95954-1248
Reenactments, other events. Participates in many civic functions.

SHENANDOAH NATIONAL HISTORY ASSOCIATION
540-999-3581
540-999-3582
3655 US Highway 211 E
Luray VA 22835-4702

SHIP'S COMPANY, INC.
410-788-7264
Lawrence Bopp, Pres.
309 Roanoke Dr
Baltimore MD 21228-4240
Official interpretive group of the USS *Constellation*, recruiting Federal sailors & marines for service aboard this 1855 war sloop - the last surviving warship to see Civil War action.

SIGNAL CORPS ASSOCIATION
410-768-3162
Lisa Christofich, Editor; Walt Mathers
13 Beach Rd
Glen Burnie MD 21060-7506
Publish monthly, multi-page newsletter - $9/yr. Sample copy - 70¢.

SONS OF CONFEDERATE VETERANS (N.C. DIVISION)
PO Box 1896
Raleigh NC 27602-1896

SONS OF CONFEDERATE VETERANS (NATL. OFFICE)
931-380-1844
http://www.scv.org
International Headquarters
PO Box 59
Columbia TN 38402
Dedicated to preserving & defending history & principles of the Old South. Recruiting male descendants of those who fought in the Confederacy. Contact for membership info.

SONS OF SHERMAN'S MARCH TO THE SEA
1725 S Farmer Ave
Tempe AZ 85281-6533
Formed for direct descendants of Sherman's troops & others interested in Sherman. Membership - $3.

SONS OF UNION VETERANS OF THE CIVIL WAR (INDIANA)
153 Connie Dr
Pittsburgh PA 15214-1251
Founded by the GAR (1881). Chartered by Act of Congress (1954). Keep your heritage/ancestors' memory alive.

SONS OF UNION VETERANS OF THE CIVIL WAR (MICHIGAN)
810-659-4999
PO Box 618
DeWitt MI 48820-0618
Recruiting decendents of Civil War soldiers & sailors who honorably served the Union, 1861-1865.

SONS OF UNION VETERANS OF THE CIVIL WAR (NY CITY)
718-426-8740
SVC Cliff Henke
Oliver Tilden Camp No. 26
8269 61st Dr
Middle Village NY 11379-1448
Welcome descendants of Union veterans in the NYC metropolitan area. Meet last Tuesday of month at 7th Regt. Armory, 66th & Park Aves., NYC.

SONS OF UNION VETERANS OF THE CIVIL WAR (NY STATE)
516-766-2403
Joseph Pucciarelli, Commander
183 Windsor Ave
Rockville Centre NY 11570
Recruiting the sons of soldiers & sailors of the Union in New York State.

SONS OF UNION VETERANS OF THE CIVIL WAR (KENTUCKY)
Don Hackel
623 E Ormsby Ave
Louisville KY 40203-2622
Camps held in Louisville & Lexington, with many KY-wide area camps to follow.

SONS OF UNION VETERANS OF THE CIVIL WAR (CALIFORNIA BAY)
707-538-9175
Charles L. Christian
5120 Oak Park Way
Santa Rosa CA 95409-3740
Camp #23 meets bi-monthly in Sonoma County.

SONS OF UNION VETERANS OF THE CIVIL WAR (PACIFIC NORTHWEST)
John Williamson
672 Redmond Ave NE
Renton WA 98056-3902
Gov. Isaac Stevens Camp #1 is recruiting sons of soldiers & sailors of the Union.

SOUTH CAROLINA BATTLEGROUND PRESERVATION TRUST, INC.
803-762-3563
PO Box 12441
Charleston SC 29422-2441
Seeks to preserve & restore SC's Civil War battlefields.

J.E.B. STUART BIRTHPLACE, INC.
540-251-1833
PO Box 240
Ararat VA 24053-0240
Memberships to help preserve the birthplace of J.E.B. Stuart begin at $25.

THE TURNER ASHBY SOCIETY
804-232-3406
Patricia Walenista
810 W 30th St
Richmond VA 23225-3515
Organization whose mission is to honor, preserve & promote the name of Gen. Turner Ashby. Gather to study & appreciate Ashby's life & times.

UNITED STATES CAVALRY ASSOCIATION
Mrs. Patricia S. Bright
PO Box 2325
Fort Riley KS 66442-0325
"We Remember." Proud sponsors of the US Cavalry Museum, Memorial Research Library & Memorial Foundation.

WEST VIRGINIA REENACTORS ASSOCIATION
304-472-5964
PO Box 2133
Buckhannon WV 26201-7133
Participates in reenactments & educational presentations; sponsors special events.

WINTER WEEKEND OF THE LIVING HISTORY SOCIETY
612-431-4760
ekatuin@compuserve.com
Elaine M. Katuin
7624 157th St W Apt 208
Apple Valley MN 55124-9166
Weekend gala featuring mid-19th-century dancing & civilian activities, workshops, ice skating & sledding. Period attire requested. Annual event - February.

MIKE WOSHNER
412-884-9299
mwoshner@bellatlantic.net
2306 Spokane Ave
Pittsburgh PA 15210-4414
Author of reference book & historical presentations on "India-rubber & gutta-percha in the Civil War era," encompassing history, patents, military trials & award-winning display of rare artifacts.

AMERICAN MILITARY ANTIQUES
410-465-6827
Courtney B. Wilson & Assoc.
8398 Court Ave
Ellicott City MD 21043-4514
Appraisers & dealers in fine 19th-century military Americana. Civil War memorabilia, books, photos, swords, forearms, relics. Buys/sells.

BACK IN TIME PORTRAIT & FINE ART STUDIO
800-484-1163 x2119 • 770-631-6533
P. Hardin
PO Box 181 • Tyrone GA 30290-0181
"Go Back in Time." Your photo converted into a B/W or full color portrait as CW soldier, mountain man, etc. Any era. Oil, pencil, acrylic. Start at $75.

BLACK & WHITE CUSTOM LAB, INC.
804-272-3345
804-744-2624
804-330-9003 Fax
MXHW21A@prodigy.com
Midlothian Festival Shopping Center
9550 Midlothian Tpke Apt 113
Richmond VA 23235-4900
Let us preserve your treasured Civil War photos with repairs, reproductions, custom printing. Digital imaging.

MIKE BRACKIN
203-647-8620
PO Box 23
Manchester CT 06045-0023
Large assortment of Civil War & Indian War autographs, accoutrements, memorabilia, insignia, medals, buttons, GAR, documents, photos & books. Catalog - $6/yr for 5 issues.

BUDGET FRAMER
888-343-7263
Larry Skaff - Photographry
940 North Ave
Grand Junction CO 81501
Civil War living history fine art prints & photography. Catalog - $1 (ref. w/ order).

DOUG BYRUM/CUSTOM ART
614-459-2622
Creative Illustration & Graphic Design
5413 Bennington Woods Ct
Columbus OH 43220-2221
Historical & reenactor portraits, battle scenes, home-front life. CW photos rendered as custom color art, contemporary art. Commissions accepted, fees based on B&W/color, size, media/subject matter. Prints available.

CONFEDERATE CALENDAR WORKS
PO Box 2084
Austin TX 78768-2084
Illustrated with previously unpublished & researched photos of Confederate soldiers, 1861-65 events, etc. $11.95.

HENRY DEEKS
978-263-1861
PO Box 2260
Acton MA 01720-6260
Vintage prints in carte de visite format of all participants in the Civil War era. Semi-annual catalog - offered without charge. (See ad page 272)

ELM TREE COLLECTIBLES, INC.
800-639-9886
17 Parkstone Ct
Stone Mountain GA 30087-2513
Archival source for rare Civil War photographs. Requests taken & items located. Custom-developed 8"x10" Grant or Lee photograph $39.95 + $4 S&H ea. Immediate shipping.

FEDERAL HILL ANTIQUITIES
410-584-8185 / 8329
14 Glen Lyon Ct
Phoenix MD 21131-1212
Purveyors of fine autographs & collectibles. Letters & documents, photos, relics & artifacts, ephemera. Buy/sell/trade.

GARLAND STUDIOS
504-261-2840
9165 Sullivan Rd
Baton Rouge LA 70818-5208
Specializes in restoring B&W photos, hand-tinting & customized B&W printing. Free estimates.

GIBSON'S CIVIL WAR COLLECTIBLES
423-323-2427
423-323-8123 Fax
Paul, Linda & Bryan Gibson
PO Box 948
Bristol TN 37621-0948
Autographs, CSA bonds & currency, diaries, flags, letter groups, newspapers, photos, slave items, uniforms, any other paper items.

DR. JOSEPH G. GOMEZ
413-533-3702
PO Box 823
Holyoke MA 01041-0823
Detailed B/W pearl finish prints from original unaltered glass plate, ca.1863.

GRAVE CONCERNS
PO Box 20094
Cincinnati OH 45220-0094
Sell/trade photographs of burial sites of Civil War generals blue & gray, politicians, spies, notables - many hard to find. 5,000 photos on hand; send SASE & needs. Catalog - SASE.

HEART OF HISTORY & VARIABLE HEART
540-234-9031 (mall)
John & Miriam Heatwole, Dick Swanson
Simonetti's Antique Center
Rt 11, off exit 235 on I-81
Weyers Cave VA 24486
One of the best Civil War shops in the Shenandoah Valley - museum-quality photos & artifacts, wrought iron, pharmaceutical relics, buttons, books, documents, & much more.

GARY HENDERSHOTT
501-224-7555
PO Box 22520
Little Rock AR 72221-2520
Autographs, photographs, imprints, flags & memorabilia of the Civil War era. Catalog - $3.

HISTORICAL COLLECTIBLE AUCTIONS
336-570-2803
336-570-2748 Fax
PO Box 975
Burlington NC 27215
Quarterly auctions of Civil War collectibles including photography, manuscripts, autographs, weapons, etc. Consignments encouraged. Catalog - $20/issue; next 3 for $45.

HISTORICAL RESOURCES PRESS
888-BOOK4US
414-469-5582 Fax
Karin K. Ramsay
7704 Castle Grn
San Antonio TX 78218-2309
Photographer ... Under Fire: The Story of George S. Cook (1819-1902). Mathew Brady's ex-partner photographed opening shots at Fort Sumter. 40 photos, limited ed. hardcover - $29.95. Brochure.

THE HISTORICAL SHOP
504-467-2532
504-464-7552 Fax
Yvonne & Cary Delery
PO Box 73244
Metairie LA 70033-3244
Photos, documents, autographs, CSA currency, letters, slavery ads & items, relics, framed displays & other collectibles. Buys/sells. Illus. catalogs - $8/yr.

THE HORSE SOLDIER
717-334-0347
717-334-5016 Fax
http://www.bmark.com/horsesoldier.antiques
hsoldier@mail.wideopen.net
PO Box 184 • Cashtown PA 17310-0184
Buying, selling & appraising Civil War military antiques: firearms, edged weapons, photographs, documents, battlefield relics & more! All items unconditionally guaranteed. Soldier research service available. Semi-annual catalog - $10/yr.

IMAGES ETC.
http://www.collectorsnet.com/imagesetc/index.htm
imagesetc@collectorsnet.com
David Cress
PO Box 493 • 141 Circle Loop
Eden NC 27288-0493
Civil War photos - more than 40 quality images, Union & Confederate. Buy/sell/trade. Catalog - $1.

IRISH BRIGADE GIFT SHOP
504 Baltimore St
Gettysburg PA 17325-2605
T-shirts, sweatshirts, jackets, books, flags, recruiting posters, photos, pins, stationery, prints, figurines & more - all relating to the Irish Civil War service. Detailed item list - send business-size SASE.

JACQUES NOEL JACOBSEN, JR.
718-981-0973
60 Manor Rd
Staten Island NY 10310-2626
Antiques & military collectibles, insignia, weapons, medals, uniforms, Kepis, relics, photos, paintings, & band instruments. Catalog - $12 for 3 issues. $15 overseas.

GLENN JAMES
PO Box 268 • Rancocas NJ 08073-0268
Wartime waist-up images of George E. Lowery, Co. C, 138th Pa. Volunteers, in uniform. 8"x10" repros - $15.

JOHN'S RELICS
843-549-7751
cwrelics@lowcountry.com • John Steele
227 Robertson Blvd
Walterboro SC 29488-2752
Civil War & colonial relics, arms accoutrements, veteran memorabilia, newspapers, books, CW tokens, photography, buttons & related memorabilia. Catalog - $1 (ref. w/ purchase).

KEYA GALLERY
212-366-9742
800-906-KEYA Orders only
http://www.KeyaGallery.com • Key15@aol.com
110 W 25th St Gallery 304A
New York NY 10001-7401
Excavated relics - bullets, tokens, buckles, buttons, insignia, & more. Catalog.

KRAINIK & WALVOORD
703-536-8045
PO Box 6206 • Falls Church VA 22040-6206
A Collector's Guide to Photographic Cases. Definitive reference on plastic ("Gutta Percha") daguerreotype cases. Hardcover - 800 illus. & price guide - $90 ppd.

MIKE KREMAN PHOTOGRAPHS
310-837-7756
PO Box 34242 • Los Angeles CA 90034-0242
Orig. limited edition platinum/palladium photo prints of Civil War sites & battle positions as they appear today - $95. Each print is titled, signed & numbered. Call for more info.

PHILLIP B. LAMB, LTD.
504-899-4710 • 800-391-0115 Orders
504-891-6826 Fax
http://www.LambRarities.com
lambcsa@aol.com
PO Box 15850 • 2727 Prytania St
New Orleans LA 70175-5850
Buy/sell Confederate memorabilia; CDVs, currency, documents, photos, art, bonds, slave items, swords, buttons, bullets, autographs, & much more.

LIVING IMAGES
304-274-0153
1104 Evergreen Cir
Falling Waters WV 25419-9745
Photography by Tim Johnson. Civil War sites with ghosted images. All photos hand-printed, matted & signed. From $19. Free catalog.

MC GOWAN BOOK CO.
919-968-1121
800-449-8406
919-968-1644 Fax
http://www.mcgowanbooks.com
mcgowanbooks@mindspring.com
R. Douglas Sanders
PO Box 4226
106 S Christopher Rd
Chapel Hill NC 27515
Always buying. Highest prices paid for fine & rare Civil War books, autographs, documents, photographs, etc. Catalog subs. - $3.

DON MEREDITH'S CIVIL WAR ART
813-962-1225
PO Box 370020
Tampa FL 33697-0020
Ordinary photos turn into extraordinary CW-era portraits, with strict attention to detail. Prices vary from $75. Discounts for photos showing proper uniform, gear, pose, etc. Color brochure - free.

THE MILITARY COLLECTION
PO Box 830970M
Miami FL 33283-0970
Helmets, uniforms, field gear, awards, medals, flags, weapons, swords, photos, etc. Catalog - $8.

MILITARY IMAGES
http://www.civilwar-photos.com
milimage@csrlink.net
RR 1 Box 99A
Henryville PA 18332-9726
Estab. 1979. Publication presenting great photographs of Yanks, Rebs & Indian War soldiers. Subscriptions - $24/yr. for 6 issues.

MOTTS MILITARY MUSEUM
614-836-5781
Warren Motts, Director
5761 Ebright Rd • Groveport OH 43125-9744
Civil War items & exhibits.

MOUNTAIN MAGIC IN METAL
719-486-8166
517 W Chestnut St • Leadville CO 80461
Pictures engraved on zinc plates, taken from original photos. Lincoln, Grant, Lee ($295 ea.) or Gettysburg Address ($375). S&H - $25. Custom photographic engraving.

THE MUSEUM OF THE CONFEDERACY
804-649-1861 • 804-644-7150 Fax
http://www.moc.org/
Janene Charbeneau
1201 E Clay St • Richmond VA 23219-1615
Maintains most comprehensive collection of military, political & domestic artifacts & art associated with the Confederacy. Adjacent to White House of the Confederacy, restored to its CW appearance.

SUSAN A. NASH
304-876-3772
PO Box 1011 • Shepherdstown WV 25443
Paper conservation. Specialist in historic documents, photographs, prints, drawings, maps, letters, broadsides. Cleaning, mending, deacidification, museum matting. By appt.

NATIONAL HERITAGE ARTS
8301 Alvord St
Mc Lean VA 22102-1736
Actual photographs, collectors' items. Satin-finished antique prints produced from archive negatives by noted Civil War photographers. 11" x 14" from $16.95.

NORTH STREET STUDIO
410-392-0630
118 E Main St • Elkton MD 21921-5907
Framed generals: Grant, Sherman, Buford, Chamberlain, Lee, Jackson, Stuart, Longstreet. 8"x10" hand-printed sepia-toned photos, double matted, walnut or silver frame.

NORTHERN CO. ARCHIVES/ACQUISITIONS
800-432-8777
18640 Mack Ave • PO Box 36793
Grosse Pointe Woods MI 48236-0793
Buyers of autographs, documents, photo collections, stock certificates, letters, contracts, etc. Lifetime member MS&D Society. Top $ paid.

HOWARD L. NORTON
PO Box 22821
Little Rock AR 72221-2821
Buy/sell/appraise. Autographs, Civil War items, Americana, historical documents, photographs, coins, currency, stamps, postal history. All transactions confidential. Catalog.

OLD PHOTO RESTORATION
815-227-0651
Civil War collectors - allow me to bring back the memories. Multimedia, photocollage, webpages.

OLDE SOLDIER BOOKS, INC.
301-963-2929
301-963-9556 Fax
Warbooks@erols.com
Dave Zullo
18779 N Frederick Ave Ste B
Gaithersburg MD 20879-3158
Largest selection of rare & hard-to-find books. Documents, letters, photographs, autographs, manuscripts. Buy/sell. Free catalog.

PANORAMICS
612-332-3912
James O. Phelps
17 S 1st St Apt A1210
Minneapolis MN 55401-1831
Panoramic, seamless battlefield photos of Gettysburg & Antietam battlefields, with maps & text. Free brochure.

PHOTOGRAPHY OF YESTERYEAR
423-510-9306
cwphotogpr@aol.com
Frank or Rita Harned
1 Prior Dr
Chattanooga TN 37421-2168
Photograph birthplaces, churches, cemeteries, landmarks. Photograph CW battlefields of approximate location of your ancestor's unit. Limited unit research available for TN, GA, KY.

PICTURE THAT ANTIQUES & COLLECTIBLES
414-361-0255
414-361-2992 Fax
107 W Huron St
Berlin WI 54923-1516
Large selection of tintypes, CDVs, ambrotypes & cabinet cards of Civil War soldiers & civilians. Books.

JOHN I. PISARCIK
1500 Annette Ave
Library PA 15129-9735
Reenactors - will draw your portrait from photo in "Battlefield Style." Special attention paid to details of uniforms, clothing & equipment.

PROFILES IN HISTORY
800-942-8856 • 310-859-7701
310-859-3842 Fax
345 N Maple Dr Ste 202
Beverly Hills CA 90210-3859
Autographs wanted. Also buying original letters, documents, vintage photos, manuscripts, & rare books (signed). Illus. catalog - $45/yr. Sample - $10.

STEVEN S. RAAB AUTOGRAPHS
800-977-8333 • 610-446-4514 Fax
http://www.raabautographs.com
raab@netaxs,com
PO Box 471
Ardmore PA 19003-0471
Serious collectors, respected dealers. Top dollars paid for collection & quality individual autographs, documents, manuscripts, signed photos, & interesting letters. Catalog sample - $5; $15/yr.

RIENZI PRESS
802-888-3439
Brad & Sue Limage
RR 2 Box 630 • Morrisville VT 05661-9802
"Vermont Soldiers in the Civil War" - calendar printed annually with large prints of Vermont brigades, CDUs, letter excerpts & battles on corresponding dates. $10 + S&H.

RON'S PHOTOGRAPHY
419-886-4835
rburgesssr@aol.com
770 State Route 97 E
Bellville OH 44813-1230
For all your photographic needs. Reasonable rates. Personalized service. Experienced photo-journalist, reenactor.

SELECTED CIVIL WAR PHOTOGRAPHS
http://rs6.loc.gov/cwphome.html
Resource providing views of 1,118 historic photos.

JOHN SICKLES
7880 Madison St
Merrillville IN 46410-4615
Buy/sell/trade cavalry images, specializing in Michigan Cavalry Brigade (1st, 5th, 6th, 7th regiments) & images depicting carbines.

DALE S. SNAIR
660-747-0341
904 Deer Run Apt C
Warrensburg MO 64093-8633
Civil War images, paper items, weapons, accoutrements. $4 for next 4 price lists.

SOUTHERN HISTORICAL SHOWCASE
800-854-7832
615-321-0639
http://www.southernhistorical.com
southernhistorical@nashville.com
1907 Division St
Nashville TN 37203-2705
Southern military art & books, prints, original documents & autographs, photos, engravings. Artists: Prechtel, Reeves, Kunstler, Kidd, Gallon, Summers, Heron, Garner, Rocco. Catalog - $5.

STOKES IMAGING SERVICES
800-856-4498
512-458-2201
7000 Cameron Rd
Austin TX 78752
Selected Civil War photographs, 1861-1865. Tapes CD-ROM for IBM or PC compatible - $79.95.

SUTLERS WAGON
Stamatelos Bros, Prop.
PO Box 390005
Cambridge MA 02139-0001
Fine quality American military items, 1775-1900. Civil War uniforms, headgear, accoutrements, buckles, tack, photos, swords, documents. Buy/sell.

TAILORED IMAGES
804-272-3345
804-744-2624
804-330-9003 Fax
MXHW21A@prodigy.com
3108 Quail Hill Dr
Midlothian VA 23112-4426
Photo restoration. Custom B&W archival quality prints. Digital imaging. Let us preserve your treasured Civil War photos. Repairs, reproductions, custom printing.

TEKNOVATION
540-548-4128
660 Montei Dr
Earlysville VA 22936-9690
Images of the Civil War, Vol. 1. Selected Civil War photographs 1861-1865. Interactive PC images. Use as screensaver, with printout capability. $24.95.

THEME PRINTS, LTD.
800-CIVL WAR
718-225-4067
PO Box 610123
Bayside NY 11361-0123
Books, antique arms, historic documents, photographs, letters & autographs from Revolutionary era to early Hollywood. Includes Civil War memorabilia. Fully illus. catalog - $5, or $12/yr. (5 issues).

CAROLE THOMPSON, FINE PHOTOGRAPHS
901-278-2741
901-726-5533 Fax
ctfp@ix.netcom.com
1515 Central Ave
Memphis TN 38104-4907
Gardner's Sketchbook of the Civil War, 100 museum quality albumen photos by Alexander Gardner & Timothy O'Sullivan. Buys/sells/appraises.

TIME LINE PHOTOS
717-337-0055
Old Gettysburg Village • 777 Baltimore St
Gettysburg PA 17325-2600
Reenactor portraits, featuring reproduction period backdrops. New, larger studio.

TRUE TO LIFE, INC.
800-847-6788 • 703-440-5062
7406 Alban Station Ct Ste B203
Springfield VA 22150-2310
Photo restoration, low cost, fast service. Old or damaged images. Consultations free & encouraged.

WAR BETWEEN THE STATES MEMORABILIA
717-337-2853 • Len Rosa
PO Box 3965 • Gettysburg PA 17325-0965
Buy/sell soldiers' letters, envelopes, documents, CDVs, photos, autographs, newspapers, badges, ribbons, relics, framed display items, currency, & more. Estab. 1978. Illus. catalogs - $10/yr for 5 issues. Active buyers receive future subscriptions free.

WELL-TRAVELED IMAGES
414-896-0555
http://www.globaldialog.com/~eicher/index.htm
eicher@globaldialog.com
Lynda Eicher
S60 W24160 Red Wing Dr
Waukesha WI 53186-9508
Color photos of CW battlefields, sites. Books. Matted color prints of 10,000+ CW-related images, also available for publication. Call or email for catalog. See internet home page for samples & info. on books.

GEORGE F. WITHAM
901-465-6722 Ph & Fax
155 Raspberry Cv • Eads TN 38028-3003
Catalog of Civil War Photographers - alphabetical listing by state of more than 5900 Civil War-era photographers. Softcover - $16.50 ppd.

CRAIG WOFFORD ANTIQUES
2101 Harrison Ave
Orlando FL 32804-5467
Civil War memorabilia bought/sold, appraisals; specializing in autographs, letters, documents, diaries, photographs. Identifies items, soldiers groupings. Est. 1975.

WRITE-TO-PRINT
245 East St Apt 203
Honeoye Falls NY 14472-1236
Extensive photos of men & battles. Maps showing placement of the regiments in battles, 24th, 81st, 110th, 147th, 184th NYV Infantry & 24th Cavalry, their stories - $20.

YANKEE CAMP STUDIO
412-238-2776
404 E Main St • Ligonier PA 15658-1420
Ltd. ed. Civil War art prints & photos.

YANKEE FORAGER
517-263-3925
137 Park St • Adrian MI 49221-2528
Civil War specialty books, documents, photos, relics, & more. Catalog - $2.

ZANGRONIZ PHOTOGRAPHY
301-924-2539
Fax 301-924-4986
marzan@idsonline.com
4011 Muncaster Mill Rd Ste 601
Rockville MD 20853-1426
U.S. Civil War reenactment postcards. First of series. Images of actual events. 4 cards in each set. 4 sets @ $1.50/set + $2 S&H. (See ad page 261)

ZIGZAG MULTIMEDIA
800-561-2765
100 professional quality photos on CD-ROM, with extensive text history to print into your own documents & presentations. Heritage of America series, incl. Civil War Battlefields. $49.95/CD.

BLITZKRIEG PRESS
21 Meridian Cir • Newtown PA 18940-1742
Stationery, notepads, etc. For sutlers, Civil War enthusiasts; personal or business use. Any design you request or have. Send $1 for more info.

CHAMBERLAIN PRESS
355 Kingsbury Way Apt 33
Westminster MD 21157-9471
Professional desktop publisher will produce 1st-rate materials for your needs. Catalogs, calendars, certificates, manuals, newsletters, programs, special documents. Specializing in Civil War materials. Free brochure.

GALLAGHER PRINTING
716-873-2434 • 716-873-0809 Fax
2507 Delaware Ave
Buffalo NY 14216-1792
For all your printing needs. Letterheads, envelopes, business cards, brochures, fliers, posters, etc. Call/write.

HUMMEL PRINTING
610-286-0399
PO Box 171 • Geigertown PA 19523-0171
12 Civil War-theme Christmas cards (4 dif. styles) with envelopes - $8 + $1.50 S&H. Special occasion & ladies' notecards, Civil War-theme writing paper & envelopes. Catalog - $1.

MHR & SONS
7387 Bethany Ridge Rd
Guysville OH 45735
Personalized bookplates. CW theme: 50 for $14, 100 for $24. Add 10% S&H.

PATRICK A. SCHROEDER PUBLICATIONS
804-376-1865
PO Box 455
Brookneal VA 24528-9304
Civil War books. New titles include *Civil War Soldier Life*; *We Came to Fight* (5th NY Vol. Inf.); & Belle Boyd. Archives research, prints, notecards, postcards available. Free catalog.

PAUL WILSON
Civil War Labels Unlimited
46 Sawmill Rd
Springfield MA 01118-1719
Personalized name/address labels, bookplates, bookmarks, notecards & scratch pad stationery - featuring your favorite CW personalities (more than 220 available). Illus. price list - $1 (checks payable to Paul Wilson).

Rockbridge Publishing

an imprint of Howell Press, Inc.

CIVIL WAR, VIRGINIA GUIDE BOOKS,
GHOSTS, & REGIONAL TITLES

EDITORIAL OFFICES
Post Office Box 351
Berryville, VA 22611
(540) 955-3980 • cwpub@visuallink.com

ON-LINE TRIVIA CONTEST • GREAT PRIZES!
http://rockbpubl.com

ADENIRAM PUBLICATIONS
3722 W 50th St # 328
Minneapolis MN 55410-2016
Brackett's Battalion: Minnesota Cavalry 1861-1866 (Bergemann). Softcover, 164 pp. - $12.99 + $2 S&H.

AMERICAN POLITICAL BIOGRAPHY
39 Boggs Hill Rd • Newtown CT 06470-1971
Presidential biographies. Send 32-cent stamp for monthly listing of available titles.

AYER COMPANY PUBLISHERS
603-922-5105 • 603-922-3348 Fax
Educational_Edge@msb.com
Haven Haynes
Lower Mill Rd • North Stratford NH 03590
Black Brigade, Folks from Dixie, David Glasgow Farragut: Admiral in the Making, Minutes of the Proceedings of the National Negro Convention. More than 60 other titles. Catalog - $24.95 on CD-ROM. 25% restocking fee if not prepaid.

BELLE GROVE PUBLISHING CO.
800-861-1861
PO Box 483 • Kearny NJ 07032-0483
Titles include *History of the 57th Pennsylvania, Four Years Campaigning in the Army of the Potomac*. Videos of "lost" films from silent movie era - *CW Cinema* Vols I-III. Call/write for more info.

BIG SHANTY PUBLISHING CO.
PO Box 80641 • Chamblee GA 30366-0641
Ghost Trains & Depots of Georgia (1833-1933), by Les R. Winn. Complete story of all Georgia's passenger carrying railroads. 400 pp., hardcover - $65 + $4 S&H.

BLACKSMITH PUBLISHERS
800-531-2665
bcbooks@northlink.com
PO Box 1752 • Chino Valley AZ 86323-1752
Sea Officer, historical novel based on lesser-known Civil War naval actions - $22.95 ppd. Free booklist.

JOHN F. BLAIR, PUBLISHER
800-222-9796 • 336-768-1374
336-768-9194 Fax
blairpub@aol.com
1406 Plaza Dr
Winston-Salem NC 27103-1485
Civil War Blunders: Amusing Incidents from the War, by Clint Johnson; *The Lee Girls*, by Mary Price Coulling; other regional & Civil War titles. Catalog.

BLUE ACORN PRESS
304-733-3917
5589 Shawnee Dr • PO Box 2684
Huntington WV 25726-0084
Book publishers: *Blood & Sacrifice, The 72nd Indiana: Wilder's Lightning Brigade, How Soldiers Were Made*, & many more.

BNR PRESS
800-793-0683 Orders & Fax
419-732-NOTE (6683)
http://www.dcache.net/~bnrpress
bnrpress@dcache.net
Fred Schwan • 132 E 2nd St
Port Clinton OH 43452-1115
Comprehensive Catalog of Confederate Paper Money by Grover Criswell & other titles of interest to collectors. Hardcover - $35; dealer discounts. Advertising opportunities.

BOGG & LAURENCE PUBLISHING CO., INC.
800-345-5595 • 305-866-3600
305-866-8040 Fax
1007 Kane Concourse
Bay Harbor Islands FL 33154-2105
The new *Dietz Confederate States Catalog and Handbook*, 2nd printing. Most comprehensive treatment of Confederate stamps & postal history; reorganized & expanded for easier use. Hardcover, 300 pp. - $75.

BOYD PUBLISHING CO.
800-452-4035
912-452-4020 after 6pm EST
tignall@accucomm.net
PO Box 367 • Milledgeville GA 31061-0367
100s of new historical publications & genealogical references. Computer software. *Official Record of the War of the Rebellion* - all 127 vols. on CD-ROM, $89.95 + $5 S&H.

BPC PUBLISHERS
PO Box 436 • Mahomet IL 61853-0436
Total War in Carolina. Story of Sherman's 1865 Carolina's campaign as told by its participants. 125 pp. - $16.00 ppd.

BROADFOOT PUBLISHING COMPANY
910-686-4816
910-686-4379 Fax
http://broadfoot.wilmington.net
Tom Broadfoot
1907 Buena Vista Cir
Wilmington NC 28405-7892
Sell rare & out-of-print material, own publications by catalog. In-print catalog - $2. Out-of-print catalog - $5 (ref. w/ order).

BROWN PUBLICATIONS
BrianB1578@aol.com
PO Box 25501 • Little Rock AR 72221-5501
In the Footsteps of the Blue & Gray - $24.95 + $2 S&H. Describes CW-related research sources in state archives, National Archives & LDS collection. History of ea. corps & hard-to-find technical information.

BUDD PRESS
71 66th St • Glendale NY 11385
President Lincoln's Third Largest City: Brooklyn & the Civil War. Fascinating reading - $13.95 ppd.

BURD STREET PRESS
888-WHT MANE • 717-532-2237
717-532-7704 Fax
Harold Collier • PO Box 152
Shippensburg PA 17257-0152
Publisher of military history with core interest in U.S. Civil War. Write for titles. Free catalog.

BUTTERNUT AND BLUE
410-256-9220 • 410-256-8423 Fax
Jim McLean
3411 Northwind Rd
Baltimore MD 21234-1250
Offer 5 to 6 comprehensive book catalogs each year. Librarian from prestigious college proclaimed that ours was "the best CW catalog." Catalog - $2 ($5 outside US) - free after order or $10 for 1-yr. subs. with no order.

BUTTERNUT PUBLICATIONS
304-267-0540
Susan Crites • PO Box 1851
Martinsburg WV 25402-1851
Civil War titles; ghost books.

C. W. HISTORICALS
609-854-1290 Ph & Fax
cwhist@erols.com
PO Box 113
Collingswood NJ 08108-0113
Civil War Spoken Here. Dictionary of mispronounced people, places & things of 1860s. 216 pp. - $14 ppd. Other titles.

CAISSON PRESS
607-547-1080
81 Lake St
Cooperstown NY 13326-1038
Fields of Gray: The Battle of Griswoldville, 232 pp. *Cradled in Glory: Georgia Military Institute, 1851-1865*, 224 pp. *Among the Best Men the South Could Boast: The Fall of Fort McAllister*, 160 pp. All hardcover - $25 ea. (ppd.)

CAMP CHASE PUBLISHING
http://nemesis.cybergate.net/~civilwar
CampChase@compuserve.com
PO Box 707 • Marietta OH 45750-0707
How to Get Started in Civil War Reenacting - 36-pg. handbook, by veteran reenactor. $5.

CAMP POPE BOOKSHOP
319-351-2407 • 319-339-5964 Fax
http://members.aol.com/ckenyoncpb
ckenyoncpb@aol.com
PO Box 2232 • Iowa City IA 52244-2232
Largest selection of in-print titles, including reprints, on trans-Mississippi theater of the Civil War. Free catalog.

CAPPER PRESS
800-678-5779 x4316
1503 SW 42nd St • Topeka KS 66609-1265
Authentic Memoirs of Civil War Soldiers. Softcover - $6.95.

CHICKASAW BAYOU PRESS
103 Trace Harbor Rd
Madison MS 39110-9754
To Live and Die in Dixie: A History of the 3rd Regiment Mississippi Infantry, CSA - 660 pp., hardcover, $42.50 + $3 S&H. *Hill of Death: The Battle of Champion Hill* - softcover, $5 + $1.50 S&H. Ltd. eds.

STAN CLARK MILITARY BOOKS
717-337-1728 • 717-337-0581 Fax
915 Fairview Ave
Gettysburg PA 17325-2906
Buys/sells Civil War books, ltd. edition prints, autographs, letters, documents, postcards, soldiers' items; special interest in U.S. Marine Corps items.

COBBLESTONE PUBLISHING
800-821-0115
http://www.cobblestonepub.com
custsvc@cobblestone.mv.com
7 School St Unit A
Peterborough NH 03458-1454
Two-volume Civil War Era set. Vol. I - *A House Divided*; Vol. II - *A New Nation.* $44.95/set. Forewords by Ken Burns & James McPherson. Free catalog.

COLLECTORS' LIBRARY
541-937-3348
PO Box 263 • Eugene OR 97440-0263
THE publisher for key reference books on accoutrements, guns, saddles, edged weapons, etc., for pre-Civil War, Civil War, Indian War & post-1900 period. Free catalog.

COMBINED PUBLISHING
610-828-2595
800-418-6065
610-828-2603 Fax
http://www.dca.net/combinedbooks
combined@dca.net
476 W Elm St
PO Box 307
Conshohocken PA 19428-0307
Titles include *Gettysburg, July 1*; *In Search of Robert E. Lee*; *Civil War Firearms*; *The Appomattox Campaign*; *The Antietam Campaign*; *The Gettysburg Campaign*, etc. Free catalog.

CUMBERLAND HOUSE PUBLISHING
615-832-1171
615-832-0633 Fax
CumbHouse@aol.com
431 Harding Industrial Park Dr
Nashville TN 37211
Best Little Stories from the Civil War by C. Brian Kelly, incl. "Varina: Forgotten First Lady," by Ingrid Smyer. A must-read. Softcover - $14.95 + $2.50 S&H.

DA CAPO PRESS
800-321-0050
233 Spring St
New York NY 10013-1522
The Rise of U. S. Grant; My Enemy, My Brother, *The Antietam and Fredericksburg;* many more. From $13.95.

DETROIT BOOK PRESS
901 W Lafayette Blvd
Detroit MI 48226-3013
Michigan Regimentals facsimile hardcover reprints.

THE DIETZ PRESS
800-391-6833
804-733-3514 Fax
Wert Smith
903 Winfield Rd
Petersburg VA 23803
Cornbread and Maggots, Cloak and Dagger: Union Prisoners and Spies in Civil War Richmond, by David D. Ryan - $24.95. Trials & tribulations from Union & Confederate sources.

THE DIXIE PRESS
615-831-0776 Ph & Fax
PO Box 110783
Nashville TN 37222-0783
Publisher, wholesaler & retailer of Southern books & genealogy products. Free catalog.

DOBI PUBLISHING
716-372-8687
1662 Haskell Pkwy
Olean NY 14760-9510
New edition of *Directory of Buyers* - lists 1000s of collectors & dealers who are anxious to buy. $14.95 + $3 S&H.

DOVER PUBLICATIONS
31 E 2nd St
Mineola NY 11501-3582
Civil War books, including *Personal Memoirs of U.S. Grant*. Many others. Free catalog.

DOWN EAST BOOKS
800-685-7962
PO Box 679
Camden ME 04843-0679
A Distant War Comes Home: Maine in the Civil War Era - Softcover, 384 pp., $21.45 ppd.

EAKIN PRESS
800-880-8642 • 512-288-1771
512-288-1813 Fax
http://www.lsjunction.com
EAKINPUB@SIG.NET
Edwin M. Eakin, Pres.
8800 Tara Ln
PO Box 90159
Austin TX 78709-0159
Boy Soldiers of the Confederacy, Reprint; 1st published in 1805. Other titles. Catalog - $1.25 (ref.).

THE EASTON PRESS
800-367-4534
47 Richards Ln • Norwalk CT 06851-3422
Own the finest editions of the 35 best Civil War books - the leather-bound Library of the Civil War.

EDINBOROUGH PRESS
612-415-1034 • 612-631-8080 Fax
edinborough@juno.com
PO Box 13790 • Roseville MN 55113-2293
Our Army Nurses: Stories from Women in the Civil War, by Mary Gardner Holland - 320 pp., softcover, $19.95. Other Civil War titles. Catalog.

EDMONSTON PUBLISHING, INC.
315-824-1965
PO Box 38 • Hamilton NY 13346-0038
While My Country Is in Danger, 12th NJ. *No Middle Ground*, Union Artillery. $22.95 ea. *Memoirs of the 149th NYV* - $35.95. *Unfurl the Flags* - $4.95. S&H - $3.50/$1.50/$1.00. Other new & used titles. Free catalog.

ELLIOTT & CLARK PUBLISHING
800-959-3245 • 334-265-8880 Fax
http://www.blackbeltpress.com
sales@blackbeltpress.com
PO Box 551
Montgomery AL 36101-0551
Titles include *A Guide to Civil War Washington* - $12.95, *Mapping for Stonewall: The Civil War Service of Jed Hotchkiss* - $29.95, *Fallen Soldiers: Memoir of a Civil War Casualty* - $14.95.

FABER & FABER PUBLISHERS
53 Shore Rd • Winchester MA 01890-2821
Featuring Civil War books such as *Battlefield: Framing a Civil War Battleground*, by Peter Svenson. Clothbound - $21.95.

FIVE CEDARS PRESS
540-877-2796
Allan Tischler • 841 Wardensville Grade
Winchester VA 22602-2058
The History of the Harpers Ferry Cavalry Expedition (Sept. 14 & 15, 1862) Ltd. ed. Hardcover book, illus., maps - $24.95 ppd.

FORDHAM UNIVERSITY PRESS
718-817-4782 • 800-247-6553 Orders
718-817-4785 Fax
cboyle@murray.fordham.edu
Cormac Boyle
2546 Belmont Ave • University Box L
Bronx NY 10458-5106
Scholarly books in the humanities. Two continuing Civil War series: *The Irish in the Civil War* and *The North's Civil War*. Free catalog.

FRANKLIN BOOKSELLERS
615-370-5737 Publisher • 615-790-1349 Store
118 4th Ave S • Franklin TN 37064-2622

FREE PRESS
212-702-2000
866 3rd Ave • New York NY 10022-6221
A Woman of Valor: Clara Barton and the Civil War. 1994, 527 pp., illus., etc. - $27.95.

FULCRUM PUBLISHING
303-277-1623 • 303-279-7111 Fax
fulcrum@concentric.net
350 Indiana St Ste 350
Golden CO 80401-5093
Publisher of books & calendars including *Mapping the Civil War*, collection of rare maps from the Library of Congress. Free catalog.
(See ad page 270)

G W SPECIALTIES
816-356-7457
George Scheil
7311 Ditzler Ave
Raytown MO 64133-6439
Civilian reprints of magazines & schoolbooks from mid-1800s. Free catalog.

GENEALOGICAL PUBLISHING CO.
800-296-6687
1001 N Calvert St
Baltimore MD 21202-3897
Publishers of the *Index to the Roll of Honor*, an incredible guide to the 228,639 Union dead listed in the *Roll's* 27 vols. 1164 pp. $75. On CD-ROM, incl. entire Roll of Honor - $49.99. Free catalog.

GIBBS SMITH, PUBLISHER
800-743-5439
http://www.gibbs-smith.com
info@gibbs-smith.com
PO Box 667
Layton UT 84041-0667
Returning to the Civil War: Grand Reenactments of an Anguished Time - living history at its best in full-color photography. 96 pp., softcover - $21.95. Free catalog.

GUILD PRESS OF INDIANA
317-848-6421 • 800-913-9563 Orders
http://www.guildpress.com
435 Gradle Dr • Carmel IN 46032-2535
The Civil War CD-Rom; *Iron Men, Iron Will*;*The Road to Glory*; *Rebel Sons of Erin*; *Field Surgeon at Gettysburg*. Other titles.

GUTS & GLORY PUBLICATIONS
3319 Dorado Pl • Carlsbad CA 92009-7706
The Battle of Antietam and *Life in the South During the Civil War*. $20 ea. + $3 S&H.

THE HEARTHSIDE PUBLISHING CO.
301-963-0141 • PO Box 2773
Staunton VA 24402-2773
Valor in Gray: The Recipients of the Confederate Medal of Honor, by Gregg S. Clemmer. 496 pp., $29.95 + $3.50 S&H.

J.W. HENRY PUBLISHING, INC.
703-404-0543 Fax
75361.755@compuserve.com
PO Box 1501 • Ashburn VA 20146-1501
Corporal Si Klegg and His Pard - Col. Wilbur Hinman's classic account of day-to-day life of Civil War enlisted man. $34.95 + $3.50 S&H.

HERITAGE BOOKS, INC.
800-398-7709 • 301-390-7709
http://www.heritagebooks.com
1540 Pointer Ridge Pl Ste E
Bowie MD 20716-1800
Books on history, Americana, Civil War, & genealogy. Free catalog.

HIGH WATER PRESS
315 S Arrawana Ave
Tampa FL 33609-3209
Recent books by Harris Mullen - *10 Incredible Mistakes at Gettysburg* and *Confederate Generals at Gettysburg* $5.95 ea. + $1.50 S&H. Both books - $11.90; no extras.

HISTORICAL RESOURCES PRESS
888-BOOK4US
414-469-5582 Fax
Karin K. Ramsay
7704 Castle Grn
San Antonio TX 78218-2309
Photographer ... Under Fire: The Story of George S. Cook (1819-1902). Mathew Brady's ex-partner photographed opening shots at Fort Sumter. 40 photos, limited ed. hardcover - $29.95. Brochure.

H. E. HOWARD, INC.
PO Box 4161
Lynchburg VA 24502-0161
Many Civil War titles.

HOWELL PRESS
804-977-4006
howellpres@aol.com
1713-2D Allied Lane
Charlottesville VA 22903-5336
Civil War titles, as well as books on history, transportation, cooking & gardening. (See ad page 267)

INDEPENDENT PUBLISHERS
3535 E Coast Hwy
Corona del Mar CA 92625-2404
War & Warriors series. Books, videos, audiotapes. Men, machines, strategies, battles, & politics of war. Catalog - send SASE.

INDIANA UNIVERSITY PRESS
812-855-6553
800-842-6796 Orders
http://www.indiana.edu/~iupress
601 N Morton St
Bloomington IN 47404-3778
The Men Stood Like Iron: How the Iron Brigade Won Its Name - hardcover, $24.95. Other titles.

JAMES RIVER PUBLICATIONS
804-220-4912
http://www.erols.com/jreb/civilwar.htm
102 Maple Ln
Williamsburg VA 23185-8106
The Chronological Tracking of the American Civil War per the Official Records, 2nd ed., fully indexed, foreword by Dr. Arthur W. Bergeron, Jr. The ultimate Civil War reference manual - $39.95.

THE JOHNS HOPKINS UNIVERSITY PRESS
800-537-5487
http://jhupress.jhu.edu/home.html
Hampden Station
Baltimore MD 21211
The Long Roll (softcover - $15.95) and *Cease Firing* (softcover - $14.95), both by Mary Johnston, a Civil War novelist rediscovered.

JOHN KALLMAN, PUBLISHERS
717-258-0919
717-258-4161 Fax
701 W North St
Carlisle PA 17013-2227
Titles include *Bull Run: Its Strategy & Tactics*, by Robert M. Johnson. 293 pp., hardcover, $29.95 ppd.

KANSAS HERITAGE PRESS
913-242-9243
PO Box 503 • Ottawa KS 66067-0503
Books dealing with Kansas' heritage & the Civil War. *Rebel Invasion of Missouri and Kansas*, *The Union Indian Brigade*, *The Civil War on the Border*, etc.

KENIMAR PUBLISHING
3137 Flowers Rd S Apt C
Atlanta GA 30341-6110
The History of Stone Mountain, memorial to the valor of soldiers, sailors & women of the Confederacy. $6 ppd.

WILLIAM KENNANN PUBLICATIONS
562-597-7384
2016 Fidler Ave
Long Beach CA 90815-2931
William Newby: A Civil War Soldier's Return.

KENNESAW MOUNTAIN PRESS, INC.
616-456-8115
75 Sheldon Blvd SE Ste 103
Grand Rapids MI 49503-4224
Melton & Pawl's Guide to CW Artillery Projectiles. Must-have pictorial handbook for collectors & researchers. Softcover - $9.95 + $3 S&H. Hardcover - $19.95.

THE KENT STATE UNIVERSITY PRESS
800-247-6553 x198
PO Box 5190 • Kent OH 44242-0001
No Sorrow Like Our Sorrow, Holding the Line, A Surgeon's Civil War, April '65, Red River Campaign, The First Day at Gettysburg, others.

SGT. KIRKLAND'S MUSEUM & HISTORICAL SOCIETY, INC.
540-899-5565 • 540-899-7643 Fax
Civil-War@msn.com
912 Lafayette Blvd
Fredericksburg VA 22401-5617
Non-profit museum, association & press devoted to preservation of historical documents, artifacts, & texts; education; publication of meritorius books; & research & recovery of CW soldiers' records. Free catalog.

LAND & LAND PUBLISHERS
504-344-1059 • Ken Land
196 S 14th St
Baton Rouge LA 70802-4752
Civil War books by William A. Spedale. *Where Bugles Called & Rifles Gleamed* - battle of Port Hudson, La. Hardcover, $17.95. *Historic Treasures of the American Civil War* - hardcover, $21.95. $2 S&H.

LENZ DESIGN & COMMUNICATIONS
404-633-0501 • 404-633-0047 Fax
Lenz_Design@msn.com
Sheila J. Lenz
2882 Delcourt Dr
Decatur GA 30033-2440
Civil War in Georgia: An Illustrated Traveler's Guide - 116 pp., softcover, $19.95

THE LIBRARY OF AMERICA
212-308-3360 • 212-750-8352 Fax
Libamerica@aol.com
Karen Iker
14 E 60th St
New York NY 10022-1006
Independent, non-profit publisher dedicated to preserving America's most significant writing in hardcover. Over 90 vols. in print, including Grant, Sherman & Lincoln. Free catalog.

LILLIBRIDGE PUBLISHING CO.
520-775-4681
Laurence F. Lillibridge
5313 N Western Blvd
Prescott Valley AZ 86314-4255
Hard Marches, Hard Crackers, & Hard Beds - reveals a soldier's hard life in his own letters & diaries of 3 yrs. $29.95 (ppd).

LOUISIANA STATE UNIVERSITY PRESS
504-388-6666
504-388-6461 Fax
uppress@lsuvm.sncc.lsu.edu
Margaret Hart
PO Box 25053
Baton Rouge LA 70894-5053
Great Civil War titles, incl. *The Battles for Spotsylvania Court House and the Road to Yellow Tavern* (Rhea) and *The Life of Billy Yank* (Wiley). Free catalog.

MADISON HOUSE PUBLISHERS, INC.
800-604-1776 Orders • 608-244-6210
608-244-7050 Fax
http://www.globaldialog.com/~mhbooks
info@mhbooks.com
PO Box 3100
2016 Winnebago St
Madison WI 53704-0100
Independent scholarly press dedicated to publishing fine books of enduring significance on American history & culture. Free catalog.

MAIL CALL JOURNAL
http://www.HistoryOnline.net
mcj@historyonline.net
PO Box 5031, Dept. B1
South Hackensack NJ 07606-4231
Actual letters & journals written by Civil War soldiers. Excerpts from books; original essays & poetry. 6 issues/yr. - $24.95. Sample - send SASE.

MC FARLAND & CO., INC.
910-246-4460 • 800-253-2187 Orders
http://www.mcfarlandpub.com
PO Box 611
Jefferson NC 28640-0611
Civil War books, Union & Confederate.

MC GUINN & MC GUIRE PUBLISHING
PO Box 20603 • Bradenton FL 34204-0603
In the Defense of This Flag: CW Diary of Pvt. Ormond Hupp. 309 pp. - $19.95 ppd.

MEDICAL STAFF PRESS
616-363-8655 Ph & Fax
http://www.iserv.net/~civilmed
CIVILMED@aol.com
Bradley P. Bengtson, MD
4286 Knapp Valley Ct NE
Grand Rapids MI 49505-9738
Orthopaedic Injuries of the Civil War - Softcover, $9.95 + $3 S&H; and *Photographic Atlas of Civil War Injuries* - Hardcover, $125 + $5 S&H.

MEHERRIN RIVER PRESS
919-398-3554
301 E Broad St • Murfreesboro NC 27855
Gatling: A Photographic Remembrance - book on the Gatling gun - $25.

MERCER UNIVERSITY PRESS
800-637-2378 x2880 • 912-752-2264 Fax
http://www.mupress.org
mupressorders@mercer.edu
6316 Peake Rd • Macon GA 31210-3960
The Lion of the South: Gen. Thomas C. Hindman $17.95; *Col. Burton's Spiller & Burr Revolver* $22.95; *The Forgotten "Stonewall of the West"* $32.95; *Rebel Georgia* $24.95 (HB), $15.95 (PB). *Carved in Stone* $32.95.

MERIT PRESS
1937 Robertson Rd SW
Albuquerque NM 87105-4057
Rebels on the Rio Grande, the Civil War journal of A.B. Peticolas with the Sibley Brigade in New Mexico (4th Texas Vols.). 187-pg softcover - $14.50 ppd.

MEYER PUBLISHING
800-477-5046 • 319-477-5041
319-477-5042 Fax • gfdchief@netins.net
PO Box 247 • Garrison IA 52229-0247
Iowa Valor - 250 firsthand accounts of IA troops in Civil War combat - $37.50. *Dark Days of the Rebellion* - Firsthand account, commentary of Civil War soldier in Salisbury Prison, a place worse than Andersonville - $24.95. Other titles. Free catalog.

MICHIGAN STATE UNIVERSITY PRESS
517-355-9543 • 800-678-2120 Fax
http://www.msu.edu/unit/msupress
1405 S Harrison Rd Ste 25
Manly Miles Bldg
East Lansing MI 48823-5243
Many titles. Write or call for complete list, including *The Ewing Family Civil War Letters*, *Trials and Triumphs*, *Women of the American Civil War*, etc.

MINERVA CENTER ON WOMEN & THE MILITARY
410-437-5379
http://www.MinervaCenter.com
mouseminer@aol.com
20 Granada Rd • Pasadena MD 21122-2708
Non-profit education foundation & publisher presents the 3rd printing of *An Uncommon Soldier: The Civil War Letters of Sarah Rosetta Wakeman, alias Pvt. Lyons Wakeman.* $25.

MISSOURI RIVER PRESS
573-446-3764
Phil Gottschalk, Pres.
1664 Highridge Cir Ste C
Columbia MO 65203-1930
In Deadly Earnest - the Missouri Brigade CSA which fought in the Vicksburg, Atlanta, & Tennessee campaigns - $30.

MORNINGSIDE BOOKSHOP
800-648-9710 • 937-461-4260 Fax
http://www.morningsidebooks.com
msbooks@erinet.com • Bob Younger
PO Box 1087 • Dayton OH 45401-1087
Editor & publisher of Civil War books & *Gettysburg* magazine. Catalog: ours & other publishers' CW books - $4 (free w/ order).

ANDREW MOWBRAY PUBLISHERS
800-999-4697 • 401-726-8011
401-726-8061 Fax
http://users.ids.net/~manatarm
smowbray@aol.com
PO Box 460 • Lincoln RI 02865-0460
New Civil War weapons book - Civil War Arms Makers and Their Contracts, facsimile report, 608 pp., $39.50 + $4.50 S&H. Catalog.

NAVAL INSTITUTE PRESS
800-233-8764 • 410-224-3378
410-224-2406 Fax
http://www.usni.org
2062 Generals Hwy
Annapolis MD 21401-6780
Fascinating facts & references to ships, battles & prominent people in military history; many titles on Civil War ships & battles. Free catalog.

NORTH SOUTH TRADERS CIVIL WAR
540-67-CIVIL
540-672-7283 Fax
nstcw@msn.com
PO Box 631
Orange VA 22960-0370
Illustrated, bi-annual *Civil War Collectors' Price Guide* - $25 + $3 S&H. Bi-monthly magazine, heavily illustrated - $25/yr.

THE NUGGET PUBLISHERS
812-866-4456
2146 S Logans Point Dr
Hanover IN 47243-9250
Civil War books, incl. *The Alford Brothers: "We All Must Die Sooner or Later"* - 356 pp., softcover, $23.95. Other titles.

O'DONNELL PUBLICATIONS
7217 Popkins Farm Rd
Alexandria VA 22306-2448
American Military Belt Plates - 1,000+ front & back views of plates, many photos. 616 pp., hardcover - $49.95 + $4.50 S&H.

OAK HILLS PUBLISHING
moreb@pcis.net • Rick Norton
The Story of Cole Younger, by Himself - $12.95.

PALADIN PRESS
800-392-2400
http://www.paladin-press.com
pala@rmii.com • Tina Mills
PO Box 1307 • Boulder CO 80306-1307
American Swords and Sword Makers. Definitive book for all edged weapons. Collectors, dealers, etc. 664 pp. - $79.95. Catalog - $2.

PARKWAY PUBLISHERS
704-265-3993 Ph & Fax
aluri@netins.net
PO Box 3678 • Boone NC 28607-5578
Across the Dark River/Clyde Ray - 56th NC Inf. Authentic in detail. Author recreates Civil War period in words & experiences of men & women who lived it - $21.95 (ppd.). Free catalog. (See ads pages 260 & 268)

PEA RIDGE PRESS
M. Dunnavant
PO Box 1068 • Athens AL 35612-1068
The Railroad War - Ride with N.B. Forrest on a daring raid against Sherman's railroad supply lines. 180 pp. - $20 (ppd).

PELICAN PUBLISHING CO.
888-5-PELICAN • 800-843-1724
http://www.pelicanpub.com
sales@pelicanpub.com
PO Box 3110
Gretna LA 70054-3110
Offers books on the Civil War era, history, the Confederacy, & war heroes, including the award-winning *Weep Not for Me, Dear Mother.* Free catalog.

PENTLAND PRESS, INC.
800-948-2786
5124 Bur Oak Cir
Raleigh NC 27612-3101
The Last Full Measure of Devotion: The Saga of an Irish Freemason, by Doby. Historical novel; letters from Shiloh, Corinth, Stoneman's Raid. 233 pp., softcover - 18.95.

PICTORIAL HISTORIES PUBLISHING CO.
888-WVA-PHPC • 304-342-1848
304-343-0594 Fax • PHPC@newwave.net
1416 Quarrier St
Charleston WV 25301-3010
Pictorial histories & Civil War titles, including *Last Sleep: The Battle of Droop Mountain*, *Civil War Medical Instruments* Vol. 1-3, & *Civil War in West Virginia.* Free catalog.

PIONEER PRESS
901-885-0374 • 901-885-0440 Fax
Sherry Stribling
PO Box 684 • Union City TN 38281-0684
Confederate Cannon Foundries, by Daniel/Gunter, 114 pp., softcover - $15. Many books on firearms.

PIONEER PUBLISHING
702-438-6565 Ph & Fax • Gloria Shepard
PO Box 43474 • Las Vegas NV 89116-1474
Private Lives of Civil War Heroes series. Vol. 1: *The Journal* - 48 pp., $5.95 + $1.50 S&H. Vol. 2: *Once Patriots* also available.

POCAHONTAS PRESS
800-446-0467 • 540-951-0467
540-961-2847 Fax
PO Box F • Blacksburg VA 24063-1020
Montgomery White Sulphur Springs -- a history of the resort, hospital, cemeteries, markers, and monument -- describes its time as a Confederate hospital & the nuns, doctors, soldiers, & others who lived & worked there.

PONDER BOOKS
Janice Ponder
PO Box 792 • Mason TX 76856-0792
Publisher of books on Civil War, history & genealogy. Trans-Mississippi region. Free booklist.

PRIDE PUBLICATIONS
888-902-5983
http://members.aol.com/pridepblsh/pride.html
PridePblsh@aol.com
18113 36th Ave W Apt J108
Lynnwood WA 98037-3877
The Redemption of Cpl. Nolan Giles, novel by Jeane Heimberger Candido. 245 pp., softcover - $11.95 + $2 S&H.

PUBLISHERS GROUP WEST
800-788-3123 • PO Box 8843
Emeryville CA 94662-0843
Shrouds of Glory by Winston Groom. 320 pages, 30 pp. of photos & maps by the author of Forrest Gump - $23. Many other titles.

R & L PUBLISHING
28 Vesey St Ste 2116C
New York NY 10007-2906
Bottles of Old New York and *New York City's Buried Past* dealing with Civil War & Rev. War bottles. $22.95 & $27.95 ppd.

R. L. SHEP PUBLICATIONS
707-964-8662 Ph & Fax
fsbks@mcn.org • Fred Struthers
PO Box 2706
Fort Bragg CA 95437-2706
Publishes reprints of important sewing & tailoring manuals as an aid to accurate reproduction of period dress.

RANK & FILE PUBLICATIONS
310-540-6601
310-540-1599 Fax
http://www.thirdwave.net/~rank
books@thirdwave.net
1926 S Pacific Coast Hwy Ste 228
Redondo Beach CA 90277-6146
Pickett's Charge: Eyewitness Accounts, Paperback - $21; Hardcover - $38. *The Damned Red Flags of the Rebellion: The Confederate Battle Flag at Gettysburg*, Hardcover - $41.95. Other titles. Free catalog.

RARE BOOK REPUBLISHERS
703-573-5116 • 703-573-5897 Fax
http://www.raredocs.com
paconose@erols.com
PO Box 3202 • Merrifield VA 22116-3202
The Cook's Own Book (1832), premier cooking reference used by families on both sides of the Civil War. More than 2,500 recipes. Hardcover - $28.95 + $3.50 S&H.

THE REPRINT COMPANY, PUBLISHERS
PO Box 5401
Spartanburg SC 29304-5401
4-volume set contains alphabetical roll of 90,000 Louisiana Confederate army members. In-depth, many vital statistics. Call/write.

ROCKBRIDGE PUBLISHING
an imprint of Howell Press, Inc.
800-868-4512 Orders
540-955-3980 Editorial
540-955-4126 Fax
http://www.rockbpubl.com
cwpub@visuallink.com
PO Box 351
Berryville VA 22611-0351
Our own & hard-to-find titles from other small presses. Free catalog. (See ad page 267)

ROKARN PUBLICATIONS
800-869-0563
PO Box 195 • Nokesville VA 20182-0195
A Southern Yarn and *Brothers in Gray* by R.W. Richards. $12.95 each.

RSG PUBLISHING
607-563-9000
217 County Highway 1
Bainbridge NY 13733-9307
Historical Addresses of the Civil War. 22nd NYV Cavalry, 2nd Brigade, 3rd Div. Reprint of 1894 original. $20. Other titles, incl. the History & Record of the 114th NYV Infantry. Free catalog.

RUTLEDGE HILL PRESS
800-234-4234
211 7th Ave N
Nashville TN 37219-1823
Civil War titles, including *Civil War Journal: The Leaders* and *Mort Kunstler's Civil War*. Books worth fighting for. (See ad page 266)

RYAN PLACE PUBLISHERS, INC.
800-871-0563
2525 Arapahoe Ave Ste E4-231
Boulder CO 80302-6720
Civil War Campaigns and Commanders, unique series of books on great battles, leaders, & failures of the Civil War. Call/write for complete list of titles.

J.S. SANDERS & CO.
615-790-8951
800-350-1101 Orders
615-790-2594 Fax
PO Box 50331
Nashville TN 37205-0331
Nashville 1864: The Dying of the Light, by Madison Jones. Other titles.

SANDLAPPER PUBLISHING, INC.
800-849-7263 • 800-337-9420 Fax
PO Box 730
Orangeburg SC 29116-0730
Regional publisher of books on the history, literature, culture & cuisine of the South, incl. Civil War titles.

J. M. SANTARELLI
215-576-5358
Civil War Books & Publishing
226 Paxson Ave • Glenside PA 19038-4612
Antique, reprint & out-of-print books. Also publishes new material. More than 300 Civil War titles. Catalog - $2.

SAVAS PUBLISHING CO.
800-848-6585
1475 S Bascom Ave Ste 204
Campbell CA 95008-0629
Original books. Features battles & campaigns, unit histories, & quarterly journal - *Civil War Regiments*. Distributed by Stackpole Books (800-732-3669). Free catalog.

SCHOLAR OF FORTUNE PUBLICATIONS
434 Bowman Dr
Kent OH 44240-4510
Friend Alice: CW Letters of Capt. David D. Bard, 7th & 104th Regts, Ohio Vol. Inf. 1862-1864. 112 pp. - $7.95 ppd. Other titles. Brochure - send large SASE.

PATRICK A. SCHROEDER PUBLICATIONS
804-376-1865
PO Box 455
Brookneal VA 24528-9304
Civil War books. New titles include *Civil War Soldier Life*; *We Came to Fight* (5th NY Vol. Inf.); & Belle Boyd. Archives research, prints, notecards, postcards available. Free catalog.

SCS PUBLICATIONS
PO Box 3832
Fairfax VA 22038-3832
Civil War Artifacts: A Guide for the Historian. More than 1700 items pictured, common to very rare. Data includes history, issuance, etc. 240 pp. $39.95.

SOUTHERN HERITAGE PRESS
615-895-5642
John McGlone, Editor
4035 Emerald Dr
Murfreesboro TN 37130-6801
Publisher of books on Confederate history, genealogy, black Confederates, Andersonville, Pat Cleburne. Winner of John Newman Edwards Award for preserving Southern history. Free catalog.

SOUTHERN ILLINOIS UNIVERSITY PRESS
800-346-2680 • 800-346-2681 Fax
grpruett@siu.edu
Gordon Pruett
PO Box 3697
Carbondale IL 62902-3697
Personal Memoirs of John H. Brinton, Army Life of an Illinois Soldier, "Black Jack" John A. Logan and Southern Illinois in the Civil War Era, & *A History of the Ninth Regiment Illinois Volunteers*, with the Regimental Roster.

SOUTHERN LION BOOKS, INC.
770-963-6776
solionbook@aol.com
J. H. Segars
PO Box 347163
Atlanta GA 30334-7163
Fine books about Southern history, 1861-1865. *In Search of Confederate Ancestors: The Guide*. Critically acclaimed by SCV & UDC. 112 pp., illus. - $10 + $1.50 S&H.

ST. MARTIN'S PRESS
800-288-2131
Publisher's Book & Audio
PO Box 70059
Staten Island NY 10307-0059
Books on the Civil War including *Mountains Touched with Fire: Chattanooga Besieged, 1863,* by Wiley Sword.

STACKPOLE BOOKS
800-732-3669
5067 Ritter Rd
Mechanicsburg PA 17055-6921
Publishers of quality Civil War books, including *Debris of Battle: The Wounded at Gettysburg* and *Portals to Hell: Military Prisons of the Civil War*, new for 1997.

STONE EAGLE PRESS
209-661-4030
PO Box 838
Madera CA 93639-0838
Manual of arms for the rifle & musket, from original text (*U.S. Infantry & Rifle Tactics, 1861*) - $10.25.

SUNFLOWER UNIVERSITY PRESS
800-258-1232
PO Box 1009
Manhattan KS 66505-1009
Since 1977, publisher of military & Western American history titles. *A Price Beyond Rubies*, Civil War novel, softcover - $25.95. *W.W. Loring: Florida's Forgotten General* - $35.95 (CL); $21.95 (PB). $2.50 S&H. Free catalog.

SYRACUSE UNIVERSITY PRESS
800-365-8929
1600 Jamesville Ave
Syracuse NY 13210-4243
The Iroquois in the Civil War (Hauptman). In-depth study of Iroquois tribes in CW. Documents service records & war's impact on tribe. $34.95. Other titles.

TACITUS PUBLICATIONS
612-644-6691 • 612-644-2265 Fax
tacitus@gte.net
Beverly A. Rude
PO Box 14412 • Saint Paul MN 55114-0412
CW biographies quoting original correspondence & describing where & how individuals fought. Information on historic sites dedicated to each individual. Illus. $5.95 ea. Free catalog. 30% disc. to retailers. (See ad page 259)

TEXAS A&M UNIVERSITY PRESS CONSORTIUM
800-826-8911 • 409-847-8752 Fax
FDL@tampress.tamu.edu
Gayla Christiansen
PO Box C • College Station TX 77843-0001
Mighty Stonewall, Make Me a Map of the Valley, Fallen Guidon, Confederate General of the Southwest. From $12.95 to $35. Also *Voices of Valor* (audio) $10.95 cassette, $17.95 CD. Free catalog.

THOMAS PUBLICATIONS
800-840-6782 • 717-334-1921
717-334-8440 Fax
Dean S. Thomas
353 Buford Ave
Gettysburg PA 17325-1138
Publishers of Civil War books. Many titles. *Ghosts of Gettysburg* series videos. Free catalog.

TRAC PRESS
313 E Strawberry Dr
Mill Valley CA 94941-2508
Yours in Love follows daily life of Iowa foot soldier in collection of letters - 285 pp., $21.95 ppd.

TRIPHAMMER PUBLISHING
PO Box 45
Scottsville NY 14546-0045
The Beau Ideal of a Soldier and a Gentleman: The Life of Col. Patrick Henry O'Rorke from Ireland to Gettysburg - softcover, 220 pp., $22.95 + $4 S&H.

TUNSTEDE PRESS
615-385-7258
500 Elmington Ave Apt 430
Nashville TN 37205-2525
Letters to Laura: A Confederate Surgeon's Impressions of Four Years of War - 304 pp., hardcover, $36 + $4 S&H. Only in-print letter collection written by a Confederate surgeon, Urban Grammar Owen, MD. (See ad page 259)

TWO TRAILS PUBLISHING
http://www.erspros.com/2trails
cwbklady@aol.com
7295 Houston St
Shawnee Mission KS 66227-2430
The Forgotten Men: The Missouri State Guard, 406 pp. Hardcover - $42.95; Softcover - $32.95. *Sterling Price's Lieutenants*, 362 pp. Softcover - $27.50. Catalog.

UNION PUBLISHING CO.
415 Miller Rd
Union ME 04862-3610
The 16th Maine Regiment in the War of the Rebellion, 1861-1865. Riveting reading about the famed 16th Maine Regt. at Gettysburg & their subsequent capture. $12.95 ppd.

THE UNIVERSITY OF ALABAMA PRESS
800-825-9980
205-348-5180
205-348-9201 Fax
http://www.uapress.ua.edu
Box 870380
University of Alabama
Tuscaloosa AL 35487-0380
Complete selection of military history titles, including the "Top 100 Classics of Civil War Literature" featuring *Attack and Die*, *Cracker Culture*, etc.

THE UNIVERSITY OF ARKANSAS PRESS
800-626-0090 • 501-575-6044 Fax
http://www.uark.edu/campus-resources/uaprinfo/public_html/
uapressinfo@cavern.uark.edu
201 N Ozark Ave
Fayetteville AR 72701-4041
Civil War in the West series: books on the trans-Mississippi & Western theaters. Portraits of Conflict series: photographic histories of individual Southern states in the Civil War. Free catalog.

UNIVERSITY OF CALIFORNIA PRESS
800-822-6657
1445 Lower Ferry Rd
Ewing NJ 08618-1424
The Frontier in American Culture, *Wagner Nights*, etc. Call for a complete listing.

UNIVERSITY OF GEORGIA PRESS
706-369-6163
300 Research Dr • Athens GA 30605-2726
To the Manor Born: The Life of Gen. William H.T. Walker. First complete biography of the general. Available at bookstores or direct. $50. Many other titles.

UNIVERSITY OF ILLINOIS PRESS
800-545-4703
http://www.press.uillinois.edu
1325 S Oak St • Champaign IL 61820-6903
Titles include *The Civil War in Books: An Analytical Biography*, by David J. Eicher. Fully annotated bibliography of the 1,100 most important books on the CW.

UNIVERSITY OF IOWA PRESS
800-235-2665
Iowa City IA 52242
Titles include *Soldier Boy: CW Letters of Charles O. Musser, 29th Iowa* - 272 pp. $24.95.

UNIVERSITY OF MAINE PRESS
207-581-1408
51 Public Affairs Bldg • Univ. of Maine
Orono ME 04469-0001
Dear Friend Anna. Civil War letters from common soldier, home to his future wife - $21.95. Other titles.

UNIVERSITY OF MISSOURI PRESS
800-828-1894 • 573-882-0180
573-884-4498 Fax
http://www.system.missouri.edu/upress
2910 LeMone Blvd • Columbia MO 65201
Shades of Blue & Gray: Introductory Military History of the Civil War, by Herman Hattaway - 296 pp., $29.95. "... best clear, brief military history of the Civil War available..." (George Rable).

THE UNIVERSITY OF NEBRASKA PRESS
800-755-1105 • 402-472-3581
http://nebraskapress.unl.edu
press@unlinfo.unl.edu
312 N 14th St
Lincoln NE 68508-1623

UNIVERSITY OF NEW MEXICO PRESS
800-249-7737
800-622-8667 Fax
Bloody Valverde: A Civil War Battle on the Rio Grande, February 21, 1862, by John M. Taylor - 1st complete account of the largest battle in New Mexico. Hardcover, 200 pp. - $29.95.

THE UNIVERSITY OF NORTH CAROLINA PRESS
800-848-6224 • 800-272-6817 Fax
http://sunsite.unc.edu/uncpress/
Chapel Hill NC
The Darkest Days of the War: The Battles of Iuka & Corinth; *The Wilderness Campaign*; many more titles.

UNIVERSITY OF OKLAHOMA PRESS
800-627-7377
ldraper@uoknor.edu
Ms. Lennie Draper, Publicity Mgr.
1005 Asp Ave
Norman OK 73019-6050
Publisher of books about military history, including number of titles about the Civil War. Free catalogs. (See ad page 262)

UNIVERSITY OF SOUTH CAROLINA PRESS
800-768-2500 Orders • 800-868-0740 Fax
718 Devine St
Columbia SC 29208
Titles include *Writing the Civil War* and *Soldiers Blue and Gray*.

UNIVERSITY OF TENNESSEE PRESS
423-974-3321
http://sunsite.utk.edu/utpress
293 Communications
Knoxville TN 37996-0001
Voices of the Civil War series. *From Huntsville to Appomattox: R.T. Cole's History of the 4th Regiment, Alabama Volunteer Infantry, CSA* - 304 pp., hardcover, $32.95.

UNIVERSITY PRESS OF KANSAS
785-864-4155 • 785-864-4586 Fax
upkansas@kuhub.cc.ukans.edu
2501 W 15th St
Lawrence KS 66049-3905
The Union Soldier in Battle: Enduring the Ordeal of Combat/Hess. *Stonewall of the West; Patrick Cleburne and the Civil War*/Symonds. Other Civil War & military titles. Free, complete listing available.

UNIVERSITY PRESS OF KENTUCKY
800-839-6855 Orders • 800-666-2211
800-870-4981 Fax
http://www.uky.edu/UniversityPress/
663 S Limestone
Lexington KY 40508-4008
With Charity for All: Lincoln and the Restoration of the Union, by William C. Harris - 336 pp., hardcover, $37.95.

UNIVERSITY PRESS OF MISSISSIPPI
800-737-7788 • 601-982-6217 Fax
press@ihl.state.ms.us
Claudette Murphree
3825 Ridgewood Rd
Jackson MS 39211-6463
John Wilkes Booth - $20. *Tracing Your Mississippi Ancestors* - $14.95. *We Saw Lincoln Shot* - $17.95. *Pemberton* - $32.50. Other titles. Free catalog.

UNIVERSITY PRESS OF VIRGINIA
804-924-3469
804-982-2655 Fax
http://www.upress.virginia.edu/
upressva@virginia.edu
PO Box 3608
University Station
Charlottesville VA 22903-0608
Several books & studies on the Civil War including *Lee's Young Artillerist*, *Longstreet's Aide*, *Black Confederates & Afro-Yankees in CW Virginia*, etc.

URE PRESS
636 Piney Forest Rd
Danville VA 24540-2800
Confederate Treasure in Danville - documented, clues to 196,000 silver dollars buried in Danville, Va. Hardcover - $26.07 ppd.

VANBERG PUBLISHING
800-799-0470
614-689-0471 Fax
http://www.vanberg-ent.com
PO Box 983
Lancaster OH 43130-0983
Annals of the 6th Pennsylvania Cavalry, by Chaplain Samuel L. Gracey. "Rush's Lancers" - $24.95. *History of the 9th Massachusetts Battery*. "Bigelow's Battery" - $29.95. Add $3.95 S&H.

WARWICK HOUSE PUBLISHING
804-846-1200
720 Court St
Lynchburg VA 24504-1406
Memoirs of Life in and out of the Army in Virginia During the War Between the States - annotated letters from the Blackford family. Leatherbound, 2 vol. set - $95 + $6 S&H.

WHITE MANE PUBLISHING CO.
888-WHT-MANE
717-532-2237 • 717-532-7704 Fax
Harold Collier
PO Box 152
Shippensburg PA 17257-0152
America's Civil War publisher offers variety of military history titles with special interest in the Civil War. Free catalog.

WILLOW CREEK PRESS OF WASHINGTON
888-830-5612
PO Box 3730
Silverdale WA 98383-3730
Kope's *Everything Civil War* - 304 pp., softcover. $19.95 + $2 S&H.

WRITE WAY PUBLISHING
800-680-1793
10555 E Dartmouth Ave Ste 210
Aurora CO 80014-2633
Featuring such books as *The Sherman Letter*, mixing history & mystery. Excellent reading. $18.95. Call for a complete listing.

WSU PRESS
800-354-7360
509-335-3518
509-335-8568 Fax
http://www.publications.wsu.edu/wsupress
jslynn@wsu.edu
Jenni Lynn
PO Box 645910
Pullman WA 99164-5910
Confederate Raider in the North Pacific: The Saga of the C.S.S. Shenandoah, *1864-65.* Reprint, 350-pp. paperback - $19.95 + $2.50 S&H. Other titles. Free catalog.

1ST WEST VA. LIGHT ARTILLERY, BATTERY D
304-242-2490
Capt. Joe Johnson
57 Greenwood Ave
Wheeling WV 26003-1448
Participate in reenactments, living history, encampments. Experience thrill of "booming" cannon. Recruits sought; receive training on full-scale artillery pieces.

2ND MARYLAND INFANTRY, CO. A, CSA
410-531-3586
http://www.sutler.com/2ndMD/2ndMD.htm

4TH NORTH CAROLINA REGT., CSA, INC.
410-795-6282
joep@schmitzpress.com
Recruiter: Joe Pearson
4473 Bartholow Rd • Sykesville MD 21784
Authentic infantry unit with members in Md., Va., & Pa. Living history emphasized. Reenactments, talks, displays, etc. Well-researched unit with uniform documentation. Registered 501.C nonprofit corporation.

5TH NEW YORK, DURYEE'S ZOUAVES
http://www.zouave.org/index.html
PO Box 1601 • Alexandria VA 22313-1601
Enlist in the 5th NY for authentic living history & reenacting.

8TH REGT. NJ VOLUNTEER INFANTRY
609-654-5561 Days • 609-654-7168 Eves
Capt. Earl Aversano
226 Sunny Jim Dr • Medford NJ 08055-9249
Honorary reactivated NJ unit which participates in reenactments & historical events throughout the eastern U.S.

13TH VIRGINIA INFANTRY, CO. H
540-877-2483 • Capt. David Melton
128 Susquehanna Trl
Winchester VA 22602-1735
Members participate in battle reenactments, living history, camp & drill demonstrations, memorials/ceremonies/dedications & help preserve historical sites & Confederate battle flags. Recruits welcome & encouraged.

THE 17TH CONNECTICUT VOL. INFANTRY
407-295-7510
Maj. Jeff H. Grzelak
7214 Laurel Hill Rd • Orlando FL 32818-5233
Retrace the steps of the 17th Conn.; after 135 years, the regiment is once again on the march. Enlist today & see a part of U.S. history firsthand.

19TH ALABAMA INFANTRY REGT., ARMY OF TENN.
http://fly.hiwaay.net/~dsmart/index.html
Reenactment organization. Website provides many links to pages of related topics.

AMERICAN CIVIL WAR ASSOCIATION
http://www.acwa.org
CSA contact: AdjCSAACWA@aol.com ; Union contact: MajorAWH@aol.com
Arthur Henrick
PO Box 61075 • Sunnyvale CA 94088-1075
Private, non-profit educational organization & reenactment society which uses living history to help the public gain better understanding of the Civil War. 350 current members. More info - send SASE.

ARMIES OF TENNESSEE
317-548-2594
PO Box 91 • Rosedale IN 47874-0091
Confederate & Union reenactors. Also involved in preservation. Annual memb. - $20.

ARMY OF THE PACIFIC
http://chaos.alchemy.net/AOP/
PO Box 1863
Santa Barbara CA 93116-1863
Infantry reenactors, specifically Union. "Authenticity and Pardships."

ASSOCIATED VIDEO PRODUCTIONS
770-425-1530 • 770-419-8033 Fax
jack@freewwweb.com
2511 Kingswood Dr Ste SB-398
Marietta GA 30066-6256
See & hear in-depth discussions about muskets, uniforms, accouterments, equipment and more,insuring historically accurate & correct impressions. *Mastering Reenacting* video - $24.95 + $4 S&H.

AVALON FORGE
410-242-8431
John White, Owner
409 Gun Rd • Baltimore MD 21227-3824
Replica goods for 18th-century "living history." Items for military, farm & home. Catalog - $2.

BATTLE AT NARCOOSSEE MILL
John Holmes
PO Box 430178
Kissimmee FL 34743-0178
Annual event held on shores of East Lake Tohopeliga, east of St. Cloud, FL. Sponsored by SCV Camp 1516. Authentic CW reeanctors welcome.

BATTLE CRY
810 Gales Ave
Winston-Salem NC 27103-3704
Multi-period reenacting publication covering Civil War & others. $8/yr. for 4 issues.

BATTLE OF AIKEN
803-642-2500
Barnard E. Bee Camp SCV
PO Box 1863
Aiken SC 29802-1863
Annual February reenactment of the battle against Sherman's invasion. Camps, cannon duels & cavalry charges. Period crafts, music & food.

BATTLE OF BLUE SPRINGS
423-638-4111
Greeneville/Greene Co. Chamber of Commerce
115 Academy St
Greeneville TN 37743-5601
Battle scenarios with all branches, full dress ball, church services. Annually - October. Spectator fee - $2, ages 12 & under free.

BATTLE OF CAMP WILDCAT & LIVING HISTORY ENCAMPMENT
606-878-6242
Fred Gillum
166 Middleground Way Apt 3
London KY 40744-8154
Reenactments, tacticals, ladies' tea, military demonstrations, pig roast, barn dance, fashion show, parade, review, & more. Registration $2. Annual event - April.

BATTLE OF GRAND LAKE
419-586-5294
106 Haig St
Celina OH 45822-2708
Reenactment on shores of Lake St. Mary's. Earthworks among best in OH. Artillery, infantry, cavalry, medical, civilians. Battles, tactical events, ladies' activities. Annually - July.

BATTLE OF OLUSTEE (OCEAN POND)
904-397-2733
904-397-4262 Fax
http://extlabl.entnem.ufl.edu/Olustee
emcgrath@alltel.net
Olustee Battlefield State Historic Site
PO Box G
White Springs FL 32096-0435
Reenactment with parade, skirmish & ball. Full-scale artillery only. Open to all authentic 1864 impressions as found in actual battle. No fees. Annual event - February.

BATTLE OF PALATKA
2171 Hoffman St
Jacksonville FL 32211-3217
Annual March reenactment on site at St. Johns River Community College. Authentic impressions welcome. Company drills, live mortar fire, ladies' tea, military ball, living history camps.

BATTLE OF PLEASANT HILL
Mason City Parks & Recreation
22 N Georgia Ave
Mason City IA 50401-3435
Battles, ladies' tea & fashion show, military ball, children's presentation, period music, competitions, ribbons. Annual event - June.

BATTLE OF POISON SPRING
501-685-2748
Annual March reenactment at Poison Spring State Park, Arkansas.

BATTLE OF RESACA
PO Box 3336
Cumming GA 30028-6519
Annual May reenactment on 600 acres of original battlefield. Battles, tactical, ladies' tea, evening social with period music.

BILLIE CREEK VILLAGE REENACTMENT
765-569-3430
765-569-5226
http://www.coveredbridges.com/bilcreek.htm
RR 2 Box 27
Rockville IN 47872-9503
Indiana's largest Civil War event. 30 historic buildings to tour. Battles & military events; extensive ladies', children's & medical events, ball. Annual event - June.

BLUE & GRAY HERITAGE COMMITTEE
912-896-3258
Adel GA
Annual April reenactment & living history site. Live-fire artillery, cavalry, & firearms competitions. Memorial & worship services. Proceeds benefit the non-profit committee's fund for permanent living history site.

BRANDYWINE CREEK REENACTMENT
Jack Pickett
116 W Main St
Middletown DE 19709-1040
Annual May reenactment of the "Campaigns of 1862." Tacticals, seminars, demonstrations, night artillery firing. Authentic camping.

BROOKSBY FARMS CIVIL WAR ENCAMPMENT
Edward Certusi
16 Maitland St
Milton MA 02186-4511
Battles, tours, lectures, displays, civilian activities, CW dance. Annual event - July.

BROOKSVILLE RAID
352-683-3700
Greater Hernando Co. Chamber of Commerce
101 E Fort Dade Ave
Brooksville FL 34601-2611
Florida's Best Event! Beautiful 1500-acre site. Battle, ball. All units & branches welcome. Annual event.

BROTHERS-IN-ARMS
52 Monarch Cir
Basking Ridge NJ 07920-3144
Reenactors, find out what units are local to you. 100s of CSA/Union infantry, artillery, & cavalry units. Men, women, children welcome. 3 units - $5 & SASE.

C & D COMMERCIAL PRODUCTIONS, INC.
800-600-6578
100 Dixie Ln
Wilmington DE 19804-2312
A Call to Arms: Your Guide to Becoming a CW Reenactor. 52-min. video - excellent recruiting tool. $19.95.

THE CALENDAR PEOPLE
800-758-2751
2083 Springwood Rd
PO Box 125
York PA 17403-0125
Civil War reenactment calendar featuring pictures of 12 reenactment groups (CSA/USA). $12 + S&H.

CAMP CHASE PUBLISHING
http://nemesis.cybergate.net/~civilwar
CampChase@compuserve.com
PO Box 707
Marietta OH 45750-0707
How to Get Started in Civil War Reenacting - 36-pg. handbook, written by veteran reenactor. Great tips. $5.

THE CANNONADE
PO Box 20601
Rochester NY 14602-0601
Nice Boom: The Amerian Civil War Artillery Reenactor's Handbook, Sean McAdoo, ed. 100+ pp., including drill, living history, tactics, NCO training & more. $10.95 + $3 S&H.

CASTLE KEEP, LTD.
630-801-1696
630-801-1910 Fax
http://www.Reenact.com
ernie@Smartgate.com
Ernest Klapmeier
83 S La Salle St
Aurora IL 60505-3331
Reenactor supplies; clothing & equipment to put man or woman into the field. Owner has 20 yrs. reenacting experience & understands concept of authenticity.

CEDAR CREEK BATTLEFIELD FOUNDATION, INC.
540-869-2064
540-869-1438 Fax
http://www.winchesterva.com/cedarcreek
Suzanne Lewis
PO Box 229
Middletown VA 22645-0229
Visitors Center & bookshop overlooking battlefield. October reenactment. Reference library, large CW book selection, flags, prints, maps & square foot certificates. All proceeds go to preservation of battlefield.

CENTER FOR LIVING HISTORY PRESERVATION
573-288-3995 • 573-288-4470
Route B / Old Highway 61
Canton MO 63435
1800s village of Cedar Falls; Civil War camp. Visitor center. Open 9 AM-5 PM. Admission - $1-2.

CENTRAL GEORGIA CASTING
3445 Osborne Pl
Macon GA 31204-1843
Hand-painted/unpainted miniatures. Fast service, custom work. Reenactor miniatures from photograph. Sample infantry figure, brochure & $5 credit - send $5.75 for 25 mm or $9.75 for 54 mm. Brochure only - $2.

THE CITIZENS' COMPANION
614-373-1865
Camp Chase Publishing
PO Box 707 • Marietta OH 45750-0707
Magazine for civilian side of reenacting. Info. on clothing, behavior, living history impressions & more. $20/yr. for 6 issues.

CIVIL WAR ADVENTURES
800-624-4421
3-day encampments for all Civil War enthusiasts. Come live the life of a Civil War soldier. Free brochure.

CIVIL WAR DAY
803-722-2996
The Charleston Museum
360 Meeting St
Charleston SC 29403-6235
Harbor & land tours in historic Charleston, SC, nationally recognized speakers, reenactors, period music. Annual event - April. Brochure.

CIVIL WAR LIVING HISTORY & BATTLES
860-526-4993
C. Quist
233 Main St
Deep River CT 06417-2055
Reenactment in Madison, NY. Shiloh scenarios. Annual event - May.

CIVIL WAR LIVING HISTORY REENACTMENT
910-371-6613
Fort Anderson NC
Reenactment on grounds of Brunswick Town State Historic Sites. Tours of earthwork fort remains, small arms & military demonstrations, civilian interpretations. Lectures/talks. Annual event - February. No admission fee.

CIVIL WAR WEEKEND AT STOEVER'S DAM PARK
717-933-4294
Capt. Dennis R. Shirk
RR 3 Box 415A
Myerstown PA 17067-1644
Battles, tactical, living history, entertainment, candlelight tours. Annual event, Lebanon, PA. Contact for dates.

GENERAL NEWTON MARTIN CURTIS WEEKEND
David H. Ellis
81 Pleasant Valley Rd
Hammond NY 13646-3253
Honors St. Lawrence County's contributions to war effort & memory of Gen. Curtis. Period encampment, skirmish, talks, living history. Open to all CW enthusiasts. Annual event - September.

DEPARTMENT OF THE SOUTH, INC.
352-394-7206
PO Box 680784
Orlando FL 32868-0784
"Hilton Head Dispatch" - official newsletter for reenactment community. Latest info. on events, book reviews, battle reports, unit history, life in trenches & on home front. $17/yr. for 6 issues.

ENCAMPMENT AT LAUREL HILL
540-251-1833
J.E.B. Stuart Birthplace, Inc.
PO Box 240
Ararat VA 24053-0240
Encampment just outside Mt. Airy, NC, to benefit the Stuart birthplace. Annual event - June. Free registration.

FORT DODGE CIVIL WAR DAYS
515-573-4231
http://www.fort.org
thefort@frontiernet.net
David Parker
Fort Museum
PO Box 1798
Fort Dodge IA 50501-1798
Annual reenactments at Fort Museum & Fort Dodge. Military ball, civilian impressions, family activities. Call for dates.

FORT MIFFLIN ON THE DELAWARE
215-492-3395
Fort Mifflin Rd
Philadelphia PA 19153
Revolutionary fort which served as prison during the Civil War; reenactments held. Museum.

GALLIA COUNTY FEDERAL ARMY HOMECOMING
800-765-6482
Gallipolis OH 45631
Living history encampment at original army campsite. Ladies' tea & workshops, period entertainment. Authentic Union infantry, artillery, medical, signal corps, engineering, civilians, sutlers welcome. Annual event - April.

GIBBS SMITH, PUBLISHER
800-743-5439
http://www.gibbs-smith.com
info@gibbs-smith.com
PO Box 667
Layton UT 84041-0667
Returning to the Civil War: Grand Reenactments of an Anguished Time - living history at its best in full-color photography. 96 pp., softcover - $21.95. Free catalog.

GRANBURY CONVENTION & VISITORS BUREAU
800-950-2212
100 N Crockett St
Granbury TX 76048-2127
Sponsors reenactments & other events. Tourist info.

GRAND ANNAPOLIS CITY BALL
Stephen Bockmiller
101 Fitz Ct Apt 204
Reisterstown MD 21136-3327
Annual March ball with orchestral music & refreshments. Period military or civilian attire required. Attendance limited. Co-sponsored by 4th NC Infantry & 5th US Cavalry.

HERITAGE DRUM CO.
256-533-5498
http://fly.hiwaay.net/~tpalmer/heritage2.htm
ropedrum@juno.com
Terry Cornett
4021 Apollo Dr SW
Huntsville AL 35805-5601
Custom order, period repro snare & bass drums. Hand-crafted.

HILTON HEAD DISPATCH
407-295-7510
7214 Laurel Hill Rd
Orlando FL 32818-5233
Publication indicating where to find reenactments, shows, & book fairs dealing in history. Covering the Southeast. $15/yr. for 6 issues.

HISTORIC HAMPTON
800-800-2202
757-727-1102
http://www.hampton.va.us/tourism
710 Settlers Landing Rd
Hampton VA 23669-4035
Historic reenactments, world-class museums, Chesapeake Bay seafood, Fort Wool, Casemate Museum at Fort Monroe, new site on the Va. Civil War Trail. Minutes from Williamsburg. Free guide.

JACKSON'S FOOT CAVALRY
804-780-3373
800-833-5522
B. Brenner Wood
Now mustering "F" Company, 21st Regt., Virginia Volunteer Cavalry. We are historians who interpret the Civil War by authentically portraying the common soldier.

LADIES' SOLDIER'S FRIEND SOCIETY
Donna Wilson, Pres.
PO Box 150223
Nashville TN 37215
Living history participation. Publish "The Ladies' Companion" bi-monthly. Annual dues - $15.

LAKE CHICOT STATE PARK CIVIL WAR WEEKEND
800-264-2430 • Don R. Simons
Lake Chicot State Park • 2542 Highway 257
Lake Village AR 71653-9515
Reenactment of Battle of Ditch Bayou, camp tours, living history demonstrations, tactical, period ball. Annual event - October.

LIVING HISTORY & RAID OF QUEEN ANNE'S RAILROAD
410-836-2642 John C. Houck
Lewes DE
2 train raids & battles. Candlelight camp tours. All period impression welcome. Annual event - August. Admission - $3 over age 12.

LIVING HISTORY ASSOCIATION, INC.
PO Box 1389
Wilmington VT 05363-1389
Reenactors' Liability Insurance, covering reenactments, encampments, black powder, cavalry, artillery; personal injury, equipment insurance. Edu. programs, workshops, full historical museum. Newsletter, events & info - $3.

LIVING HISTORY ENCAMPMENT
Larry S. Hoffman
3000 State Route 18
Hookstown PA 15050-1605
Annual May encampment includes Revolutionary War, Civil War, Lewis & Clark, the world wars, & modern armed forces. Daily drills, firing, crafts. Pioneer crafts & music.

MALTA ENCAMPMENT
Dr. Robert Richmond
4455 State Route 37 • Malta OH 43758-9756
Skirmish & battle, parade, ball, ladies' tea. Annual event - July. No fees.

MC LEAN COUNTY CIVIL WAR WEEKEND
309-827-5416
Ron Montgomery
711 E Wood St• Bloomington IL 61701-6847
Annual event. All branches of military & civilian welcome.

MICHAELS & PERRIN
717-922-1065 • 717-922-1245
tperrin@sunlink.net
414 Main St • PO Box 29
Hartleton PA 17829-0029
Uniforms & period clothing for men & women. Equipment for reenactors. Catalog.

MISSISSIPPI (COLUMBUS) CONVENTION & VISITORS BUREAU
800-327-2686 • Columbus MS
Annual February Battle of West Point & Prairie reenactment & authentic dance. Call for info. & dates.

NEVADA CIVIL WAR VOLUNTEERS
http://pw2.netcom.com/baugh1/index.html
PO Box 11033 • Reno NV 89510-1033
Living history & other programs devoted to Civil War study, such as "Soldier for an Hour." Educational presentations. Union, Confederate & civilian groups. Annual membership - $15 (individ.); $25 (family).

NORTH-SOUTH SKIRMISH ASSOCIATION
http://mh004.infi.net/~nssa/
Phil Spaugy
501 N Dixie Dr • Vandalia OH 45377-2011
Team competition in high-level marksmanship with original or approved reproduction muskets, carbines, revolvers, & artillery at breakable targets in a timed match. Period regimental uniforms worn.

NORTHWEST REENACTMENTS
800-624-4421
Civil War Adventures, Inc.
1532 Lakeway Pl
Bellingham WA 98226-5133
The ultimate Civil War experience. Reenactments, encampments for everyone. Call for info.

OGLEBAY PARK REENACTMENT
304-845-1893
Don McNabb
RR 1 Box 107A
Moundsville WV 26041-9801
Scored interactive tactical, ladies' tea, dance, children's activities. Annual event - June.

PIONEER VILLAGE REENACTMENT
319-355-0898
Bruce Kindig
3923 Forest Rd • Davenport IA 52807-2350
2 battles on 30-acre field, dance. Annual event - September.

PRAIRIE GROVE BATTLEFIELD STATE PARK
501-846-2990
PO Box 306
Prairie Grove AR 72753-0306
Battlefield museum, historic houses. Self-guided tours. Bi-annual December reenactment. Located on U.S. Route 62. Various fees.

REENACTOR'S JOURNAL
309-463-2123
309-463-2188 Fax
PO Box 1864
Varna IL 61375-1864
For the "Who, what, where, when and how-to" of Civil War Reenacting. 12 issues - $24. Sample issue - $3.

REENACTOR'S WEB MALL
http://rampages.onramp.net/~lawsonda/mall
Links to directories of sutlers, basic 19th-century supplies, etc.

REENACTORS HOMEPAGE
http://www.cwreenactors.com
"Dedicated to the brave souls, North & South, who fought & died in the War Between the States."

REENACTORS OF THE AMERICAN CIVIL WAR
PO Box 1248
Magalia CA 95954-1248
Reenactments, other events. Participates in many civic functions.

SAMUELL FARM CIVIL WAR WEEKEND
Kevin Keim
380 Country Ln
Haslet TX 76052-4312
Annual March weekend near Dallas, featuring 3 battles, dance, period worship service. No reenactor fee.

KELLY SCHULTZ FARM REENACTMENT
716-839-3200
716-885-3755
Maj. Richard J. Rosche
840 W Delavan Ave
Buffalo NY 14209-1113
Battle of Five Forks reenactment & living history event, including trench warfare. Authentics only. Extensive civilian activities. Sutlers welcome. Annual event - June.

SHIP'S COMPANY, INC.
410-788-7264
Lawrence Bopp, Pres.
309 Roanoke Dr
Baltimore MD 21228-4240
Official interpretive group of the USS *Constellation*, recruiting Federal sailors & marines for service aboard this 1855 war sloop - the last surviving warship to see Civil War action.

STONEWALL JACKSON MEMORIAL WEEKEND
540-972-7215
Bethel Baptist Church
10530 Beaver Ln • Spotsylvania VA 22553
May reenactment where Pegram's artillery battalion encamped after Chancellorsville. Tacticals, church hospital, burials, auction, candlelight camp tour, recreation of 1863 memorial service held at church for Jackson.

STUHR MUSEUM LIVING HISTORY ENCAMPMENT
308-385-5316 • 308-385-5028 Fax
Gail Stoklasa • Nebraska
2 major battles, skirmishes, candlelight tours. All branches & units welcome. Encampment at Stuhr Museum of the Prairie Pioneer.

TOWN PARK LIVING HISTORY & REENACTMENT
410-836-2642
Maj. Gen. John C. Houck
402 Schucks Rd • Bel Air MD 21015-4916
Battles, demonstrations, camp life. Period music & dancing, memorial & church services. All branches & impressions welcome. Annual event - October. Admission - $3 over age 12.

USHER'S FERRY REENACTMENT
319-355-0898
Bruce Kindig
3923 Forest Rd • Davenport IA 52807-2350
3 battles, ball. Annual July reenactment of battle fought in 1860s town in Cedar Rapids.

VIDALIA REENACTMENT
912-537-7667 • Vidalia GA
Annual March battle reenactment & living history encampment.

WEST VIRGINIA REENACTORS ASSOCIATION
304-472-5964
PO Box 2133 • Buckhannon WV 26201-7133
Participates in reenactments & educational presentations; sponsors special events.

WINTER WEEKEND OF THE LIVING HISTORY SOCIETY
612-431-4760 • ekatuin@compuserve.com
Elaine M. Katuin
7624 157th St W Apt 208
Apple Valley MN 55124-9166
Weekend gala featuring mid-19th-century dancing & civilian activities, workshops, ice skating & sledding. Period attire requested. Annual event - February.

YUMA CROSSING QM DEPOT HISTORIC SITE
520-329-0471
Wells Twombly
Yuma Crossing Foundation
PO Box 2768
Yuma AZ 85366-2768
Civil War encampment, 2 battles daily. Camping & some horses allowed. Ladies' fashion contest, lectures. No reenactor fee. Annual event - January.

HUDSON ALEXANDER
911 Velma Ln
Murfreesboro TN 37129-2367
Will research your soldier/unit from Tennessee.

ANTIQUE AMERICAN FIREARMS
847-304-GUNS
PO Box 1861 • Barrington IL 60011-1861
Civil War weapons search - match your weapon's serial number with our database to identify issuance. Annual membership.

BATTLEFIELDS REVISITED
BattRev@aol.com
Patricia Watt
PO Box 231 • New Cumberland PA 17070
Research Civil War soldiers, sailors - all nationalities. Reports, records, histories.

BRODERBUND
39500 Stevenson Pl Ste 204
Fremont CA 94539-3103
Family Tree Maker CD-Rom - solid starting point for genealogical research. PC compatible with Windows programs, 386 or higher, 4MB RAM (8MB recommended).

BROWN PUBLICATIONS
BrianB1578@aol.com
PO Box 25501 • Little Rock AR 72221-5501
In the Footsteps of the Blue & Gray - $24.95 + $2 S&H. Describes CW-related research sources in state archives, National Archives & LDS collection. History of ea. corps & hard-to-find technical information.

PAUL BUCHER
703-243-6654
PO Box 17304 • Arlington VA 22216-7304
Civil War military service records, Union & Confederate, army & navy. 10-day turnaround, reasonable fee.

THE CIVIL WAR GARRISON
PO Box 1681 • Springfield IL 62705-1681
Will research the veteran you designate & write his personal story in the War Between the States, or produce a Civil War plaque of his experiences.

CIVIL WAR RESEARCH
219-483-0640
PO Box 8355
Fort Wayne IN 46898-8355
Will research your Civil War soldier through the official records. Provides brief report & extracts from the official records - $34.95.

COLLECTORS' LIBRARY
541-937-3348
PO Box 263
Eugene OR 97440-0263
THE publisher for key reference books on accoutrements, guns, saddles, edged weapons, etc., for pre-Civil War, Civil War, Indian War & post-1900 period. Free illus. catalog.

CONFEDERATE DESK
812-948-5057
rebeldesk@aol.com
201 Virginia Ct
New Albany IN 47150-5076
New online research service. Most major archives & manuscript depositories accessed immediately. Call, write or access e-mail.

CONFEDERATE DIRECTORY
915-446-4439
David Martin
PO Box 61 • Roosevelt TX 76874-0061
Reference for vendors of Confederate currency, books, tapes, flags, stationery, memorabilia, reenactors' supplies, services, memorials, etc.; includes COMPLETE Confederate Constitution. $12 (ppd.).

THE CONFEDERATE RESEARCH CENTER & MUSEUM
817-582-2555
Hill College
PO Box 619 • Hillsboro TX 76645-0619
Exhibits include flags, artillery pieces, ephemera & other items. Research center contains capsule histories of all CSA regiments & special units, as well as ships; other research material.

CORTLAND COUNTY HISTORICAL SOCIETY, INC.
607-756-6071
25 Homer Ave • Cortland NY 13045-2056
Hosts Suggett House Museum & Kellogg Memorial Research Library. *A Regiment Remembered: 157th New York Volunteers* - Lt. William Saxton's diary, 157 pp. - $20 + $3.40 S&H. NYS - add 8% sales tax.

COWLES HISTORY GROUP
http://www.thehistorynet.com
Attn: Military History Index
PO Box 3242 • Leesburg VA 20177-8111
Cross-referenced index of more than 3,000 entries, through 1000s of years of battle. Every subject addressed in *Military History* magazines - $24.95.

CW BATTLES
1943 N Grimes St Ste B229
Hobbs NM 88240-2722
Handbook of 230 major Civil War battles; when, where, who, what index. $9.95 + S&H.

R. DAMBRISI
1231 Ten Oaks Rd
Baltimore MD 21227-1314
Search service; will locate & print text from Official Records US/CS Army - $25/topic.

JOHN EMOND
PO Box 44625
Washington DC 20026-4625
Will research military & pension records at National Archives. Reasonable fees - no charge until found.

FORT WARD MUSEUM & HISTORIC SITE
703-838-4848
4301 W Braddock Rd
Alexandria VA 22304-1008
Museum in pattern of Union headquarters building, w/ various exhibits; tours. Research library available. Free admission. Closed Mon.

GRAVE CONCERNS
PO Box 20094
Cincinnati OH 45220-0094
Sell/trade photographs of burial sites of Civil War generals blue & gray, politicians, spies, notables - many hard to find. 5,000 photos on hand; send SASE & needs. Catalog - SASE.

E. GREISSER
771D E Main St
Bridgewater NJ 08807-3339
Civil War soldiers from Philadelphia & New Jersey. Pension, family & church records when available.

W.D. GRISSOM, SR.
medals@cei.net
PO Box 59
Cabot AR 72023-0059
Medals, documents, related items. Regimental research, reasonable price. Specialist for US & foreign military medals. Catalog - $1 (ref.).

JOHN GROSS
305-512-9542
PO Box 5645
Hialeah FL 33014-1645
Confederate research - info. on 1 million soldiers! Speedy reply. $8/soldier. Unit rosters, pensions, service records, etc. Send SASE for more info.

H-BAR ENTERPRISES
800-432-7702
205-622-3040 Fax
http://www.hbar.com
hbar@oakman.tds.net
1422 Davidson Loop
Oakman AL 35579-5820
Official Records - every word indexed, both reports & correspondence included. Custom CDs available - choose your books. Create own computer databases, add personal notes. Call for info.

THE HANDLEY LIBRARY ARCHIVES
540-662-9041 x22
PO Box 58 • Winchester VA 22604-0058
Contain numerous historical documents & personal records.

HEIRLINES
800-570-4049
James W. Petty, Genealogist
PO Box 893
Salt Lake City UT 84110-0893
Will help you find your ancestors & begin learning about your genealogy. Search censuses, church, court, & land records, military files, etc., in America & other countries.

HILL COLLEGE CONFEDERATE RESEARCH CENTER & MUSEUM
PO Box 619 • Hillsboro TX 76645-0619
Civil War displays & exhibits; extensive collection of research material.

HOFFMAN RESEARCH SERVICES
412-446-3374
http://www.abebooks.com/home/hoffsrch
hoffsrch@westol.com
Ralph Hoffman
PO Box 342 • Rillton PA 15678-0342
Free international book search. Professional bookfinders since 1965; members of Interloc, Advanced Book Exchange & Virtual Book Shop. Please send SASE w/ mail requests.

THE HORSE SOLDIER
717-334-0347
717-334-5016 Fax
http://www.bmark.com/horsesoldier.antiques
hsoldier@mail.wideopen.net
PO Box 184 • Cashtown PA 17310-0184
Buying, selling & appraising Civil War military antiques: firearms, edged weapons, photographs, documents, battlefield relics & more! All items unconditionally guaranteed. Soldier research service available. Semi-annual catalog - $10/yr.

THE INDEX PROJECT, INC.
2525 10th St N Apt 621
Arlington VA 22201-1966
Non-profit group preparing computerized index of 100,000 Union court-martials.

INFO CONCEPTS, INC.
800-747-1861 • 505-298-1528 Fax
11024 Montgomery Blvd NE Ste 284
Albuquerque NM 87111-3962
CW Regimental Info. System - computer-based information source detailing 2,550 Confederate units, 50 orders of battle, 6,000 officers' names, maps, portraits, flags, etc. $99.95 + $7 S&H. Call for info.

INKLINGS BOOKSHOP
804-845-BOOK
1206 Main St
Lynchburg VA 24504-1818
New & used books, out-of-print searches. Civil War, South, Literature, History, Religion, etc.

INSTITUTE FOR CIVIL WAR RESEARCH
ICWRJohn@aol.com
7913 67th Dr
Middle Village NY 11379-2908
Histories of more than 7,500 Civil War units, Union & Confederate. Organizational data, engagement lists, maps, etc. $15/unit. Other services.

JAMES RIVER PUBLICATIONS
804-220-4912
http://www.erols.com/jreb/civilwar.htm
102 Maple Ln
Williamsburg VA 23185-8106
The Chronological Tracking of the American Civil War per the Official Records, 2nd ed., fully indexed, foreword by Dr. Arthur W. Bergeron, Jr. The ultimate Civil War reference manual - $39.95.

TED JONES, CIVIL WAR VETERANS
tedjones@epix.net
RR 1 Box 1317
Little Meadows PA 18830-9730
Let me find your Civil War ancestors. Write for info.

KANSAS STATE HISTORICAL SOCIETY
785-272-8681 x117
http://history.cc.ukans.edu/heritage/kshs/kshs1.html
Library & Archives Division
6425 SW 6th Ave
Topeka KS 66615-1099
Genealogy

RICHARD A. LA POSTA
860-828-0921
154 Robindale Dr
Kensington CT 06037-2054
Civil War books. Regimental histories. First editions. Search service. Buy/sell/trade. Next 2 price lists - $1.

MAC MILLAN GENERAL REFERENCE
800-428-5331
201 W 103rd St
Indianapolis IN 46290-1093
The Atlas of the Civil War - puts the entire Civil War at your fingertips. At bookstores or order direct.

JAMES MEJDRICH
630-668-0384
128 N Knollwood Dr
Wheaton IL 60187-4731
Will check the register of Confederate graves in Mississippi for $1/name & SASE.

MERIDIAN STREET USED BOOKS
317-482-4882
126 S Meridian St
Lebanon IN 46052-2523
Buy/sell/trade used books on all subjects, including military history. Search service.

MERTIN RESEARCH SERVICES
888-248-7166
PO Box 1323
Summit NJ 07902-1323
Experienced genealogist will research Civil War ancestors. Pensions, service records, Union or Confederate.

JUDY MINGUS
30 Pleasant St
Methuen MA 01844-3119
Experienced researcher will research any military records available in Washington, DC, or regional material in Boston area. Send SASE.

GEORGE TYLER MOORE CENTER FOR THE STUDY OF THE CIVIL WAR
304-876-5399
304-876-5429
304-876-5079 Fax
Shepherd College
Shepherdstown WV 25443
For continuing study/education of the most pivotal time in American History - the Civil War. Research being compiled on CW soldiers through a sophisticated database.

THE MUSEUM OF THE CONFEDERACY
804-649-1861 • 804-644-7150 Fax
http://www.moc.org/
Janene Charbeneau
1201 E Clay St • Richmond VA 23219-1615
Maintains most comprehensive collection of military, political & domestic artifacts & art associated with the Confederacy. Adjacent to White House of the Confederacy, restored to its CW appearance.

NATIONAL ARCHIVES & RECORDS ADMIN.
202-501-5400 • 202-501-5410
http://www.nara.gov
inquire@arch2.nara.gov
7th St & Pennsylvania Ave
Washington DC 20408-0001

NEBRASKA STATE HISTORICAL SOCIETY
402-471-4751
http://www.nebraskahistory.org
Library/Archives Division
PO Box 82554 • 1500 R St
Lincoln NE 68501-2554
Checks GAR memberships & burials, rosters of Nebraska soldiers, & the 1890 Census of veterans & widows. Research fee.

OUT-OF-STATE-BOOK-SERVICE
PO Box 3253
San Clemente CA 92674-3253
Books located, out-of-print free search service. No obligation.

PALMETTO HISTORICAL WORKS
803-699-6746
Tim Bradshaw
120 Branch Hill Dr
Elgin SC 29045-9383
Civil War researcher. Union & Confederate letters, 6th East Tenn VI muster roll, tintypes.

PHOTOGRAPHY OF YESTERYEAR
423-510-9306
cwphotogpr@aol.com
Frank or Rita Harned
1 Prior Dr
Chattanooga TN 37421-2168
Photograph birthplaces, churches, cemeteries, landmarks. Photograph CW battlefields of approximate location of your ancestor's unit. Limited unit research available for TN, GA, KY.

CLAUDE V. REICH, PhD
1516 N 14th St
Reading PA 19604-1850
Open-ended database of more than 35,000 Pa. Volunteers at the Battle of Gettysburg.

RESEARCH DATABASE
http://www.civilwardata.com/acw
Don't miss the Civil War again! Visit the largest, most in-depth, & fully searchable research database of U.S. Civil War history. See website for free demonstration.

DAVID B. ROBINSON
PO Box 35926
Richmond VA 23235-0926
Complete listing of every engagement in Virginia referenced to the Official Records. 79 pp. - $12 ppd.

SAUERS HISTORY SHOP
800-510-1108
3531 Martha Custis Dr
Alexandria VA 22302-2002
Eagerly awaited research guide to Civil War material in the *National Tribune*, 1877-1884. $19.95 ppd. (In KY, $20.97).

PATRICK A. SCHROEDER PUBLICATIONS
804-376-1865
PO Box 455
Brookneal VA 24528-9304
Civil War books. New titles include *Civil War Soldier Life*; *We Came to Fight* (5th NY Vol. Inf.); & Belle Boyd. Archives research, prints, notecards, postcards available. Free catalog.

S. SCHUMACHER
425-259-1641
103505.1733@compuserve.com
4027 Rucker Ave Ste 747
Everett WA 98201-4839
CW pension & bountyland packets researched - $20/name. Send name, state mustered in, wife's name, & regiment (if known). Union soldier's burial place researched; 200,000+ names - $10/name. Send details & SASE.

D. SEADLER
3426 Queensborough Dr
Olney MD 20832-2552
Researches Official Records. Regiment, battle reports pension, POW records - $10 for search + first 10 xeroxed pages. 15¢/page thereafter.

SEAWEED'S SHIPS OF HISTORY
800-SEA-WEED
304-652-1525 Fax
PO Box 154, Dept M
Sistersville WV 26175-0154
Histories of U.S. naval, army transports, most Coast Guard, sunken ships, etc. $8 & up.

SOLDIER SEARCH
PO Box 1492
Culpeper VA 22701-1492
Pension & military records of individual soldiers who fought in the Civil War. Records are from the National Archives - $49.95/soldier.

PAUL SPERLING
160 E 38th St # 25
New York NY 10016-2651
Still looking for a book? Free search.

STATE HISTORICAL SOCIETY OF MISSOURI
573-882-7083
1020 Lowry St
Missiouri University
Columbia MO 65201
Research libraries; historical & genealogical materials.

THE UNITED STATES CIVIL WAR CENTER
504-388-3156
504-388-4876 Fax
http://www.cwc.lsu.edu
David Madden, Director
Louisiana State University
Baton Rouge LA 70803-0001
Facilitates the creation of a database encompassing *all* Civil War interests; promotes CW studies from multiple perspectives. Website: best comprehensive index to historic & Civil War-related websites.

GEOFF WALDEN
35197 23 Mile Rd # 4
New Baltimore MI 48047-3639
Will research your ancestor who served with the Kentucky Infantry or Artillery for $3/name. Capsule unit histories for $8/regt. or battery.

JAMES & KAREN WARD
9906 Warson Ct
Richmond VA 23237-3908
Virginia Confederates. Photocopies of your ancestors' military records from the Virginia State Archives. Send soldier's name, county or brigade & $40.

STEVEN J. WRIGHT
7644 Burholme Ave
Philadelphia PA 19111-2411
Civil War & Plains Indian Wars historian.

95TH ILLINOIS CIVIL WAR ROUND TABLE
Tom Steinkamp
1500 East Ave
Belvidere IL 61008-4563

ADIRONDAK CIVIL WAR ROUND TABLE
PO Box 2656
Glen Falls NY 12801-6656

ALABAMA CIVIL WAR ROUND TABLE
DPEACE6499@aol.com
Dan Peace
PO Box 531305
Birmingham AL 35253-1305

AMERICAN CIVIL WAR ROUND TABLE OF AUSTRALIA, INC.
http://www.health.latrobe.edu.au/hs/ss/cu/ACWRTA/Home/cw1page
Barry Crompton, Pres.
14 Sunlight Crescent
East Brighton Victoria, 3187 AUSTRALIA

ANN ARBOR CIVIL WAR ROUND TABLE
http://www.izzy.net/~michaelg/aacwrt.htm
michaelg@izzy.net
Tom Nanzig
PO Box 995
Ann Arbor MI 48106-0995

ARIZONA CIVIL WAR COUNCIL
George Kuckworth
12602 N 20th Ave
Phoenix AZ 85029-2610

ASH COUNTY CIVIL WAR ROUND TABLE
Richard Waters
73 W Jefferson St
Jefferson OH 44047-1027

ATLANTA CIVIL WAR ROUND TABLE
devanetr@argold.com
Thomas R. Devaney
1358 Brawley Cir NE
Atlanta GA 30319-1709

AUGHWICK CIVIL WAR ROUND TABLE
PO Box 41
Three Springs PA 17264-0041

AUSTIN CIVIL WAR ROUND TABLE
110 Wild Basin Rd S Ste 290
Austin TX 78746-3337

BONNIE BALDWIN CIVIL WAR ROUND TABLE
7305 Inzer St
Springfield VA 22151-3007

BALTIMORE CIVIL WAR ROUND TABLE
410-661-4479
Don Macreadie
1809 Wendover Rd
Baltimore MD 21234-6122
Meets 2nd Tuesday, 7:30 pm, Tall Cedars Hall, Putty Hill Shopping Center, Putty Hill Ave. & Old Harford Rd. Free newletter & other info. (incl. dues).

BATESVILLE AREA CIVIL WAR ROUND TABLE
Ken Spencer
7 Buckeye St
Batesville AR 72501-9198

BATON ROUGE CIVIL WAR ROUND TABLE
hildamax@intersurf.com
Charles Elliott
4025 Floyd Dr
Baton Rouge LA 70808-3724

BAY COUNTY CIVIL WAR ROUND TABLE
7th_nhrc@interoz.com
J.K. Lacey
PO Box 1331
Youngstown FL 32466-1331

BENTON CIVIL WAR ROUND TABLE
http://www.civilwarbuff.org
pamray@aol.com
Pam Ray
520 Virginia St
Benton AR 72015-3839

BLUE & GRAY CIVIL WAR ROUND TABLE OF PRINCE GEORGES COUNTY
John Wyrick
5608 Woodland Dr
Forest Heights MD 20745-1329

BRYAN / COLLEGE STATION CIVIL WAR ROUND TABLE
Bill Vance
714 Encinas Pl • College Station TX 77845

BUCKS COUNTY CIVIL WAR ROUND TABLE
PO Box 1868 • Doylestown PA 18901-0369

BULL RUN CIVIL WAR ROUND TABLE
703-330-1965
http://osf1.gmu.edu/~cgrymes/brcwrt/brcwrthp.html • fit2prnt@erols.com
Karen Fojt
PO Box 196 • Centreville VA 20122-0196
Lecture and discussion group devoted to the historical study of the years 1861-65.

DAN BUTTERFIELD CIVIL WAR ROUND TABLE
wh_ref@midyork.lib.ny.us
Cheryl Pula
57 New Hartford St
New York Mills NY 13417-1503

CAMP OLDEN CIVIL WAR ROUND TABLE
609-275-0143
http://www.trenton.edu/~sirak/cocwrt/coindex.html
sirak@tcnj.edu
PO Box 11060
Hamilton NJ 08620-0060

CAMP TIPPECANOE CIVIL WAR ROUND TABLE
http://www.dcwi.com/~yannerdr/ctcwrt.html
yannerdr@dcwi.com
Wells Cultural Center
7th & North Sts
Lafayette IN 47901

CAPE FEAR CIVIL WAR ROUND TABLE
blakedp@wilmington.net
PO Box 10535
Wilmington NC 28405-0535

CAPITAL DISTRICT CIVIL WAR ROUND TABLE
http://pages/prodigy.com/WNUW97A
WNUW97A@prodigy.com
PO Box 14871
Albany NY 12221-4871

CAPITOL AREA CIVIL WAR ROUND TABLE
David Finney
316 Thompson St
Howell MI 48843-1222

CAPITOL HILL CIVIL WAR ROUND TABLE
http://www.geocities.com/Athens/1799/cwrt9612.html
800 11th St NW
Washington DC 20001-4514

CENTRAL DELAWARE CIVIL WAR ROUND TABLE
PO Box 328
Odessa DE 19730-0328

CENTRAL OHIO CIVIL WAR ROUND TABLE
http://www.qn.net/~wittenberg/roundtable.html
ejwlaw@qn.net
Eric Wittenberg
923 E Broad St
Columbus OH 43205-1101

JOSHUA L. CHAMBERLAIN CIVIL WAR ROUND TABLE
Warren B. Randall
PO Box 1046
Brunswick ME 04011-1046
Usually meets 7 PM, 2nd Thursdays, Sept.-June at Junior High. Membership & monthly newsletter: reg. $20, family $30, non-resident associate $10. $50 members receive audio-tapes of year's speakers.

CHICAGO CIVIL WAR ROUND TABLE
8417 W Johanna Dr
Niles IL 60714-1850

CINCINNATI CIVIL WAR ROUND TABLE
http://members.aol.com/CintiCWRT/index.html
CintiCWRT@aol.com
PO Box 1336
Cincinnati OH 45201-1336

CIVIL WAR ROUND TABLE
RR 3 Box 135-60
Strafford MO 65757-9314

CIVIL WAR ROUND TABLE ASSOCIATES
501-255-3996
jlrussell@civilwarbuff.com
PO Box 7388
Little Rock AR 72217-7388
Est. 1968; oldest national CW battlefield preservation organization. Publishes *CWRT Digest*, newsletter devoted to news of contemporary activities, inspired by interest in CW history & historic preservation. $12.50/yr.

CIVIL WAR ROUND TABLE OF ALEXANDRIA / FORT WARD
4301 W Braddock Rd
Alexandria VA 22304-1007

CIVIL WAR ROUND TABLE OF ARKANSAS
http://www.civilwarbuff.org
PO Box 7281
Little Rock AR 72217-7281

CIVIL WAR ROUND TABLE OF BIRMINGHAM
3648 Kingshill Rd
Birmingham AL 35223-1424

CIVIL WAR ROUND TABLE OF BUFFALO
benedict@ns.moran.com
5559 Broadway St
Lancaster NY 14086-2223

CIVIL WAR ROUND TABLE OF CAPE MAY, NJ
http://www.jerseycape.com/users/cole/index.htm
billc@jerseycape.net
40 Secluded Ln • Rio Grande NJ 08242-1527

CIVIL WAR ROUND TABLE OF CENTRAL FLORIDA
Karl Eichorn
PO Box 255 • Sharpes FL 32959-0255

CIVIL WAR ROUND TABLE OF CHARLOTTE
William Quinn
1018 Heather Ln
Charlotte NC 28209-2540

CIVIL WAR ROUND TABLE OF CHATTANOOGA
620 S Sanctuary Rd
Chattanooga TN 37412-4150

CIVIL WAR ROUND TABLE OF COLORADO
1920 Bluebell Ave
Boulder CO 80302-8024

CIVIL WAR ROUND TABLE OF D.C.
R. Warner
1550 Brookshire Ct
Reston VA 20190-4201

CIVIL WAR ROUND TABLE OF DALTON
PO Box 2316
Dalton GA 30722-2316

CIVIL WAR ROUND TABLE OF EASTERN PENNSYLVANIA
http://www.enter.net/~cwrt
holubowsky@mail.enter.net
Jayne Holubowsky
PO Box 333
Allentown PA 18105-0333

CIVIL WAR ROUND TABLE OF FAIRFIELD COUNTY
Guy Desmond
108 Diamondcrest Ln
Stamford CT 06903-4932

CIVIL WAR ROUND TABLE OF FORT MYERS
1821 Llewellyn Dr
Fort Myers FL 33901-5821

CIVIL WAR ROUND TABLE OF FREDERICKSBURG
PO Box 491
Fredericksburg VA 22404-0491

CIVIL WAR ROUND TABLE OF GREATER BOSTON
http://k12.oit.umass.edu/masag/1092o.html
Monthly meetings on the last Friday of each month. Field trips. 37th year.

CIVIL WAR ROUND TABLE OF HAWAII
219 Kuuhale St
Kailua HI 96734-2943

CIVIL WAR ROUND TABLE OF KANSAS CITY
Richard Southall
5730 W 81st Ter
Shawnee Mission KS 66208-4807

CIVIL WAR ROUND TABLE OF KENTUCKY
Nicky Hughes
PO Box 1792
Frankfort KY 40602-1792

CIVIL WAR ROUND TABLE OF LAKE COUNTY
Tracy Cripps
101 N Grandview St Apt 312
Mount Dora FL 32757-5675

CIVIL WAR ROUND TABLE OF MILWAUKEE
John H. Thompson
505 E Henry Clay St Apt 104
Milwaukee WI 53217-5656

CIVIL WAR ROUND TABLE OF MONTGOMERY COUNTY
Vicki Heiling
11843 Summer Oak Dr
Germantown MD 20874-1942

CIVIL WAR ROUND TABLE OF NAPLES
Mary Den Dooven
619 Binnacle Dr
Naples FL 34103-2725

CIVIL WAR ROUND TABLE OF NE ARKANSAS
Randy F. Philhours
414 W Court St
Paragould AR 72450-4246

CIVIL WAR ROUND TABLE OF NEBRASKA
John Higgins
4201 Fran Ave
Lincoln NE 68516-1705

CIVIL WAR ROUND TABLE OF NEW ALBANY
PO Box 1087
New Albany IN 47151-1087

CIVIL WAR ROUND TABLE OF NEW HAMPSHIRE
Barry Burnham
PO Box 369 • Epping NH 03042-0369

CIVIL WAR ROUND TABLE OF NEW ORLEANS
Charles J. Nunez
3220 Lake Trail Dr • Metairie LA 70003-3433

CIVIL WAR ROUND TABLE OF NEW YORK
217-677-2200
175 5th Ave # 2209
New York NY 10010-7703
Monthly Manhattan meetings, guest lecturers, battlefield tours. Dues $40/yr.

CIVIL WAR ROUND TABLE OF NW ARKANSAS
http://www.tcac.com/~bunderdn/cwrt.htm
bunderdn@tcac.com
Bob Underdown
PO Box 2947
Fayetteville AR 72702-2947

CIVIL WAR ROUND TABLE OF OKLAHOMA CITY
James Caster
3401 NW 24th St
Oklahoma City OK 73107-1807

CIVIL WAR ROUND TABLE OF RACELAND
Jon Lowry
409 Highland Ave
Raceland KY 41169-1023

CIVIL WAR ROUND TABLE OF SOUTH CENTRAL CT
Albert S Redway
100 Woodlawn St
Hamden CT 06517-1339

CIVIL WAR ROUND TABLE OF SOUTH FLORIDA
Arlyn Austin Katims
6801 SW 79th Ave • Miami FL 33143-2637

CIVIL WAR ROUND TABLE OF SPRINGFIELD
David Preston
1314 N 2nd St
Springfield IL 62702-3834

CIVIL WAR ROUND TABLE OF ST. LOUIS
http://home.stlnet.com/~cwrtstl
cwrtstl@stlnet.com • Hugh Johns
1783 Heffington Dr
Chesterfield MO 63017-5424

CIVIL WAR ROUND TABLE OF STUTTGART
wolfgang.hochbruck@po.uni-stuttgart.de
Deutsch-Amerikanisches Zentrum
Charlottenplatz 17
D - 70173 Stuttgart GERMANY

CIVIL WAR ROUND TABLE OF THE NW CORNER
PO Box 35
Hotchkiss School
Lakeville CT 06039-0035

CIVIL WAR ROUND TABLE OF THE OZARKS
Rick Gorman
606 N 7th Ave
Ozark MO 65721-9320

CIVIL WAR ROUND TABLE OF VANDERBURGH COURTHOUSE
Robert Leach
PO Box 869
Evansville IN 47705-0869

CIVIL WAR ROUND TABLE OF WAYNE COUNTY
TyeTurning@aol.com
Tyrone Turning
1062 Douglas Dr
Wooster OH 44691-2771

CIVIL WAR ROUND TABLE OF WEST CENTRAL INDIANA
http://www.thnet.com/~liggetkw/cwrt/cwrtwci.htm
Emmaline Henry
404 Linwood Dr
Greencastle IN 46135-1137

CIVIL WARRIORS ROUND TABLE
818-224-2001
http://www.dentistry.com/cwrt
c/o Jeffrey L. Wissot, DDS
23067 Ventura Blvd Ste 101
Woodland Hills CA 91364-1153
Join this round table discussion group in the West San Fernando Valley, Los Angeles, Calif.

CLAY COUNTY CIVIL WAR ROUND TABLE
Larry Kramer
RR 2
Flora IL 62839-9803

CONNECTICUT VALLEY CIVIL WAR ROUND TABLE
A W Whyte
25 Murphy Ter
Northampton MA 01060-1610

COOPERSTOWN CIVIL WAR ROUND TABLE
Thomas Malone
5 Susquehanna Ave
Cooperstown NY 13326-1220

COTEAU CIVIL WAR ROUND TABLE
David Rambow
113 S Hiawatha Ave
Pipestone MN 56164-1664

CUMBERLAND VALLEY CIVIL WAR ROUND TABLE
D Hartmann
PO Box 663 • Chambersburg PA 17201-0663

CUYAHOGA VALLEY CIVIL WAR ROUND TABLE
Thomas L. Vince
49 E Main St • Hudson OH 44236-3003

DALLAS CIVIL WAR ROUND TABLE
214-368-6230
sdavis@why.net
Pax Glenn, President
3800 Lovers Ln • Dallas TX 75225-7101

DAYTON CIVIL WAR ROUND TABLE
http://www.infinet.com/~lstevens/a/ohcwrt.html
biggsk@aol.com
Karel Lea Biggs
106 Haig St
Celina OH 45822-2708

DC CIVIL WAR ROUND TABLE
1740 Bay St SE
Washington DC 20003-1646

DECATUR CIVIL WAR ROUND TABLE
Sharon Lee
138 S Delmar Ave
Decatur IL 62522-2506

DELAWARE VALLEY CIVIL WAR ROUND TABLE
http://www.ourworld.compuserve.com/homepages/paulag/homepage.htm
PO Box 63006
Philadelphia PA 19114-0806

ELK GROVE CIVIL WAR ROUND TABLE
PO Box 1864
Elk Grove CA 95759-1864

FORT SMITH CIVIL WAR ROUND TABLE
Bob Vick
1102 Wofford Lake Rd
Fort Smith AR 72916-3611

FORT WAYNE CIVIL WAR ROUND TABLE
http://www.thnet.com/~liggetkw/cwrt/ftwayne.cwrt.htm
dfboyle@juno.com
Robert Johnsonbaugh
6818 Woodcrest Dr
Fort Wayne IN 46815-5571

FORT WORTH CIVIL WAR ROUND TABLE
Jim Rosenthal
3952 Thistle Ln
Fort Worth TX 76109-3425

FREDERICK COUNTY CIVIL WAR ROUND TABLE
http://members.aol.com/Fredcocwrt/private/index.htm
FredCoCWRT@aol.com
PO Box 4101
Frederick MD 21705-4101

CAPT. HENRY GALPIN CIVIL WAR CIVIL WAR ROUND TABLE
RR 1 Box 319
Little Falls NY 13365-9634

GENESSEE VALLEY CIVIL WAR ROUND TABLE
DTKTT@aol.com
Donna Payne
PO Box 451 • Pavilion NY 14525-0451

GETTYSBURG CIVIL WAR ROUND TABLE
Barbara Angstadt
201 Hills Dr
Gettysburg PA 17325-2435

GLOVERSVILLE CIVIL WAR ROUND TABLE
James Morrison
95 Lincoln St • Gloversville NY 12078-2017

GRAND RAPIDS CIVIL WAR ROUND TABLE
Ron Farra
666 Four Mile Rd NE
Grand Rapids MI 49525-2106

GRANVILLE CIVIL WAR ROUND TABLE
http://www.infinet.com/~lstevens/a/ohcwrt.html
PO Box 129 • Granville OH 43023-0129

GREATER TOLEDO CIVIL WAR ROUND TABLE
http://www.infinet.com/~lstevens/a/ohcwrt.html
http://www.netcom.com/~jobuford/CWRT/main.html
jobuford@ix.netcom.com
4325 Commonwealth Ave
Toledo OH 43612-2040

GREEN MOUNTAIN CIVIL WAR ROUND TABLE
http://members.aol.com/vtcw150/gmcwrt.htm
auntis@aol.com
PO Box 653 • Woodstock VT 05091-0653

MAJ. ANDREW J. GROVER CIVIL WAR ROUND TABLE
41 Creamery Rd • Richford NY 13835-1001

HAMPTON ROADS CIVIL WAR ROUND TABLE
127 W Lorengo Ave
Norfolk VA 23503-4313

HARPERS FERRY CIVIL WAR ROUND TABLE
PO Box 355
Harpers Ferry WV 25425-0355
Meets 2nd Wed. of each month, Sept-June at Camp Hill United Methodist Church, Harpers Ferry, W.Va. Dues - $15/yr.

HARRISBURG CIVIL WAR ROUND TABLE
William Matter
3621 Brookridge Ter Apt 101
Harrisburg PA 17109-2131

HARTFORD CIVIL WAR ROUND TABLE
R D Wolff
105 Hedgehog Ln
West Simsbury CT 06092-2107

HAYWARD CIVIL WAR ROUND TABLE
2753 Meadowlark Dr
Union City CA 94587-3142

HIAWATHA VALLEY CIVIL WAR ROUND TABLE
Patrick Lewis
412 Laird St
Winona MN 55987-4030

HOOSIER BLUE & GRAY CIVIL WAR ROUND TABLE
http://www.thnet.com/~liggetkw/cwrt/b&g.htm
James Gibson
PO Box 292
Cambridge City IN 47327-0292

HOUSTON CIVIL WAR ROUND TABLE
http://members.aol.com/Houstcwrt/index.html
reyork@ibm.net
Dean Letzring
PO Box 4215
Houston TX 77210-4215
Website: information, programs & schedule of events.

IMPERIAL VALLEY CIVIL WAR ROUND TABLE
510 W Main St
El Centro CA 92243-2900

INDIANAPOLIS CIVIL WAR ROUND TABLE
http://www.thnet.com/~liggetkw/cwrt/indmain.htm
Beverly Roberts
10006 E Washington St Ste A
Indianapolis IN 46229-2624

INLAND EMPIRE CIVIL WAR ROUND TABLE
Don McCue
A.K. Smiley Public Library
125 W Vine St
Redlands CA 92373-4761

THE JACKSON CIVIL WAR ROUND TABLE
PO Box 3475
Jackson MS 39207-3475

JEFFERSON COUNTY CIVIL WAR ROUND TABLE
http://www.thnet.com/~liggetkw/cwrt/jccwrt.htm
Eric Losey
3940 W Prall Ln
Scottsburg IN 47170-7811

KANAWHA VALLEY CIVIL WAR ROUND TABLE
888 S Washington St
Saint Albans WV 25177-3784

KNOXVILLE CIVIL WAR ROUND TABLE
PO Box 313
Knoxville TN 37901-0313

LAUREL HILL CIVIL WAR ROUND TABLE
Gary Birkett
PO Box 701
Stuart VA 24171-0701

ROBERT E. LEE CIVIL WAR ROUND TABLE
http://nj5.injersey.com/~mbwick
augn61a@prodigy.com or
mbwick@injersey.com
1162 Saint Georges Ave Ste 194
Avenel NJ 07001-1263

GEORGE W. LEE CIVIL WAR ROUND TABLE
Michael Yost
PO Box 500
Howell MI 48844-0500

ABRAHAM LINCOLN CIVIL WAR ROUND TABLE OF MICHIGAN
lstringer@ameritech.net
Liz Stringer, Pres.
23959 Brookplace Ct
Farmington Hills MI 48336-2728

LINCOLN CIVIL WAR SOCIETY
John Bloom
127 Mansfield Rd
Landsdowne PA 19050-1513

LINCOLN CLUB OF DELAWARE
David H. Burdash
1111 Bayview Rd
Middletown DE 19709-9625

LINCOLN GROUP OF BOSTON
Thomas Turner
27 Forest Trl
East Bridgewater MA 02333-1612

LITTLE FORT CIVIL WAR ROUND TABLE
Torlief Homes
2636 W Vermont Ave
Waukegan IL 60087-3648

LONG BEACH CIVIL WAR ROUND TABLE
9813 Via Sonoma • Cypress CA 90630-3437

LONG ISLAND CIVIL WAR ROUND TABLE
Richard Cashman
18 Dillmont St • Smithtown NY 11787-1602

LOUDOUN COUNTY CIVIL WAR ROUND TABLE
540-338-7550
PO Box 18 • Lincoln VA 20160-0018
Meets monthly at Douglass Community School, Route 7 E & Sycolin Rd., Leesburg.

LOUISVILLE CIVIL WAR ROUND TABLE
PO Box 1861
Louisville KY 40201-1861

MADISON COUNTY HISTORICAL SOCIETY CWRT
http://www.thnet.com/~liggetkw/cwrt/mchscwrt.htm
Gerald Jones
2812 E 100 S
Anderson IN 46017-1802

MAHONING VALLEY CWRT
David Badger
RR 1 Box 389
New Galilee PA 16141-9619
Meets 2nd Tues., Sept-May.

MANITOWOC COUNTY CIVIL WAR ROUND TABLE
dmoore@lakefield.net
Dennis R Moore
1232 Arlington Ave
Manitowoc WI 54220-2628

MICHIGAN REGIMENTAL CIVIL WAR ROUND TABLE
junskimos@aol.com
John Moore
2119 Van Antwerp St
Grosse Point Woods MI 48236-1624

MID-ATLANTIC CONFERENCE OF CIVIL WAR ROUND TABLES
610-262-1614
CWRT of Eastern PA
PO Box 333 • Allentown PA 18105-0333
Special speakers. Annual conference - April.

MIDWEST CWRT CONFERENCE
Cincinnati CWRT
PO Box 1336
Cincinnati OH 45201-1336
Annual April conferences with several speakers, book sales, raffles, tours.

MURFREESBORO CIVIL WAR ROUND TABLE
Pennie Jekot
2115 Shannon Dr
Murfreesboro TN 37129-1334

NASSAU COUNTY CIVIL WAR ROUND TABLE
Walter Anthony
150 Lincoln Ave
Rockville Centre NY 11570-5901

NATIONAL CONGRESS OF CWRTs
501-225-3996 • jlrussell@civilwarbuff.com
CWRTA
PO Box 7388 • Little Rock AR 72217-7388
Speakers & tours. Annual October conference sponsored by Civil War Round Table Associates.

NORTH CAROLINA CIVIL WAR ROUND TABLE
4109 Charles G Dr • Raleigh NC 27606-9237

NORTH COUNTY CIVIL WAR ROUND TABLE
315-386-8133 • 315-386-8134 Fax
slcha@northnet.org
St. Lawrence Co. Historical Assn.
PO Box 8 • Canton NY 13617-0008

NORTH LOUISIANA CIVIL WAR ROUND TABLE
http://www.prysm.net/~garyj/NLCWRT/nlcwrt.htm
garyj@prysm.net
Mary Margaret & Allan Richard or Garry D. Joiner
245 Forest Ave • Shreveport LA 71104-4506

NORWICH CIVIL WAR ROUND TABLE
Dave Manzer
594 Lyon Brook Rd • Norwich NY 13815-3427

OHIO VALLEY CIVIL WAR ROUND TABLE
740-425-3201
Joe Atkinson
321 N Broadway St
Barnesville OH 43713-1109
Meetings held at 7 PM, 4th Monday of every month, at Ohio Valley Mall Bonanza restaurant. Dues - $15/yr. All CW buffs welcome.

OLD BALDY CWRT OF PHILADELPHIA
215-735-8196
Steven Wright, Mike Cavanaugh, or Pat Purcell
1805 Pine St
Philadelphia PA 19103-6601
Monthly meetings, speakers, field trips, heavily into preservation.

OLDE COLONY CIVIL WAR ROUND TABLE
David Kenney
43 Fairview St
Dedham MA 02026-3223

ONONDAGA CIVIL WAR ROUND TABLE
Tom Hunter
311 Montgomery St
Syracuse NY 13202-2009

ORLANDO CIVIL WAR ROUND TABLE
Hal K. Litchford
PO Box 1549
Orlando FL 32802-1549

OTTAWA NATIONAL CAPITAL CIVIL WAR ROUND TABLE
Mr. Cliff Forsythe
1002 Driftwood Cres
Gloucester, Ontario Canada K1C 2P1
Also Confederate Historical Association of Canada. Monthly meetings.

PALM BEACH CIVIL WAR ROUND TABLE
James Roberts
829 Salem Ln
Lake Worth FL 33467-2764

WILLIAM DORSEY PENDER CIVIL WAR ROUND TABLE
John Derbyshire
PO Box 7828
Rocky Mount NC 27804-0828

PENINSULA CIVIL WAR ROUND TABLE
PO Box 1274
San Carlos CA 94070-1274

PENSACOLA CIVIL WAR ROUND TABLE
http://members.aol.com/PENCWRT/index.html
pencwrt@aol.com
Thomas R. Long, Jr.
4204 Rosebud Ct
Pensacola FL 32504-8448

PIEDMONT CIVIL WAR ROUND TABLE
William Stafford
150 Riley Forest Ct
Winston Salem NC 27127-7574

PLATTE VALLEY CIVIL WAR ROUND TABLE
Lawrence Lefler
1835 E Military Ave # 127
Fremont NE 68025-5465

PORTER COUNTY CIVIL WAR ROUND TABLE
Jeff Sandlin
103 E Mound St
Knox IN 46534-1133

PORTSMOUTH AREA CIVIL WAR ROUND TABLE
Jessie Hines
641 Mount Vernon Ave
Portsmouth VA 23707-2018

PUGET SOUND CIVIL WAR ROUND TABLE
D P Richardson
6614 NE Windermere Rd
Seattle WA 98115-7943

RANDOLPH COUNTY CIVIL WAR ROUND TABLE
http://www.thnet.com/~liggetkw/cwrt/RCCWRT.htm
Meet at 101 W. Franklin St., Winchester, Indiana.

RAPPAHANNOCK VALLEY CIVIL WAR ROUND TABLE
540-786-2470
Mwyckoff@pop.erols.com
Mac Wyckoff
PO Box 7632 • Fredericksburg VA 22404

RICHMOND CIVIL WAR ROUND TABLE
Sandra V. Parker, Sect.
PO Box 37052
Richmond VA 23234-7052
Meets 2nd Tuesday each month at Boulevard Methodist Church, Boulevard & Stuart Ave., Richmond, Va., at 8 PM.

ROANOKE CIVIL WAR ROUND TABLE
Clive Rich
PO Box 11882
Roanoke VA 24022-1882

ROCHESTER CIVIL WAR ROUND TABLE
Jerry Poslusny
118 Burrows Hills Dr
Rochester NY 14625-2129

ROCKBRIDGE CIVIL WAR ROUND TABLE
PO Box 7
Brownsburg VA 24415-0007
Monthly meetings. Dues - $15. Bob Driver, president.

ROCKLAND CIVIL WAR ROUND TABLE
Ken Dudonis
95 Hunt Ave
Pearl River NY 10965-1868

SACRAMENTO CIVIL WAR ROUND TABLE
7713 Las Lilas Ct
Citrus Heights CA 95621-1722

SALT CREEK CIVIL WAR ROUND TABLE
http://www.civilwar-saltcreek-rt.com
Donald A. Sender, Pres.
PO Box 4873
Wheaton IL 60189
125-150 members. Has recently contributed more than $10,000 to battlefield preservation through auctions, book drawings & special events. Est. 1962. Monthly newsletter.

SAN ANTONIO CIVIL WAR ROUND TABLE
Rusy Mahan
13643 Princes Knls
San Antonio TX 78231-1948

SAN DIEGO CIVIL WAR ROUND TABLE
CWDAVE@aol.com
PO Box 22369
San Diego CA 92192-2369

SAN FRANCISCO CIVIL WAR ROUND TABLE
PO Box 2389
Livermore CA 94551-2389

SAN GABRIEL VALLEY CIVIL WAR ROUND TABLE
PO Box 80680
San Marino CA 91118-8680

SAN JOAQUIN VALLEY CIVIL WAR ROUND TABLE
8665 N Cedar Ave Unit 112
Fresno CA 93720-1823

SAVANNAH GRAYS CIVIL WAR ROUND TABLE
PO Box 15238
Savannah GA 31416-1938

SHENANDOAH VALLEY CIVIL WAR ROUND TABLE
George Hansbrough
209 F St
Shenandoah VA 22849-1126

SOUTH BAY CIVIL WAR ROUND TABLE
1475 S Bascom Ave Ste 204
Campbell CA 95008-0629

SOUTHERN MINNESOTA CIVIL WAR ROUND TABLE
1104 7th St SW
Rochester MN 55902-2005

SOUTHERN ONTARIO CIVIL WAR ROUND TABLE
quee@netrover.com
Dave Carney
28 James St
Georgetown Ontario, CANADA L7G 2H4

STILLWATER CIVIL WAR ROUND TABLE
http://www.infinet.com/~lstevens/a/ohcwrt.html
Dr. David R. Hayes
PO Box 366 • West Milton OH 45383-0366

SUFFOLK CIVIL WAR ROUND TABLE
Robert Hardy
5085 Indian Trl • Suffolk VA 23434-7322

TENNESSEE VALLEY CIVIL WAR ROUND TABLE
http://members.aol.com/TVCWRT/index.html
jfepperson@aol.com
Brian Hogan
11202 Suncrest Dr SE
Huntsville AL 35803-1620

TRI-VALLEY CIVIL WAR ROUND TABLE
PO Box 5076
Pleasanton CA 94566-0576

TWIN CITIES CIVIL WAR ROUNDTABLE, INC.
612-933-6696 • Paul Olson
14699 Beacon Cir
Minnetonka MN 55345-4707
Meets monthly September-May for dinner & guest speaker on Civil War topics.

TWIN TIER CIVIL WAR ROUND TABLE
Michael S. Winicki
PO Box 1108 • Olean NY 14760-6108
Sponsors of seminars, talks, presentations & other Civil War activities. Supports preservation efforts. Est. 1990.

ULSTER COUNTY CIVIL WAR ROUND TABLE
UCCWRT@mhv.net
PO Box 120
Stone Ridge NY 12484-0120

VILLANOVA CIVIL WAR ROUND TABLE
International Studies
Villanova University
Villanova PA 19085

WACO CIVIL WAR ROUND TABLE
Jerry Powell
Baylor Univ Continuing Ed
Box 97288
Waco TX 76798-7288

WATERTOWN CIVIL WAR ROUND TABLE
Richard Kraemer
871 Leray St
Watertown NY 13601-1353

WEST CENTRAL OHIO CIVIL WAR ROUND TABLE
http://www.infinet.com/~lstevens/a/ohcwrt.html
302 N Wayne St
Van Wert OH 45891-1328

WESTCHESTER NY CIVIL WAR ROUND TABLE
PO Box 1861
Croton Falls NY 10519

WESTERN OHIO CIVIL WAR ROUND TABLE
http://www.infinet.com/~lstevens/a/ohcwrt.html
PO Box 511
Celina OH 45822-0511

WESTMORELAND COUNTY CIVIL WAR ROUND TABLE
Jack Burger
323 N Maple Ave
Greensburg PA 15601-1818

WICHITA CIVIL WAR ROUND TABLE
pjhjr@juno.com
John Handley
PO Box 1654
Wichita KS 67201-1654

WICHITA FALLS CIVIL WAR ROUND TABLE
Bill Spears
PO Box 780
Wichita Falls TX 76307-0780

WILLIAMSBURG CIVIL WAR ROUND TABLE, INC.
757-838-1685
JPHA1982@aol.com or bowers5@erols.com
Peggy Vogtsberger
7 Carmel Ter • Hampton VA 23666-2807
Meets monthly, 2nd Thurs. 7:30 PM, Bruton Parish Church Center, Duke of Gloucester St., Williamsburg. Excellent speakers, field trips. Active in battlefield preservation & historical interpretation. Dues - $20/yr.

WILMINGTON DE CIVIL WAR ROUND TABLE
Robert Widenor
2211 Beaumont Rd
Wilmington DE 19803-3016

WYOMING VALLEY CIVIL WAR ROUND TABLE
PO Box 613
Dallas PA 18612-0613

AIKEN LEE-JACKSON BANQUET
803-649-9475
SCV
PO Box 1863 • Aiken SC 29802-1863
Annual January banquet. Hosted by Brig. Gen. Banard E. Bee Camp #1575, SCV, to benefit preservation.

CAPITAL OF THE CONFEDERACY CIVIL WAR SHOW
804-737-5827
Central VA Relic Hunters Assn
Richmond VA
More than 450 tables of original weapons, uniforms, relics, currency, documents, & personal soldier items. Hourly presentations by Museum of the Confederacy. Annual event - November.

CAROLINA TRADER PROMOTIONS
704-282-1339
http://www.trellis.net/carotrader
carotrader@trellis.net
Esther & Richard Shields
PO Box 769
1902 Plyler Mill Rd
Monroe NC 28111-0769
Promoters of military collectible shows. Contact for locations & other info.

CELEBRATE HISTORY
800-748-9901
http://www.celebratehistory.com
PO Box 70332
Port Richmond CA 94807-0332
Held annually every President's Day holiday weekend (Feb. 13-15, 1998) at South San Francisco Conference Center. Includes complete Civil War round table & symposium.

CELEBRATION DINNER DANCE
616-349-6195 • 616-349-1480 Fax
tmselem2@net-link.net
Pam Boudreau
3330 S Rose St
Kalamazoo MI 49001-4723
Dinner dance with period music, dance instruction; 3rd Saturday in March. Period dress optional. Annual event sponsored by 3rd Battery, 1st Michigan Light Artillery.

CENTRAL NC RELIC HUNTERS CIVIL WAR SHOW
704-463-5439 Terry Teff
704-289-4212 Mick Aderholdt
Salisbury NC
Civil War relics. Annual show - February.

CHRISTMAS AT THE FORT
334-861-6992
Fort Gaines Historic Site
PO Box 97
Dauphin Island AL 36528-0097
Annual living history weekend; 1998 dates - December 5-6. Experience 1861 Christmas at the fort with Confederate soldiers -- authenticity stressed. Candlelight tour, feast, dance, drills, camp life, etc.

CIVIL WAR MEMORABILIA, RELIC & BOOK SHOW (SC)
803-577-7766
Ray Davenport
Charleston SC
Hosted by Lowcountry CW Collectors Assn. Display awards. Annual show - January. Admission - $4 over age 12.

CIVIL WAR MEMORABILIA, RELIC & BOOK SHOW (VA)
703-823-1958 John Graham
Northern Va. Relic Hunters Assn.
Fairfax VA
More than 275 tables of finest Civil War & earlier military effects, memorabilia, relics & books for sale or trade. Exhibitor awards. Annual show - March. Admission - $4 over age 12.

CIVIL WAR SCULPTURE EXHIBITION & SEMINAR
800-438-5800
Grove Park Inn Resort
Asheville NC
Annual March exhibition. Vignettes, auctions, discussions & more. Call for info. & free brochure.

COASTAL CAROLINA MILITARY ANTIQUES SHOW
704-282-1339
Wilmington NC
Arms & memorabilia of Civil War, Indian Wars, world wars, etc. Annual July event.

COHASCO, INC.
914-476-8500
914-476-8573 Fax
E. Snyder
Postal 821
Yonkers NY 10702
Semi-annual mail/phone auction catalogs containing varied CW memorabilia: generals, maps, letters, photos, ephemera, etc. Our 50th year in business. Catalog - $5.

COLUMBUS-BELMONT STATE PARK
502-677-2327
502-677-4013 Fax
Bill Stevens, Park Mgr.
PO Box 8 • Columbus KY 42032-0008
Civil War museum, activities, special events.

CONFERENCE ON WOMEN & THE CIVIL WAR
800-473-3943 • roslin@nfs.com
12728 Martin Rd
Smithsburg MD 21783-9337
Through lectures on various topics, recognizes & honors the services performed by women for their country & its people during the 1860s.

EARLY AMERICAN HISTORY AUCTIONS, INC.
619-459-4159
800-473-5686
619-459-4373 Fax
http://www.cts.com/browse/ean
PO Box 3341
La Jolia CA 92038-3341
Mail bid auctions every two months; approx. 1,000 lots in each. Historic Americana & Civil War-related material. Always buying collections & accepting important consignments. Catalog - $36/yr. for 6 issues. Free on Internet.

FIREARMS SKIRMISH NATIONAL COMPETITION
North-South Skirmish Assn.
Winchester VA
More than 3,600 competitors on 200 teams competing with muskets, carbines, revolvers, mortars & cannon. Largest event of its kind. Sutlers, food, free admission. Annual event - May.

FORKS OF THE DELAWARE ANTIQUE & MODERN ARMS SHOWS
610-588-8305
Forks of the Delaware Historical Arms Society, Inc.
97 Johnson Rd
Bangor PA 18013-9274
Antique & modern arms, & related items. Presented 4 times/yr. $5 donation at door.

FREDERICK CIVIL WAR SHOW
301-253-4961
Ed Dishman
PO Box 246
Damascus MD 20872-0246
Annual April CW show, sponsored by Frederick Co., MD, CWRT & Central MD Heritage League. Admission - $4 over age 12.

GETTYSBURG BATTLEFIELD PRESERVATION ASSOCIATION
717-337-0031
Dr. Walter L. Powell, Pres.
PO Box 1863
Gettysburg PA 17325
Bi-annual newsletter "Battle Lines" (for $10 annual membership). Various Civil War books & prints available for donations. Annual Civil War Book Show.

GRAND ANNAPOLIS CITY BALL
Stephen Bockmiller
101 Fitz Ct Apt 204
Reisterstown MD 21136-3327
Annual March ball with orchestral music & refreshments. Period military or civilian attire required. Attendance limited. Co-sponsored by 4th NC Infantry & 5th US Cavalry.

HARRISBURG CIVIL WAR EXPOSITION & SEMINARS
717-780-2587
vlgentze@hacc01b.hacc.edu
Harrisburg Area Community College
1 HACC Dr
Harrisburg PA 17110-2903
Showcases reenactor demonstrations, living historians, historical societies' displays, merchants. Seminars feature many topics, guest speakers. Advance registration required. Annual March-April event. Call to be placed on mailing list.

HEART OF THE CONFEDERACY SPRING CIVIL WAR RELIC SHOW & SALE
707-477-8159
Steve E. Lister
PO Box 1014
Jonesboro GA 30237-1014
Civil War relics. More than 300 tables. Annual event, south of Atlanta - March.

HILTON HEAD DISPATCH
407-295-7510
7214 Laurel Hill Rd
Orlando FL 32818-5233
Publication indicating where to find reenactments, shows, & book fairs dealing in history. Covering the Southeast. $15/yr. for 6 issues.

HISTORICAL COLLECTIBLE AUCTIONS
336-570-2803 • 336-570-2748 Fax
PO Box 975 • Burlington NC 27215
Quarterly auctions of Civil War collectibles including photography, manuscripts, autographs, weapons, etc. Consignments encouraged. Catalog - $20/issue; next 3 for $45.

INTERNET CIVIL WAR EXPO
815-458-2029
http://www.bmark.com/cw.show
World's 1st Civil War Expo on the Internet, 24 hrs./day, 365 days/yr. Many major dealers. One month ads available for your extra relics, books, & other items.

KALAMAZOO ANTIQUE ARMS & PIONEER CRAFT SHOW
616-327-4557
Kalamazoo County Fair Grounds MI
Annual March show, featuring pre-1890 firearms, accoutrements, period fashions, living history.

KENTUCKIANA ARMS COLLECTORS ASSN., INC.
PO Box 1776
Louisville KY 40201-1776
Sponsors annual gun show in July; has resurrected John Hunt Morgan show. 200 tables, weapons, relics, accoutrements, displays, photos, memorabilia.

LEE/JACKSON CEREMONY
410-296-9235 Elliott Cummings
410-747-3271 Bob Lyons
Col. Harry W. Gilmor Camp #1388 SCV
Baltimore MD
Honors Lee & Jackson on their birthdays. Reenactors, UDC, period civilians, spectators invited. Held annually in January, at the Lee/Jackson monument, Art Museum & Wyman Park Drive, Baltimore.

LIVING HISTORY ASSOCIATES, INC.
804-788-1493
804-788-1489 Fax
PO Box 4914
Richmond VA 23227
Providing history-related services to clients; Richmond-area tours, 1860s speakers bureau, special events, living history workshops, film & TV project consultants.

LOONEY'S TAVERN AMPHITHEATER & PARK
205-489-5000
205-489-3500 Fax
PO Box 70
US Highway 278 E
Double Springs AL 35533-0070
Performances in amphitheater relate local Civil War stories, Thurs.-Sat. 8 PM. Park boasts Civil War show, riverboat cruises & other activities.

LOW COUNTRY CIVIL WAR SHOW
770-972-4904
Mike Kent
PO Box 336
Grayson GA 30017-0336
Annual memorabilia, relic & book show, held in Charleston, SC.

MARCH FOR GETTYSBURG
717-334-0772
717-334-3118 Fax
Friends of Natl. Parks at Gettysburg
10 Lincoln Sq
PO Box 4622
Gettysburg PA 17325-2205
Fundraiser for Land Acquisition Fund. March follows route of Law's 15th Ala. Infantry to Little Round Top. Prizes & seedlings. Reenactors welcome. Annual event - April.

MID SOUTH CIVIL WAR SHOW
901-362-2874
James R. Chalmers Camp 1312, SCV
PO Box 161254
Memphis TN 38186-1254
Annual Civil War show - February. Admission - $4 age 13 & over; $2 ages 12 & under.

MIDWEST CIVIL WAR COLLECTOR SHOW
773-539-8432
608-884-3237 Fax
hawkeye@jvlnet.com
Robert Nowak
3238 N Central Park Ave
Chicago IL 60618-5306
450+ tables of American militaria, antiques, books & art to 1898. Period uniforms & costumes welcome. Non-profit annual September event, Wheaton, IL. Admission - $5 over age 12; under 12 - free.

MISSISSIPPI VALLEY CIVIL WAR SYMPOSIUM
800-298-1861
CW Education Assn.
PO Box 78
Winchester VA 22604-0078
Special speakers. Annual event - September.

NATIONAL CIVIL WAR ARTILLERY & INFANTRY SCHOOL
315-483-9284
Frank Cutler
6343 Kelly Rd • Sodus NY 14551-9502
Training & classes in Youngstown, NY, under top instructors from around the country. Live & train inside historic fort. $6 fee. Annual in May.

NEW HOPE ANTIQUE ARMS FAIR
610-588-8853
New Hope PA
Semi-annual, invitational event featuring firearms, swords, photos, uniforms, & more. June & October. Admission - $5.

OHIO CIVIL WAR ASSOCIATION
419-586-5294
419-586-6763 Fax
106 Haig St • Celina OH 45822-2708
Hosts annual Civil War conference & other events.

OHIO CIVIL WAR COLLECTORS & ARTILLERY SHOWS
419-289-3120
Mansfield OH
Annual May encampment, field hospital scenarios, period music, sutlers, artillery displays, firing demonstrations.

OLD DOMINION GUN SHOWS
540-238-1343 • 540-238-1453 Fax
PO Box 289
Woodlawn VA 24381-0289

OLDE AMERICAN COLLECTIBLES, INC.
13 Nathalie Ct
Peekskill NY 10566-6240
Semi-annual auctions, mail/telephone. Collections purchased outright or accepted on consignment. Fully illus. catalog - $20 for 2-issue subscription.

OLE NORTH STATE MILITARY SHOWS
704-282-1339
carotrader@trellis.net
Carolina Trader Promotions
PO Box 769
Monroe NC 28111-0769
Semi-annual shows of arms & memorabilia of Civil War & other periods. Admission - $4.

POTOMAC ARMS COLLECTOR'S ASSN.
301-921-9673
PO Box 1812
Wheaton MD 20915-1812
Sponsors of annual October gun show, Frederick, MD. Guns, knives, & related items. Donation - $4.

RETURNING HEROES BALL
Patri & Barbara Pugliese
39 Capen St
Medford MA 02155-5824
Annual March ball featuring contra-dances, quadrilles, waltzes, polkas, & schottisches.

SHARPSBURG HERITAGE FESTIVAL: WHERE HISTORY COMES ALIVE
301-432-4065 Sid Gale
PO Box 456
Sharpsburg MD 21782-0456
Remembrance march, encampments, scripted vignettes. Period camping on sites Confederates held during battle. Barn dance at Piper Farm. Annual event - September.

VANISHING GLORY
601-634-1863
717 Clay St
Vicksburg MS 39180-2933
Historical, wide-screen, half-hour drama depicting Union's siege of Vicksburg, from writings of soldiers & civilians.

VICKSBURG CONVENTION & VISITORS BUREAU
800-221-3536
601-636-4642 Hayes Latham
http://www.vicksburg.org/cvb
PO Box 110
Vicksburg MS 39181-0110
Annual March "Run Through History" through Vicksburg NMP. 10K race, 5K walk, 1-mile run. Refreshments, music.

WAR BETWEEN THE STATES MEMORABILIA & ANTIQUE GUN SHOW
910-784-0301 Jerry Hart
Brig. Gen. Wm. R. Boggs Chapter, MOSB
Winston Salem NC
Memorabilia & guns. Annual event - March. Admission - $4, children under 12 - $1.

WEST VIRGINIA REENACTORS ASSOCIATION
304-472-5964
PO Box 2133
Buckhannon WV 26201-7133
Participates in reenactments & educational presentations; sponsors special events.

WILDERNESS ROAD REGIONAL MUSEUM
540-674-4835
540-639-0351
PO Box 373
Newbern VA 24126-0373
Collection of Civil War artifacts & ephemera. Hosts Civil War events.

97th REGIMENTAL STRING BAND
813-391-4565
PO Box 2208 • Largo FL 33779-2208
Cassettes & CDs of the 80 most popular Civil War songs. Many vols. Coffee cups, T-shirts, & spoken history cassettes. Catalog - SASE.

ADDISON WORLDWIDE INC.
PO Box 3691
Pembroke NC 28372-3691
"Don't blame me, I voted for Jefferson Davis." Bumper stickers - $3 ea., quantity discounts. T-shirts - $17.95 ea. (specify size).

AMERICAN AFGHAN COMPANY
410-744-5470
1074 Craftswood Rd
Baltimore MD 21228-1312
50" x 60" cotton weave Confederate battle flag afghan. $49.95 ea. Other products.

AMERICANA SOUVENIRS & GIFTS
http://www.americanagifts.com
302 York St
Gettysburg PA 17325-1930
Most complete line of Civil War souvenirs & memorabilia for both USA & CSA. Cannons, bullets, patches, toys, books, flags, videos, documents, insignias, & much more.

ANCIENT AMERICAN ART
601-566-2778
601-566-4925
http://www.pointsouth.com/aaa.htm
aaart@dixie-net.com
PO Box 1745
Verona MS 38879-1745
Handmade reproductions of battle & regimental flags of the Civil War. T-shirts $20. Prints $25. Wholesale discounts.

ANTIETAM GALLERY
301-432-5868
17320 Shepherdstown Pike
Sharpsburg MD 21781-1626
Distinctively framed & displayed prints by Kunstler, Strain, Troiani & others. Battlefield gift items.

APPALACHIAN ART STAMPS
678-377-1324
678-377-1320 Fax
aplchnarts@stampcity.com
584 Cedars Ct
Dacula GA 30019
Selection of Civil War-related stamps, incl. seals, personalities, cannon, flags, etc. Catalog - send 52¢ business-size SASE.

B.FORM CREATIVE MEDIA
908-846-5725
bform4@tribeca.ios.com
116 Park Pl
Highland Park NJ 08904-2202
Heavyweight, short-sleeve, hand screen-printed gray T-shirts. Image of Longstreet or Forrest in black. $11 + $3.50 S&H.

BARTLETT'S COLLECTIBLES
PO Box 545
Mechanicsburg PA 17055-0545
Civil War trading cards; superb photography, educational, collectible. Sample card & catalog - free.

BATTLEZONE, LTD.
PO Box 266
Towaco NJ 07082-0266
Military patches, pins, decals, planes, books. 5,000+ items. Color catalog - $4.50 ppd. ($2 ref. w/ 1st order)

BELLE & BLADE
201-328-8488 • 201-442-0669 Fax
124 Penn Ave
Dover NJ 07801-5335
Send for catalog of war books, videos, toys, swords, knives, & gifts. Catalog - $3; free w/ order.

BLITZKRIEG PRESS
21 Meridian Cir
Newtown PA 18940-1742
Stationery, notepads, etc. For sutlers, Civil War enthusiasts; personal or business use. Any design you request or have. Send $1 for more info.

THE BLUE & GRAY SHOP
800-454-7104
531 Baltimore St
Gettysburg PA 17325-2606
Reasonably priced T-shirts of *The Killer Angels*, Gettysburg, etc. Videos, cassettes, CDs, calendars, etc.

BLUE MOON IMAGES
18 Washington St Ste 210
Canton MA 02021-4004
Set of 8 Civil War watercolor notecards - 4 scenes. $8.95 ea. set + $2.50 S&H.

BOOKMARK
414-646-4499 • 414-646-4427 Fax
PO Box 335 • Delafield WI 53018-0335
Mort Kuntsler's Civil War & *Legends in Gray* calendars & notecards. Catalog - $2.

THE BRADFORD EXCHANGE
9345 N Milwaukee Ave
Niles IL 60714-1393
The Heart of Plate Collecting. Limited edition collector's plates featuring historic events.

BRANDYWINE TEE
1099 Parkerville Rd
West Chester PA 19382-7036
Robert E. Lee, "Stonewall" Jackson, Colt pistols & powder flask T-shirts & mugs. Mugs - $3.50 ea. + $1 S&H.

BUFFALO ROBE TRADING POST
520-457-2322
George Henry
9 N 5th St
PO Box 741
Tombstone AZ 85638-0741
Civil War, local history, American Indian, western lawmen & outlaws. Gift shop, artifacts, video & audio tapes. Historian in attendance.

THE CALENDAR PEOPLE
800-758-2751
2083 Springwood Rd
PO Box 125
York PA 17403-0125
Civil War reenactment calendar featuring pictures of 12 reenactment groups (CSA/USA). $12 + S&H.

CARDS WITH MY PARDS (TM)
877-443-1863 (toll free)
cardswithmypards@yahoo.com
Tony & Pat Fantilli
PO Box 6186
Clearwater FL 33758-6186
Buys & sells CW playing card decks; repro CW card decks. Historically accurate, colorful & informative "Civil War Playing Cards" newsletter. (See ad page 263)

CAVALIER SHOPPE
800-227-5491
Rex Jarrett, Owner
PO Box 511
Bruce MS 38915-0511
Confederate flag apparel - 100% cotton. Shirts, slacks, shorts, skirts, boxers, belts, ties, watches, flags. Free catalog.

CHRIS & JACKIE'S
410-741-1909
PO Box 717
Dunkirk MD 20754-0717
Civil War designs on decorative light switch plates - $9.95-$14.95.

CIVIL WAR SOLDIERS MUSEUM
850-469-1900
850-469-9328 Fax
http://www.cwmuseum.org
info@cwmuseum.org
108 S Palafox Pl
Pensacola FL 32501
Explore the life of the Civil War soldier through exhibits of personal, religious, medical, musical, military, political & social aspects of the War. Tours available.

COLUMBIA GAMES, INC.
800-636-3631
http://www.columbiagames.com/
questions@columbiagames.com
PO Box 3457
Blaine WA 98231-3457
"Dixie" - a tactical CW card game consisting of collectible cards - $7.95/deck of 60 random cards. 1 for each regiment, battery & brigade officer at Bull Run, Shiloh, Gettysburg. Free catalog.

CONFEDERATE CALENDAR WORKS
PO Box 2084
Austin TX 78768-2084
Illustrated with previously unpublished & researched photos of Confederate soldiers, 1861-65 events, etc. $11.95.

CONFEDERATE ENTERPRISES
800-996-8883
Flags, jackets, bumper stickers. Keep it flying!

CONFEDERATE GRAY
615-320-1715
615-320-3272 Fax
http://www.dixienet.org/conf_gray/default.htm
congray@home.com
Meeks Booker
PO Box 121984
Nashville TN 37212-1984
Hand-carved music boxes that play "Dixie" when opened; other tunes available. Named for great Southern leaders or battles. Refer to Source Book for 10% discount. Catalog - $2 (ref.).

CONFEDERATE MEMORIES
PO Box 261 • Midlothian VA 23113-0261
Set of 12 Southern Christmas cards - 4 scenes, $11.95 + S&H. Illus. flier - SASE.

CONFEDERATE PRODUCTS
301-863-7870
PO Box 974 • California MD 20619-0974
10oz. coffee mug with imprint of Confederate seal & flag - $6 ea. + $3 S&H.

THE CONFEDERATE SHOPPE
205-942-8978
928 Delcris Dr • Birmingham AL 35226-1953
Books, audio & video tapes, flags, bumper stickers, auto tags; modern clothing & linens. What we don't have, we try to find.

CONFEDERATE SUPPLY CO.
PO Box 2012 • Murfreesboro TN 37133-2012
Confederate flag souvenirs - bandanas, license plates. Conf. battleflag - $15 + $2.50 S&H. Catalog - $1.

THE CORPORAL'S COLOURS
106 Haig St • Celina OH 45822-2708
Confederate Commemorative Series Battleflag T-shirts. Designs based on solid research. Portion of proceeds earmarked for flag preservation. $15. Free list.

COTTON & CO.
800-994-5366
4 Penny Ct • Hendersonville NC 28739-6871
Tapestries picturing Lee, with Lt. Col. Marshal, leaving McLean House at Appomattox CH. Choose wall hanging ($39.95) or afghan throw ($45). Machine washable 100% cotton.

COWLES HISTORY GROUP CALENDARS
800-358-6327
PO Box 921
North Adams MA 01247-0921
1998 Civil War & Military History calendars. Perfect gifts for history buffs - $14.95.

CROSSROADS COUNTRY STORE
540-433-2084
Shenandoah Heritage Farmer's Market
Route 11 S • VA
Shenandoah Valley's premier Civil War store; books, flags, music, souvenirs, crafts, gifts, jewelry. Part of the Shenandoah Heritage Farmer's Market. Open Mon-Sat 10am-6pm.

W.S. DAVIS DESIGNER
205-851-0839
http://www.e-pages.com/flagtag
PO Box 143 • Clay AL 35048-0143
License tags - proudly display the Great Seal & the Flags of the Confederacy. $8 (ppd.). Dealer discounts.

DEERFIELD VALLEY WOOD CARVING
6 King Philip Ave
South Deerfield MA 01373-1127
Historic wood carvings. Patriotic Civil War themes, North & South; eagles, flags, etc. Quality custom work. Free catalog.

DIXIE DEPOT
706-265-7533
706-265-3952 Fax
http://www.ilinks.net/~dixiegeneral
Dixie_Depot@stc.net
John Black
PO Box 1448
72 Keith Evans Rd
Dawsonville GA 30534-0027
Pro-Southern educational products: video/audio tapes, new/old books, bumper stickers, flags, wearables, lapel pins, exclusive Great Seal items. More than 600 items! Catalog. (See ad page 260)

THE EARLY AMERICAN HISTORY SHOPPE
603-772-7973
225 Water St
Exeter NH 03833-2417
Books (antiquarian & in-print), ephemera, prints, antique memorabilia & collectibles, T-shirts, CD-Rom, flags, games, tapes, maps, mugs, miniatures, genealogies & more. Specialize in the Civil War. Free catalogs.

EXCELSIOR PRESS
516-475-7069
516-874-2489 Fax
Don Roberts
PO Box 926
Bellport NY 11713-0926
Civil War Cabinet Cards. Color art prints of 24 famous regiments include period battle maps & regimental histories. Boxed set - $23.95 + $3.50 S&H (30-day money-back guarantee). Catalog/brochure - $1 (ref. w/ purchase).

FREDERICKSBURG MONOGRAMMING & EMBROIDERY
540-373-3937
540-373-4006 Fax
525 Caroline St
Fredericksburg VA 22401-6013
Custom embroidery of favorite Civil War designs. Casual clothing, fast delivery; quantity orders/dealers welcomed. All work on-site, from artwork to finished garment.

GETTYSBURG CIVIL WAR & ANTIQUE CENTER
717-337-1085
705 Old Harrisburg Rd
N Gettysburg Plaza
Gettysburg PA 17325-3401
Multi-dealer complex in heart of antique country. Civil War memorabilia, military art, antiques & fine collectibles. Open 7 days/wk. Free parking.

GOLDBENDERS
540-373-4573
110 Hanover St
Fredericksburg VA 22401-5929
Handmade Civil War rings, silver or gold. Available with either Confederate or Union flag.

GOSPEL TRUTH/CIVIL WAR ROOM
412-238-7991
228 W Main St
Ligonier PA 15658-1130
Full-service Christian bookstore & Civil War room. Kunstler calendars, patterns, pewter figurines, books, videos, music, hats, accessories, shirts, Woolrich wool & much more.

GRANNIE'S ATTIC SHURT HAUS
800-827-5127
717-337-8704
922 Johns Ave
Gettysburg PA 17325-2901
Souvenirs, printed & embroidered T-shirts, including Gnatek color portrait shirts. Flags & accessories. 2nd shop located at 13 Steinwehr Ave., Gettysburg.

THE GREAT T-SHIRT CO.
717-334-8611
65 Steinwehr Ave
Gettysburg PA 17325-2811
Souvenir T-shirts, sweatshirts & hats; exclusive Civil War designs.

GREENBRIAR PRESS
PO Box 703
Marietta GA 30061-0703
Notepads & notecards with envelopes. 2 color notepads with Union or Confederate flag with "From the desk of..." - 8-1/2"x 5-1/2". Write for details & prices.

RICHARDS GREGORY
PO Box 2342
Lancaster SC 29721-2342
S.C.A.R.Y. (Southern Citizens Advocating Relocation of Yankees). 100% cotton T-shirts (L & XL) - $12. + $3.50 S&H. South Carolina flag on front.

HALLOWED GROUND
717-337-0010
PO Box 3983
Gettysburg PA 17325-0983
T-shirts - Army of Northern Virginia, Army of Potomac, Forrest, Lee's Lts, Iron Brigade, Cleburne, Stonewall Brigade, etc. 100% cotton. $14.50 ppd.

THE HAMILTON COLLECTION
4810 Executive Park Ct
PO Box 44051
Jacksonville FL 32231-4051
Collectible plates, featuring Civil War Generals.

HEARTFELT DESIGNS
301-729-2974
PO Box 206
Pinto MD 21556-0206
Blue & gray samplers of major Civil War battles. Kits - $24.50; patterns - $4.50. Brochure - $2.

CARL A. HEDIN
3562 Antarctic Cir
Naples FL 34112-5041
3 Civil War bookmarks (U.S. commemorative stamps). Battles, generals. Laminated. 2-3/4"x8-1/2". $3.50 ea. or 3 for $9.95 ppd.

HERITAGE BOOKS
Dale Curry
313 Woodlawn Ave
Zanesville OH 43701-4939
Civil War books & gifts. Free catalog.

HERITAGE EMBROIDERY
402-488-7913
402-488-8167 Fax
http://WWW.CivilWarMall.com/Image.htm
Heritage@navix.net
Tom & Dorothy Rivett
PO Box 22424
Lincoln NE 68542-2424
Exclusive Mort Kunstler art images embroidered on quality American-made garments. Personalization available for reenactors, round tables, museums & galleries. Visit our online catalog.

HISTORIC IMPRESSIONS
8394 Creek St
Jonesboro GA 30236-3923
T-shirts & caps. Quality shirts, 8 selections - $15 ea. ppd. Caps, 3 selections - $19 ea.

HISTORIC SPORTSWEAR
615-754-4334
611 Oakwood Ter
Mount Juliet TN 37122-2107
Beautiful silk necktie! Show your pride with Southern Banners, crafted with Southern pride of the finest silk. Free brochure & dealer list.

HISTORICAL IMPRESSIONS
888-603-0100 • 970-256-0157 Fax
lskaf@iti2.net
PO Box 60323
Grand Junction CO 81506-8758
PC & Mac standard & multimedia Civil War screensavers for Union, South or mixed versions. Limited ed. art, posters, bookmarks, magnets, postcards. Dealer inquiries welcome. Catalog. (See ad page 264)

HUMMEL PRINTING
610-286-0399
PO Box 171 • Geigertown PA 19523-0171
12 Civil War-theme Christmas cards (4 dif. styles) with envelopes - $8 + $1.50 S&H. Special occasion & ladies' notecards, Civil War-theme writing paper & envelopes. Catalog - $1.

INDY SCREEN PRINT
800-344-9899
1700 Georgetown Rd
Speedway IN 46224-5723
"Heroes in Blue & Gray" - American Anthem Collector's Series #1, 100% cotton T-shirt. S-XL - $14.95 ea. + $5 S&H. XXL/XXXL - add $2.

IRISH BRIGADE GIFT SHOP
504 Baltimore St • Gettysburg PA 17325-2605
T-shirts, sweatshirts, jackets, books, flags, recruiting posters, photos, pins, stationery, prints, figurines & more - all relating to the Irish Civil War service. Detailed item list - send business-size SASE.

J.J.B. LTD.
PO Box 507
Shamokin PA 17872-0507
Civil War print/calendar of the year 1861. Day-to-day events. 20"x17-1/2" - $29.95.

W. E. JACKSON & COMPANY
401-232-3570 Fax
PO Box 3842
North Providence RI 02911-0042
Civil War engravings, awards. Series of 3D embossed notecards from handcut dies. Lee, Jackson, Meade, artillery action, etc. 10 cards & envelopes per box.

JKG HANDCRAFTS
PO Box 667
Glade Spring VA 24340-0667
Handmade Confederate battle flag quilts - $150-$350. Others flag quilts available - send SASE for descriptions.

JM COMICS
PO Box 56982
Jacksonville FL 32241-6982
First & only historically accurate Civil War comic series. "Southern Blood" takes you from Fort Sumter to Appomattox. 1 yr/12 issues - $22.50.

KATE GALLERY
652 Great Plain Ave
Needham MA 02192-3305
18th-20th century architecture, furniture & decorative art prints. Framed & unframed. Fine notecards. Illus. catalog - $2.

LANG GRAPHICS
414-646-2211
PO Box 99
Delafield WI 53018-0099
Mort Kunstler's new Civil War calendar & notecards. Beautifully done, fully illustrated. $12.95 + $5 S&H. Catalog - $2.

LEGACY TIE WORKS
888-851-1122 Orders
635 Bonnie Pl
Franklin TN 37064-2954
"The Five Flags of the Confederacy Collection" ties - 100% Italian silk, jacquard weave. $34.50 ea. ppd.

MABELS CARD SHOP
203-698-0029
http://www.mabels.com
mabels@futuris.net
PO Box 331
Old Greenwich CT 06870-0331
Play Cards with History. Outstanding selection of Civil War & American History playing cards. Catalog.

MAGNOLIA T-SHIRT LTD.
PO Box 121
Malvern PA 19355-0121
Gettysburg T-shirt; 1st in Civil War Battles series, using victor's colors, names of commanding generals, dates & more. M/L - $17.95 ppd.; XL/XXL - $19.95 ppd.

TY MAWR CLASSICS, INC.
800-998-7051
PO Box 4221
Martinsville VA 24115-4221
Civil War coverlet by artists at Ty Mawr Classics. 100% cotton throw, triple weave, multi-color. 50"x70" - made in USA. $53.95.

DON MEREDITH'S CIVIL WAR ART
813-962-1225
PO Box 370020 • Tampa FL 33697-0020
Ordinary photos turn into extraordinary CW-era portraits, with strict attention to detail. Prices vary from $75. Discounts for photos showing proper uniform, gear, pose, etc. Color brochure - free.

MHR & SONS
7387 Bethany Ridge Rd
Guysville OH 45735
Personalized bookplates. CW theme: 50 for $14, 100 for $24. Add 10% S&H.

NEWFIELD PUBLICATIONS
PO Box 16613 • Columbus OH 43272-0001
Set of Civil War cards. Many scenes, incl. *Battle of Gettysburg: Pickett's Charge*, by Mort Kunstler.

OHIO SILVER
301-834-5389
PO Box 124 • Brunswick MD 21716-0124
Silver bullet key chains & necklaces. Minie bullet replicas (.575 cal.) on key ring or sterling silver chain.

OLD GUARD, INC.
215-572-7913
7511 Sycamore Ave
Elkins Park PA 19027-1053
Gettysburg generals on 100% cotton T-shirts. Pickett, Hood, Longstreet, Armistead, McLaws, etc. $12. Catalog - $3.

OLDE SOUTH, LTD.
T. R. Meetze
PO Box 11302 • Columbia SC 29211-1302
Classic check design - Confederate flag background. Send void check & deposit slip with $13.95 (incl. S&H) for 200. Script lettering & personal message available.

PEPPERELL STAMP WORKS
800-752-4656
Bradford PA 16701-0527
Collectible rubber stamps. Offering learning with stamping. Current sets include Victorian Flowers, Civil War, Sailing Ships, Endangered Species, Railroads. $4.95/stamp + $3.50 S&H.

PIXELCHROME PROFESSIONAL
4304 Standridge Dr
The Colony TX 75056-4033
Gettysburg commemorative posters - 11"x17" - full color. Art prints of the Penn. & Va. monuments. Both posters - $15 + $3.95 S&H.

PORKCHOP & HAMBURGER HILL
PO Box 191
Honeoye Falls NY 14472-0191
Civil War license frames - $9.95-$29.95 + $4.95 S&H for 1st frame, $1 ea. add'l. Frame includes: regiment, 1 year, USA or CSA flag, & blue/gray force decal. 120-pg. military catalog - $2.95.

PYRAMID AMERICA
901-452-1323 • 800-737-1323
Quality USA, Texas or Confederate flags & flag apparel. Jackets, shorts, T-shirts, bandanas, backpacks, knives, framed/unframed prints, more. Call for more info.

RAINBOW CARD CO.
800-473-5213 • 516-367-6790
516-367-3063 Fax
717 E Jericho Tpke Ste 315
Huntington Station NY 11746-7502
Official Currier & Ives "Civil War" card set. Limited edition (5,000 sets), individually serial numbered, 16 full-color cards - $14.95/set. Catalog - $1.

RBM ENTERPRISES
502-893-5057
PO Box 6374, Dept A
Louisville KY 40206-0374
Updated version of our classic necktie. Confederate battle flags with red stripes on navy or gray background - $18.50.

THE REBEL CO.
770-947-1863
PO Box 15191 • Atlanta GA 30333-0191
Ships more than 30 traditionally Southern Rebel products. Delicious syrups, preserves, dressings, honey, sauces, relish, jams, chutney, peanuts, pecans & more. Free catalog.

REGIMENTAL FLAG & BANNER
919-496-2888 • 919-496-7720 Fax
rebelflags@aol.com
1909 Seven Paths Rd
Louisburg NC 27549-7015
Flags - historical to modern. Civil War theme shirts, caps. Free catalog.

RIENZI PRESS
802-888-3439
Brad & Sue Limage
RR 2 Box 630 • Morrisville VT 05661-9802
"Vermont Soldiers in the Civil War" - calendar printed annually with large prints of Vermont brigades, CDUs, letter excerpts & battles on corresponding dates. $10 + S&H.

RIVERDALE DECORATIVE PRODUCTS
PO Box 4959
1920 S Court St
Montgomery AL 36103-4959
Civil War battle scene pillows by Mort Kunstler. From $15.

RUFFIN FLAG COMPANY
706-456-2111 • 706-456-2112 Fax
http://www.mindspring.com/~micromgt/ruffin.htm
241 Alexander St NW
Crawfordville GA 30631-2804
Auto tags, bumper stickers, books, T-shirts, crew sweatshirts, polo shirts, regulation battle flags, etc. Jeff Davis, Dixie's Pride, N.B. Forrest, etc. Retail/wholesale. Catalog - $1.

SARAH ADAMS PRODUCTIONS
717-432-2752
717-432-8820 Fax
Civil War wrapping paper - photographic scenes of Manassas, Shiloh, Gettysburg, Antietam & others. 2 sizes. Coordinating ribbon also available.

SCENIC EFFECTS, INC.
510-235-1955
510-235-9901 Fax
Wendy Schuldt
PO Box 70332
Port Richmond CA 94807-0332
Ltd. ed. of historically accurate buildings, ea. handmade. Some include figures & are hand-painted; unpainted available. Catalog/listing - send SASE.

SCHOOLHOUSE ANTIQUES
717-334-4564
Gettysburg PA 17325
Antique guns, relics, swords, uniforms, souvenirs. Close to battlefield - 5 mi. on Business Rt. 15 South.

PATRICK A. SCHROEDER PUBLICATIONS
804-376-1865
PO Box 455
Brookneal VA 24528-9304
Civil War books. New titles include *Civil War Soldier Life*; *We Came to Fight* (5th NY Vol. Inf.); & Belle Boyd. Archives research, prints, notecards, postcards available. Free catalog.

SCREEN PRINT IMAGE
9302 S Mooreland Rd
Richmond VA 23229-8126
Lee, Jackson, Stuart, Mosby, Forrest, Flags of the Confederacy, other multicolor designs on first quality T-shirts, sweatshirts. From $12.

SCRIBNER'S
800-303-8337
907 4th St SE
Roanoke VA 24013-2351
Confederate T-shirt with flag & inscription, "It's a Southern Thing, You Wouldn't Understand." Prices vary by size, $11.95-15.95 + $3 S&H.

SENECA RIDGE GALLERY
412-828-0240
426 Allegheny River Blvd
Oakmont PA 15139-1725
Civil War & 18th-century art, books, videos, games, music, more!

SILVERWOOD INDUSTRIES, INC.
813-662-1075
11756 Browning Rd # 300
Lithia FL 33547-1915
Personalized unit wall plaques with your photo, name & unit. 6"x5", walnut grain, gold lettering & stars. $19.95 (ppd.). 10% discount on 6 or more.

SOUTHERN HERITAGE PRINTS
256-539-3358
George Mahoney, Jr.
PO Box 503
Huntsville AL 35804-0503
Civil War flags, memo pads, envelopes, bookmarks, paperweights, chronology chart/map, prints. *Last Charge at Brandy Station*, ltd. ed. print by C.E. Monroe, Jr. - $135 inc. S&H. Portion of proceeds goes to APCWS.

STARMASTER
http://www.iboutique.com/starmaster/index.htm
2500 Laurelhill Ln
Fort Worth TX 76133-8112
Playing cards featuring Civil War generals, battles, armaments & trivia. 3 decks - $18. Free catalog.

STARS & BARS GIFT SHOP AT BEAUVOIR
601-388-9074
601-388-1313
2244 Beach Blvd
Biloxi MS 39531-5002

STRATFORD'S NOVELTY, LTD
843-797-8040
Kent Stratford
PO Box 1860
Goose Creek SC 29445-1860
Civil War-related novelties & gifts. Confederate flag imprinted products & merchandise. Large selection. Bumper stickers. Free list & pricing.

STRICKLAND ENTERPRISES, INC.
800-454-7104 • 717-334-2472
531 Baltimore St
Gettysburg PA 17325-2606
Shirts, hats, clothing. Outfitters of popular Civil War culture. Novelty slogans. Custom embroidering. Free catalog.

STRICTLY SOUTHERN
912-454-1860
912-453-8483 Fax
http://www.accucomm.net/~theSouth
Ken Simpson
PO Box 1945
Milledgeville GA 31061
Confederate shop featuring books, T-shirts, souvenirs, Kunstler prints, jewelry. Mail orders available.

TARA HALL, INC.
800-205-0069
212-802-6423 Fax
http://www.fighting69th.com
tarahall@earthlink.net
Vic Olney
PO Box 2069
Beach Haven NJ 08008-0109
Meagher's Irish Brigade, Fighting 69th, Corcoran's Irish Legion memorabilia, shirts, jackets, hats, sweaters, steins, pins, flags, books, miniatures, poster, belt buckles, NINAs, etc. Free catalog. (See ad page 272)

THE TEE SHIRT GUY
609-547-9486 Ph & Fax
1225 Keswick Ave
Haddon Heights NJ 08035-1213
Custom-printed T-shirts, sweatshirts, hats, jackets, bumper stickers. Designs include armies of the Potomac & Northern Virginia, 69th Irish Brigade, Jackson, Lee, Longstreet, Chamberlain. M/L/XL - $13 ppd. XXL - $15.

TL SPECIALTIES
RR 4 Box 336B
Wynantskill NY 12198
Civil War clocks & plaques. Reproduced prints from *Leslies* and *Harpers* magazines of 1860s. Walnut/burnt wood stain. Free brochure - SASE.

THE TURNING POINT
800-454-7104
240 Steinwehr Ave
Gettysburg PA 17325-2814
Reasonably priced T-shirts of *The Killer Angels*, Gettysburg, etc. Full color & one color. Videos, cassettes, CDs, calendars, etc.

U.S. SURPLUS SALES
888-794-6296
http://www.dixienet.org/ads/commercial/us_surplus_sales/usss.html
1184 W Highway 436 • Forest City FL 32714
Confederate T-shirts, sure to inspire friends of the South everywhere. Free flier.

THE VILLAGE SHOPPE
800-454-7104
Old Gettysburg Village • Gettysburg PA 17325
T-shirts reasonably priced of *The Killer Angels*, Gettysburg, etc. Full color & one color. Videos, cassettes, CDs, calendars, etc.

VILLAGE SURPLUS
PO Box 530931 • Mountain Brook AL 35253
Confederate flag magnets - $5 ppd.

VIRGINIA STEREOSCOPIC EMPORIUM, INC.
PO Box 1718 • Stafford VA 22555-1718
Civil War Stereoscopic cards. Beautiful 3D image when viewed through stereo viewer. Set of 6 cards - $19.95 + S&H. Catalog - $2.

N. WASSERMAN & CO.
800-USPS-492
490 City Park Ave • Columbus OH 43215
1995 CW postage stamps come to life on 5 beautifully decorated 11 oz. porcelain coffee mugs - "The Women," "The Battles," "The Union," "The Confederate," & "War Heroes." $9.95 ea. + $1.50 S&H.

PAUL WILSON
Civil War Labels Unlimited
46 Sawmill Rd • Springfield MA 01118-1719
Personalized name/address labels, bookplates, bookmarks, notecards & scratch pad stationery - featuring your favorite CW personalities (more than 220 available). Illus. price list - $1 (checks payable to Paul Wilson).

X FACTOR PUBLISHING
511 Alondra Dr
Huntington Beach CA 92648-3711
Series 1-100 high gloss, color, 3.75" sq. collectors cards of "Great Battles of History" - $24.95.

ZANGRONIZ PHOTOGRAPHY
301-924-2539
4011 Muncaster Mill Rd Ste 101
Rockville MD 20853-1426
U.S. Civil War reenactment postcards. First of series. Images of actual events. 4 cards in each set. 4 sets @ $1.50/set + $2 S&H.

BLACKJACK TRADING COMPANY
Chuck Hanselmann
PO Box 707 • Blythewood SC 29016-0707
Buyer of family Confederate paper, stamps, letters, autographs, currency, slave documents, slave tags, & estates.

BOGG & LAURENCE PUBLISHING CO., INC.
800-345-5595 • 305-866-3600
305-866-8040 Fax
1007 Kane Concourse
Bay Harbor Islands FL 33154-2105
The new *Dietz Confederate States Catalog and Handbook*, 2nd printing. Most comprehensive treatment of Confederate stamps & postal history; reorganized & expanded for easier use. Hardcover, 300 pp. - $75.

CIVIL WAR STORE
504-522-3328
212 Chartres St • New Orleans LA 70130
Mail order catalog - weapons, currency, bonds, stamps, letters, diaries, CDVs, prints, slave broadsides & bills of sale, autographs, photos. Catalog - $4.

CONFEDERATE POSTMASTER
PO Box 1864 • Middletown CT 06457-8364
Repro stamps, 60 different envelopes. Regimental envelopes on special order. 2 stamps, stationery available to match: U.S. Corps w/ division stationery; framed C.S. stamps. Finest quality now available. Catalog - $2 (credit on order); send SASE.

FLEETWOOD
800-443-3232 • 800-628-3123 Fax
http://www.unicover.com/fleetwoo.htm
James A. Willms
1 Unicover Ctr
Cheyenne WY 82007-2109
First-day Civil War covers (20). U.S. Postal Service's "Classic Collection" series. Stamps, cancellation marks, & custom envelopes. $51.45 - 1st edition.

BRIAN & MARIA GREEN, INC.
336-993-5100
336-993-1801 Fax
http://www.collectorsnet.com/bmg/index.shtml
bmgcivilwar@webtv.net
PO Box 1816J
Kernersville NC 27285-1816
Civil War autographs, letters, documents, diaries, CSA stamps, covers, currency, etc. Catalog - $5/yr for 4 issues.

CARL A. HEDIN
3562 Antarctic Cir
Naples FL 34112-5041
3 Civil War bookmarks (U.S. commemorative stamps). Battles, generals. Laminated. 2-3/4"x8-1/2". $3.50 ea. or 3 for $9.95 ppd.

HARDIE MALONEY
504-522-3328
212 Chartres St
New Orleans LA 70130-2215
Civil War store. Confederate currency, bonds, stamps, covers, CDV.s, letters, diaries, documents, autographs, pistols & swords.

MYSTIC STAMP CO.
Camden NY 13316
Giant grabbag of more than 200 U.S. stamps includes obsolete issues - $2. Adults only, limit 1 per address. Price lists.

HOWARD L. NORTON
PO Box 22821
Little Rock AR 72221-2821
Buy/sell/appraise. Autographs, Civil War items, Americana, historical documents, photographs, coins, currency, stamps, postal history. All transactions confidential. Catalog.

OSBORNE-KAUFMANN
800-WE DO BUY (933-6289)
Trish@webuystamps.com
522 Old State Rd • Lincoln DE 19960-9767
Buy/sell collectible Confederate stamps & envelopes.

PINE BARREN STAMPS
609-978-0373
PO Box 779 • Barnegat NJ 08005-0779
Est. 1954. Genuine mint Confederate stamps, Civil War Centenary stamps, Union stamps. Deluxe price list - $5.

POSTAL COMMEMORATIVE SOCIETY
47 Richards Ln
Norwalk CT 06851-3422
Civil War Stamp Collection & art print of *Sheridan's Men* by Mort Kunstler. Limited edition.

STAMP OF APPROVAL
800-808-0567
10 Kendall Green Dr
PO Box 2157 • Milford CT 06460-3068
Original Battle of Gettysburg decorated envelope, postmarked the first day the Gettysburg stamp was issued - 7/1/1963. Call for details.

TARGET AUCTIONS
816-965-0013 Orders
http://www.usbusiness.com/target/us.htm
PO Box 17841
Kansas City MO 64134-0141
"Tattered Flags" - the most fun you'll ever have fighting the Civil War! Original game for the PC, $14.95 + $3 S&H. Other Civil War games, stamps.

TWO COLONELS ENTERPRISES
330-745-2888 Ph & Fax
http://www.webchamps.com/twocolonels
twocolonels@webchamps.com
Daniel P Sens
1287E Sevilla Ave
Akron OH 44314-1457
Patriotic reproduction stamps & stationery. Many designs. Union & Confederate. Genuine stamps, covers, & paper. Prices on request. Wholesale & retail catalogs - free.

N. WASSERMAN & CO.
800-USPS-492
490 City Park Ave
Columbus OH 43215-5780
1995 CW postage stamps come to life on 5 beautifully decorated 11 oz. porcelain coffee mugs - "The Women," "The Battles," "The Union," "The Confederate," & "War Heroes." $9.95 ea. + $1.50 S&H.

AMAZON DRY GOODS
319-322-6800 • 319-322-4138
319-322-4003 Fax
J. Burgess, Pres.
407 Brady St • Davenport IA 52801-1510
Victorian apparel & accessories. Corsets, bonnets, hoop skirts, fans & snoods, hats, paper dolls, flags, books, patterns, shoes & boots. Sutlers' wholesale catalog. Retail catalogs (pattern, shoe, & general) - all 3 for $15.

ARROWHEAD FORGE
605-938-4814
RR 1 Box 25 • Wilmot SD 57279-9718
Tools, fire irons, candleholders, grills, eating utensils, tomahawks, & much more.

AVALON FORGE
410-242-8431
John White, Owner
409 Gun Rd • Baltimore MD 21227-3824
Replica goods for 18th-century "living history." Items for military, farm & home. Catalog - $2.

THE BAG MAN
615-859-9658
Patrick Strickland
588 Dividing Ridge Rd
Goodlettsville TN 37072
Best possible reproductions. Knapsacks - $50 & up; S&K copper or tin canteens - $39 & $55.

BENCKENDORF PIPES
515-255-0838
PO Box 30062
Des Moines IA 50310-9402
Finest reproduction & collectible pipes & smoking accoutrements. Free catalog.

BERMAN LEATHER
617-426-0870 • 617-357-8564 Fax
Robert S. Berman
25 Melcher St • Boston MA 02210-1516
Leather hides like Civil War era for belts, straps, clothing, bags, even footwear. Full catalog of hardware, tools, buckles & kits - $3 (ref.).

THE BLOCKADE RUNNER
931-389-6294
http://www.blockaderunner.com
103 Blackman Blvd
Wartrace TN 37183
18th-19th c. goods. Custom work & fitting, all types uniforms, civilian & ladies' wear; standard & custom tents. All work done in-house. Catalog - $2.

BONNET BRIGADE
Pat Wullenjohn
PO Box 28
Fremont CA 94537-0028
Civil War-period clothing, equipment, weapons, accoutrements, & camping equipment. Catalog - $3.

BOOKS & COMPANY
PO Box 1046
Dunkirk NY 14048-6046
Historical recipes & cooking info. from Civil War era. Recipes from notable figures & soldiers. History of some classic recipes. $7 ppd.

BORDER STATES LEATHERWORKS
501-361-2642
501-361-2851 Fax
1158 Apple Blossom Ln
Springdale AR 72762-9762
Civil War collectibles, original weapons & equipment. Reproduction cavalry saddles & equipment. Custom hand-forged bits.

WILLIAM H. BOYDEN
198 W Plumstead Ave
Lansdowne PA 19050-1307
Hand-rolled & tied cartridge tubes made from Frankford Arsenal pattern; paper matches close to original color. 20 tubes - $5 + $2 S&H.

KEN BROWN
614-498-8379
17261 Sligo Rd
Kimbolton OH 43749-9604
Quality, handmade, reproduction cavalry tack, equipment & accoutrements. Free brochure.

C & C SUTLERY
208-388-0973
208-384-9523 Fax
CLOX@RMCI.NET
3353 Fuller Rd
Emmett ID 83617-9514
Full-service Civil War supplier. Uniforms, etc.

C & D JARNAGIN
601-287-4977 • 601-287-6033 Fax
http://www.jarnaginco.com
Robin Jarnagin
PO Box 1860 • 103 Franklin St
Corinth MS 38834-1860
Military & historical outfitters. Research, develop, & manufacture high quality uniforms, leather gear, footwear, & tinware for American troops, 1750-1865. 18th-century & CW catalogs - $3 each. (See ad page 257)

C & H SUTLERY
10619 W Atlantic Blvd # 145
Coral Springs FL 33071-5610
Authentic, all natural, no perfume, hypo-allergenic, homemade lye soap. Great for reenactors, naturalists. 3 bars - $5.98.

THE CARRIAGE HOUSE
918-367-6425
PO Box 8 • Slick OK 74071-0008
Wooden wheels for cannon, old auto, carriage & decor.

CARRICO'S LEATHERWORKS
316-922-7222 • 316-922-3311 Fax
David Carrico
811 5000 Rd • Edna KS 67342
Authentic reproduction Civil War cavalry equipment & accoutrements. Saddles, bridles, holsters, belts, etc. Free price list.

CARTRIDGES UNLIMITED
314-664-4332
Mike Watson
4320 Hartford St # A
Saint Louis MO 63116-1917
Cartridges - blank, dummy & live; tubes; labels; trapezoids for rifle, carbine & pistol. Authentically rolled. Catalog - free w/ SASE.

CASTLE KEEP, LTD.
630-801-1696 • 630-801-1910 Fax
http://www.Reenact.com
ernie@Smartgate.com
Ernest Klapmeier
83 S La Salle St • Aurora IL 60505-3331
Reenactor supplies; clothing & equipment to put man or woman into the field. Owner has 20 yrs. reenacting experience & understands concept of authenticity.

CIVIL WAR EMPORIUM, INC.
408 Mill St • Occoquan VA 22125
From harmonicas to working cannons. Working repros. Decorator models. Consignments welcome. Buy/sell.

CONFEDERATE GRAY
615-320-1715 • 615-320-3272 Fax
http://www.dixienet.org/conf_gray/default.htm
congray@home.com
Meeks Booker
PO Box 121984 • Nashville TN 37212-1984
Hand-carved music boxes that play "Dixie" when opened; other tunes available. Named for great Southern leaders or battles. Refer to Source Book for 10% discount. Catalog - $2 (ref.).

COON CREEK
602-886-8273
601 S Desert Steppes Dr
Tucson AZ 85710-5940

CRANE MERCANTILE & MFG. CO.
314-231-4163
1212 Allen Ave
Saint Louis MO 63104-3914
Purveyor of finest cavalry saddle hardware. Iron frame coat strap buckles. McClellan saddle kit, tree & all hardware. Brochure - $2.

CRESCENT CITY SUTLER
812-983-4217
17810 Highway 57
Evansville IN 47711-9318
Reproduction & original Civil War uniforms & equipment. Catalog - $3.

DEAD HORSE FORGE
1220 Price Station Rd
Church Hill MD 21623-1315
All types of knives, Hawks & other ironware, powder horns & gourd canteens. Brochure - send SASE.

DIXIE FASHIONS
804-527-2028
George Dunn
11300 Cedar Hill Ct
Richmond VA 23233-1847
Confederate & Union exact reproduction uniforms, made to fit, museum-quality work, including all leather accessories, shell jackets, sashes, frocks, trousers, Kepis, shirts. Catalog - $3.

DIXIE GUN WORKS, INC.
800-238-6785 Orders only
901-885-0700 • 901-885-0440 Fax
PO Box 130 • Union City TN 38281-0130
The source for firearms, parts, shooting supplies, leather goods, uniforms, books, patterns & cannons. 600-pg catalog with more than 8,000 items - $5.

THE DIXIE SUTLER
PO Box 5162 • Mobile AL 36605
Specializing in Civil War-period supplies & collectibles for the reenactor or collector.

DONNA'S STITCHES BACK IN TIME
800-808-7685
We stitch for sutlers. High-quality muslin shirts - $13.50 wholesale. Also sell retail. Price list on request.

THE EMPORIUM
417-683-2764
Ed & Maryln Peterka
RR 1 Box 363 • Ava MO 65608-9726
Supplies for the muzzleloader & living history participant. Patterns, hosiery, ladies' straw hats. Catalog - $3 (ref.).

FAIR OAKS SUTLER, INC.
540-972-7744 Noon-9 PM
540-972-3256 24-hr Fax
9905 Kershaw Ct
Spotsylvania PA 22553-3768
High-quality replica Civil War uniforms, accoutrements, equipment & muskets; Kepi & bummer caps our specialty. Satisfaction guaranteed. Catalog - 2 stamps.

FALL CREEK SUTTLERY
765-482-1861
765-482-1848 Fax
http://fcsutler.com
AJF5577@aol.com or fcsutler@aol.com
Andy Fulks
PO Box 92
Whitestown IN 46075-0092
Authentic reproduction Civil War & mid-19th-century uniforms, leather goods, weapons, shoes, tents, insignia, reference books & more. 32-pg catalog - $3. (See ad page 271)

FAMILY HEIRLOOM WEAVERS
717-246-2431 Ph & Fax
familyheirloom@mindspring.com
775 Meadowview Dr
Red Lion PA 17356-8608
Reproduction fabrics - historically accurate ingrain carpets & jacquard coverlets. Uniforms, shirtings, etc. Brochure & swatches - $4.

FOUR SEASONS TENTMASTERS
517-436-6245
4221 Livesay Rd
Sand Creek MI 49279-9702
Est. 1968. Hand-crafted tent dwellings for Civil War & other time periods. Full line of accoutrements from ground up - poles, stakes, ropes, transport bags. Guide & catalog - $2.

FRAZER BROTHERS' 17TH REGIMENT
214-696-1865
214-426-4230 Fax
5641 Yale Blvd Ste 125
Dallas TX 75206-5026
Uniforms & equipment, artillery hardware, & side arms. Civilian clothing (men only). Handmade leather goods. Large supply of tinware. Boots. American products.

FRENCH'S STORE & TRADING COMPANY
717-530-5037
PO Box 454
Shippensburg PA 17257-0454
Authentic Civil War reproductions of trade goods, 17th-19th century. Specializing in cavalry & leather goods & saddles. Catalog - $1.

FRONTIER SADDLE
941-322-2560
Gabriel Libraty
5530 Juel Gill Rd
Myakka City FL 34251-9234
Replica saddles of the Old West & military; from mountain man to Civil War to classic Western saddles. Free catalog.

GDR ENTERPRISES
803-889-6360
PO Box 807
Hollywood SC 29449-0807
Wooden ammunition crates; shipping containers, chests, officer's desk, & more. Handcrafted reproductions for military historians since 1982. Photo-illus. catalog - $2.

CARL GIORDANO, TINSMITH
330-336-7270
tinsnip@newreach.net
PO Box 74 • Wadsworth OH 44282-0074
18th- & 19th-century reproductions. Hand-wrought, custom work. Brochure - send SASE.

GREAT CIRCLE FORGE
PO Box 9040 • Lexington OH 44904-9040
Hand-forged ironwork: tent stakes, tripods, potted plant stands, coat racks, decorative hooks, trammel hooks, & more. Catalog - $1.50.

GREY OWL INDIAN CRAFT SALES CORP.
718-341-4000 • 718-527-6000 Fax
Wes Cochrane
13205 Merrick Blvd • PO Box 340468
Jamaica NY 11434-0468
Green River knives, powder flasks, military buttons, buckskin, leathers, dags, strikers, books, tapes, videos, recordings, etc. 200 custom kits/4000+ items. Catalog - $3.

THE HAVERSACK DEPOT
210-620-5192
1236 River Acres Dr
New Braunfels TX 78130-3529
Museum-quality products at reasonable prices, incl. US haversack, CS cartridge box sling & CS leather belt with Ga. frame brass buckle. Satisfaction guaranteed.

HEARTLAND HOUSE
540-672-9267 • 540-672-4963 Fax
neocelt@earthlink.net
Nick Nichols
Old Blue Ridge Tpke • Rochelle VA 22738
Troiani calls us "the *Stradivarius* of historical leather craftsmen." Full line of Victorian-era saddlery, tack & equestriana (U.S., C.S., British military, & civilian). Illus. catalog - $4 (ref.).

HILLBILLY SPORTS, INC.
410-378-4533
PO Box 70 • Conowingo MD 21918-0070
Leather goods, period firearms, uniform items, camp items & much more. Catalog - $3.

HIS LADY & THE SOLDIER SUTLERY
517-435-3518 Summer
352-583-4627 Winter
851 Kaypat Dr • Hope MI 48628-9615
Period hair goods & accessories for the lady & gentleman reenactor. Catalog - $2.

HOOP & HAVERSACK SUTLERY
517-643-5368
PO Box 415 • Merrill IL 48637-0415

THE HOUSE OF TIMES PAST
864-834-0061
634 W Darby Rd
Greenville SC 29609-7121
Period shop with authentic clothing, rifles, muzzleloading supplies & accessories for living historians & reenactors. Catalog - $2.

HUSS MACHINE WORKS
RR 3 Box 216
San Augustine TX 75972-9227
Iron reproduction of camping, cooking & other blacksmithed gear for the Civil War reenactor. Catalog - $2.

J & J WAGONS
PO Box 363 • Orlando FL 32802-0363
Authentic wagons for reenactments, living history/special events. QM Wagons, Reg. AO Wagons, & U.S. Grant-style wagons. All for rent in the Southeast.

J. K. LEATHER
540-955-0301
Dave Allen
RR 2 Box 3026
Berryville VA 22611-9501
Repairs & restoration of all leather goods, esp. antique saddles & tack. Custom-made leather products. Handmade saddles.

JAMES COUNTRY MERCANTILE
816-781-9473
816-781-1470 Fax
JAMESCNTRY@aol.com
Del Warren or Michael Gooch
111 N Main St
Liberty MO 64068-1639
For your military & civilian reenacting needs - weapons, accoutrements, clothing, patterns. Illus. catalog - $6 ppd.

GORDON WILSON JENKS & CO.
800-835-7933
Goex black powder - all granulations, incl. authentic new cartridge powder.

K & P WEAVER
kpweaver@aol.com
Ken & Paula Weaver
PO Box 1131, Dept J
Orange CT 06477-7131
Historically accurate repro men's clothing for military or civilian impression. Custom-made with handsewn buttonholes. Quality accessories; cherry dominoes, checkers with canvas board. Early leather baseballs, bats, uniforms & books. Catalog with swatches - $1.

LEVI LEDBETTER, SUTLER
704-485-4746 Orders
Frank Lanning, Prop.
7032 Mineral Springs Rd
Oakboro NC 28129-8855
Uniforms are our specialty. Tentage, knapsacks, accoutrements, canteens, tinware, blankets, buttons, buckles & brogans. Price list - send long SASE.

LOG CABIN SHOP
800-837-1082
330-948-1082
330-948-4307 Fax
http://www.logcabinshop.com
logcabin@logcabinshop.com
8010 Lafayette Rd
PO Box 275 • Lodi OH 44254-0275
Full line of muzzleloading guns, kits, components, supplies, accessories, books, cookware, blankets, etc. 200-pp. catalog - $5.

HEIDI MARSH PATTERNS
3494 N Valley Rd
Greenville CA 95947-9604
Authentic patterns & how-to books of the CW era (1855-1865) for all ages. Ballgowns, blouses, undergarments, hoops, boning, etc. Playing cards & other sundries; books. Catalog - $3.

TY MAWR CLASSICS, INC.
800-998-7051
PO Box 4221 • Martinsville VA 24115-4221
Civil War coverlet by artists at Ty Mawr Classics. 100% cotton throw, triple weave, multi-color. 50"x70" - made in USA. $53.95.

MECHANICAL BAKING COMPANY
309-353-2414
http://www.mechanical-bakery.com
jlarkin@mtco.com
Jeanie Larkin
PO Box 513P • Pekin IL 61555-0513
Bakers of army-style hardtack. Great for reenactors & living histories. Edible teeth dullers. Price list & sample - $1.50. 4-6 weeks for delivery.

MENDELSON'S LEATHER
501 Short St • Grants Pass OR 97527-5443
Master leather craftsman makes moccasin boots, full spectrum of custom goods you can't find anywhere else.

MERCURY SUPPLY CO.
409-327-3707
101 Lee St • Livingston TX 77351-4226
Civil War uniforms, reproduction equipment, tents, accoutrements, leather goods, firearms military & civilian. Catalog - $2.

MICHAELS & PERRIN
717-922-1065 • 717-922-1245
tperrin@sunlink.net
414 Main St
PO Box 29
Hartleton PA 17829-0029
Uniforms & period clothing for men & women. Equipment for reenactors. Catalog.

MJN BOOT & LEATHER SHOP
605-368-2922
Mick Nesseim
PO Box 351
27210 468th Ave.
Tea SD 57064-0351
Custom-made, fine officers' boots, 1859 light artillery boot & brogans. Catalog - $2.

NASHVILLE DEPOT
615-833-2275
141 Neese Dr • 500 Zodiac Bldg
Nashville TN 37211-2750
Authentically reproduced carpetbag in colorful period designs. Lined interior with pockets & enclosed rigid bottom. Leather handles & straps. 18"Lx18"Dx"8"W - $79.50 + $6.75 S&H.

NINETEENTH CENTURY MERCANTILE
508-398-1888 Ph & Fax
Barbara A. Amster
2 N Main St
South Yarmouth MA 02664-3151
Hard-to-find goods recreated in ca.1800s fashion. Housewares, dry goods, toiletries, remedies, hardware, fashion accessories, etc. All presented in 19th-century mercantile atmosphere. Hundreds of items.

THE NORTHWOOD SUTLERY
715-381-0288
Phillip Cudd
415B Wisconsin St N
Hudson WI 54016-1036
Sales of original & reproduction Civil War-era military & civilian equipment & supplies. Specialize in medical items. Free catalog.

OLD SUTLER JOHN
607-775-4434 Ph & Fax
Westview Station
PO Box 174 • Binghamton NY 13905-0174
Full line of quality reproduction Civil War guns, bayonets, swords, uniforms, leather items, & other collectibles. Catalog - $3. (See ad page 260)

OLD WEST SADDLE SHOP
307-577-1356
http://www.trib.com/SADDLESHOP
mattsee@trib.com
6584 Hummingbird Ln
PO Box 4300
Casper WY 82604
Selection of period saddles.

PANTHER LODGES
304-462-7718 • 304-462-7755 Fax
PO Box 32-CB
Normantown WV 25267-0032
Famous for Civil War tentage & gear for reenactors. Our A-frames, wall tents, & sibleys set the standard for quality tentage. Catalog - $2 (ref. w/ 1st order).

PRESERVATION PRODUCTS
608-839-4038
preservprod@yahoo.com
Jeffery C. Remy
3813 Bass Ln
Cottage Grove WI 53527
Wooden ammunition boxes, shipping containers, traveling chests, offiers' & regimental desks, & more. Historically accurate reproductions of Civil War & Indian War. Photo-illus. catalog - $2 (ref.).

R & K SUTLERY
217-732-8844
1015 1200th St
Lincoln IL 62656-5047
Complete line of military uniforms & civilian clothing for both men & women; coats, pants, skirts, blouses, dresses, etc. Top quality tents, Officer's Wall, A-frames, dog tents & sibley. Catalog - send SASE.

RARE BOOK REPUBLISHERS
703-573-5116
703-573-5897 Fax
http://www.raredocs.com
paconose@erols.com
PO Box 3202
Merrifield VA 22116-3202
The Cook's Own Book (1832), premier cooking reference used by families on both sides of the Civil War. More than 2,500 recipes. Hardcover - $28.95 + $3.50 S&H.

REB'S TRADING POST
3608 Alta Vista Dr
Waco TX 76706-3741
Canvas goods, lodges, tents, flys, bags, etc. Blanket rifle sheaths, antler products, leather products, belt blanks, holsters, etc. Catalog - $1.

THE REBEL CO.
770-947-1863
PO Box 15191
Atlanta GA 30333-0191
Ships more than 30 traditionally Southern Rebel products. Delicious syrups, preserves, dressings, honey, sauces, relish, jams, chutney, peanuts, pecans & more. Free catalog.

RED WILLOW CANVAS COMPANY
319-628-4815
John Honn
131 W Main
PO Box 188
Oxford LA 52322-0188
Makers of quality authentic shelters for reenactors including common shelters, officers' tents & guards' tents. Catalog - $1.

THE REGIMENTAL QUARTERMASTER
215-672-6891
215-672-9020 Fax
PO Box 553
Hatboro PA 19040-0553
Civil War repro muskets, carbines, revolvers, swords, uniforms, shoes, boots, buckles, buttons, tents, tapes, tinware, equipment, accoutrements, accessories. Catalog - $2 ($1 ref.).

RICHMONVILLE TINWARE
800-501-1675
541-678-1675
PO Box 407
21328 Highway 99E
Aurora OR 97002-0407
Highest quality, historically correct tinware obtainable. Custom orders welcome. Catalog - $3.

S & S FIREARMS
718-497-1100
718-497-1105 Fax
7411 Myrtle Ave • Glendale NY 11385-7433
Military Americana. Antique gun parts, carbines, Enfield, buttons, insignia, books, equipment, appendages, headdress, etc. Reenactor supplies. Original & reproduction. Photo-illus. catalog - $3.

S & S SUTLER OF GETTYSBURG
717-677-7580 •717-337-0438 Fax
Tim Sheads
PO Box 218
Bendersville PA 17306-0218
Reproduction Civil War uniforms, leather goods, insignia, tinware, & more. Free catalog.

SANTA FE SALES
1 Ranch Club Rd Ste 3402-R
Silver City NM 88061-7862
Replicas. Relive American History through us for hard-to-find historical accessories, books, reprints, tinware, numerous historical items. Catalog - $3.

SARAH ADAMS PRODUCTIONS
717-432-2752 • 717-432-8820 Fax
Civil War wrapping paper - photographic scenes of Manassas, Shiloh, Gettysburg, Antietam & others. 2 sizes. Coordinating ribbon also available.

EDWARD SEMMELROTH
517-278-2214
415 Fleming Rd • Tekonsha MI 49092-9660
Antique iron sales, restoration & reproductions, incl. 1820s-1870s style kitchen cookstove. Custom casting & restoration in any medal; no job too big or small.

TOM SMITH
716-337-0181
12101 New Oregon Rd
Springville NY 14141-9619
US Cavalry Horse Equipment, 1859-1917. Custom work. Correct hardware & leather spec's (no harness leather). Color cat. $7.

STALEY'S SUNDRIES
540-899-6464
540-373-2469 Fax
710 Caroline St
Fredericksburg VA 22401-5904
Largest collection of Civil War music anywhere. Military insignia, flags, hats, clothing, patterns, buttons, buckles, miniatures, books, magazines & gift items.

SUTLERS OF THE SIXTEEN
905-338-9427
Lorne & Nancy Weller
1359 White Oaks Blvd #906
Oakville Ontario L6H 2R8 CANADA
Period footwear, 19th-century historical clothing, pine boxes & more.

SUTLERS WAGON
Stamatelos Bros, Prop.
PO Box 390005
Cambridge MA 02139-0001
Fine quality American military items, 1775-1900. Civil War uniforms, headgear, accoutrements, buckles, tack, photos, swords, documents. Buy/sell.

SWAMP FOX SUTLERY
816-364-2150
Craig Pierce, Prop.
RR 1 Box 3090
De Kalb MO 64440-9801
Civil War reenactor supply, original & reproduction.

T5 ENTERPRISES
208-788-3348
Larry & Wende Thornton
4 Freedom Loop
Bellevue ID 83313-5012
Buy/sell/trade U.S. cavalry & horse-related equipment (1833-1943).

TARA HALL, INC.
800-205-0069
212-802-6423 Fax
http://www.fighting69th.com
tarahall@earthlink.net
Vic Olney
PO Box 2069
Beach Haven NJ 08008-0109
Meagher's Irish Brigade, Fighting 69th, Corcoran's Irish Legion memorabilia, shirts, jackets, hats, sweaters, steins, pins, flags, books, miniatures, poster, belt buckles, NINAs, etc. Free catalog. (See ad page 272)

TENTSMITHS
603-447-2344
603-447-1777 Fax
PO Box 1748
Conway NH 03818-1748
Authentic period tentage of unsurpassed quality. Each tent made to your specifications by people who care.

TIMELESS TEXTILES
717-930-0201
Mary Harkless
321 N Union St
Middletown PA 17057-1442
Historically correct fabric, retail & wholesale, for reenactors of all eras. Carry both civilian & military, ladies' & men's fabrics.

TIPPECANOE FRONTIER TRADING CO.
937-667-1816
114 E Main St
Tipp City OH 45371-1962
Thousands of items serving reenactors, hunters, history buffs. Gunsmith for restorations, information, minor repairs (1700s-1900s). Long-range shooting supplies. Catalog - $4.

JAMES TOWNSEND & SON, INC.
219-594-5852
http://www.jastown.com/
PO Box 415
Pierceton IN 46562-0415
Large selections of reenactment supplies, 1740-1840. Clothing, blankets, eyeglasses, cookware, trade silver, shoes, hats, lanterns, tentage, knives, kegs, etc. Catalog - $2.

TURKEY FOOT TRADING CO.
419-832-1109
Allen & Colleen Schroll
PO Box 58
Grand Rapids OH 43522-0058
18th- & 19th-century merchandise: beads, clothing, iron work, tinware, more. Catalog.

TWIN OAKS SADDLERY
407-790-2461
11580 46th Pl N
Royal Palm Beach FL 33411-9141
American-made Civil War goods/reproductions. Cartridge box plates, carbine box, cap box, sword belts, sashes, holsters, saddlebags, saddles & parts, belts & buckles, tinware. Catalog - $2.

UPPER MISSISSIPPI VALLEY MERCANTILE CO
319-322-0896 • 319-383-5549 Fax
1607 Washington St
Davenport IA 52804-3613
Top quality goods & supplies for Civil War reenactors; uniforms, tinware, tents, leather goods, muskets, books, weapons, patterns, more. 100-pp., illus. catalog - $3.

USA HISTORY STORE
508-947-8866
http://www.usahistorystore.com
PO Box 109
Middleboro MA 02346-0109
Authentic brass camp candlesticks perfect for 19th-century impression. Set of 2 - $13.95 + $3 S&H. Books, games, flags & period clothing.

V.C.R.
675-794-4652
888-794-4652
RR 5 Box 77
Crawfordsville IN 47933-9719
Quality handmade chairs for all occasions. Free brochure.

VILLAGE TINSMITHING WORKS
336-468-1190
330-468-1191 Fax
Bill & Judy Hoover
PO Box 539
Hamptonville NC 27020-0539
Quality reproduction & period items. Lead-free solder on potable items. More than 80 items. Custom orders. Catalog - free w/ long SASE.

THE WINCHESTER SUTLER, INC.
540-888-3595
540-888-4632 Fax
270 Shadow Brook Ln
Winchester VA 22603-2071
Reproduction Civil War firearms, uniforms, camp gear, accessories, shoes, boots, hats, etc. Catalog - $4.

WORLD EXONUMIA
815-226-0771
815-397-7662 Fax
http://www.exonumia.com
Rich Hartzog
PO Box 4143BWX
Rockford IL 61110-0643
Civil War & sutler tokens, medals, slave tags, Civil War dog tags, corps badges, sutler paper, GAR reunion badges, etc. Buy/sell; mail bid sales. Publisher of *Sutler Paper Money*.

20TH MAINE, INC.
207-865-4340 • 207-865-9575 Fax
Patricia Hodgdon
49 West St • Freeport ME 04032-1127
Specialized bookstore devoted to Civil War with new & old books, art, music, videos, antiques & much more.

AMERICAN HERITAGE MARKETING GROUP, INC.
5904 Welborn Dr • Bethesda MD 20816-3422
Longstreet! Civil War video on the war's most controversial general; in-studio film version of live stage play - $29.95 + $4.95 S&H.

THE AMERICAN LISTENERS' THEATRE
888-283-4695
PO Box 50056 • Austin TX 78763-0056
Listen to the Civil War tales of Ambrose Bierce. 2 cassette set, 3 hrs. $22.50 (ppd.).

AMERICANA SOUVENIRS & GIFTS
http://www.americanagifts.com
302 York St
Gettysburg PA 17325-1930
Most complete line of Civil War souvenirs & memorabilia for both USA & CSA. Cannons, bullets, patches, toys, books, flags, videos, documents, insignias, & much more.

ASSOCIATED VIDEO PRODUCTIONS
770-425-1530
770-419-8033 Fax
jack@freewwweb.com
2511 Kingswood Dr Ste SB-398
Marietta GA 30066-6256
See & hear in-depth discussions about muskets, uniforms, accouterments, equipment and more,insuring historically accurate & correct impressions. *Mastering Reenacting* video - $24.95 + $4 S&H.

BATTLEFIELD VIDEO PRODUCTIONS
6374 Larch Ln
Macungie PA 18062-9380
Civil War guns video. 47-min. video of the guns of the Civil War, their makers, & those who used them. Live fire demonstration. $29.95 ppd.

BELLE & BLADE
201-328-8488
201-442-0669 Fax
124 Penn Ave
Dover NJ 07801-5335
Send for catalog of war books, videos, toys, swords, knives, & gifts. Catalog - $3; free w/ order.

BELLE GROVE PUBLISHING CO.
800-861-1861
PO Box 483 • Kearny NJ 07032-0483
Titles include *History of the 57th Pennsylvania, Four Years Campaigning in the Army of the Potomac.* Videos of "lost" films from silent movie era - *CW Cinema* Vols I-III. Call/write for more info.

BETWEEN THE BULLET & THE BATTLEFIELD
814-695-9893
PO Box 511 • Hollidaysburg PA 16648-0511
Historically correct video presents the "Truth & Myths of CW Medicine." Visit actual aid stations & field hospitals in Gettysburg & Antietam. $21.95 + $3 S&H.

BLACKSTONE AUDIO BOOKS
800-729-2665
PO Box 969 • Ashland OR 97520-0033
More than 600 titles, rentals by mail, unabridged recordings. Free catalog.

THE BLUE & GRAY SHOP
800-454-7104
531 Baltimore St • Gettysburg PA 17325-2606
Reasonably priced T-shirts of *The Killer Angels*, Gettysburg, etc. Videos, cassettes, CDs, calendars, etc.

BOOKCASSETTE SALES
800-222-3225
1704 Eaton St • PO Box 887
Grand Haven MI 49417-0887
Fragments of the Ark, by Louise Meriwether - audiocassette, unabridged. Peter Mango delivered the stolen gunboat *Swanee* to the U.S. navy & brought with him a group of runaways united by love & painful histories. ISBN 1-56100-556-8, $23.95.

BOOKS ON TAPE
Ed Mauss, Dir. of Publication
123 Briarwood Ln
Aliso Viejo CA 92656-2966
Unabridged audiobooks for rental or purchase. Large selection of Civil War accounts & biographies, acclaimed authors. Catalog - $5 (ref.).

BRIGADE BUGLER
609-589-3901 • George Rabbai
PO Box 165 • Pitman NJ 08071-0165
Civil War infantry bugle calls, book & cassette, $19.95 ppd. for set. *Teach Yourself How to Play the Bugle* - for all levels of buglers, includes exercises, tonguing & lip flexibility. $8 ppd.

BUFFALO ROBE TRADING POST
520-457-2322
George Henry
9 N 5th St • PO Box 741
Tombstone AZ 85638-0741
Civil War, local history, American Indian, western lawmen & outlaws. Gift shop, artifacts, video & audio tapes. Historian in attendance.

C & D COMMERCIAL PRODUCTIONS, INC.
800-600-6578
100 Dixie Ln • Wilmington DE 19804-2312
A Call to Arms: Your Guide to Becoming a CW Reenactor. 52-min. video - excellent recruiting tool. $19.95.

CAROLINA VIDEO PRODUCTIONS, INC.
PO Box 751 • Isle of Palms SC 29451-0751
Video on Fort Sumter. 1-hour documentary of authentic photos & full-color action. Historian narrated. Unusual facts & opinions. $24.95.

CATHEDRAL AUDIO BOOKS, INC.
800-479-0099
Steven Kalb
341 Beirut Ave
Pacific Palisades CA 90272-4625
The Killer Angels, classic novel by Michael Shaara, on 9 audiocassettes with selected music soundtracks from the film *Gettysburg*. Must-have for *Gettysburg* buffs - $49.95.

CLASSIC IMAGES
800-888-5359
Jack Foley
PO Box 2399 • Columbia MD 21045-1399
Video series; live-action footage with archival photos, animated maps, narration, & music. Includes Shiloh, Manassas, Vicksburg. Free catalog.

COLLECTING THE CIVIL WAR
800-440-8478
PO Box 18844
Denver CO 80218-0844
2 videotapes - "Collecting the Union Soldier" vol. 1, & "... Confederate Soldier" vol. 2. Expert descriptions, close-up color photography. 100s of items. $19.95 ea.; set $29.95. Add $4 S&H.

COMMAND POST
201-627-6272
201-627-6627 Fax
PO Box 1015
Denville NJ 07834-0615
Books & videos on the Civil War, including the role of women. Free catalog.

COMMUTERS LIBRARY
800-643-0295 • 703-827-8937 Fax
commlib@aol.com
Joseph Langenfeld
PO Box 3168
Falls Church VA 22043-0168
Superb narrations of Lincoln's writings. *Lincoln's Letters* ("audio best of the year" - Publishers Weekly). *Lincoln's Prose* (includes Gettysburg Address). Beautiful editions - 2 cass. $16.95 ea. Free catalog.

THE CONFLICT BOOKSHOP
800-847-0911
EPETE1731@aol.com
213 Steinwehr Ave
Gettysburg PA 17325-2801
Latest in Civil War titles, as well as fine collection of used & rare books, audio & video tapes & other memorabilia. Free flyer.

CRITTENDEN SCHMITT ARCHIVES
http://www.erols.com/tyrannus/archives/csavideo.html
PO Box 4253 / Courthouse Station
Rockville MD 20849-4253
Technical & historical books & videotapes relating to weapons & ammunition of all types & eras.

DIXIE DEPOT
706-265-7533 • 706-265-3952 Fax
http://www.ilinks.net/~dixiegeneral
Dixie_Depot@stc.net
John Black
PO Box 1448 • 72 Keith Evans Rd
Dawsonville GA 30534-0027
Pro-Southern educational products: video/audio tapes, new/old books, bumper stickers, flags, wearables, lapel pins, exclusive Great Seal items. More than 600 items! Catalog. (See ad page 260)

DONALD DREW
PO Box 422 • Stillwater MN 55082-0422
Basic training video for the beginner. Directly from Harde's. Professional production. All facings, rifle movements, load/fire procedure, etc. VHS - $27 ppd.

THE FLAG GUYS
914-562-0088 x307
http://www.flagguys.com • Flagguys@aol.com
283 Windsor Hwy Dept 307
New Windsor NY 12553-6909
Flags of all types & sizes. Books, Kepis, accessories, swords, cassettes, CDs, novelties. Free catalog. (See ad page 263)

FUSION VIDEO
800-959-0061
100 Fusion Way
Country Club Hills IL 60478-3115
Videos on the Civil War & American history. Contact for complete listing.

GARRETT PRODUCTIONS
800-870-9626
Thomas A. Garrett
185A Newberry Commons
Etters PA 17319-9362
Insight to the Battle of Gettysburg, 28-pg book. Great for first-timers or refresher - $10.97 ppd. *The Monuments of Gettysburg* 40-min. videotape - $32 ppd.

GETTYSBURG NMP BOOKSTORE
800-JULY 3 1863 • 717-334-1891 Fax
Robert Housch
Visitor Center Electric Map
95 Taneytown Rd
Gettysburg PA 17325-2804
Complete Civil War bookstore specializing in books, tapes, CDs & videos. Free catalog.

GREY OWL INDIAN CRAFT SALES CORP.
718-341-4000 • 718-527-6000 Fax
Wes Cochrane
13205 Merrick Blvd
PO Box 340468
Jamaica NY 11434-0468
Green River knives, powder flasks, military buttons, buckskin, leathers, dags, strikers, books, tapes, videos, recordings, etc. 200 custom kits/4000+ items. Catalog - $3.

GREYSTONE'S HISTORY EMPORIUM & GALLERY
717-338-0631
717-338-0851 Fax
http://www.GreystoneOnline.com
461 Baltimore St
Gettysburg PA 17325-2623
Producers of *CW Journal* have created a store, gallery & museum. Military miniatures, books, videos, collectibles, art, exhibits, story theatre. Unique merchandise.

HISTORY IN PRINT
800-816-3571 • 219-465-5778 Fax
PO Box 1295 • Valparaiso IN 46384-1295
World's largest seller of Civil War books, videos, audio tapes, maps & fine art prints. Delivered to your door - select from 100s of titles! Free catalog.

INDEPENDENT PUBLISHERS
3535 E Coast Hwy
Corona del Mar CA 92625-2404
War & Warriors series. Books, videos, audiotapes. Men, machines, strategies, battles, & politics of war. Catalog - send SASE.

INSTITUTE FOR PUBLIC AFFAIRS
217-786-6799
217-786-6542 Fax
University of Illinois at Springfield
Springfield IL 62794
The Lincolns of Springfield, Illinois, a video documentary distributed nationally by PBS - $24.95.

T.R. KOBA & COMPANY
419-588-2938
11918 Berlin Rd
Berlin Heights OH 44814-9667
Rebel Fire/Yankee Ice, The Johnson's Island Story, video documentary featuring the music of Bobby Horton. VHS. $28.45. The story of the Confederate POW camp.

THE LEXINGTON CIVIL WAR COMPANY
540-464-1100
Lexington, Virginia: Auto Tape Guide to Civil War Sites. Drive at your own pace. Featuring music by Bobby Horton.

MAJOR VISTA MEDIA, INC.
800-554-3108
2715 W Stein Rd
La Salle MI 48145-9797
Custer's Monroe - narrated 30-min. video tour around hometown of George & Libbie Custer, featuring homes, sites & photos. $29.95 + $4 S&H.

MARILL PRODUCTIONS
PO Box 460820
San Francisco CA 94146-0820
Video documentaries on Colt revolvers (1836-1869) & Bowie knives (1820-1870), in-depth, exquisite. $29.95 ea. or both for $45.

MARY LOU PRODUCTIONS
800-774-8511
PO Box 17233
Minneapolis MN 55417-0233
"Gift of Heritage" - how-to video showing you the process of creating your own family documentary, including tips on researching, organizing, & combining info. - $32.95. Call for more info.

MEDIA MAGIC
517-393-3100 • 517-393-3338 Fax
3120 Pine Tree Rd
Lansing MI 48911
3 new feature-length Civil War video programs - *School of the Soldier*, *The Battle of the Wilderness*, & *The Battle of Fort Stedman*.

MODEL EXPO, INC.
PO Box 229140
Hollywood FL 33022-9140
Video catalog of historic ship model kits. Video & color catalog - $5.

JOHN S. MOSBY HERITAGE AREA
540-687-6681
PO Box 1178
Middleburg VA 20118-1178
Maps of Mosby Heritage Area - $20. Audiotape driving tour "Prelude to Gettysburg" - $17. Free "Drive Through History" brochure.

MOVIETECH
2590 NE 201st St
Miami FL 33180-1910
Relive the Battle of Olustee & the 20th annual reenactment with video narrated by Luke Halpin. Reenactor interviews. Captures the solemnity & excitement of the 3-day event. $19.95 + $4 S&H.

MUSEUM OF HISTORIC NATCHITOCHES
318-357-0070
840 Washington St
Natchitoches LA 71457-4728
The Forgotten March: the Red River Campaign. Video documenting the largest campaign west of the Mississippi. $22.50 ppd. (Proceeds benefit museum)

PRESERVATION ENTERPRISES
412-285-6995
228 E Pearl St
Butler PA 16001-4472
A Visit from a Civil War Soldier - video. Extraordinary one-man show based on Pvt. Hinchberger's diary & recollections. Color, VHS, 50 min. $22.95 ppd.

RECORDED BOOKS, INC.
800-638-1304
http://www.RecordedBooks.com
RecordedBooks@RecordedBooks.com
270 Skipjack Rd
Prince Frederick MD 20678-3410
More than 1,800 titles narrated by experts. Unabridged, studio recordings. Free brochure. Call for info. on special discounts.

S. B. PRODUCTIONS
509-682-2616
PO Box 548
Chelan WA 98816-0548
Full hour of the soldier's story from camp life to first battle to letters home. Written & narrated by Scott Brundage. Tape - $14.95.

SANGAMON STATE UNIVERSITY
217-786-6799
217-786-6542 Fax
Springfield IL 62794
The Lincolns of Springfield, Illinois, a video documentary distributed by PBS. Not the myth, but the midwestern, middle-class, & victorian. $24.95.

THE SCHOLAR'S BOOKSHELF
609-395-6933 • 609-395-0755 Fax
http://www.scholarsbookshelf.com
books@scholarsbookshelf.com
110 Melrich Rd
Cranbury NJ 08512-3511
A major book catalog company that produces three 88-pp. Military History catalogs each year. Catalogs feature a substantial variety of Civil War books & videos. Free catalog.

THE SOUTHERN ARMY ALBUM!
John Mills Bigham
4833 Arcadia Rd
Columbia SC 29206-1307
Christopher Memminger's homeplace. 4 families share Confederate oral histories & images. Military headstones 1776+ recorded in 3 antebellum churchyards. Lasting regional 1992 video production. $21.95.

TEXAS A&M UNIVERSITY PRESS CONSORTIUM
800-826-8911 • 409-847-8752 Fax
FDL@tampress.tamu.edu
Gayla Christiansen
PO Box C • College Station TX 77843-0001
Mighty Stonewall, *Make Me a Map of the Valley*, *Fallen Guidon*, *Confederate General of the Southwest*. From $12.95 to $35. Also *Voices of Valor* (audio) $10.95 cassette, $17.95 CD. Free catalog.

THOMAS PUBLICATIONS
800-840-6782 • 717-334-1921
717-334-8440 Fax
Dean S. Thomas
353 Buford Ave • Gettysburg PA 17325-1138
Publishers of Civil War books. Many titles. *Ghosts of Gettysburg* series videos. Free catalog.

TIME-LIFE VIDEO
800-843-1199
PO Box 85571
Richmond VA 23285-5571
Civil War Journal - video cassettes of the critically acclaimed series, from $9.99 to $19.99.

TN RELEASING CO.
800-289-6682
400 S Farrell Dr Ste B205
Palm Springs CA 92262-7960
Out of the Wilderness and *Black Easter* - video documentaries of Abraham Lincoln's life & assassination. 75 min. & 50 min. - $29.95 ea.; both for $54.95.

THE TURNING POINT
800-454-7104
240 Steinwehr Ave
Gettysburg PA 17325-2814
Reasonably priced T-shirts of *The Killer Angels*, Gettysburg, etc. Full color & one color. Videos, cassettes, CDs, calendars, etc.

VIDEO PORTRAITS
800-378-8764
PO Box 108
Vinton IA 52349-0108
New Market video. Largest assembly of troops, cavalry & artillery since the original 1864 battle. 90-min., professional produced - $19.95 ppd.

THE VILLAGE SHOPPE
800-454-7104
Old Gettysburg Village
Gettysburg PA 17325
T-shirts reasonably priced of *The Killer Angels*, Gettysburg, etc. Full color & one color. Videos, cassettes, CDs, calendars, etc.

VOYAGER VIDEO, INC.
800-786-9248
PO Box 1122
Darien CT 06820-1122
Video catalog designed specifically for educational enrichment. History, world culture, African Americans, etc. Catalog.

STEVE WARREN
1612 S 126th Ave E
Tulsa OK 74128
Last Raid at Cabin Creek - 90-min. documentary of South's greatest victory in the Indian nations. $15.99 ppd.

ALABAMA BUREAU OF TOURISM & TRAVEL
800-ALABAMA
334-242-4554 Fax
http://www.touralabama.org
info@touralabama.org
Russell A. Nolen
401 Adams Ave
PO Box 4927
Montgomery AL 36103-4927
Birthplace of the most dramatic chapter in American history. Site of historic battles, parks, politics, & much more. Free travel guide.

AMERICANA TOURS
800-220-7609
http://www.telepath.com/amtour
amtour@telepath.com
Les Rodman
Visit historical sites of the CW: Gettysburg, Fredericksburg, Manassas, Virginia Capitol, White House of the Confederacy, & others. Notebook containing historical narrative provided.

BATTLEFIELD TOURS
800-972-5858
4638 N Ravenswood Ave Ste 204
Chicago IL 60640-4510
In-depth, slow-paced Civil War walking tours.

BELLE GROVE PLANTATION
540-869-2028
PO Box 727
336 Belle Grove Rd
Middletown VA 22645-0727

BILLIE CREEK VILLAGE REENACTMENT
765-569-3430 • 765-569-5226
http://www.coveredbridges.com/bilcreek.htm
RR 2 Box 27
Rockville IN 47872-9503
Indiana's largest Civil War event. 30 historic buildings to tour. Battles & military events; extensive ladies', children's & medical events, ball. Annual event - June.

BLUE & GRAY EDUCATION SOCIETY
804-797-4535
416 Beck St • Norfolk VA 23503-5302
Non-profit organization which interprets battlefields for public visitation. North Anna is most recent achievement. More than 600 members via tax-exempt donation. Seminars, tours, symposiums & debates.

CAMP MOORE CONFEDERATE MUSEUM & CEMETERY
504-229-2438
70640 Camp Moore Rd
PO Box 25
Tangipahoa LA 70465
440 of Camp Moores soldiers buried in cemetery. Museum contains artifacts from the camp, which was destroyed by Union forces in 1864. Walking tours offered.

CAMPAIGN TOURS
800-343-6768
508-750-9692 Fax
Brian Crowley
435 Newbury St
Danvers MA 01923-1065
Many fascinating Civil War tours: Shenandoah Valley, Atlanta & Vicksburg campaigns. Call/write for info. Free catalog.

CENTER STATE 29
800-732-5821
"Virginia's Civil War Connection." Follow Highway 29 to sample sites rich in Civil War heritage & history. Call for free brochure.

CHARLES COUNTY
800-766-3386
PO Box B
La Plata MD 20646-0167
Historic inn with visitors like John Wilkes Booth. Dr. S.A. Mudd's house. Rolling meadows, forests, coastline, & Maryland seafood. Bird watching guide available.

THE CHARLESTON MUSEUM
803-722-2996
360 Meeting St
Charleston SC 29403-6297
Harbor & land tours, reenactments. Nationally recognized speakers. Period music. Call or write for upcoming events, exhibits, tours, & more. Free brochure.

CHRISTMAS AT THE FORT
334-861-6992
Fort Gaines Historic Site
PO Box 97
Dauphin Island AL 36528-0097
Annual living history weekend; 1998 dates - December 5-6. Experience 1861 Christmas at the fort with Confederate soldiers -- authenticity stressed. Candlelight tour, feast, dance, drills, camp life, etc.

CIVIL WAR DAY
803-722-2996
The Charleston Museum
360 Meeting St
Charleston SC 29403-6235
Harbor & land tours in historic Charleston, SC, nationally recognized speakers, reenactors, period music. Annual event - April. Brochure.

CIVIL WAR DRIVING TOUR
757-886-7777 • 888-493-7386
757-886-7981 Fax
13560 Jefferson Ave
Newport News VA 23603
Self-guided tour of major Peninsula Campaign sites. Map.

CIVIL WAR EDUCATION ASSOCIATION
800-298-1861 • 540-667-2339 Fax
21 N Loudoun St
Winchester VA 22601-4715
Non-profit organization presenting the finest seminars, symposia, & tours. Develops educational materials, publishes/distributes Civil War books. Contact for extensive calendar of events.

CIVIL WAR LIVING HISTORY REENACTMENT
910-371-6613
Fort Anderson NC
Reenactment on grounds of Brunswick Town State Historic Sites. Tours of earthwork fort remains, small arms & military demonstrations, civilian interpretations. Lectures/talks. Annual event - February. No admission fee.

CIVIL WAR SOCIETY
800-247-6253 • 540-955-1176
540-955-2321 Fax
cwmag@mnsinc.com
PO Box 770 • Berryville VA 22611-0770
Membership includes award-winning *Civil War Magazine*, calendar, newsletters, membership cert., preservation & education activities, ancestors research guide, tours, seminars, discounts & camaraderie. Call for brochure & free sample magazine.

CIVIL WAR SOLDIERS MUSEUM
850-469-1900 • 850-469-9328 Fax
http://www.cwmuseum.org
info@cwmuseum.org
108 S Palafox Pl • Pensacola FL 32501
Explore the life of the Civil War soldier through exhibits of personal, religious, medical, musical, military, political & social aspects of the War. Tours available.

CIVIL WAR TOURS, INC.
770-908-8410
888-678-8942
Deaj95@aol.com
Tour battlefields of the Atlanta Campaign with an historian. Stand in trenches, see Soldier-Life Demonstrations of either side. Step-on-guide service/group rates available. Mon-Sat., 1/2 or full day.

CIVIL WAR TOURS OF TENNESSEE, INC.
615-356-7537
Stuart M. Moore, President
PO Box 1298
Fairview TN 37062-1298
Daily tours of Confederate invasion of Tennessee in 1864, culminating in battle of Franklin & Nashville. Free brochure.

CLASSIC QUESTS
800-458-5394
2 Federal St • Saint Albans VT 05478-2035
Escorted tours, many with multi-night stays in fine hotels/inns. Quality historic & scenic tours. Escorted rail tours. Free catalog.

CONFEDERATE HISTORICAL INSTITUTE
501-225-3996
jlrussell@civilwarbuff.org
PO Box 7388
Little Rock AR 72217-7388
Est. 1979 to promote study of Confederate history. Speakers & tours, annual institute - April. Newsletter. Membership - $20/yr.

THE CORINTH CIVIL WAR CENTER
601-287-9501
http://www.corinth.org/
civilwar@tsixroads.com
PO Box 45 • Corinth MS 38835-0045
Offers 12-minute video of Corinth's role in the Civil War. Walking/driving tour maps available. Small gift shop.

CSS NEUSE STATE HISTORIC SITE
919-522-2091 • PO Box 3043
2612 W Vernon Ave
Kinston NC 28502-3043
Remains of Confederate ironclad, artifacts. Guided tours of the gunboat.

DAVIS CREEK CAMP
406-342-5423 • 406-665-3538
Sarpy Route • Hysham MT 59038
Ride the actual trails of Custer. Authentic equipment. Tours ride through Custer's Last Stand reenactment, Reno Creek & Little Big Horn (all on horseback).

DAYS INN
301-739-9050
900 Dual Hwy
Hagerstown MD 21740-5913
Conveniently located near several major battlefields: Gettysburg, Antietam, Harpers Ferry. Outdoor pool & playground. Full service restaurant.

THE DELTA QUEEN STEAMBOAT CO.
800-347-4318
30 Robin St Wharf
New Orleans LA 70130-1890
Civil War Vacations - special cruises aboard an authentic paddlewheeler explore the war's strategies & turning points on the mighty rivers with special guest historians, authors, & CW experts. Call for more info.

DIXIANA
800-272-3589
Private Southern Pride Airline club for weekend getaways. Affordable air transportation for members only. Call for more info. on membership requirements & application.

EDGERTON'S TRAVEL SERVICE, INC.
800-643-4604
Civil War cruise - relax & enjoy the beautiful Tennessee & Cumberland rivers on the Mississippi Queen. Visit Shiloh, Florence, Paducah, Decatur, Dover, & famous battlefields. Noted lecturers. Free brochure.

FARNSWORTH HOUSE INN
717-334-8838
401 Baltimore St
Gettysburg PA 17325-2623
"Showplace of the Civil War." Daily house tours, fine dining. Bed & breakfast - Victorian elegance, private baths. Tavern, bookstore.

FORT CLINCH STATE PARK
904-277-7274
904-277-7225 Fax
2601 Atlantic Ave
Fernandina Beach FL 32034-2299
Living history demonstrations, tours of fort which fell into Union hands in 1862.

FORT FISHER STATE HISTORIC SITE
910-458-5538
910-458-0477 Fax
PO Box 169
1610 Fort Fisher Blvd S
Kure Beach NC 28449-0169
Guided tours of fort's remains; visitor center.

FORT WOOL
800-800-2202
757-727-1102
Hampton Visitor Center
710 Settlers Landing Rd
Hampton VA 23669
Civil War island fort, open Apr.-Oct. to pleasure boaters.

GETTYSBURG ADDRESS VISITOR'S GUIDE
717-334-6296
http://www.gettysburgaddress.com
gbtours@mail.cvn.net
778 Baltimore St
Gettysburg PA 17325-2610
"Where History Comes Alive." The center of everything & all within walking distance. Package & group plans available.

GETTYSBURG CONVENTION & VISITORS BUREAU
717-334-6274 • 717-334-1616 Fax
http://www.gettysburg.com
35 Carlisle St • Gettysburg PA 17325-1802
Helps promote various events such as collectors' shows, Civil War book shows, etc. Contact for a complete listing of all yearly events.

GETTYSBURG GROUP RESERVATIONS
717-334-6020 • 800-447-8788
grpres@mail.cvn.net
200 Steinwehr Ave
Gettysburg PA 17325-2814
Offer years of service & professionals to arrange tours your group will long remember & cherish. Tours planned for Gettysburg & surrounding areas.

GETTYSBURG SCENIC RAIL TOURS
717-334-6932
106 N Washington St
Gettysburg PA 17325-1423
Ride into history, April-October. Special events include Civil War train raids, Lincoln weekend, fall foliage trips, dinner trips, & Santa trains. Group rates available.

GETTYSBURG TOUR GUIDES
717-334-1124
Gettysburg National Military Park
97 Taneytown Rd
Gettysburg PA 17325-2804
Licensed battlefield guides, tested & licensed by Natl. Park Service to ensure quality/accuracy. Personal tour in your car; short/long tours. Over 75 years experience.

GRACE HALL B&B
334-875-5744 • 334-875-9967 Fax
506 Lauderdale St
Selma AL 36701-4527
Mayor's home occupied by Union forces in 1865. 6 rooms. Tours available.

GRANBURY CONVENTION & VISITORS BUREAU
800-950-2212
100 N Crockett St • Granbury TX 76048-2127
Sponsors reenactments & other events. Tourist info.

GREAT EXPEDITIONS LTD.
800-353-8256
http://www.astanet.com/get?grtexpd
81 High Path Rd
Guildford GU1 2QL England
Several annual 9-12-day Civil War tours.

GULFSTREAM VANGUARD
804-288-9700 • 804-288-0916 Fax
Richmond VA 23232
Follow the route of the "Final Campaign." Limousines, sedans, 14 passenger vans.

HISTORIC AIR TOURS, INC.
800-VA BY AIR
Williamsburg-Jamestown Airport
PO Box 681
Williamsburg VA 23187-0681
See the battlefields on historic air tours. See the Lower Peninsula, Richmond, Petersburg, etc. Reasonable & reliable. Expert commentary.

HISTORIC HAMPTON
800-800-2202
757-727-1102
http://www.hampton.va.us/tourism
710 Settlers Landing Rd
Hampton VA 23669-4035
Historic reenactments, world-class museums, Chesapeake Bay seafood, Fort Wool, Casemate Museum at Fort Monroe, new site on the Va. Civil War Trail. Minutes from Williamsburg. Free guide.

HISTORIC HAUNTS OF WINCHESTER
540-662-3424 Ph & Fax
Mac Rutherford / Keith Toney
PO Box 1415
Winchester VA 22604-7915
Ghost & history walking tours in Winchester, Va.; 7 PM Sat. from Cork St. Tavern, April-Oct. Adults $8, Children 6-12 $4. Info. on Gettysburg & Antietam historic tours.

HISTORIC JONESBOROUGH VISITORS CENTER
423-753-1012
117 Boone St
Jonesborough TN 37659-1345
Guided tours to Civil War sites. Maps available.

HISTORIC RICHMOND FOUNDATION TOURS
804-780-0107 • 804-788-4244 Fax
707 E Franklin St
Richmond VA 23219-2313
Civil War guided riding tour (includes battlefields). Reservations required. Open April-Oct. Call for prices.

HISTORIC TRAVELER MAGAZINE
717-657-9555
102430.410@compuserve.com
6405 Flank Dr
Harrisburg PA 17112-2750
Bi-monthly magazine guide to historic sites. Travel, routes, background, etc. $11.97/yr.

HISTORY AMERICA TOURS
800-628-8542 • 972-713-7173 Fax
PO Box 797687
Dallas TX 75379-7687
Specializing in Civil War tours & cruises, accompanied by historians. From motor coach to clipper ship. Call for details & free brochure.

CRAIG HOWELL
202-462-0535
chowell@erols.com
1825 T St NW • Washington DC 20009-7135
Eastern battlefield guide for individuals or groups, single or multiple day. Custom-tailored tours for battlefields of your choice. Free brochure.

HUNT-PHELAN HOME
901-344-3166 • 800-350-9009
533 Beale St
Memphis TN 38103-3201
Discover a Civil War treasure. Built in the 1800s; filled with the family's original furnishings & documents. Free brochure.

JEFFERSON DAVIS STATE HISTORIC SITE
912-831-2335 • 912-831-2060 Fax
338 Jeff Davis Park Rd
Fitzgerald GA 31750-6343
Confederate memorial & museum, containing relics from a Ga. battle flag to rare uniforms. Davis family's capture at this site on May 10, 1865, marked official end of the Confederacy.

KENNESAW MOUNTAIN NATL BATTLEFIELD PARK
770-422-3696
900 Kennesaw Mountain Dr
Kennesaw GA 30152-4854

KENTUCKY HERITAGE TOUR GUIDE
800-225-TRIP
Capital Plaza Tower • 500 Mero St Fl 22
Frankfort KY 40601-1957
Contains all the info. you'll need to conduct your own visit to Kentucky. Civil War battle reenactments, historic outdoor dramas, driving tours. Free guide.

KURTZ CULTURAL CENTER
2 N Cameron St • Winchester VA 22601-4728
Welcome center for historic Winchester Civil War Information Center, Patsy Cline display, rotating exhibits. Open daily.

THE LEXINGTON CIVIL WAR COMPANY
540-464-1100
Lexington, Virginia: Auto Tape Guide to Civil War Sites. Drive at your own pace. Featuring music by Bobby Horton.

LIVING HISTORY ASSOCIATES, INC.
804-788-1493 • 804-788-1489 Fax
PO Box 4914 • Richmond VA 23227
Providing history-related services to clients; Richmond-area tours, 1860s speakers bureau, special events, living history workshops, film & TV project consultants.

LOTZ HOUSE WAR BETWEEN THE STATES MUSEUM
615-791-6533
http://www.phoenix.w1.com/lotz
Lotzrebel@aol.com
Ronny Mangrum, Dir.
1111 Columbia Ave • Franklin TN 37064-3616
Area's most comprehensive Civil War collection. Tours of Lotz House, which was used as hospital after Battle of Franklin; genealogy services.

THE MADISON HOUSE B&B
800-828-6422
804-528-1503
Dale & Irene Smith
413 Madison St
Lynchburg VA 24504-2435
Lee surrendered here. Longstreet recuperated here. Early, Dearing, Garland, Rodes buried here. Elegant accommodations. "Dedicated to Yesterday's Charm with Today's Convenience." Civil War Library. Tour packets.

MAJOR VISTA MEDIA, INC.
800-554-3108
2715 W Stein Rd
La Salle MI 48145-9797
Custer's Monroe - narrated 30-min. video tour around hometown of George & Libbie Custer, featuring homes, sites & photos. $29.95 + $4 S&H.

MANSFIELD PLANTATION
800-355-3223
1776 Mansfield Rd
Georgetown SC 29440-6923
Historic bed & breakfast combining the best of the old & the new South. $75-$95/night, double occupancy. Guided tours for groups of 12 or more with advance registration - $6/person.

PATRICK MC DONALD
912-748-6286
PO Box 366
Pooler GA 31322-0366
Civil War tours of the low country, battlefields, skirmish sites, forts, historic homes, etc. of Savannah, Ga., Beaufort, S.C., Hilton Head Is., Ridgeland, S,C., & environs. Long/short tours. Licensed guide.

MILITARY HISTORICAL TOURS, INC.
703-739-8900
800-722-9501
703-684-0193 Fax
PJ4MHT@aol.com
4600 Duke St Ste 420
Alexandria VA 22304-2517
Tours with leading Civil War historians.

MISSISSIPPI (COLUMBUS) CONVENTION & VISITORS BUREAU
800-327-2686
Columbus MS
Annual February Battle of West Point & Prairie reenactment & authentic dance. Call for info. & dates.

MISSISSIPPI TOURISM
800-WARMEST • PO Box 1705
Ocean Springs MS 39566-1705
Free Civil War guide to the battlegrounds & other historic places of Mississippi.

MISSOURI DIVISION OF TOURISM
800-777-0068
Convention & Visitors Bureau
Cape Girardeau MO 63701
"Hearts of Blue & Grey" Civil War sites - Fort D, Union Monument & fountain, Confederate War memorial, CW hospital.

MONOCACY BATTLEFIELD & BOOKSTORE
301-662-3515
Parks & History Association
4801 Urbana Pike # B
Frederick MD 21704-7307

JOHN S. MOSBY HERITAGE AREA
540-687-6681
PO Box 1178 • Middleburg VA 20118-1178
Maps of Mosby Heritage Area - $20.
Audiotape driving tour "Prelude to Gettysburg" - $17. Free "Drive Through History" brochure.

NATIONAL CONGRESS OF CWRTs
501-225-3996 • jlrussell@civilwarbuff.com
CWRTA • PO Box 7388
Little Rock AR 72217-7388
Speakers & tours. Annual October conference sponsored by Civil War Round Table Associates.

NEWPORT NEWS, VA
888-493-7386
Battlefield tours, historic houses, harbor tours, museum exhibits & living history events. Free visitor guide & Civil War tour brochure.

OATLANDS PLANTATION & GIFT SHOP
703-777-3174
20850 Oatlands Plantation Ln
Leesburg VA 20175-6572

PAGE ONE
PO Box 4232 • Richmond VA 23220-8232
Guide to Virginia Civil War - all the Civil War trail sites.

PAMPLIN PARK: NATL. MUSEUM OF THE CIVIL WAR SOLDIER
804-861-2408 • 804-861-2820 Fax
http://www.pamplinpark.org
pamplinpark@mindspring.com
6523 Duncan Rd
Petersburg VA 23803-7449
Site of 1865 battle - preserved fortifications, walking trails, guided tours, living history, gift shop, restaurant. New high-tech museum (May 1999) focuses on common soldier. Website features museum gift shop.

PARKERSBURG/WOOD CO. VISITORS & CONVENTION BUREAU
800-752-4982
http://wvweb.com/www/parkersburg.html
350 7th St • Parkersburg WV 26101-4610
Uncover wonderful, unexpected surprises in Greater Parkersburg, W.Va. Historic Victorian-style homes, river of intrigue.

JOHN PELHAM HISTORICAL ASSOCIATION, INC.
757-838-1685
http://members.aol.com/JPHA1982
JPHA1982@aol.com
Peggy Vogtsberger
7 Carmel Ter
Hampton VA 23666-2807
Bi-monthly newsletter, "The Cannoneer." Annual convention & tour of Fredericksburg; commemorative ceremony at Kelly's Ford. Supports preservation; active in erecting monuments. Archives located at Jacksonville Public Library, Jacksonville, Ala.

PENN STATE ALUMNI ASSN.
814-865-7679
Mary Jane Stout
105 Old Main
Pennsylvania State University
University Park PA 16802-1501
Penn State-sanctioned lecturers & battlefield walking tours by leading historians/authors. Also available over the Internet. A continuing & distance education service.

PENNSYLVANIA
800-VISIT-PA x606
Full color guide to all the sites & attractions of historic Pennsylvania.

PETERSBURG VISITOR CENTER, OLD TOWNE
800-368-3595
804-733-2400
425 Cockade Alley
Petersburg VA 23803
Tourism info on the City of Petersburg & Lee's Retreat, one of 5 VA Civil War Trails.

TIMOTHY J. REESE
301-834-6261
118 E Main St
PO Box 458
Burkittsville MD 21718-0458
Crampton's Gap & South Mountain Battlefield tours - customized, individual or group, by author, historian & professional tour guide. Also tour sites peripheral to 1862 MD Campaign.

RICHMOND NEWSPAPERS SUPPLE MENTARY PUBLICATIONS
800-422-4434
PO Box 85333
Richmond VA 23293-5333
The Insider's Guide to the Civil War (Eastern Theater), Travel Guide - $9.95.

ROOTS & WINGS EXCURSIONS
800-722-9005
Walk in the footsteps of Civil War heroes. See the war's most important sites with expert guides. Gettysburg, Antietam, Richmond, more.

ROSEHILL CEMETERY
312-561-5940
5800 N Ravenswood Ave
Chicago IL 60660-3195
Self-paced & guided Civil War walking tours, visiting graves of 500 Union soldiers & sailors, incl. 14 generals.

SCHRIVER HOUSE
717-337-2800
309 Baltimore St • Gettysburg PA 17325-2602
Civil War House Tour of George Washington Schriver's private residence built in 1860. Presents civilian point of view.

SELBY HOUSE
540-373-7037
226 Princess Anne St
Fredericksburg VA 22401-6039
Four spacious rooms, private bath, full breakfasts. Official tour guide for battles of Fredericksburg, Chancellorsville, Wilderness, Spotsylvania Court Hse. Member APCWS.

STEAMBOATIN' VACATIONS
800-214-2579
Travel America's rivers on 3-14 night steamboating cruise. Free brochure.

STONEWALL JACKSON HOUSE
540-463-2552 • 540-463-4088 Fax
http://www.stonewalljackson.org
Michael A. Lynn
8 E Washington St • Lexington VA 24450
The Confederate general's only home with restored garden & museum shop. Tours every half hour Mon-Sat 9-5, Sun 1-5; last tour begins 4:30PM. Open until 6PM June-August (last tour 5:30PM). Closed major holidays.

SURRATT HOUSE MUSEUM & GIFT SHOP
301-868-1121 • 301-868-8177 Fax
http://www.clark.net/pub/surratt/surratt.html
Laurie Verge, Director
PO Box 427 • 9118 Brandywine Rd
Clinton MD 20735-0427
1852 home of Surratt family. Served also as tavern, hostelry, post office & link in Confederate spy network. Played role in Lincoln assassination. Offsite bus tours. (See ad page 258)

TENNESSEE ANTEBELLUM TRAIL
931-486-9055 • 800-381-1865
5700 Main St
Spring Hill TN 37174
90-mile, self-driving tour encompassing more than 54 historic sites & Civil War battlefields.

TIME TRAVELERS ANTIQUES
717-337-0011
http://www.tias.com/stores/gettysburg
gettysburg@mail.wideopen.net
312 Baltimore St
Gettysburg PA 17325-2601
Fine general line of quality Americana, collectibles & decorative arts in ca.1901 Victorian house. Costumed Civil War walking tours of Old Baltimore Street sites.

M. TRACEY TODD
803-571-6036
mttodd@mindspring.com
Walk Charleston, SC - the "cradle of secession" - with local historian & museum administrator.

TRAVEL AMERICA, INC.
800-225-2553
131 Dodge St Ste 5
Beverly MA 01915-1861
Seminars & trips on such topics as the American Revolution, the Old West, the Civil War, American History. Contact for info.

VALENTINE RIVERSIDE
800-365-7272
550 E Marshall St
Richmond VA 23219-1852
Richmond's innovative history park at the falls of the James River. Civil War tours, sound/light show, vintage carousel, high-tech exhibits, African-American history/tours, archeological digs, living history.

VICKSBURG CONVENTION & VISITORS BUREAU
800-221-3536
601-636-4642 Hayes Latham
http://www.vicksburg.org/cvb
PO Box 110
Vicksburg MS 39181-0110
Annual March "Run Through History" through Vicksburg NMP. 10K race, 5K walk, 1-mile run. Refreshments, music.

VIRGINIA CIVIL WAR TRAILS
888-CIVIL WAR
Tourism info on the 5 VA Civil War Trails, Lee's Retreat, Lee vs. Grant, & Overland Campaign.

VIRGINIA DIVISION OF TOURISM
800-321-1865
804-371-8164
804-786-1919 Fax
http://www.VIRGINIA.org
901 E Byrd St
Richmond VA 23219-4069
Call for free Civil War brochure, "Virginia Is for Lovers" travel guide & state highway map.

WAYFARING TRAVELERS
410-666-7456
http://www.gorp.com/wayfaring
Elizabeth Coxe
27 Sunnyview Dr
Phoenix MD 21131-2036
Walking tours along the backroads & hidden corners of historic Shenandoah Valley & colonial Virginia.

WHITE ELEPHANT B&B INN
901-925-6410
http://www.bbonline.com/tn/elephant
Sharon & Ken Hansgen
304 Church St
Savannah TN 38372-2014
Victorian home, 10 miles to Shiloh battlefield. Full breakfasts, private baths. Owner leads guided tours of Shiloh & nearby Civil War sites.

WILSON'S CREEK NATL. BATTLEFIELD
417-732-2662
6424 W Farm Rd 182
Highway ZZ
Republic MO 65738
Site of 1861 battle. Exhibits, tours, visitor's center with 13-min. film. Admission - $2/person or $4/car. Open year-round.

WINCHESTER-FREDERICK CO. VISITORS CENTER
540-662-4135
1360 S Pleasant Valley Rd
Winchester VA 22601-4447

YANKEE FLEET DRY TORTUGAS NATIONAL PARK FERRY
800-634-0939
305-294-7009
PO Box 5903
Key West FL 33045-5903
Cruise to remote Fort Jefferson, Union military prison that housed Dr. Samuel Mudd, aboard air-conditioned 100' yacht. Complimentary breakfast, lunch, guided tour.

7TH REGIMENT, TEXAS VOLUNTEER BRIGADE
303-221-3099
Capt. E. Roy Jordan
300 E Harmony Rd
Fort Collins CO 80525-3237
Civil War gun club to promote family fun through black powder shooting & safety.

THE AMERICAN HISTORICAL FOUNDATION
800-368-8080 • 804-353-1812
804-359-4895 Fax
http://www.ahfrichmond.com
1142 W Grace St
Richmond VA 23220-3613
Firing reproductions of Lee's 1851 Navy Revolver (Limited). Colt's 34d Model Dragoon Revolvers, Jackson LeMat, JEB Stuart Le Mat, Lee/Grant Henry Rifles, etc.

DALE C. ANDERSON CO.
4 W Confederate Ave
Gettysburg PA 17325
Firearms, edged weapons, uniforms, accoutrements, & 1000s of other objects touching all periods & significant events, 1776-1945. Emphasis on Civil War era. Our 37th year. Photo-illus. militaria catalog issued bi-monthly - $12/yr.

ANDERSONVILLE ANTIQUES
912-924-2558
912-924-1044
Peggy & Fred Sheppard
PO Box 26
Andersonville GA 31711-0026
Authentic Civil War guns, swords, buttons, documents; books on the Civil War.

ANTIQUE AMERICAN FIREARMS
847-304-GUNS
PO Box 1861
Barrington IL 60011-1861
Civil War weapons search - match your weapon's serial number with our database to identify issuance. Annual membership.

THE ARTILLERYMAN
800-777-1862
802-889-3500
802-889-5627 Fax
firetec@firetec.com attn.artilleryman
RR 1 Box 36, Monarch Hill Rd
Tunbridge VT 05077-9707
Quarterly magazine dealing with artillery, 1750-1898. Safety, places to visit, history, workshops, & more. $18/yr. Sample - $2.

ATLANTA ARSENAL
6005 State Bridge Rd Apt 1434
Duluth GA 30097-6463
Reproduction Confederate painted canvas accoutrements, copy from originals, incl. cartridge boxes, cap boxes, bayonet scabbards, slings, belts. Free price list.

ATLANTA CUTLERY CORP.
800-883-0300 • 770-388-0246 Fax
PO Box 839
2143 Gees Mill Rd
Conyers GA 30013-0839
Knives, Civil War swords, exotic & historical edged weapons, knifemaking supplies & many exclusives.

AUTAUGA ARMS, INC.
800-262-9563 • 331-361-2950
331-361-2931 Fax
817 S Memorial Dr
Prattville AL 36067-5734
Brass tube scope, 6x15 magnification. Scope length 382 mm. $149.95 + $10.95 S&H includes mounts.

BATTLEFIELD VIDEO PRODUCTIONS
6374 Larch Ln
Macungie PA 18062-9380
Civil War guns video. 47-min. video of the guns of the Civil War, their makers, & those who used them. Live fire demonstration. $29.95 ppd.

ROBERT L. BAXTER
1207 Nettie Dr
Miamisburg OH 45342-3428
New muzzleloader brass castings, parts, & supplies. Dealer inquiries invited. Catalog - $2.

BELL CONSULTING, INC.
352-753-0219
Ted & Pat Bell
PO Box 579 • Lady Lake FL 32158-0579
Antique handguns, Bowie knives, cartridge belts & holsters, rifles, deringers, swords. Buy/sell/trade. Catalog - send #10 SASE.

BELLINGER'S MILITARY ANTIQUES
770-992-5574
Bill Bellinger
PO Box 76371-SB
Atlanta GA 30358-1371
FULL-TIME DEALER of antique firearms, edged weapons, belt plates, leather goods, books & miscellaneous from the 17th-19th century. Civil War a specialty. Catalog - $3; 4 issues - $10 (overseas - $20).

BLACK CREEK GUN SHOP
540-888-3349
863 Chestnut Grove Rd
Winchester VA 22603
Black powder & percussion caps at huge savings. Musket caps, pistol caps, rifle & cannon powder. Can be shipped by UPS with certain limitations.

BLACKSWORD ARMOURY, INC.
352-495-9967
102 Depot Rd
Hawthorne FL 32640-5613
Replicas of historical weapons & armor from ancient to Civil War. Catalog - $3.

THE BLADESMITH
George M. Sweeney
171 Dean St
Mansfield MA 02048-2421
Handcrafted frontier & Native American knives. Copper-bladed knives, battlefield daggers, custom Bowies, Civil War Bowies, all with sheathes - $90-$200. For more info, send $1 & SASE.

BORDER STATES LEATHERWORKS
501-361-2642
501-361-2851 Fax
1158 Apple Blossom Ln
Springdale AR 72762-9762
Civil War collectibles, original weapons & equipment. Reproduction cavalry saddles & equipment. Custom hand-forged bits.

BOWDOIN EXPLOSIVES, INC.
207-737-2630
RR 1 Box 1799
Litchfield ME 04350-9601
Elephant black powder - now 10% faster burning with easy pour tin spouts. Supply your event with the best. Call for pricing.

BOXER GALLERY & FRAME CO.
330-494-2348 Ph & Fax
PO Box 2362
North Canton OH 44720-0362
Prints by Troiani, Kunstler, Strain. Mounted officers (15"H) & other Gettysburg figures (9"H) in full color. Free list of swords, bayonets, belts, buckles, insignia.

WILLIAM H. BOYDEN
198 W Plumstead Ave
Lansdowne PA 19050-1307
Hand-rolled & tied cartridge tubes made from Frankford Arsenal pattern; paper matches close to original color. 20 tubes - $5 + $2 S&H.

WALTER BUDD
3109 Eubanks Rd • Durham NC 27707-3622
Finest selection of US military antiques, firearms, swords, uniforms, head gear, cavalry equipment, McClellan saddles, mess gear, horse-drawn army wagons & rolling stock, etc. Subscription rate - $5 for 8 issues.

CALDWELL & CO. COLLECTIBLES
765-482-6280
civilwr@in-motion.net
816 Pleasant St • Lebanon IN 46052-2853
Edged weapons, firearms, Civil War items & general antiques. Buy/sell. Free catalog.

KEITH CANGELOSI
4201 Frenchman St
New Orleans LA 70122-3839
Civil War military antiques. Longarms, carbines, handguns, edged weapons. List - $2.

CANNON, LTD.
740-667-6896
http://www.florentine.com/cannonltd
25249 W Hornsby Rd • Coolville OH 45723
1/8 through full-scale cannons - 150 firing models, bronze & steel-lined ductiles & solid steel barrels. Museum kiln-dried oak carriages. Video & catalog - $12. (See ad page 271)

THE CANNONADE
PO Box 20601 • Rochester NY 14602-0601
Nice Boom: The Amerian Civil War Artillery Reenactor's Handbook, Sean McAdoo, ed. 100+ pp., including drill, living history, tactics, NCO training & more. $10.95 + $3 S&H.

CARTRIDGES UNLIMITED
314-664-4332
Mike Watson
4320 Hartford St # A
Saint Louis MO 63116-1917
Cartridges - blank, dummy & live; tubes; labels; trapezoids for rifle, carbine & pistol. Authentically rolled. Catalog - free w/ SASE.

CHATTAHOOCHEE B.P.S. CO.
770-889-6738
PO Box 2543 • Cumming GA 30028-6506
Colt muskets! N-SSA approved.

CIVIL WAR ANTIQUES
419-878-8355 • 419-882-5547
David W. Taylor
PO Box 87 • Sylvania OH 43560-0087
Pedigreed Civil War antiques, guns, swords, uniforms, buckles, flags, drums, letters, diaries, etc. Bought/sold. Catalog - $10.

CIVIL WAR EMPORIUM, INC.
408 Mill St • Occoquan VA 22125
From harmonicas to working cannons. Working repros. Decorator models. Consignments welcome. Buy/sell.

CIVIL WAR STORE
504-522-3328
212 Chartres St
New Orleans LA 70130-2215
Mail order catalog - weapons, currency, bonds, stamps, letters, diaries, CDVs, prints, slave broadsides & bills of sale, autographs, photos. Catalog - $4.

COLLECTOR'S ARMOURY
800-544-3456 x515 • 703-684-6111
703-683-5486 Fax • James W. Hernly
PO Box 59, Dept CWB
Alexandria VA 22313-0059
Full line of "non-firing" reproduction pistols, rifles, cannons, Civil War swords, knives, bayonets, canteens, cap boxes, bugles & flags. Free catalog.

COLLECTORS HERITAGE, INC.
PO Box 355 • Bernardsville NJ 07924-0355
Reproduction museum-quality military swords, knives, & bayonets. Catalog - $5 (ref.).

COLT BLACKPOWDER ARMS CO.
718-499-4678
718-768-8056 Fax
110 8th St
Brooklyn NY 11215
Genuine Colt revolvers, muskets & accessories; signature series. The tradition lives on! Free catalog.

COLUMBUS ARMORY
706-327-1424 Ph & Fax
David S. Brady
1104 Broadway
Columbus GA 31901-2429
Complete Civil War store featuring books, relics, art, muskets & supplies. Buy/sell/trade. Free price list.

COMPANY QUARTERMASTER
716-693-3239 • 716-693-3237 Fax
Terry Schultz
258 Zimmerman St
North Tonawanda NY 14120-4509
Enfield 3-band, bright barrel, lock & bands, Italian markings removed, 1860s proofs, 1862 TOWER lock, BSAT stock cartouch, stock darkened, square-eared screw escutcheons & more. $455 + $10 S&H.

DAVID CONDON, INC.
540-687-5642
800-364-8416 Orders only
540-687-5649 Fax
PO Box 7
Middleburg VA 20118-0007
Dealing in fine antique firearms since 1957. Store located at 109 E Washington St (Route 50), Middleburg, Va.

THE CONESTOGA CO., INC.
800-987-BANG (2264)
PO Box 405
Bethlehem PA 18016-0405
Carbide cannons from 9" to 25", starting at $49.95 ppd. Free catalog.

CONFEDERATE STATES ARSENAL
910-960-2466
Robert M. Schaber
1305 Spring Ave
Spring Lake NC 28390-2239
Antique artillery reproductions, sights, accessories, parts. Full-scale only. Restorations, work on original cannons. Free catalog.

CRITTENDEN SCHMITT ARCHIVES
http://www.erols.com/tyrannus/archives/csavideo.html
PO Box 4253 / Courthouse Station
Rockville MD 20849-4253
Technical & historical books & videotapes relating to weapons & ammunition of all types & eras.

DEAD HORSE FORGE
1220 Price Station Rd
Church Hill MD 21623-1315
All types of knives, Hawks & other ironware, powder horns & gourd canteens. Brochure - send SASE.

DR. K. DIETRICH
PO Box 994
Stockbridge MA 01262-0994
Buy/sell Civil War memorabilia, soldiers' letters, weapons & accoutrements, images. Listing - 2 stamps.

DIXIE GUN WORKS, INC.
800-238-6785 Orders only
901-885-0700 • 901-885-0440 Fax
PO Box 130
Union City TN 38281-0130
The source for firearms, parts, shooting supplies, leather goods, uniforms, books, patterns & cannons. 600-pg catalog with more than 8,000 items - $5.

DIXIE LEATHER WORKS
502-442-1058 • 800-888-5183 Orders only
502-448-1049 Fax
PO Box 8221 • Paducah KY 42002-8221
Military & civilian museum-quality repros. 60+ hard-to-find leather items. Documents, maps, printed labels & stationery. Swords, firearms, & hats. Handmade chairs, desks; leather medical cases & bottle roll-up kits. Photo- illus. catalog - $6.

R. STEPHEN DORSEY ANTIQUE MILITARIA
541-937-3348
PO Box 263 • Eugene OR 97440-0263
Largest western dealer in pre- & post-Civil War, Civil War, & post-1900 U.S. militaria. Guns, accoutrements, edged weapons, etc. Catalog - $8 for 4 issues.

DONALD DREW
PO Box 422
Stillwater MN 55082-0422
Basic training video for the beginner. Directly from Harde's. Professional production. All facings, rifle movements, load/fire procedure, etc. VHS - $27 ppd.

DRUMMER BOY AMERICAN MILITARIA
717-296-7611
Christian Hill Rd
RR 4 Box 7198
Milford PA 18337-9713
Civil War repro goods: uniforms, buttons, leather goods, insignia, firearms, tinware, canteens, flags, books, blankets, sabers, etc. Catalog - $1.

DYNAMIT NOBEL-RWS, INC.
81 Ruckman Rd
Closter NJ 07624-2102
Caps for muzzleloaders. Ignites black powder & substitutes non-corrosive, non-erosive, non-mercuric, & non-toxic. A cap to fit any black-powder gun.

EITNIER RIFLES
765-798-3525
Jerry Eitnier
PO Box 125
Hillsboro IN 47949-0125
Iron-mounted Southern guns.

ELF HOLLOW FORGE
910-763-7903
504 Woodlawn Ave
Wilmington NC 28401-7226
Hand-forged knives & tomahawks. Replica & original design. Color photo brochure - $2.

FALL CREEK SUTTLERY
765-482-1861
765-482-1848 Fax
http://fcsutler.com
AJF5577@aol.com or fcsutler@aol.com
Andy Fulks
PO Box 92
Whitestown IN 46075-0092
Authentic reproduction Civil War & mid-19th-century uniforms, leather goods, weapons, shoes, tents, insignia, reference books & more. 32-pg catalog - $3. (See ad page 271)

FIREARMS SKIRMISH NATIONAL COMPETITION
North-South Skirmish Assn.
Winchester VA
More than 3,600 competitors on 200 teams competing with muskets, carbines, revolvers, mortars & cannon. Largest event of its kind. Sutlers, food, free admission. Annual event - May.

N. FLAYDERMAN & CO., INC.
305-761-8855
PO Box 2446
Fort Lauderdale FL 33303-2446
Antique guns, swords, & knives. Nautical, western & military collectibles from Revolutionary through Spanish-American wars. Catalog - $15.

THE FLINTLOCK ROOM
201-543-1861 • 201-543-1865 Fax
http://www.flintlockroom.com
6 Hilltop Rd
Mendham NJ 07945-1238
Collectibles for Connoisseurs - classic firearms, fine cigars, military figurines, prints & militaria, Victorian miniatures.

FRAZER BROTHERS' 17TH REGIMENT
214-696-1865 • 214-426-4230 Fax
5641 Yale Blvd Ste 125
Dallas TX 75206-5026
Uniforms & equipment, artillery hardware, & side arms. Civilian clothing (men only). Handmade leather goods. Large supply of tinware. Boots. American products.

GOEX, INC.
318-382-9300
PO Box 659 • Doyline LA 71023-0659
Last American manufacturer of authentic black powder for reenactors, target shooters, hunting & competition. Goex black powder (FFg). Quality & consistency to make every shot your best shot.

WILL GORGES CIVIL WAR MILITARIA
919-636-3039 • 919-637-1862 Fax
http://www.collectorsnet.com/gorges/index.htm
rebel!@abaco.coastalnet.com
2100 Trent Blvd • New Bern NC 28560-5326
Largest active inventory of authentic items in the Southeast. Fine quality uniforms & weapons our specialty. Buy/sell/appraise/broker. Catalog - $10.

GREEN RIVER TRADING CORP.
502-531-3115 Ph & Fax
ekelle@scrtc.net
PO Box 2 • Bonnieville KY 42713-0002
Original & repro Civil War relics, clothing, weapons.

GREY OWL INDIAN CRAFT SALES CORP.
718-341-4000 • 718-527-6000 Fax
Wes Cochrane
13205 Merrick Blvd • PO Box 340468
Jamaica NY 11434-0468
Green River knives, powder flasks, military buttons, buckskin, leathers, dags, strikers, books, tapes, videos, recordings, etc. 200 custom kits/4000+ items. Catalog - $3.

THE GUN REPORT
309-582-5311
309-582-5555 Fax
John Mullen
PO Box 38
Aledo IL 61231-0038
The new *Gun Report Index* - your guide to 35 years of collectible firearm history. 128 pp., $24.95 + $3.50 S&H.

DENNIS HEATH
919-569-8781
RR 1 Box 55A • Deep Run NC 28525
Civil War weapons, relics, accoutrements. Catalog - $7/yr.

HILLBILLY SPORTS, INC.
410-378-4533
PO Box 70
Conowingo MD 21918-0070
Leather goods, period firearms, uniform items, camp items & much more. Catalog - $3.

HISTORIC FRAMING & COLLECTIBLES
410-465-0549
Joe Parr
8344 Main St • Ellicott City MD 21043-4653
Civil War weaponry & assorted items. Military art by all major artists, including aviation & WWII. True conservation-quality framing.

HISTORIC MIDWAY MUSEUM STORE
606-846-4214
PO Box 4592
124 E Railroad St
Midway KY 40347-4592
Civil War newspapers, books on Kentucky. Scale model cannons.

THE HORSE SOLDIER
717-334-0347
717-334-5016 Fax
http://www.bmark.com/horsesoldier.antiques
hsoldier@mail.wideopen.net
PO Box 184
Cashtown PA 17310-0184
Buying, selling & appraising Civil War military antiques: firearms, edged weapons, photographs, documents, battlefield relics & more! All items unconditionally guaranteed. Soldier research service available. Semi-annual catalog - $10/yr.

THE HOUSE OF TIMES PAST
864-834-0061
634 W Darby Rd
Greenville SC 29609-7121
Period shop with authentic clothing, rifles, muzzleloading supplies & accessories for living historians & reenactors. Catalog - $2.

HUNTERDON IMPORTING CO.
304-728-7730
PO Box 187
192 High St
Harpers Ferry WV 25425-0187
Engraved swords - US Foot Officer's & CSA Cavalry Officer's.

JACQUES NOEL JACOBSEN, JR.
718-981-0973
60 Manor Rd
Staten Island NY 10310-2626
Antiques & military collectibles, insignia, weapons, medals, uniforms, Kepis, relics, photos, paintings, & band instruments. Catalog - $12 for 3 issues. $15 overseas.

JAMES COUNTRY MERCANTILE
816-781-9473
816-781-1470 Fax
JAMESCNTRY@aol.com
Del Warren or Michael Gooch
111 N Main St
Liberty MO 64068-1639
For your military & civilian reenacting needs - weapons, accoutrements, clothing, patterns. Illus. catalog - $6 ppd.

GORDON WILSON JENKS & CO.
800-835-7933
Goex black powder - all granulations, incl. authentic new cartridge powder.

JOHN'S RELICS
843-549-7751
cwrelics@lowcountry.com
John Steele
227 Robertson Blvd
Walterboro SC 29488-2752
Civil War & colonial relics, arms accoutrements, veteran memorabilia, newspapers, books, CW tokens, photography, buttons & related memorabilia. Catalog - $1 (ref. w/ purchase).

K & P VALLEY COLLECTIBLES
540-635-8564
499 Osprey Ln
Front Royal VA 22630-8336
Original, Civil War excavated relics & artifacts, incl. weapons & newspapers. Specialize in original Harper's Weekly issues. List available.

KAWARTHA MARKETING COMPANY
705-639-2572
705-639-1809 Fax
RR 1 Station W
Norwood Ontario, KOL 2VO Canada
Firearms, cannons, knives, helmets, bayonets, daggers, swords, surplus, uniforms, etc. Including originals that have seen battle. Catalog - $4 (ref. w/ order).

KINGSTON MILITARY ANTIQUES
770-336-9354
Jerelhook@aol.com
Jere Hook
PO Box 217 • Kingston GA 30145-0217
Buy/sell/trade pre-1898 militaria, mostly Civil War. By appt. only. Catalog - 32¢.

L & G EARLY ARMS
2049 Clermont Laurel Rd
New Richmond OH 45157-9557
Authentic Civil War guns. Free list w/ business-size SASE.

GEORGE LAYMAN
55 Littleton Rd Apt 24F
Ayer MA 01432-1762
1866 Peabody Breech-Loading Rifle Catalog, new repro. *Rolling Block Rifle* and *A Guide to the Maynard Breech Loader*. Single shot books.

LEGEND PRODUCTS CORPORATION
21218 Saint Andrews Blvd
Boca Raton FL 33433-2435
"Black Canyon Powder" solves the problem of sulfur corrosion & fouling. Direct weight-for-weight replacement for black powder.

LEGENDARY ARMS, INC.
800-528-2767
908-788-7330
908-788-8522 Fax
PO Box 479
Three Bridges NJ 08887-0479
Museum-quality, authentic duplication. Finest repros: swords, knives, battle axe, & bugle, uniforms of the Civil War.

LEGENDARY ARMS, INC.
800-875-7967
212-532-ARMS
Greeley Square Station
PO Box 20198
New York NY 10001-9992
High-quality reproduction swords, sabers, spurs, entrenching tools, bayonets, cutlasses. Officers', Cav., NCOs, etc. Call for price list.

LODGEWOOD MFG.
414-473-5444
414-473-8970 Fax
William V. Osborne II
494 Ventura Ln
Whitewater WI 53190-1500
Civil War guns & parts. United States martial arms 1780-1898.

LOG CABIN SHOP
800-837-1082
330-948-1082
330-948-4307 Fax
http://www.logcabinshop.com
logcabin@logcabinshop.com
8010 Lafayette Rd
PO Box 275
Lodi OH 44254-0275
Full line of muzzleloading guns, kits, components, supplies, accessories, books, cookware, blankets, etc. 200-pp. catalog - $5.

HARDIE MALONEY
504-522-3328
212 Chartres St
New Orleans LA 70130-2215
Civil War store. Confederate currency, bonds, stamps, covers, CDV.s, letters, diaries, documents, autographs, pistols & swords.

MARILL PRODUCTIONS
PO Box 460820
San Francisco CA 94146-0820
Video documentaries on Colt revolvers (1836-1869) & Bowie knives (1820-1870), in-depth, exquisite. $29.95 ea. or both for $45.

JOSEPH L. MARTIN
1125 Kennesaw Springs Ct
Kennesaw GA 30144
Buying, selling, trading fine Civil War swords, guns, uniforms, flags, etc. Over 35 yrs of experience in dealing military items. Competent appraisals available.

MATUSZEK'S
847-253-4685 • Frank Matuszek
126 E Wing St # 210
Arlington Heights IL 60004-6064
Civil War & Indian War firearms, swords, uniforms & other collectibles. Sample catalog - $2. Mention the Civil War Source Book!

MERCURY SUPPLY CO.
409-327-3707
101 Lee St • Livingston TX 77351-4226
Civil War uniforms, reproduction equipment, tents, accoutrements, leather goods, firearms military & civilian. Catalog - $2.

MILES OF HISTORY (CIVIL WAR AUCTION)
423-337-2540
http://www.collectorsnet.com/miles
huskey@usit.net
Miles Huskey
PO Box 599 • Sweetwater TN 37874-0599
Buy/sell/trade Civil War items. Images, buttons, weapons, documents, personal items, & authentic period jewelry available through internet auction on website.

THE MILITARY COLLECTION
PO Box 830970M • Miami FL 33283-0970
Helmets, uniforms, field gear, awards, medals, flags, weapons, swords, photos, etc. Cat. $8.

MOUNTAIN STATE MUZZLELOADING SUPPLIES, INC.
800-445-1776
304-375-7842
304-375-3737 Fax
Terry Lambert
RR 2 Box 154-1 Dept CW
Williamstown WV 26187-9540
Everything for muzzleloading hunters, shooters, & builders. Guns, parts, shooting/cleaning supplies, casting supplies, books, bags, etc. Catalog - $4 (ref.).

MUSEUM OF AMERICAN CAVALRY
540-740-3959
Peter & Jane Comtois
298 Old Cross Rd
New Market VA 22844
History of the Horse Soldier from colonial times through Vietnam & modern times. Gift shop with books, flags, weapons, relics, other items. Formerly Indian Hollow Antiques.

MUSEUM OF HISTORICAL ARMS, INC.
2750 Coral Way Ste 204
Miami FL 33145-3200
Catalog-reference book contains more than 1600 imported items for sale. Firearms & edged weapons, all periods. Catalog - $10.

MUSEUM REPLICAS LIMITED
800-883-8838
770-388-0246 Fax
PO Box 840
2143 Gees Mill Rd
Conyers GA 30012-0840
Reproductions of authentic museum quality, historically accurate replicas of weapons & period battle wear. Catalog - $3.

NAVY ARMS CO.
201-945-2500
689 Bergen Blvd
Ridgefield NJ 07657-1499
Finest in quality replica firearms. Revolvers, Sharps rifles & carbines, Enfields, leather goods.

NESHANIC DEPOT
610-847-5627
610-847-8618 Fax
283 Durham Rd
PO Box 367
Ottsville PA 18942-0367
Historic artifacts, muzzleloading guns & supplies, originals, reproductions, & historic flags.

NMC ENTERPRISES
800-591-2999 (24 hrs.)
913 18th St Apt 2
Santa Monica CA 90403-3251
Civil War blackpowder accessories; fine, handcrafted leather. Holsters, belts, pouches, bags, buckles. Free catalog.

THE NOBEL COLLECTION
800-806-6253
PO Box 3444
Merrifield VA 22116-3444
Historic reproductions & collectible swords. From King Arthur to Samurai. Free catalog.

OLD SOUTH MILITARY ANTIQUES
919-523-7181
Dennis Heath
403A E New Bern Rd
Kinston NC 28504-6737
Full line of Civil War muskets, swords, accoutrements & artifacts at reasonable prices. Shop open Mon-Sat. Catalog - $7/yr.

OLD SUTLER JOHN
607-775-4434 Ph & Fax
Westview Station • PO Box 174
Binghamton NY 13905-0174
Full line of quality reproduction Civil War guns, bayonets, swords, uniforms, leather items, & other collectibles. Cat. $3. (See ad page 260)

OSAGE PRESS
815-398-0602
PO Box 5082 • Rockford IL 61125-0082
Repro of 1860 Spencer Repeating Rifle Patent Drawings - start at $13.95. Free catalog.

PALADIN PRESS
800-392-2400
http://www.paladin-press.com • pala@rmii.com
Tina Mills
PO Box 1307 • Boulder CO 80306-1307
American Swords and Sword Makers. Definitive book for all edged weapons. Collectors, dealers, etc. 664 pp. - $79.95. Catalog - $2.

PAULSON BROS. ORDINANCE CORP.
715-263-3300
715-263-3301 Fax
PO Box 121
Clear Lake WI 54005-0121
Limber & chest parts.

PENINSULA FIREARMS
813-547-6471 • 813-547-6175 Fax
7116 78th St
Pinellas Park FL 33781-3733
Civil War reproduction muskets, revolvers & accessories. Catalog - $3.

PETRO-EXPLO, INC.
800-588-8282 • 817-478-8888
817-478-8891 Fax
http://www.fastlane.net/~petro
petro@fastlane.net
7650 US Hwy 287 #100
Arlington TX 76017
Elephant black powder for use in Flintlock/Caplock rifles & shotguns. Performs excellently in rifles & shotguns in all weather conditions.

THE PICKET POST
540-371-7703
Tim Garrett & Bill Henderson
602 Caroline St
Fredericksburg VA 22401-5902
Civil War military antiques: canteens, buttons, swords, guns, images, buckles, uniforms. Buys/sells. Photo-illus. catalog - $10 for 3 issues.

PLAINESMAN GUN SHOP
24101 Empire Ave
Tomah WI 54660-4265
Civil War & Indian War rifles & carbines. No mail order, so stop in & see the Plainesman Gun Shop.

POWDER HORNS
PO Box 397
Fletcher OH 45326-0397
Make powder horns from start to finish, including engraving them for your use, gifts, display, or sale - $12.95.

R & R BOOKS
716-346-2577
3020 E Lake Rd
Livonia NY 14487
Books on weapons, featuring *The British Soldier's Firearm*, *Spencer Repeating Firearms*, *Confederate Edged Weapons*, etc.

RAPINE BULLET MANUFACTURING CO.
215-679-5413
9503 Landis Ln
East Greenville PA 18041-2541
Civil War bullet molds. Catalog - $2.

RED BULL ANTIQUES
304-535-2259
staneagl@intrepid.net
Stan Hadden
PO Box 131
Harpers Ferry WV 25425-0131
Civil War bullets, swords, muskets, pistols, buttons, belt buckles, etc. Original Schneider & Glassick Revolver.

THE REGIMENTAL QUARTERMASTER
215-672-6891
215-672-9020 Fax
PO Box 553
Hatboro PA 19040-0553
Civil War repro muskets, carbines, revolvers, swords, uniforms, shoes, boots, buckles, buttons, tents, tapes, tinware, equipment, accoutrements, accessories. Catalog - $2 ($1 ref.).

RICHMOND ARSENAL
804-272-4570 Ph & Fax
7605 Midlothian Tpke
Richmond VA 23235-5223
100% authentic Civil War antiques, from common bullets & buttons to museum quality weapons, accoutrements, uniforms, drums & flags. Photo-illus. catalog - $10 for 3 issues.

L. ROMANO'S RIFLE CO.
315-695-2066
551 Stewarts Corners Rd
Pennellville NY 13132-3234
Quality reproduction Spencers rifle & carbine 1860 models, 56/50 cal. Machined action & parts made in NY. Free catalog.

S & S FIREARMS
718-497-1100 • 718-497-1105 Fax
7411 Myrtle Ave • Glendale NY 11385-7433
Military Americana. Antique gun parts, carbines, Enfield, buttons, insignia, books, equipment, appendages, headdress, etc. Reenactor supplies. Original & reproduction. Photo-illus. catalog - $3.

SCHNEIDER ENTERPRISES
414-534-6813
1252 N Browns Lake Dr
Burlington WI 53105-9794
Lowest prices, high quality on Civil War field & naval-style cannons, & Gatling guns. Cat.$2.

SCHOOLHOUSE ANTIQUES
717-334-4564 • Gettysburg PA 17325
Antique guns, relics, swords, uniforms, souvenirs. Close to battlefield - 5 mi. on Business Rt. 15 South.

SHARPSBURG ARSENAL
301-432-7700 • 301-432-7440 Fax
101 W Main St • PO Box 568
Sharpsburg MD 21782-0568
Purveyors of fine Civil War militaria; firearms, edged weapons, buttons, bullets, leather accoutrements, battlefield relics, books, flags, personal & camp items, paper, letters, framed prints. Buy/sell. (See ad page 264)

THE SINGLE SHOT EXCHANGE MAGAZINE
803-628-5326 Ph & Fax
singleshotex@earthlink.net
PO Box 1055 • Dept B • York SC 29745-1055
Monthly magazine for black powder cartridge, silhouette & Schuetzen shooters, & antique gun collectors. Buy/sell/trade, historical & how-to articles. Antique & classic firearms only - $27.50/yr. V/MC accepted.

DALE S. SNAIR
660-747-0341
904 Deer Run Apt C
Warrensburg MO 64093-8633
Civil War images, paper items, weapons, accoutrements. $4 for next 4 price lists.

SOUTH BEND REPLICAS, INC.
219-289-4500
61650 Oak Rd
South Bend IN 46614-9345
Antique ordnance replicas since 1972. Solid cast, machine bored, sleeved & lathe turned. 128-pg., 1200-photo catalog - $7. Brochure only - SASE.

STAFFORD WHEEL & CARRIAGE
610-486-0567
Jeff Stafford
1019 Lieds Rd
Coatesville PA 19320-4837
Restoration & reproduction of Civil War cannon carriages, wheels, & rolling stock.

STARS & BARS MILITARY ANTIQUES
540-972-1863
9832 Plank Rd
Spotsylvania VA 22553-4243
Civil War militaria: edged weapons, uniforms, accoutrements, medals, weaponry, prints, etc. On Chancellorsville battlefield, est. 1976.

STEEN CANNONS
606-329-2477
http://www.wwd.net/steen
steencannons@wwd.net
10730 Midland Trail Rd
Ashland KY 41102-9679
Authentic, full-scale reproductions. All barrels cast solid, machine bored, sleeved, & lathe-turned. Several models from which to choose. Manufacturer of cannon carriages, limbers & cannon & limber hardware.

STONE EAGLE PRESS
209-661-4030
PO Box 838
Madera CA 93639-0838
Manual of arms for the rifle & musket, from original text (*U.S. Infantry & Rifle Tactics, 1861*) - $10.25.

STONEMAN TREASURERS
PO Box 15309
Philadelphia PA 19111-0309
Musket & trapdoor Springfield parts. Affordable historical collectibles, incl. bayonets, swords, tools, relics, etc. 6-pg. list - $1 + stamp.

SWORD & SABER
717-334-0205
2159 Baltimore Pike
Gettysburg PA 17325-7015
Specializing in original Confederate & Union documents, framed items, relics, weapons & swords. 5 illus. catalogs - $10.

THEME PRINTS, LTD.
800-CIVL WAR • 718-225-4067
PO Box 610123 • Bayside NY 11361-0123
Books, antique arms, historic documents, photographs, letters & autographs from Revolutionary era to early Hollywood. Includes Civil War memorabilia. Fully illus. catalog - $5, or $12/yr. (5 issues).

TIPPECANOE FRONTIER TRADING CO.
937-667-1816
114 E Main St • Tipp City OH 45371-1962
Thousands of items serving reenactors, hunters, history buffs. Gunsmith for restorations, information, minor repairs (1700s-1900s). Long-range shooting supplies. Cat.$4.

UPPER MISSISSIPPI VALLEY MERCANTILE CO
319-322-0896 • 319-383-5549 Fax
1607 Washington St
Davenport IA 52804-3613
Top quality goods & supplies for Civil War reenactors; uniforms, tinware, tents, leather goods, muskets, books, weapons, patterns, more. 100-pp., illus. catalog - $3.

W.M.B. BLACK POWDER REPLICAS
314-631-1514
PO Box 6952 • Saint Louis MO 63123-0252
The Yorktown Mortar Kit, 1/10th scale replica, barrel is 3" long with 1" bore. Walnut wood with brass hardware - $50. Catalog - $2.

WARNER LIMITED
800-371-9373
19 Seekonk Rd
Great Barrington MA 01230-1562
"Genovese: Civil War Gun series" prints. All prints shipped flat.

WHITACRE'S MACHINE SHOP
540-877-1468
519 Turtle Meadow Dr
Winchester VA 22602-1986
Rifle barrels; fit original stocks. 1842, 1855-1863 Spring, 2-Band, Carbine. Enfield barrels - Parkerhale style, Mississippi & Zouave barrels. 3-land groove, tapered depth rifling. Breech plugs. N-SSA approved.

WILDMAN'S CIVIL WAR SURPLUS
770-422-1785
2879 S Main St
Kennesaw GA 30144-5624
Rare & antique guns, books, & other Civil War collectibles. Price list - $2. (See ad page 258)

THE WINCHESTER SUTLER, INC.
540-888-3595
540-888-4632 Fax
270 Shadow Brook Ln
Winchester VA 22603-2071
Reproduction Civil War firearms, uniforms, camp gear, accessories, shoes, boots, hats, etc. Catalog - $4.

WISE CUSTOM KNIVES
910-353-1311
Michael Wise, Knifemaker
197 Charles Rd Trlr 6
Jacksonville NC 28546-4850
Custom-made knives.

YE OLDE POST OFFICE
334-928-0108
17070 Scenic Hwy 98
PO Box 9
Point Clear AL 36564-0009
Dealer in antique & military collectibles, guns, swords, uniforms, books, etc.

YESTERYEAR
615-893-3470
Larry W. Hicklen
3511 Old Nashville Hwy
Murfreesboro TN 37129-3094
Quality dug & non-dug Civil War artifacts of all types. Buckles, buttons, swords, guns, paper, leather, etc. Mail order subscription - $5/yr.

JOHN G. ZIMMERMAN
304-535-2558
PO Box 1351
1195 Washington St
Harpers Ferry WV 25425-1351
Master gunsmith; custom-made Civil War muskets. Price on request.

NOTES

NOTES

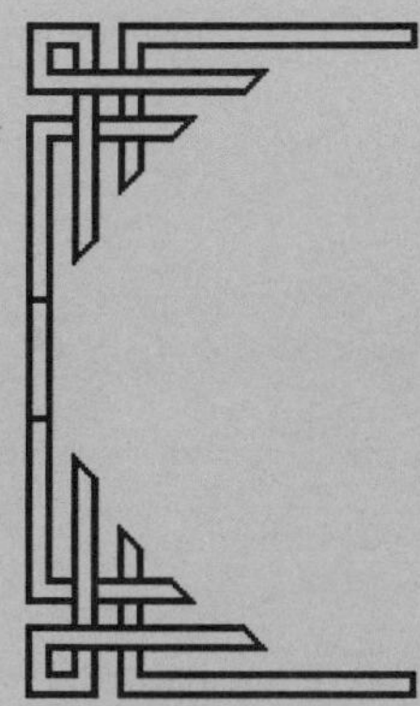

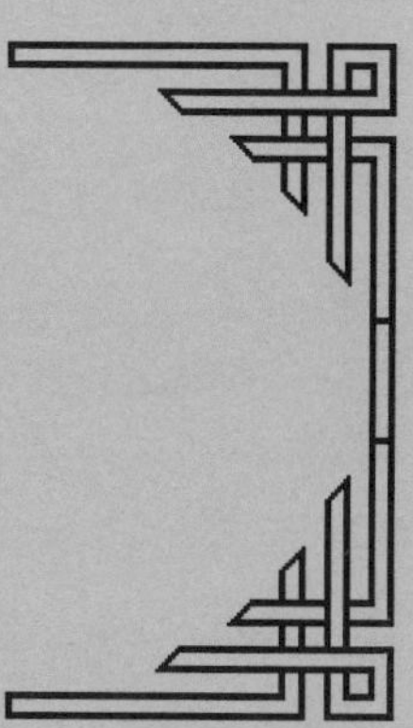

OUR ADVERTISERS

Tell 'em you saw it in the Civil War Source Book!

Historic Surratt House Museum

Where 19th-century culture mingles with the ghosts of the Lincoln assassination story.

9118 Brandywine Road
P. O. Box 427
Clinton, Maryland 20735

Phone and TTY: 301-868-1121
Fax: 301-868-8177

The Maryland-National Capital
Park and Planning Commission

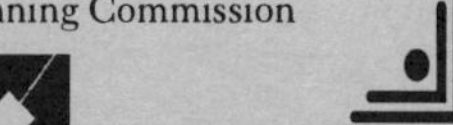

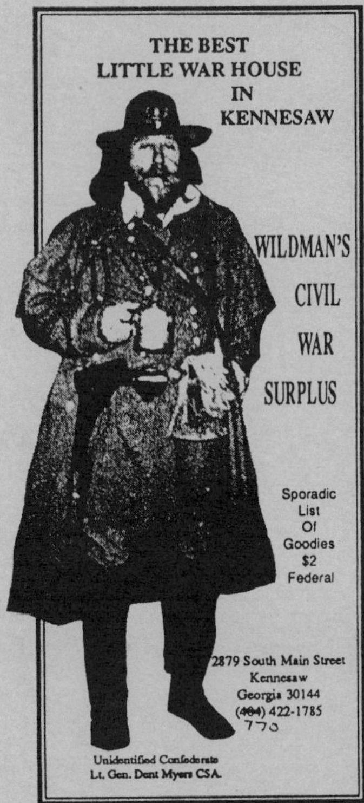

QUALITY CUSTOM FRAMING ~ CIVIL WAR ~ WILDLIFE ` AVIATION ~ AMERICANA ~ GOLF ART

Come see Original Oils by Don Stivers. Large Selection of Limited Edition Prints by Mort Kunstler, Don Stivers, John Paul Strain, Don Troiani, Dale Gallon and More! Hand Painted Pewter Figurines, Civil War Chess Set, Books Calendars and Cards.

Join us for First Friday Gallery Walk on the first Friday of each month for an artist reception. Enjoy Wine & Cheese while meeting local and regional artists. First Friday Gallery Walk is held from 6-9 p.m. each month except January.

The Potomac Gallery

family owned business since 1989

17 South King Street Old Town Leesburg, VA 703/771-8085 1/800-882-1861

Hours: Monday-Saturday 10-5:30 p.m., Sunday 12-4

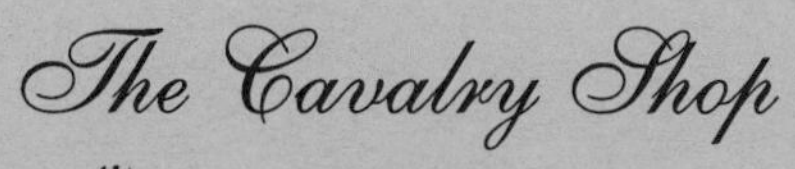

9700 Royerton Drive
Richmond, VA 23228
804-266-0898

CIVIL WAR LEATHER GOODS
—ALL AMERICAN MADE—

FOR THE BEST IN REPRO LEATHER GOODS & BUCKLES

AND MANY MORE ITEMS TOO NUMEROUS TO MENTION!

WRITE FOR
General Catalog .. $3.00

McClellan Saddles & Parts

CIVIL WAR BIOGRAPHIES

Pvt. Sam Davis, 1st Tenn., CSA
Pvt. Newt Dobson, Mabrey's Artillery, Tenn., CSA
Capt. Tacitus T. Clay, 5th Texas, CSA
Maj. Gen. Grenville M. Dodge, 4th Iowa, USA

Experience their crises. Meet their families and friends. Letters and eyewitness accounts of campaigns & battles.

$5.95 ea. **Special** - all four for $20.00.
Add $1.75 for postage/ Minnesota residents add 7% sales tax

TACITUS PUBLICATIONS
P.O. Box 14412 · St. Paul, MN 55114

SILENT SENTINEL STUDIO

Civil War
Fine Art
Prints

Joanne Marin,
Sales Mgr.

Pail Martin III,
Artist

PO Box 551
Yorktown Hts,
NY 10598

914-245-8903
Commissions Accepted

Original Frameworks

1314 S. Main, Blacksburg, VA 24060
(800) 654-1861

❧

All Civil War artists at discount. Signatures, documents, 19th-century steel engravings, relics. Will find any artwork. Always looking to purchase.

civilwar@usit.net • http://www.ptiweb.com/civilwar

Only book in print of Civil War letters-collection written by a

Confederate Surgeon

Urban Grammar Owen, M.D., Army of Tennessee
Genealogy: Owen, Dobson, Hughes, Rives
Letters to Laura: A Confederate Surgeon's Impressions of Four Years of War
304 pp., hardcover, 105 duotones, reference notes, biography, maps, drawings, bibliography, index, $28 plus $3 S&H
TUNSTEDE PRESS • 500 Elmington Avenue • Nashville, TN 37205
615-385-7258